PENGUIN CANADA

Selected Works on the Pleasures of Reading

ROBERTSON DAVIES (1913–1995) was born and raised in Ontario, and was educated at a variety of schools, including Upper Canada College, Queen's University, and Balliol College, Oxford. He had three successive careers: as an actor with the Old Vic Company in England; as publisher of the Peterborough *Examiner*; and as university professor and first Master of Massey College at the University of Toronto, from which he retired in 1981 with the title of Master Emeritus.

He was one of Canada's most distinguished men of letters, with several volumes of plays and collections of essays, speeches, and *belles lettres* to his credit. As a novelist he gained worldwide fame for his three trilogies: *The Salterton Trilogy*, *The Deptford Trilogy*, and *The Cornish Trilogy*, and for later novels *Murther & Walking Spirits* and *The Cunning Man*.

His career was marked by many honours: He was the first Canadian to be made an Honorary Member of the American Academy of Arts and Letters, he was a Companion of the Order of Canada, and he received honorary degrees from twenty-six American, Canadian, and British universities.

JENNIFER SURRIDGE worked in various administrative positions for many years before joining Robertson Davies for the last three years of his life as his research assistant. In 1996 she and Mrs. Davies formed Pendragon Ink, where she is general manager. Pendragon Ink looks after Davies's literary legacy. She has edited *The Merry Heart* and *Happy Alchemy*, and is working on editing and annotating Davies's voluminous diaries.

Also by Robertson Davies

NOVELS

Tempest-Tost

Leaven of Malice

A Mixture of Frailties

Fifth Business

The Manticore

World of Wonders

The Rebel Angels

What's Bred in the Bone

The Lyre of Orpheus

Murther & Walking Spirits

The Cunning Man

SHORT FICTION

High Spirits

CRITICISM

A Voice from the Attic

ESSAYS

One Half of Robertson Davies

The Enthusiasms of Robertson Davies

The Merry Heart

Happy Alchemy

ROBERTSON DAVIES

Selected Works on the Pleasures of Reading

Edited and with an Introduction by Jennifer Surridge

**PENGUIN
CANADA**

PENGUIN CANADA

Published by the Penguin Group

Penguin Group (Canada), 90 Eglinton Avenue East, Suite 700, Toronto, Ontario, Canada M4P 2Y3
(a division of Pearson Canada Inc.)

Penguin Group (USA) Inc., 375 Hudson Street, New York, New York 10014, U.S.A.
Penguin Books Ltd, 80 Strand, London WC2R 0RL, England
Penguin Ireland, 25 St Stephen's Green, Dublin 2, Ireland (a division of Penguin Books Ltd)
Penguin Group (Australia), 250 Camberwell Road, Camberwell, Victoria 3124, Australia
(a division of Pearson Australia Group Pty Ltd)
Penguin Books India Pvt Ltd, 11 Community Centre, Panchsheel Park, New Delhi – 110 017, India
Penguin Group (NZ), 67 Apollo Drive, Rosedale, North Shore 0632, Auckland, New Zealand
(a division of Pearson New Zealand Ltd)
Penguin Books (South Africa) (Pty) Ltd, 24 Sturdee Avenue, Rosebank, Johannesburg 2196,
South Africa

Penguin Books Ltd, Registered Offices: 80 Strand, London WC2R 0RL, England

First published 2008

(WEB) 10 9 8 7 6 5 4 3 2 1

Manufactured in Canada.

ISBN-13: 978-0-14-305566-2
ISBN-10: 0-14-305566-6

Library and Archives Canada Cataloguing in Publication data available on request.

Visit the Penguin Group (Canada) website at **www.penguin.ca**

Special and corporate bulk purchase rates available; please see
www.penguin.ca/corporatesales or call 1-800-810-3104, ext. 477 or 474

For

Miranda Davies
with love

Contents

Introduction

by Jennifer Surridge

When I was asked if I'd be interested in editing a collection of shorter pieces written by my father, Robertson Davies, I was delighted to accept. The task has been fascinating, as it has given me a chance to read pieces from all stages of his writing life. These selections are taken from *A Voice from the Attic, One Half of Robertson Davies, The Merry Heart,* and *Happy Alchemy.* Three of these books are mainly collections of speeches he gave over the years, and his favourite topics at these events were reading and writing. I have divided the material I've chosen to include these two areas, among others. It is never wise to categorize Davies too forcefully. But still, since the theme of this collection is the pleasures of reading, let us look at how these selections all relate in some way to this theme. Since the selections span decades, I've noted when each was written and have arranged them in chronological order within each section so that the reader can observe the development of the writing.

To avoid any confusion, I want to say a word about the introductions to each selection. The pieces from *A Voice from the Attic* had no introductions, so I have added them. The introductions from *One Half of Robertson Davies* were written by Davies; the introductions from *The Merry Heart* were written by Douglas Gibson of McClelland & Stewart; and the ones from *Happy Alchemy* were written by me.

Robertson Davies always loved surprises, so to begin the first section, Reading, I've chosen not a speech but rather an essay, "A Call to the Clerisy," which is an appeal for a deeper reading and understanding of books, although not necessarily in a critical manner. The word *clerisy* is defined in the *Shorter Oxford Dictionary* as "a distinct class of learned or literary persons." Davies used it because he felt that *layman* "is a word which has gained a new and disquieting currency in our language." This essay is the first in *A Voice from the Attic*, which was written at the request of Alfred Knopf and published initially in the United States. In the prologue to that book Davies explains the title this way:

A voice, certainly—any book is a voice—but why from the Attic?

In this book I want to comment and digress on some aspects of the world of books today, by no means always seriously and certainly not with any desire to impose my taste on anyone; rather, I expose my taste hoping that it may provide diversion for the reader. I do this as one who, for twenty years, reviewed books for a living (or part of a living, for I never found that it provided a whole one) and as one who has given hard knocks as a reviewer and taken them as an author. Because I am a Canadian, my outlook may possess some novelty for readers in the United States, for my country sees not only the greater part of the books produced in yours, but those published in Great Britain as well—not to speak of our own books. Canada is, I believe, the only country so blessed.

Statesmen are fond of stressing Canada's role as a mediator between the United States and Great Britain. Sometimes for us in Canada it seems as though the United States and the United Kingdom were cup and saucer, and Canada the spoon, for we are in and out of both with the greatest freedom, and we are given most recognition when we are most a nuisance. If, in these reflections, I seem not to be committed to either side, it is because I am a Canadian, and of Canada one of our poets, Patrick Anderson, has said:

... I am one and none, pin and pine, snow and slow, America's attic ...
and that is why this is A Voice from the Attic.

In the speech that follows, "A Rake at Reading," Davies asserts that "we who are committed readers may appear to choose our books, but in an equally true sense our books choose us." We continue with "Literature and Technology," a speech that was given at the Ontario Science Centre in Toronto and that offers an interesting juxtaposition for one who was a self-described techno-moron. The section ends with "Literature and Moral Purpose," which Davies delivered as the Erasmus Lecture at the Institute of Religion and Public Life in New York. The theme of the lecture is "how far literature may be expected to discuss moral problems and what contribution it can make to their solution, without being untrue to itself," and he gives his own twist to the subject.

Davies was an avid book collector, and so had many ideas on the subject of collecting, the focus of the second section. In *A Voice from the Attic* he wrote a chapter called "In Pursuit of Pornography," which considers pornography from the collector's point of view; our laws of pornography and our views of the world have changed greatly since this piece was written, so I include it to show how things haven't changed from this perspective so very much. "Painting, Fiction and Faking," given as a speech at the Metropolitan Museum of Art in New York, features some of the research Davies did for his novel *What's Bred in the Bone* as well as a discussion of his favourite painting, Bronzino's *Allegory of Love*, which hangs in the National Gallery in London. The section ends with "How to Be a Collector," a speech given in 1995 at the Pierpont Morgan Library in New York when Davies became an Honorary Fellow of the Library.

Davies loved ghost stories, but when he tried his hand at writing one for the first Massey College Gaudy Night in 1963, he couldn't keep his natural bent for humour out of it. These stories, which became a regular event at the College, were later collected in *High Spirits*. Davies was astounded by how enthusiastically the reading public responded to them, so here I've included three that aren't in that collection. The first of these, "Harper of the Stones"—originally accompanied by music written by Toronto composer Louis Applebaum—was inspired by the huge granite boulders that studded the land where my parents built their house north of Toronto. (He even decorated parts of the garden by having boulders set on end.) The second, "A Ghost Story," was written for the twenty-fifth anniversary Gaudy Night at Massey College in 1988. The third is a fragment. In 1995, when John Fraser was elected the new master of the College, he asked Davies if he'd write a ghost story for his first Gaudy. Davies accepted, though he was not well at the time. He started the outline for the story on September 30 and wrote the first two pages on October 1 and 5. I've included the fragment here because it's so exciting. It's fun to speculate on where it might have gone.

Davies was a great fan of Charles Dickens; he read all his novels many times, collected them, and enjoyed them thoroughly, although he was well aware of their faults. When he saw an opportunity to update *A Christmas Carol* it became *A Christmas Carol Re-Harmonized*. The Pierpont Morgan Library has the original manuscript of A Christmas Carol, and when they celebrated the 150th anniversary of its publication they asked Davies to speak. He revelled in the occasion, taking the audience through the book and pointing out its theatricality, and the event was topped off with a Dickensian Christmas dinner. The "Dickens and Music" piece included here was written in 1995 when Penguin U.K. wanted to publish *A Christmas Carol Re-Harmonized* as a small book for their sixtieth-anniversary celebration. Davies thought it a bit short for the purpose, and so offered this additional piece to lengthen the book.

"Masks of Satan" is a four-part lecture series given at Trinity College, Toronto, as the 1976 Larkin-Stuart Lecture. In it Davies explores the theme of evil in literature, which is a large subject even for four lectures. Halfway through he wrote in his diary: *"The second lecture … goes well indeed, and provokes real, strong enthusiasm. I feel that my tedious work of preparation is justified."* When he wrote novels Davies missed the immediate response of the audience; he was still an actor at heart and was able to use these talents in the delivery of his speeches and lectures.

In 1984 at Johns Hopkins Medical Institutions in Baltimore he gave two lectures—"Can a Doctor Be a Humanist" and "An Allegory of the Physician"—on the same day; he was there attending a seminar organized under the latter title by Dr. George Udvarhelyi. Davies talked about the role of the physician in drama, citing such plays as *Macbeth* and *The Doctor's Dilemma*. He had a good time endeavouring to convince the doctors he was addressing that they should read and reflect more in private life; this, he said, would help them in their professional life.

The final section of this book, Unusual Treatments, features examples of unexpected works written by Davies over the years. "Prologue to *The Good Natur'd Man*" was written in 1939 for a production at the Old Vic Theatre in London. When it was used in *Masque for the Master*, presented at University of Toronto's Hart House on the occasion of Davies's retirement from Massey College, he noted in his diary: *"Was astonished at how concentrated it was, how funny it often was, and how my youthful stuff—from school poems and the prologue to* The Good Natur'd Man *stood up. It was quite the most flattering and imaginative tribute to anyone I have encountered at this University, or anywhere else, for that matter."* "Animal U," a children's story, was written at the request of Jack McClelland of McClelland & Stewart for a series of children's books he was planning; however,, several people thought it was too difficult for children. Happily it was issued as an illustrated book in 1995 by Storytellers Ink of Seattle, Washington, as part of a reading initiative called Light Up the Mind of a Child Series. "The Fourth Wiseman," a short story describing a dream, is a work I discovered in Davies's 1974 diary. It demonstrates how clearly he wrote, before tinkering, as there were no corrections. (I leave its interpretation to the reader, since Davies never said what he thought it meant.) "Look at the Clock," a television play, is the retelling of the Oedipus myth, in which, as you know, Oedipus killed his father and married his mother Jocasta; when they found out their mistake Jocasta hanged herself and Oedipus put out his eyes. In this version, Jocasta decides that it's time to change her part in the myth as it needs updating in our era of women's rights. On January 3, 1976, Davies wrote this in his diary: *"Dismantle the tree, and take down most of the holiday decorations. Usually I find this melancholy work, but I am upheld today because I think I have found the way to work on my Oedipus play: to make Jocasta the principal character, and to stress the problems of spiritual, rather than physical, incest—the domination of child by parent, and the insistence that the unlived life of the parent be bodied forth by the child. Will be hard to do, but I think that is the way to attempt it."*

For a number of years now, I have been working on Davies's diaries. In them he always notes or discusses what he was reading.

This has been quite intimidating for me, and I keep lecturing myself that I should read more often and more widely. I have now come to the conclusion that I can only do what I can manage. In these pages, however, we can all benefit from his lifetime of reading. So on to the meat of the book, and I hope you enjoy this new collection of Robertson Davies's work.

*Selected Works on the
Pleasures of Reading*

Reading

1

A Call to the Clerisy

This essay about reading is in the volume *A Voice from the Attic*, which was published by Knopf in New York. When Alfred Knopf asked Davies to write the book in early 1958, Davies wrote in his diary:

Thursday, April 3: Alfred Knopf writes asking for a book of literary criticism founded on my Saturday Night *pieces—a dream come true: a conspectus of the modern literary situation: Can hardly believe this luck.*

As he went on preparing to write the book, he noted some further thoughts.

May 18, 1958: For Knopf book would like to do something Canadian, as being in main stream of both U.S. and U.K. writing: some amusing comment would surely be possible, contrasting their attitudes—especially toward one another.

October 8, 1959: ... worked on plan for Knopf book and listened to music: the book is still too stuffy, too much a series of academic essays: it must be light but not silly, and above all original.

May 29, 1960: Knopf's are using a fine Janson for Voice from the Attic: their usual handsome typographical job: but proof-reading is dismal and makes me think the books foolish and shallow.

♨

Layman is a word which has gained a new and disquieting currency in our language. For much of the five hundred years or so that it has been in use it meant simply one who worshipped, as opposed to a priest, who had knowledge of the sacred mysteries. Then, by extension, it came to mean the client or the patient, in his relation to the lawyer and the physician. But nowadays the word is used loosely for anybody who does not happen to know something, however trivial, which somebody else knows, or thinks he knows. The meat eater is a layman to the butcher, and the seeker for illumination is a layman to the candlestick maker. Most reprehensibly, the word is used among people who should meet as equals in education and general knowledge, within wide bounds. The layman is the non-expert, the outsider; the implication is still that the layman's opposite has not merely special knowledge, but a secret and priestlike vocation.

It is particularly displeasing to hear professional critics using the term "layman" to describe people who are amateurs and patrons of those arts with which they are themselves professionally concerned. The fact that the critic gets money for knowing something, and giving public expression to his opinion, does not entitle him to consider the amateur, who may be as well informed and as sensitive as himself, an outsider. Admitting that there are triflers hanging to the skirts of the arts it is generally true that we are all, critics and amateurs alike, members of a group which meets on a reasonably equal footing. The critics have their special tastes and firm opinions and are, in some cases, more experienced and sensitive than any but the most devoted of amateurs. But they should never assume that it is so; they, of all people, should know the humility which art imposes and avoid the harlotry of a cheap professionalism.

That is why I address this book, which is about reading and writing, to the clerisy, knowing that many in that large body will be my superiors, but not, for that reason, contemptuous of me, any more than I presume to dismiss those who are not so widely read, or so particular in their tastes, as I am.

DEFINING THE CLERISY

Who are the clerisy? They are people who like to read books.

Are they trained in universities? Not necessarily so, for the day has long passed when a university degree was a guarantee of experience in the humanities, or of literacy beyond its barest meaning of being able, after a fashion, to read and write.

Are the clerisy critics and scholars, professionally engaged in judging the merit of books? By no means, for there are critics and scholars who are untouched by books, except as raw material for their own purposes.

Then does the clerisy mean all of the great body of people who read? No; the name can only be applied with justice to those within that body who read for pleasure and with some pretension to taste.

The use of a word so unusual, so out of fashion, can only be excused on the ground that it has no familiar synonym. The word is little known because what it describes has disappeared, though I do not believe that it has gone forever. The clerisy are those who read for pleasure, but not for idleness; who read for pastime but not to kill time; who love books, but do not live by books. As lately as a century ago the clerisy had the power to decide the success or failure of a book, and it could do so now. But the clerisy has been persuaded to abdicate its power by several groups, not themselves malign or consciously unfriendly to literature, which are part of the social and business organization of our time. These groups, though entrenched, are not impregnable; if the clerisy would arouse itself, it could regain its sovereignty in the world of letters. For it is to the clerisy, even yet, that the authors, the publishers, and the booksellers make their principal appeal.

Has this group any sense of unity? It had, once, and this book is written in the hope that it may regain it. This is a call to the clerisy to wake up and assert itself.

READING A PRIVATE ART

Let me repeat, this is a call, not a roar; it is an attempt to arouse the clerisy, but not to incite it to violence or rancorous controversy.

Anything of the sort would be bound to fail, for by its very nature the clerisy is not susceptible of such appeals. Moral causes, good and bad, may shout in the ears of men; aesthetic causes have lost the fight as soon as they begin to be strident. Reading is my theme, and reading is a private, interpretative art. Let us have no printed shrieks about reading.

In 1944 a book by B.H. Haggin was published, called *Music for the Man Who Enjoys Hamlet*; some parts at least of this book might be called *Reading for the Man Who Enjoys Music*, for I want to write about the actual business of reading—the interpretative act of getting the words off the page and into your head in the most effective way. It is not the quickest way of reading, and for those who think that speed is the greatest good, there are plenty of manuals on how to read a book which profess to tell how to strip off the husk and guzzle the milk, like a chimp attacking a coconut. There are remedial reading courses for adults who are dissatisfied with their speed, which show you how to snatch up clumps of words with your eyes, and how to bolt paragraphs at a glance, so that a determined zealot can flip through *War and Peace* in five hours, and, like a boa constrictor, gobble up all Plato in a week. But if you read for pleasure, such gourmandizing will not appeal to you. What musician would hastily scan the pages of a sonata, and say that he had experienced it? If he did so, he would be laughed at by the others. Who among the clerisy would whisk through a poem, eyes a-flicker, and say that he had read it?

The answer to that last question must unfortunately be: far too many. For reading is not respected as the art it is.

READING AND TIME

Perhaps it would be more just to say that most people, the clerisy included, are impatient of any pace of reading except their fastest, and have small faith in their interpretative powers. They do not think of themselves as artists. But unless they make some effort to match their interpretative powers to the quality of what they would read, they are abusing their faculty of appreciation. And if they do not mean to make the most of their faculty of appreciation, why are they reading?

To kill time? But it is not time they are killing; it is themselves.

What is time? Let the philosophers and the physicists say what they will, time for most of us is the fleeting instant we call Now. Any enjoyment or profit we get from life, we get Now; to kill Now is to abridge our own lives.

Yet how many people there are who read as though some prize awaited them when they turned the last page! They do not wish to *read* a book; they want to *have read* it—no matter how. The prize they seek is to have done with the book in hand. And so, as they read, they are always straining forward toward the goal of completion. Is it astonishing that they experience so little on the way, and that while they may be "great readers" quantitatively they are wretchedly poor readers qualitatively, and that they reveal by the poverty of their minds how ill-read they truly are?

ENDS AND MEANS

Doubtless there are philosophical terms for this attitude of mind, of which hasty reading is one manifestation, but here let us call it "end-gaining," for such people put *ends* before *means*; they value, not reading, but having read. In this, as in so many things, the end-gainers make mischief and spoil all they do; end-gaining is one of the curses of our nervously tense, intellectually flabby civilization. In reading, as in all arts, it is the means, and not the end, which gives delight and brings the true reward. We laugh at tourists who dash through the Uffizi, to say that they have "done" it; we know that if they have any serious feeling for pictures, fifteen minutes with one masterpiece would far outweigh the pleasure of such dashes. But do we not dash through books, to say that we have "done" them?

THE DECORUMS OF STUPIDITY

Not all rapid reading is to be condemned. Much that is badly written and grossly padded must be read rapidly and nothing is lost thereby.

Much of the reading that has to be done in the way of business should be done as fast as it can be understood. The ideal business document is an auditor's report; a good one is finely edited. But the memoranda, the public-relations pieces, the business magazines, need not detain us. Every kind of prose has its own speed, and the experienced reader knows it as a musician knows Adagio from Allegro. All of us have to read a great deal of stuff which gives us no pleasure and little information, but which we cannot wholly neglect; such reading belongs in that department of life which Goldsmith called "the decorums of stupidity." Books as works of art are no part of this duty reading.

Books as works of art? Certainly; it is thus that their writers intend them. But how are these works of art used?

Suppose you hear of a piece of recorded music which you think you might like. Let us say it is an opera of Benjamin Britten's—*The Turn of the Screw*. You buy it, and after dinner you put it on your record player. The scene is one of bustling domesticity: Your wife is writing to her mother, on the typewriter, and from time to time she appeals to you for the spelling of a word; the older children are chattering happily over a game, and the baby is building, and toppling, towers of blocks. The records are long-playing ones, designed for thirty-three revolutions of the turntable per minute; ah, but you have taken a course in rapid listening, and you pride yourself on the speed with which you can hear, so you adjust your machine to play at seventy-eight revolutions a minute. And when you find your attention wandering from the music, you skip the sound arm rapidly from groove to groove until you come to a bit that appeals to you. But look—it is eight o'clock, and if you are to get to your meeting on time, Britten must be choked off. So you speed him up until a musical pause arrives, and then you stop the machine, marking the place so that you can continue your appreciation of *The Turn of the Screw* when next you can spare a few minutes for it.

Ridiculous? Of course, but can you say that you have never read a book in that fashion?

One of the advantages of reading is that it can be done in short spurts and under imperfect conditions. But how often do we read in conditions which are merely decent, not to speak of perfection? How often do we give a book a fair chance to make its effect with us?

9

FICTION AND FEELING

Some magazine editors say the public no longer enjoys fiction; it demands "informative" articles. But informative writing requires less effort to assimilate than does fiction, because good fiction asks the reader to feel. There is no reason to suppose that people today feel less than their grandfathers, but there is good reason to think that they are less able to read in a way which makes them feel. It is natural for them to blame books rather than themselves, and to demand fiction which is highly peppered, like a glutton whose palate is defective.

The clerisy at least want to feel. They have reached that point of maturity where they know that thought and reason, unless matched by feeling, are empty, delusive things. Foolish people laugh at those readers a century ago who wept over the novels of Dickens. Is it a sign of superior intellect to read anything and everything unmoved, in a gray, unfeeling Limbo? Happy Victorians! Perhaps their tears flowed too readily. But some of Dickens's critics—by no means men of trivial intellect—wept. If this should meet the eye of any modern critic, let me ask: When did you last weep over a book? When did you last give a book a fair chance to make you do so?

Feeling is a condition of appreciation, and there can never have been a time when people were so anxious as they now are to have emotional experiences, or sought them so consciously. On the North American continent today sensual experience is frankly acknowledged as one of the good things of life. The popularity of "mood music" shows how eagerly we seek to deepen the quality of our experience. Any shop which sells phonograph records can supply long-playing discs and tapes to accompany a dozen activities with supposedly appropriate music. There is even one called, simply, *Music For*—, and the picture on the envelope—of female bare feet, toes upward, bracketing a pair of male bare feet, toes downward—makes plain *what* it is music for. Everywhere there is evidence of this anxiety that no shade of sensual enjoyment should be missed; the emphasis, indeed, is on nursing sensual enjoyment to its uttermost power, and advertising of all sorts reveals it. Do great numbers of people feel that they are missing some of the joy of life? Who can doubt it?

Like all anxiety, this is end-gaining, and carries the seeds of its own failure. Not ends, but means must be the concern of those who seek satisfaction in the pleasures as well as the obligations of life.

THE MEANS OF READING

As this is a book about reading, let us consider the means of satisfactory reading. If we look after the means, we may be confident that the ends will take care of themselves.

It is a truism that we shall find nothing in books which has no existence in ourselves.

> Bookes give not wisdom where none was before,
> But where some is, there reading makes it more

says Sir John Harington, Elizabethan epigrammatist (and, blessed be his name, the inventor of the water closet); what is true of wisdom is true also of feeling. We all have slumbering realms of sensibility which can be coaxed into wakefulness by books. Aldous Huxley tells us that "writers influence their readers, preachers their auditors, but always, at bottom, to be more themselves." But do they know what they themselves are? Is not that what they are reading books to find out?

The best of novels are only scenarios, to be completed by the reader's own experience. They do not give us feeling: They draw out such feeling as we have. If fiction is going out of fashion (which is said from time to time but which I do not believe), it is not because fiction is any worse than it was; apart from the pepper and curry fiction already referred to, the general level of it is probably better. But great numbers of people find fault with fiction because they do not give themselves a chance to respond to it.

It is the way they read which is at fault. The great success of Emlyn Williams in reading Dickens and Dylan Thomas to large audiences showed us where the trouble lies. I have seen Mr. Williams hold a large audience spellbound as he read, in two and a half hours, an abridgment of Dickens's *Bleak House*. He had their undivided attention, and he read with all the resources of a consummate actor. He and his hearers were, for the evening, giving the best of themselves to *Bleak House*; his audience was moved to curiosity, to laughter, to horror, to tears, as audiences are not often moved by plays.

Sir John Gielgud moves audiences similarly by reading Shakespeare. Thomas's *Under Milk Wood* comes to life on phonograph records, and the catalogues of the large recording companies contain many examples of recorded plays and excerpts from books. Ah, you may say, but those are performances by actors. Yes, and if you want the best from reading, you must learn to give the best performances of which you are capable, sitting soundless in your chair, with your book before you. The gifts demanded of a good reader are less those of the critic than of the actor. You must bestir yourself, and above all you must cultivate the inward ear.

AN AGE OF THE EYE

We live in an age when the eye is feasted and the ear, if not starved, is kept on short rations. Special merit is accorded to the cartoon which makes its effect without a caption. In the theatre we expect a higher standard of scenic design, aided by elaborate lighting, than playgoers have ever known. It is not uncommon for a stage setting, at the rise of the curtain, to be greeted with a round of applause. But how long is it since you heard an actor applauded because he had delivered a fine speech particularly well? This calls attention to our comparative indifference to fine speech; it is not altogether lacking, but we do not insist upon it as we insist on the gratification of the eye. But how do the books you read reach your consciousness? By words you hear, or pictures you see?

Unless you have a visualizing type of mind, by words. And how do those words reach you?

Teachers of rapid reading are opposed to an inward vocalizing of the words read, and some of them write about it with the asperity of a Puritan divine condemning lace ruffles. But so far as I can find out, they oppose it only because it decreases reading speed. They say it adds nothing to understanding. That may be, but we are concerned here with something more subtle than simple understanding: We are talking about reading for pleasure, for emotional and intellectual extension, for the exercise of the sensibilities. For these things, some measure of vocalizing is indispensable.

In the Middle Ages readers spoke aloud the words they read, and a temporary hoarseness or loss of voice was a sufficient reason for a scholar to suspend his studies. In monasteries it was the custom for someone to read aloud during meals, and this practice persists in many religious houses. In universities a principal means of instruction was the lecture—literally "a reading aloud"—in which the master read to the undergraduates from a work of his own composition: The custom persists still, though many lectures are, in effect, speeches and exhibitions of personality—not necessarily the worse for that. Holy Writ was read aloud in churches, and a point which was greatly emphasized during the Reformation was that it should be read in a language known to all the hearers and not only to the clerisy. The reason for all this vocalizing of what was read was that it might strike inward not only through the eye but through the ear; even the most learned did not trust to the eye alone, simply because they could read. "It is voicing things that makes them real," said Miss Ivy Compton-Burnett; it is a psychological truth neglected in our day.

Neglected by readers, but not therefore unknown. Television advertisers do not scorn the medieval aids of repetition and rhyme, assonance and rhythm, in selling their goods. Whatever the content of their compositions, their techniques derive from the anonymous composer of *Beowulf*, the unknown makers of folk song, and the originators of such mnemonics as:

Thirty days hath September
April, June and November.

Our emphasis on the eye as the high road to the intellect is a new thing, and we all use our ears readily when we are asked to do so. Even when we do not desire it (as with advertising jingles), what enters our consciousness through the ear is likely to stick.

THE INWARD VOICE

Certainly it is not my purpose to suggest that we should return to all this reading aloud, creating in every library a hubbub like that which one hears when walking through the corridors of a conservatory of music. But are we not foolish to give up that inward voice in which books can speak to us? And in the pursuit of speed, of all things! What has speed to do with literary appreciation? Speed, unless some real, defensible good is achieved by it, is nothing but end-gaining, which is the death of all enjoyment of the arts. Not *ends*, but *means* bring delight and fulfillment to the reader, and his means of reading is listening to the inward, reading voice.

What is that voice like? Its quality depends on your ear. If you have a good ear and some talent for mimicry, you can read to yourself in any voice, or as many voices as you please. You have seen Sir Laurence Olivier's film of *Richard III*? Very well, can you hear him again when you read the play? If you can, and if you are a playgoer and a filmgoer, you should be able to find voices for all the characters in the books you read. James Agate, the English theatre critic, amused himself by casting the novels of Dickens, in which he delighted, with the actors whom it was his professional duty to watch; his favourite Mr. Dombey was Sir John Gielgud.

This is a game, and a very good game, but it asks for a good ear, and makes heavy imaginative demands upon the reader. You may not be able to play it; perhaps you have no desire to do so; it is not for all temperaments. Your taste may be more austere. Besides, it only works with novels and plays. What about reading history or poetry?

The inner voice is of your own choosing, of your own development. It may differ greatly from the voice in which you speak. To read Trollope in the tones of Kansas, or Joyce in the cadences of Alabama, is as barbarous as to read *Huck Finn* with a Yorkshire accent, or Edith Wharton in the voice of Glasgow. One of the most dismaying experiences of my college days was to hear the whole of *Hamlet* read by a professor whose voice was strongly nasal, and whose vocal range was well within one octave. Did he, I wondered, read to himself in that voice? Or did he hear, inside himself, a full, rich, copious, nobly modulated sound unlike the dispirited drone which came out of his mouth? There are, one presumes, utterly tone-deaf readers.

AUTHORS AS READERS

But what does literature mean to them? Good writing sets its own tune, insists on its own cadence. Joyce presents a particularly interesting example. Nothing of his, and *Finnegans Wake* least of all, can be read comfortably except in the Joycean mode. There exists a phonograph record which illustrates that mode, with Joyce himself reading, but thousands of readers have found it, or some part of it, without the record: The mode arises from the page.

The examples of authors are not always so happy. Recordings of another Irish author, Sean O'Casey, also exist; few could endure to hear a whole book in the O'Casey voice, as exemplified there. But Joyce, a singer, was also a great reader, and the musical allusions and echoes which abound in his work (so strangely missed by those of his critics who do not know the queer, second-rate nineteenth-century repertoire in which he delighted) give not only a special comic or sardonic flavor to it, but dictate the rhythms of some of his most expressive passages.

Talk of the rhythms of prose may alarm some readers who have trouble enough with the rhythms of poetry. But poetic rhythm is the rhythm of song, whereas prose rhythm is the rhythm of speech. Not always the speech of the streets or of conversation, but speech rising to nobility, to prophecy, to denunciation. It was Thomas Mann who contrasted the rhythms of verse with "the finer and much less obvious rhythmical laws of prose." Less obvious, but still to be captured by the attentive inward ear, and when so captured, to give a new and splendid dimension to the pleasure of reading.

To some of my readers it may seem that I am advising them to conjure up within themselves a host of dialect comedians, and that I want them to read with the embarrassing vehemence of old fashioned elocutionists. Nothing could be farther from my intention, and I know that many readers are happiest with a low-keyed and antitheatrical approach to their pleasure. But I do urge them to approach reading in a less passive and more interpretative spirit.

READER AS INTERPRETER

Interpretative, you will observe: Not creative. The word *creative* is used now so carelessly that its real meaning is being rubbed away. The reader cannot create; that has been done for him by the author. The reader can only interpret, giving the author a fair chance to make his impression. As Lord David Cecil makes plain in his essay *The Fine Art of Reading*, the reader allows the writer to act upon him. "Every reader is a Lady of Shalott, who, secluded in his secret chamber, forgets the hours, as he sits watching the endless procession of human thought and passion and action, as it passes, motley and tumultuous, across the gleaming mirror of literature." This cannot be done if the reader, in his secret chamber, hears what he reads declaimed at the speed and in the tones of a tobacco auctioneer.

We would not dream of judging a piece of music which we heard performed on an untuned and neglected piano by a player not up to the work, long out of practice and ill-taught. But we treat a piece of literature, too often, in a comparable fashion. Good reading is the only test of good writing. Can you read this at high speed, without inward vocalizing, and make anything of it?

Rest not in an Ovation, but a Triumph over thy Passions. Let Anger walk hanging down the head; Let Malice go Manicled, and Envy fetter'd after thee. Behold within thee the long train of thy Trophies not without thee. Make the quarreling Lapithytes sleep, and Centaurs within lye quiet. Chain up the unruly Legion of thy breast. Lead thine own captivity captive, and be *Caesar* within thyself.

You have no desire to read Sir Thomas Browne, and do not care what he has to say? Well, what about Mark Twain?

It was a real bully circus. It was the splendidest sight that ever was when they all come riding in, two and two, and gentleman and lady, side by side, the men just in their drawers and undershirts, and no shoes nor stirrups, and resting their hands on their thighs easy and comfortable—there must 'a' been twenty of them—and every lady with a lovely complexion, and perfectly beautiful, and looking just like a gang of real sure-enough queens, and dressed in clothes that cost millions of dollars, and just littered with diamonds. It was a powerful fine sight; I never see anything so lovely. And then one by one they got up and stood, and went a-weaving around the ring so gentle and wavy and graceful, the men looking ever so tall and airy and straight, with their heads bobbing and skimming along, away up there under the tent-roof, and every lady's rose-leafy dress flapping soft and silky around her hips, and she looked like the most loveliest parasol.

A CRITICAL INSTRUMENT

The second of these passages is undoubtedly easier than the first, but neither can be taken at a gallop. The difficult Browne yields his secret, and his exquisite savour, when his pace and tone have been discovered—so does Huck Finn. The reader who has cultivated his appreciation of pace and tone has at his command one of the most powerful of critical instruments, and he will not be content with "those hopelessly banal and enormous novels which are typed out by the thumbs of tense mediocrities and called 'powerful' and 'stark' by the reviewing hack"—to quote Vladimir Nabokov, a novelist himself remarkable for the individuality of his pace and tone. Attentive, appreciative reading quickly sorts good writing from bad; to the book gobbler no such discrimination is possible, for he reads so quickly that he has no time in which to discover what is not worth reading.

This is not another evangelistic book, officiously seeking to insure the literary salvation of its readers by exhorting them to read nothing save "the best." The best, as every true reader knows, is not always what one wants; there are times when one does not feel equal to the demands of the best. Indeed, one may without shame confess that for the time being one is tired of the best. Very often one wants no more than "a good read," to shut out the world while those bruises heal which the world has given. But there are degrees in all things, and degree is vastly more important in those realms which are not quite first-rate than on the level of "the best."

CRITICAL HERESY

Nor is the exercise of judgment in reading to be confused with the attitude of the journalistic or academic critic. His special heresy is that his trade makes him an explainer, rather than an experiencer, of literature. In this heresy he is followed by many of those intellectuals who are not quite intellectual enough, and who would rather be modish than individual in their taste. All too often, to this type of mind, explaining a thing robs it of value. Having discovered what makes the clock go, it is no longer a matter of interest to them that the clock can tell time.

It is not necessary, in rejecting the critical-intellectual heresy, to rush to another extreme. Nobody can say nowadays, as Thomas à Kempis said in the fifteenth century: "Take thou a book into thine hands as Simon the Just took the child Jesus into his arms to carry Him and kiss Him. And when thou hast finished reading, close the book and give thanks for every word out of the mouth of God; because in the Lord's field thou hast found a hidden treasure." But a decent book is in some measure a work of art and deserves to be treated as one. The reader should submit himself to it until it shows itself worthy of further submission or of rejection. Readers should not be, as Yeats complained, "sciolists and opinionated bitches." They should read as, were they authors, they would wish to be read.

Thomas à Kempis wrote as he did because in his day printed books were rarities; most books were still copied by hand, and the production of a single volume was too great a labour to be undertaken except in the case of works of proven value. (The books he knew were likely to be works of edification, clothed in individual beauty, which ensured them of a regard not wholly dependent on an objective critical estimate of their contents.) The ability to read, also, was restricted to a clerkly minority. In our day books appear by the score, every day; there is no limit to the number of copies which can be made, and everybody can read them; the analphabet is a rarity in our time.

THE GREAT EXPERIMENT

This uncontrolled proliferation of books is one of the consequences of an astounding experiment which has been in progress in the English-speaking world for about a century and a quarter—nothing less than an attempt to create a complete literacy. The experiment was undertaken as part of the democratic-philanthropic enthusiasm which goes with modern idealism. There is plenty of evidence that the early advocates of the experiment supposed that if everybody *could* read, everybody *would* read, and would furthermore read the best books they could lay their hands on.

Most English-speaking people today can read and write. Great Britain asserts that inability to do so is negligible within her confines; in the United States the latest available figure shows a 2.7 illiteracy, and in Canada the figure is 3.79; in Australia it is 4.7, and in South Africa it is 2.34 among the white population. The illiterates are said to be among the older people, and presumably the time is in sight when illiteracy will have no statistical existence in the English-speaking world. But although they can read, millions of these heirs of eighteenth-century idealism do not read, and of those who read, there are great numbers whose choice of books would make the injunction of Thomas à Kempis (supposing they were to act upon it) a gross blasphemy.

ITS PRESENT STATE

We need not despair because so many people, having been taught—with what staggering cost in time and money, with what wholesale creation of teachers and building of schools!—to read, read nothing at all, or read trash. The experiment is perhaps the most revolutionary in the history of mankind, and far from being done, it is hardly begun.

We have reached the point where English-speaking adults can all read, after a fashion; that is a cause for triumph. Only mad romantics can ever have expected them all to read in the same fashion.

There is no democracy in the world of intellect, and no democracy of taste. Great efforts have been made to pretend that this is not so, but they have failed. The spread of literacy has emphasized what was apparent before. Teach everybody to read, and they will read what appeals to them, what accords with their experience and ideal of life. Their wealth or poverty have little to do with the matter; the man of means who reads rubbish, and the poor man who exhausts the classics in his public library, are still among us. But in the latter throes of the great experiment the clerisy, as an entity to be reckoned with in the population, has disappeared. It is due for revival, because it is needed if the future stages of the great experiment are to go in the right direction.

THE CLERISY AS IT WAS

A century and a half ago the reading population was much smaller than it is today, and the clerisy was still a recognizable and important element in it. The education of the clerisy was on a plan which stressed study of the Greek and Latin classics almost to the exclusion of everything else; such an education was narrow in matter, but very wide in scope; it developed taste and encouraged independent thought in minds with any aptitude for such things. It had its ridiculous side, and it developed certain snobberies. Dickens's Dr. Blimber was one kind of Victorian schoolmaster, and Mr. Curdle, who defined the dramatic unities as "a kind of universal dove-tailedness with regard to place and time," typifies Dr. Blimber's duller pupils. But that classical culture—even on the Curdle level—gave a coherence to the reading public.

Classical culture was not the only one; there was a widespread Biblical culture also, and it was a powerful shaper of thought and expression. The Bible is a classical literature of history, poetry, drama, legend, and prophecy, which used to be reasonably familiar to all educated people in the great King James version. What if it were not understood completely, as modern scholarship reckons completeness? What if it were uncritically reverenced? It was understood at least as well, and reverenced little more, than Homer or Virgil. And it is characteristic of classics that their influence is not dependent so much on critical understanding as on love and familiarity. The Biblical culture of the nineteenth century had its ridiculous side, as did the classical culture, but both provided touchstones of taste to which a writer could appeal, and which he could depend upon in his audience.

The last gasps of these cultures were to be heard within the experience of living North Americans. School reading books, sixty years ago, contained sinewy passages from Shakespeare, Ben Jonson ("It is not growing like a tree, In bulk, doth make man better be"), Sir Walter Scott, Addison (well do I recall grappling with *The Vision of Mirzah* at the age of eleven), Sheridan, R.L. Stevenson, Thomas Campbell (readers in the United States probably missed this poet of British military might, but Canadian children knew him well), and of course Emerson, Longfellow, Whittier, and their New England congeners. There was much rubbish in these "readers," too, but nineteenth-century standards still set the tone for them, and set it high.

But what sets the tone now? It is not my intention to denounce modern education. If it is bad, it may be said that all education is bad which is not self-education, and quite a lot of self-education is going on today—some of it in our schools, under the very noses of the teachers! The classical culture has shrunk so that it has no appreciable influence: The Biblical culture scarcely exists, and the writer or speaker who draws a parallel or a quotation from the Bible today will not be understood by any more people than if he made his allusion to something in Homer. Nothing has replaced this culture rooted in Greek, Latin, and Hebrew classics. The kind of education which could formerly be expected in the clerisy has gone, and it is not likely to return.

THE COHERENT AUDIENCE

This is true of the North American continent in a greater degree than it is true of England. Though great changes are at work in education there, the process is slower than it is with us. Geography has some part in preserving the high standard of literacy, and the coherence and self-consciousness of the clerisy, in the British Isles. Population is dense and the land area small; no educated man is far from someone else of much his own standard of education—a comfort so completely forgotten by hundreds of thousands of people in North America that it is hard to conceive what it must mean. The tradition of a clerisy still exists in Britain. In 1958 the distinguished novelist C.P. Snow, writing in the *New Statesman*, could say this:

> It is the variety of experience of the (English) audience that gives it its authority, and so strengthens the writer's confidence. For example, Mr. Macmillan, Mr. Butler, Mr. Gaitskell are all deeply read men, interested in contemporary work; so are a good sprinkling of other members of the House. That would also be true of a surprisingly high proportion of civil servants and miscellaneous administrative bosses.
>
> So our audience scatters itself through society, quite wide and quite deep.... In England, the society is so compact that we realize this is happening; we know, almost in a personal sense, whom we are writing for. An American writer can't; he feels much more lost. Do American politicians, civil servants, school teachers read as ours do? If they do, the writers do not feel their response. That, I think, is the one great creative stimulus we have, which is denied to them.

The result is that on this continent "the writers don't really know whom they are writing for—apart from their fellow writing scholars."

REVIEWERS AND CRITICS

Their fellow writing scholars—damnable tribe! Yet it is true that the place of the clerisy as the desired audience of the writer has been taken by critics and reviewers, whose power, without being absolute, is great, and whose influence on writing is pernicious.

Lambasting critics is easy but profitless entertainment. They exist in great numbers because books drop from the presses in great numbers, and some portion of this monstrous birth must be weighed and valued. Reading reviews is an accepted way of keeping up with what is happening in the world of books. Reviewers gain reputation less by the justness of their criticism than by their own ability to write well and entertainingly, and though this may sometimes cause hardship to authors, it is inevitable. Reviewers themselves live and work under special strain. If they praise much they appear to be simple fellows, too readily pleased, for it is a widespread belief that a truly critical mind exists in a constant state of high-toned irascibility. But blame always looks well. The eighteenth-century playwright knew his business who made his critic say:

> Panegyric and praise! And what will that do with the publick? Why who the devil will give money to be told that Mr. Such-a-one is a wiser or better man than himself? No, no; 'tis quite and clean out of nature. A good sousing satire, now, well powder'd with personal pepper, and season'd with the spirit of party; that demolishes a conspicuous character, and sinks him below our own level; there, there we are pleas'd; there we chuckle and grin and toss the half-crowns on the counter.

The reviewer who does not heed this popular view of his work may find himself reproached, as Arnold Bennett was in his last years, with discovering a new genius every week. The consequence is that reviewers often fall into a state of mind which can be summed up in the phrase "but on the other hand," doling out cautious praise tempered with cautious blame, proving their impartiality to author, publisher, and public alike. They have no time to be appreciators or experiencers. Like most of us, they are end-gainers, reading a book not for itself but as article fodder, and their own neat phrases pop into their heads as they scan another man's prose. Most of them are too good-natured for sousing satire, well powder'd with personal pepper; most of them are too well-balanced to shoot cannon at sparrows; but in most of them the razor edge of appreciation has been hacked and dulled by too much exercise on the firewood which is, inevitably, what comes to them in most abundance.

I am not clamouring for a revision of the reviewing system. I do not see how, under present conditions, it can be revised. I ask for a revival of the clerisy; the existence of a more intelligently self-conscious and literate group in the vast reading public would greatly ease and elevate the reviewers' task The clerisy would also effectively review the reviewers.

SCIOLISTS AND OPINIONATED BITCHES

Beyond and above the daily, weekly, and monthly reviewers lie the university critics, who concern themselves not with the daily black flux of the presses, but with trends, with niceties not understanded of the base, and with all that area of literature which Victorians called "Poesy and Buzzem"—though Buzzem has come to be much more like Brain, of a particularly juiceless and gritty sort.

Their productions are varied in nature and value. At best they are themselves contributions to literature, works which can be read with delight, because in them minds of one rare kind shed light upon minds of another rare kind. But in their second-best rank, books of this academic sort are, of all books, the easiest to write. They chew over what has already been well chewed; they grapple with other scholars, seeking to bear them down into the academic ooze; they explore the vast caverns of the creator's spirit with no illumination save the smoky and fitful rushlight of their own critical intelligence.

The great sin of English writing of this kind is that it feigns sensibility where sensibility plainly does not exist, and pretends (often with remarkable skill) to knowledge which it does not possess. How often we hear the hum (high and fine, like the voice of a gnat) of the "survey" in such writing. How easily come the judgments of these men and women who have not read whole libraries of books, but have "examined" (*i.e.*, leafed over) and read about them! Nobody can have read everything, but to pretend to have read what one has, at best, skimmed, is a nasty dishonesty.

The American fault in these academic works of the lesser sort is more often simple ignorance. The writer knows his subject, but he knows little else; he has no base of general cultivation on which his expert knowledge may rest. He may painstakingly bone up on the historical background of his literary quarry, but he never gets the *feel* of his period, except in the clumsiest and most obvious fashion. Not long ago an American scholar wrote a worthy but juiceless book about Goldsmith in which he set forth all that goodwill and dogged toil could assemble; but he knew so little of eighteenth-century England that he seemed baffled by the term "a pair of stairs." In eighteenth- and nineteenth-century England stairs came in pairs, like scissors and trousers; the "two-pair back" was the room at the rear, two flights up; and a "three-pair back," so often mentioned with shame as the abode of a ruined heroine or a distressed author, was directly below the servants' quarters. How can a man have any light to throw on Goldsmith who has so little of the feel of Goldsmith's age and Goldsmith's vocabulary? To these writers they are themselves the measure of all things, and with honesty and goodwill they reshape great men in their own image. They do not know enough to know that they lack humility.

THE DOLL'S HOUSE

Though this academic criticism is little read by people who are not themselves, in some way or another, of the literary world, it exerts a strong influence at second hand. It sets the style. It says which authors in the past are most worthy of the notice of the present, and while this is legitimate and necessary within reason, we sometimes feel like adults overhearing a quarrel among children as to which dolls are to have places in the doll's house No, Tennyson is *not* to have a chair in the best room! His stuffing has been leaking out for years. And George Eliot is *too* ugly—though perhaps she need not still be hidden in the old dolls' box, where she has been for so long. Browning? With his horrid red face and loud, aggressive squeaker? Never! But the Dickens doll is back in favour, and seems to be made of better stuff than we supposed. And the Thackeray doll is tolerable once again. But if we are to keep the Virginia Woolf doll, we mustn't let the Arnold Bennett doll have any affection at all. Thus the doll game is played.

There is an endless rummaging in the doll box, for the need of the scholars for new or neglected material is unappeasable. But how badly the dolls wear! Of course the Shakespeare doll and the Johnson doll will stand up to any amount of rough play, but few of the others are really durable. A.E. Housman, for instance, once such a popular doll, was suddenly banished to the depths of the box, and when he was fished up recently, for another look, it was discovered that he had cherished a lifelong affection of an intense sort for his university friend Moses Jackson. And this, for reasons not wholly apparent to those not in the doll game, so invalidated his poetry that he has gone back into the box, perhaps forever. Yet other dolls with a similar idiosyncrasy, like the Wilde doll, are much cherished.

The scholar's doll game influences the literary world in some unexpected places. *The New Yorker*, in 1958, contained this:

Jane Eyre was written in 1841 by a spinster whose sophistication was largely the product of the parsonage in which she grew up. Her book was a success (Thackeray could hardly restrain his enthusiasm for it), but by depraved modern standards it is not a very good novel.

It is not necessary in writing of this kind to explain why a doll must be refused a place in the doll's house, and must lie in the darkness of the dolls' box. That has been done by the academic critics. The writer in more popular pages has only to pity, and reject, and readers who have no firm opinions of their own will acquiesce, lest their own sophistication and modernity be called in question. Thus the taste of past years is rebuked, and the great dead are snubbed across the Void.

DWINDLING LEISURE

Not all readers are prepared, at all times, to make independent judgments. But the failure of modern education to equip them to do so even when they have the inclination creates a serious gap in modern culture. The enormously increased production of books, and the appearance of an academic and journalistic junta of criticism, have robbed the reading public of most of its ability to form its own opinions.

This robbery is not the result of a plot. No cabal of professors and reviewers, meeting in secret, have vowed to cheat the reading public of its rights. The reading public has itself connived at the deprivation, and has helped to shove the junta into power. The temper of the time is unfriendly to independent literary judgment. We all lack leisure, for we tend to work longer hours than any but the proletarians of the past. And when we are not working at our jobs, the modern craze for good causes threatens our dwindling leisure; the once-sweet voice of charity has risen to an imperious bellow. We pander to the ideal of Work as few Victorians did; university students are eager for holiday jobs, and few of them seem to know that in the beginning, university vacations were made long so that students could spend them in reading which would augment their formal studies. Long toil and small leisure are part of the heavy price we pay for our North American standard of living. It is reputed to be the highest in the world, and so it should be, for it is bought at an inordinate price.

Part of that price has been the resignation of literary taste, by the intelligent reading public, into the hands of professionals, of experts, of an intelligentsia. I have no complaint against the existence of an intelligentsia; on the contrary, I favour it. But I do not favour a small, professional intelligentsia because the very nature of an intelligentsia is that it should be non-professional; belonging to it is not something at which anybody works.

IGNORING THE HIGHBROWS

Nevertheless, we have a professional intelligentsia now, and it has lost touch with most of the public. Not that determinedly anti-intellectual public which decries one presidential candidate because he is unmistakably literate, and worries about the chances of another because he has a modest skill in playing the piano. The anti-intellectual pose is one of the unforeseen results of our great experiment in complete literacy. Everybody can be made to read and write, but not everybody is going to like it. No, the public with which the intelligentsia has so unhappily lost touch is itself composed of intelligent humanists—a humanist being, by E.M. Forster's definition, a person possessed of curiosity, a free mind, a belief in good taste, and a belief in the human race. The intelligentsia has lost touch with the clerisy. As C.S. Lewis wrote in 1958 (in, curiously enough, a comic magazine, *Punch*), "the Intelligentsia (scientists apart) are losing all touch with, and all influence over, nearly the whole human race. Our most esteemed poets and critics are read by our most esteemed critics and poets (who don't usually like them much) and nobody else takes any notice. An increasing number of highly literate people simply ignore what the 'Highbrow' are doing. It says nothing to them. The Highbrows in return ignore and insult them."

What is to be done? My proposal is a revival of the clerisy. And surely those who have read thus far will know by now of what the clerisy consists.

If it is to become a more vocal and coherent body on the North American continent, the people who comprise it must do a very difficult thing—a thing from which they now shrink. They must accept the fact of their clerisy, and be ready to assert it and defend it with good manners when the need arises. This will expose them to some measure of dislike, and probably a good deal of ridicule. They will find among their ranks many people in whose company they can take no joy—the contentious, the cranks, the ax grinders, the meanly ambitious—those pests who turn up in all large groups, and who seem determined to bring shame upon the cause they espouse. The clerisy must expect to be called "intellectuals," a word which has been given both a comic and a sinister connotation of late years.

THE SHAME OF BRAINS

What is so dreadful about being an intellectual? A friend of mine, a European, was engaged by a very important United States company for an important job. He suited all the bosses who interviewed him, and was at last passed on to the high priest of personnel, for a final check. This grandee elicited from my friend that he was keenly interested in music, pictures, theatre, but knew nothing of sports; he played no games, but he liked to go for walks, alone; he read much, in English, French, and German; asked about his hobby, he said "Entertaining." What did he do when he entertained his friends? They talked. The personnel genius was by now somewhat hostile and derisive. "I guess you're what would be called an intellectual," said he "Oh, no," said my friend. "I would not make any such claim for myself; let us say, rather, that an intellectual is what I aspire to be." This naked avowal was more than the personnel man could cope with, and the interview ended.

Why are so many people ashamed of having intelligence and using it? There is nothing democratic about such an attitude. To pretend to be less intelligent than one is deceives nobody and begets dislike, for intelligence cannot be hidden; like a cough, it will out, stifle it how you may. No man has ever won commendation for standing at less than his full height, either physically, morally, or intellectually. If you are an intellectual, your best course is to relax and enjoy it.

This book is about literature (a few odd nooks and corners of it), and it is only in matters relating to literature that I may fittingly exhort my readers to assert themselves in this particular way. My advice as to how they should do so must take the form, chiefly, of prohibitions. No societies, no clubs, associations, or gangs; no buttons, grips, or other means of identification are possible or necessary. Curiosity, the free mind, belief in good taste, and belief in the human race are the marks of the clerisy, allied with a genuine love of literature, not as a manifestation of fashion, not as a substitute for life, but as one of the greatest of the arts, existing for the delight of mankind.

THE COZY BOOKMAN

"Love of literature"—I know how these words may be misunderstood. The "bookman," sunk deep in his leather chair before the fire, his feet in old and comfortable slippers, his friendly briar filled with the fragrant Nostalgia Mixture, and a cherished volume (for "bookmen" are great cherishers of volumes and never seem to read one which is not "well-worn") rises sickeningly before the eye. A pox, yea, a gleety imposthume upon all these bookmen and their snug rituals! They make the whole idea of reading nauseous to thousands of decent people. They love literature only as a kind of intellectual Turkish bath, to caress and lull them. They are the narcissists of the reading world, and their cult belongs in literary clubs dedicated to the Higher Jackassery.

But truly to love literature, to regard it as one of the necessary and occasionally noble aspects of a civilization, is not to be a cozy bookman. It is to belong to the clerisy.

What that means has already been set out in the first few pages of this chapter. It only remains to say how the clerisy can recapture the position in society and the world of letters which it has lost.

AN AWAKENED CLERISY

Obviously a revived or awakened clerisy is not going to be the one which fell asleep in the middle of the nineteenth century. We are the spiritual great-great-grandchildren of those people. Their world is not ours, nor have we their classical education or their Biblical culture; we do not live in a society so frankly class-conscious as theirs. Where they had one new book to read, we have a thousand. Where they had a splendid certainty of their own taste and learning—one recalls the Victorian clergyman who replied to a young lady who observed that his pronunciation of a particular word did not agree with the dictionary: "My dear, dictionaries exist to record the pronunciations of people of education, like myself"—we defer to the opinions of journalistic critics who are, in their turn, reflections of academic critics. We live in a world where bulk is often equated with quality, and though we know that the bestseller is not therefore the best book, we can be awed by impressive sales. Nevertheless, we of the clerisy exist; we are not fools; we can make our existence felt by authors, publishers, and critics simply by recognizing that we exist as a class which cuts across all classes, and by making our opinions better known, verbally, in public, by correspondence, and by the other means which present themselves in the course of daily life. We are people to be reckoned with.

Courteously but firmly we must refuse the outsider role, the layman label, which we have allowed the world of publishers and critics to foist upon us. By our own sheepishness we incurred this loss of our right; by our intelligence we shall reclaim it. We are not ashamed to reverse the words of Nathaniel in *Love's Labour's Lost:* we *have* fed of the dainties that are bred in a book; we *have* eat paper and drunk ink; our intellect is replenished.

2

A Rake at Reading

Robertson Davies's interesting account of a lifetime's encounter with books—ranging in sophistication from *The Little Red Hen* to *Ulysses*—encompasses his philosophy of reading before moving on to the provocative assertion that "we who are committed readers may appear to choose our books, but in an equally true sense our books choose us."

Davies chose the University of Manitoba in Winnipeg to deliver these thoughts as the 1980 Warhaft Memorial Lecture. The event had initially been arranged for October 16, 1980, but Davies came down with flu and the lecture was rescheduled for November 20. In his diary he deals frankly not only with the reaction to his talk, but also with his own reaction to hearty prairie fare at the residence breakfast table. The diary records: *Then my lecture at University College to over five hundred people: hall full. Goes extremely well and lots of people want to talk afterward. I like the pretty girls who say "Oh, you're wonderful!"—Vain old ass that I am, but what one could not attain in youth one savours in age.*

The next day: *Get some breakfast this morning, but ate Shredded Wheat as apparently the students eat three fried sausages partnered with three great stove lids of wheat cakes, drenched in maple syrup: My soul yearned after this dish, but I knew that my senile gut would never put up with it....*

✑

"People say that life is the thing, but I prefer reading." Did I say that? No, Logan Pearsall Smith said it, but I have thought it so many times that sometimes I mistake it for my own. However, as you will know by the time I have done, that is not my final, most carefully considered opinion. All my life long, reading has been my great refuge and solace, and in those words I have given myself away. What, you are thinking, does he not read for information, for enrichment, in order to acquaint himself with the best which has been thought and said in the world? Is he admitting that he reads for escape?

Alas, though necessity has driven me to read much that even Matthew Arnold would have approved, and a mountain of rubbish that nobody could approve—I mean mediocre journalism, government publications, the essays of students, and all that sort of thing—when I read for my own satisfaction, I read just as I please. That is why I have called this address "A Rake at Reading." The phrase comes from a letter written to a friend by Lady Mary Wortley Montagu: "I have been a rake at reading," says she. The word *rake*, in the middle of the eighteenth century when Lady Mary made her confession to the Countess of Bute, still meant to roam or stray, but I think she also meant it to have a hint of what was dissolute and irresponsible. So— I confess I have been a rake at reading. I have read those things which I ought not to have read, and I have not read those things which I ought to have read, and there is no health in me—if by health you mean an inclusive and coherent knowledge of any body of great literature. I can only protest, like all rakes in their shameful senescence, that I have had a good time.

It occurred to me on my last birthday that I have been reading for sixty years. Before that time people read to me. My parents chose books they supposed would be good for me. My father read from Kingsley's *The Heroes* and Hawthorne's *Tanglewood Tales*, and these adventures into classic myth frightened me out of my wits and marked me forever as a lover, and victim, of myth. My mother read Ruskin's *The King of the Golden River* and Grimm's Fairy Tales, and I have been devoted to both ever since. But my brothers read to me, as well. On the sly, they read the comics for me—in those days we called them the Funny Papers—and I had a powerful urge to live in the exciting, violent world of Mutt and Jeff and Mr. and Mrs. Jiggs. Like so many small children I longed to impress myself on the adult world—that world of gods, ogres, monsters, and inexplicable forces. I should have liked to possess one of those weapons that every hero of the mythic past called his own—a great bow or a magic sword—I would have been just as much thrilled by the power to throw spittoons and rolling pins with the deadly accuracy displayed in the Funny Paper world. You see I had no taste, no discrimination. I have developed a little of those qualities since then, but vulgarity and rough stuff still have a strong appeal for me.

Best of all, perhaps, were what may be called Family Stories—reminiscences by my parents of their own life in childhood. My mother recalled visits to her native city by Sir John A. Macdonald, when children whose parents were not of Sir John's political colour danced along the streets beside his carriage, singing—

> I wish I were in the land of cotton
> Sticking pins in Old John's bottom.

My father, who was born in North Wales, spent his childhood in a town dominated by a Castle, inhabited by a real Earl and his beautiful Countess, and these were figures of fable. But even more fascinating were the characters from Welsh low-life—his nurse Liz Duckett and her husband, John Jones, known in Welsh fashion as Jack the Jockey—to distinguish him from Jack the Skinner, who was also a Jones. These inherited memories peopled my world of fantasy, where the Earl of Powys was a hero as authentic as Hercules, and Sir John A. was a monster in no way less terrifying than the Minotaur. Thus narrative and fable entered my life much earlier than education, or reading. And so I think it must be for all lucky children.

I did not learn to read until I was six, which I believe is considered rather late. But with people ready to read to me, what inducement had I to learn? I must have had a queer notion of what reading involved, for I remember that the first day I went to school, I returned home, took a volume of the encyclopedia from the shelf, opened it, and waited for it to tell me something. I knew that reading was a skill that came of going to school, and I was humiliated to find that it involved a tedious encounter with a creature called the Little Red Hen.

Have you ever met the Little Red Hen? Hers was the first story in the *Ontario Primer*, and it was printed not in the Latin alphabet, but in the debased calligraphy which was taught to children at that time, ruining their handwriting forever. Why it was thought that children could read this script more easily than print, I do not know. In the pictures illustrating the story, the Little Red Hen was larger than the cat, the dog, and the pig with whom she shared the farmyard. Much later in life, when I became interested in the icons of the Orthodox church, I discovered the reasoning behind this apparent absurdity; the Little Red Hen was morally bigger than the cat, the dog, and the pig, so she was drawn larger, just as saints in icons are drawn larger than pagans or people of mere ordinary virtue.

The story was that the Little Red Hen found some wheat; she called on the cat, the dog, and the pig to help her plant, reap, grind, and make bread from the wheat, but they refused. But when the Little Red Hen said, "Who will help me eat the bread?" they were eager for a share. This was the Little Red Hen's finest hour. She declared: "You would not plant the wheat, you would not cut the wheat, you would not grind the wheat, you would not bake the bread; you shall not eat the bread. My little chicks shall eat the bread." And they did.

This is unexceptionable doctrine. Not Karl Marx, not Chairman Mao at his finest, not even Mrs. Thatcher could have improved on the political doctrine of the Little Red Hen. Yet—somehow I did not like it. During my life I have met a great many Little Red Hens, and they are quick to point out that they are the salt of the earth; they are always working for the good of somebody else. They are morally superior; they know best. It never occurred to the Little Red Hen that the dog had been guarding the farmyard for her; that she had been free to enjoy the physical beauty and music of the cat; that barnyard culture owed an immeasurable debt to the philosophy and general dignity of the pig; no, in the conduct of her life she was confined within the world view of a hen, and she asked no more.

Once out of the toils of the Little Red Hen things got better in the Primer. That group of little pigs who went to market, stayed at home, had roast beef, went hungry, and said "Wee, wee" (and what child ever failed to put his whole heart into reading "Wee, wee"?) came next, then Humpty Dumpty, then Jack and Jill, and then—wonder of wonders—Christina Rossetti's poem "Who Has Seen the Wind?" which was our first glimpse of poetic beauty, and to meet it at the age of six, and to be able to read it for oneself, was an adventure. Of course I did not know that it was a fine lyric, but I felt its grace, and I knew it came from a source very far away from the Little Red Hen.

Here I should like to speak in praise of the committee, as I suppose it must have been, who chose the material for those old Ontario School Readers. These were graded to meet the reading ability of children between six and twelve, but they were not confined to somebody's notion of what children at that time of life might most easily understand. The Readers contained a good deal of what was commonplace, and much that was of a narrowly moral tendency, because in the course of time the Little Red Hen changed her name to Benjamin Franklin, and we were confronted with samples of his cautious, cynical, mean-spirited attitude toward life—the boy who was warned against adults who wanted him to turn the grindstone, and the boy who paid too much for his whistle—as if the price of a really fine, heart-lifting whistle could be estimated in money. This was in the vein of the Little Red Hen, whose influence is strong. It is not commonly known that two of her chicks went into the Reader business for themselves, under the names of Dick and Jane. But there were splendid, life-enhancing things, as well. There was Aesop, whose fables were gold, whereas the Little Red Hen and Benjamin Franklin were gilded tin. There was somebody of whom I know nothing, called F.W. Bourdillon, who, when we were eight, told us that—

> The night has a thousand eyes,
> And the day but one;
> Yet the light of the bright world dies
> With the dying sun.
>
> The mind has a thousand eyes,
> And the heart but one;
> Yet the light of a whole life dies
> When love is done.

There's a mind stretcher for children! There is what I think of as an educational time bomb, for it reaches its target, and explodes later. I suppose it was fifteen years after I read that poem in school before I really understood what it meant, but when I needed it, there it was, ready to mind.

Who put these time bombs in those Readers? Some unknown teacher who would not have agreed with the later educational psychologists who were so earnest in their desire that a child should not be confronted with anything it could not fully comprehend, and who were astonishingly sure that they knew what children could comprehend, and who never understood how warmly intelligent children respond to what they partly comprehend. Another of these time bombs for me was this—

It is not growing like a tree
In bulk, doth make man better be;
Or standing long an oak, three hundred year,
To fall a log at last, dry, bald and sere:
A lily of a day
Is fairer far in May,
Although it fall and die that night;
It was the plant and flower of light.
In small proportions we just beauty see;
And in short measures life may perfect be.

Nobody told us that was a Pindaric, and a great one. Nobody said anything about the author, Ben Jonson. They simply said that it meant that you could lead a good life even as a child. That was enough for us at the time. But the splendour of expression is for a lifetime.

Of course the Readers did not always move on that high level. There was much in them that was commonplace, much that would now be hopelessly out of fashion, telling of heroic deeds and impossible aspirations, but there was very little downright trash. Even the trash had a romantic glow about it, like a bad lobster in a dark cellar. An example is a dreadful story which told how Beethoven, walking through the streets of Bonn one night, heard someone playing his Sonata in F; he investigated and found that the player was a blind girl, poor and despairing because she wanted to go to Cologne to hear the great master play in person. Rushing in, Beethoven cried, "I am a musician; I will improvise a Sonata to the Moonlight," and he did, then and there, and rushed off at once to write down the Moonlight Sonata while he could still remember it. This did not impress me, because my family was musical and I knew that composers didn't work like that; I also knew that Beethoven had been about as kindly and charitable as a bear with a thorn in its paw. Nevertheless, the romance of the story appealed to me. Not so much, however, as the romance of Don Quixote's fight with the windmills, which was in the same Third Reader.

I must not detain you over these Readers of my Ontario childhood, but I think they are worth some time as evidence of what was offered, not in a school for advanced children, or children from wealthy homes, but to all the children of the province, in its public schools. Nowadays such selections would probably be condemned as elitist, for they gave children hard nuts to crack, and it is certain that not every child cracked them. But I think that behind the selection there stood a fine ideal, which was nothing less than to create, on however modest a scale, a coherent body of literary knowledge in which everybody could share, so that in future every citizen of Ontario would know who Don Quixote was, and who Mr. Pickwick was, and Ali Baba and his Old Man of the Sea, and that Sir Walter Scott and R.L. Stevenson had written stirring ballads and romances, and that we had in Canada writers whose work was fit to stand in this distinguished company. There is an idea prevalent today that Canadian writing was scorned and neglected until quite recently, but that is not true. The Readers contained Canadian poems and tales of historic adventure, and although the bias was certainly toward English writers, and then toward American writers, with Longfellow, Lowell, and Whittier well to the fore, Canadian writers, and especially Canadian poets, were not neglected.

Later, in high school, we used a fine anthology compiled by Professor W.J. Alexander of the University of Toronto, called simply *Shorter Poems*, divided into four parts for use over four years; each part contained a generous selection of Canadian verse, and to encounter Wilfred Campbell's "How One Winter Came in the Lake Region"—

> That night I felt the winter in my veins,
> A joyous tremor of the icy glow;
> And woke to hear the north's wild vibrant strains,
> While far and wide, by withered woods and plains,
> Fast fell the driving snow.

—that was literary adventure, for there was our own weather and our own landscape transformed into poetry.

I spoke of elitism a few minutes ago; Professor Alexander seems to have been an elitist, for in his preface he writes: "Here are to be found some poems of very slight poetic merit; because something in them— their dash, their fun, even their didactic content or moralizing vein— may give them a hold upon those whose imaginative and aesthetic sensibilities are dull or undeveloped." You see, he did not expect every pupil to understand everything in his anthology at the same level of intensity. Or was he not simply a realist? I often wonder if the elitists are not those who, like the Little Red Hen, assert their judgments on the basis of what they themselves think best, relying on some inborn grace, rather than an acquaintance with a broad culture.

Permit me to refer just once more to the school Readers of my childhood, for there was a selection in the Fourth Reader, which I suppose I encountered at the age of eleven or twelve; it has remained with me through the years, not because of its romance or richness of style, but because of the chill it cast upon me then and which it casts to this day. If you wanted something for children of that age, would it occur to you to choose the 159th number of Addison's *Spectator*? It is called *The Vision of Mirzah*, and it tells of an Eastern sage who climbs into the mountains above Baghdad, and there meets the Genius of the Rocks, who shows him a vision: Far in the valley below he sees a great sea, and the Genius tells him that it is the Vale of Misery, and that the water is the great Tide of Eternity. At both ends of the water is mist, and between stretches the bridge of human life; the bridge has seven entire arches, and after that a few broken arches, and over this bridge, which is beset with many perils, Mirzah sees the procession of mankind making its stumbling way until, worn out with the journey, each figure falls into the waters below. When Mirzah grieves that the fate of man should be so wretched, the Genius dispels some of the mist at the further end of the bridge and shows him the islands where the blessed ones find peace; but the fate of those who are not among the blessed the Genius refuses to reveal. As Mirzah eagerly seeks to gain the secret of time and eternity, the Genius vanishes and the allegory of life vanishes as well, and Mirzah sees only Baghdad in the valley below.

Now, isn't that a dainty dish to set before a child of eleven? There is a good deal of Biblical material in the Readers as a whole, but this is a cold blast from the eighteenth century, and none the worse for that. When I meet contemporaries today I sometimes ask them: Do you remember the *Vision of Mirzah*? The best of them do. They are not the ones with cozy minds.

Perhaps you are wondering what was rakish about reading what I was obliged to read in school. Nothing at all; the rakishness began at home. My parents were keen readers, and had a lot of books, but they were also readers of a kind rarer in our day than it was in the early twenties. They read a lot of periodicals: the *Atlantic Monthly* and *Scribner's* came into our house, and these, with the *Saturday Evening Post*, which was a great fiction magazine at that time, were our contributions from below the border. From England came the *Strand* and *Pearson's*, as well as *Punch*, but so far as I was concerned *Punch* meant pictures. Thus a great many short stories were available to me every month, at a time when the short story engaged some of the best writers of the day. P.G. Wodehouse was a favourite, and innocent; but Somerset Maugham was not, and I devoured his supposedly cynical tales of adultery with a powerful appetite, because, although I was not sure what adultery was, I knew it was wicked. There were, even at that late date, new stories about Sherlock Holmes by Conan Doyle, and the funny stories about sailors and poachers by W.W. Jacobs.

I spoke of the readiness of children to welcome what they cannot wholly understand; I well recall my puzzled fascination with Kipling's story "Dayspring Mishandled," which I first met in one of these English magazines of fiction.

Sometimes there was a serious article on a hot topic, and I especially remember one by a bishop headed "Is Nudity Salacious?" (The bishop thought it need not be, if encountered in the proper spirit, but he gave a lot of enlightening examples of conditions under which it might be, in his word, *inflammatory*. There wasn't much nudity in our neck of the woods, and I enjoyed that article tremendously.) There were many stories with backgrounds of high life and society, which I suppose would be thought unsuitable for a child. I was not supposed to read these magazines, but as nobody supervised my reading very carefully, I read them on the sly. A magazine was taken especially for me; it was called *The Youth's Companion*; it came from Boston and was of a morally improving tendency containing stories about remorselessly grammatical boys and girls who were helpful to their parents and generally admirable. I read all the stories about girls, hoping to penetrate their secrets; I knew girls had secrets because all the girls I met were great whisperers and gigglers.

Much more fun, for a boy like me, was the bound volume I received each Christmas, of an English boys' magazine called *Chums*. It was about Anarchic Boys, who put their schools on the rocks and drove their masters to the brink of madness by their ingenious pranks; there were also Daring Boys, who had adventures with mountains, the sea, and criminal foreigners. (Foreigners were sharply divided between Good Foreigners, who might be Dutch or noble-minded East Indians and Bad Foreigners, who were German, or Russian, or evil-minded Easterners who were usually described as "rascally Lascars"). There were boys who saved the Honour of the School by sporting feats. And of course there were boys who lived in past ages of history, and did marvels at Trafalgar, or Waterloo, or even at Crecy and Agincourt.

The one thing all these boys had in common was that they were not Canadians. I did not question this; it seemed natural enough that everything interesting happened somewhere else. Many years later I was told by a reader for a great London theatrical producing company, to which I was trying to sell some of my plays—"Nobody is interested in Canada." This opinion is still strong in England, though it seems to be losing its grip elsewhere.—But I am mistaken. I had one book of Canadian adventures by William Kingston called *Snowshoes and Canoes*, and a thrilling book it was.

There was nothing rakish about these publications that were aimed at children, but I read other things, not in magazines. I read a lot of Dickens, and though there are still people who think Dickens innocuous for children, I can tell them they are wrong. I did not know quite why Quilp was pursuing Little Nell, but I sensed that it was for no good purpose. I was strongly aware of Evil, even if I could not pin it down. I was told not to read *Tess of the D'Urbervilles*, as it was, in my parents' phrase, "beyond me," and I suppose it was, because so far as I could discover Tess fell asleep under a tree in the company of the wicked Alec D'Urberville, and shortly afterward had a baby, about which there was an unholy fuss, considering what tedious creatures babies were. As you see, I was sexually uninformed. On my mother's strong recommendation I read Victor Hugo's *Nôtre Dame de Paris*, and it won an allegiance that I have not relinquished to this day; I must have read it five or six times. But I didn't know why the wicked priest was trying to get the beautiful Esmeralda into his alchemist's cell in Nôtre Dame; my interest was all in the grotesque Quasimodo, who also wanted Esmeralda, whom he presumably meant to keep as a pet. I knew about Love, of course; Somerset Maugham had made it clear that Love was dangerous and fascinating. Sex was to come later.

If there was to be any Sex, I wanted it with style and magic. And sure enough, when I was about fifteen, along came just the right book; it was *Mademoiselle de Maupin* in the Powys Mathers translation, and I read it at boarding school, after lights-out, with the aid of a flashlight. Here was the thing I wanted; the language was splendid, the story entrancing, and the descriptions of sexual encounters exquisitely managed, being at once intense and delicate in their atmosphere. The lovers were sophisticated adventurers but they were neither coarse nor yet cripplingly innocent, like Tess, who must have been, I decided, a dumbbell, as well as a Pure Woman, and I did not like the combination. Here, you see, rakishness is at last apparent; I was not impressed by conventional literary judgments. Is there a serious student of literature, I wonder, who would rank Theophile Gautier above Thomas Hardy? I was not a serious student of literature. Never was, and doubtless never will be. But I had a taste of my own, which is not a luxury every serious student of literature permits himself.

From *Mademoiselle de Maupin* I never looked back, and my next rung on the ladder of literary rakishness was Aldous Huxley. Since his death, he has been enskied and sainted by people who put heavy emphasis on his later, serious books, but when I met him he was thought to be a dangerously cynical and sophisticated fellow, and the girls I knew were all forbidden to read him. His very title pages were thought to be seminal.

What appealed to me about *Antic Hay*, which was the first of his novels to come my way, was not that it was funny—though it is very funny indeed—but that it looked at life, so to speak, through the wrong end of the binoculars, giving it a wonderful clarity, while at the same time putting it at a distance, so that compassion became an irrelevance. I had, by that time, had enough compassion in literature to last me for several years, and a holiday in the intellect, with emotion temporarily removed from the scene, was just what I needed. But Huxley was only one of the authors who won me a reputation as a rake at reading. Probably the greatest was Bernard Shaw, whose plays and prefaces I consumed by the dim illumination of my flashlight, when I should have been asleep. The father of one of my friends, having heard me speak with enthusiasm of Shaw, forbade my friend ever to ask me to the house again. I was obviously in training to become an anarchist. But I was unimpressed by this sort of disdain. I went beyond Shaw and Huxley and read Havelock Ellis.

This was in my first year at Queen's, and I had to get the book from the sulphurous region beyond the Librarian's office where the Special Collection was housed. I have never met anyone else who has read the whole of *Studies in the Psychology of Sex*; I believe they are now condemned as wrong-headed by modern psychologists, but they were admirably written, and the case histories they contained gave me an idea of the infinite variability of mankind for which I am profoundly grateful. Ellis was not obtrusively compassionate, but he was accepting of human variety, and at a time when it is fashionable to rate him rather low, I still think him a great man.

From Ellis it was an easy leap to Freud, whose major works I gobbled with a greedy appetite. The vision of life Freud presented was bleak, but the Ontario Readers had given me enough high-mindedness and aspiration to make a heavy dosage of bleakness very acceptable. Freud is tough chewing, and while I was reading him I had not time or inclination to read many other things that bulked large in the reading of my contemporaries. I never read much Hemingway. Under the urging of a friend who had read *Farewell to Arms* five times I read it once, and told him I thought it a sentimental account of an uninteresting adultery between uninteresting people. He was furious; this was blasphemy. But I spoke sincerely; under the spell of Shaw and Huxley I could find nothing of interest in Hemingway's tongue-tied, hard-breathing lovers.

Nor did I get on any better with Thomas Wolfe, whom I thought insufferably tedious. Scott Fitzgerald I considered to be attempting to do what Evelyn Waugh splendidly achieved. My friends said I could see no good in any writer who was not English. Not so. Sinclair Lewis was one of my heroes, a taste encouraged by my mother, who once told me that whenever she felt herself feeling tenderly toward the clergy she hastened to correct it by a rereading of *Elmer Gantry*. Another American writer whom I read with avidity was H.L. Mencken, and although now I can hardly bear anything of his except the great books on the American Language, I owe him a debt of gratitude for some rough eye-openers in my youth.

Not very rakish yet, you may say. Nothing really offbeat in any of this. But in 1933 I discovered an author, by no means widely popular yet, though I think him one of the giants of our century, and so do some other critics whom I respect. I speak of John Cowper Powys. It was in that year that *A Glastonbury Romance* appeared; it was just what I wanted and I read its 1,174 pages with wonderment, sometimes with bafflement, but eventually with breathtaking illumination. I had found one of my great men. He was not English, nor was he American; he declared himself to be Welsh, though he was not by any reckoning as Welsh as I was myself. Very often he described his best fictions, which I hastened to read, as romances, which is a better name for them than novels, for they break every rule that the high priests of the novel have devised. He was as great a master as Joyce—in my view greater—but he did not try to extend the confines of language as Joyce did; instead he attempted, with variable success (for he is not one of your fine-tuned writers, not a great stylist) to extend the boundaries of what language can do in evoking rare and unusual modes of feeling. His books are romances in the old Celtic sense, for in them the point of view changes whenever he pleases, the prevailing mood varies and bypaths are pursued with what is sometimes maddening caprice. But they enlarge the reader's concept of what may be comprised within a single consciousness in a way that many masters of the novel, like Henry James, cannot achieve. Yet he was not describable as a romantic; sometimes he is a realist, sometimes a cynic. He is, to put it as simply as possible, a very great man of a Blake-like breadth of perception. If I had no time for Hemingway or Faulkner or D.H. Lawrence, it was because I was greatly occupied elsewhere.

At the same time I found my bonnet giving shelter to a very fine bee. Consider this: From the age of seventeen onward I devoted a great deal of time to greedy reading of the drama of the nineteenth century. Why, I shall not explain. There is an explanation, but it belongs to another portion of my autobiography. Wedged in among Freud and Powys I was reading anything I could get my hands on of the social drama, the costume drama, the farce, and the melodrama of the period between 1800 and 1880. Of course I read Ibsen, to see what had supplanted the theatre of my favoured period, and I fell under the spell of that magnificent psychologist and have remained his devoted admirer ever since. I did not read nineteenth-century plays to jeer at them, but for the enjoyment they brought me. I never scorned them: These were plays, I reminded myself, that Dickens, Thackeray, George Eliot, and a score of other great ones had seen, and while they condemned the worst, they applauded the best; therefore there must be something in them. Our forefathers did not leave their brains at the door when they went to the theatre.

Where did I find such plays? The fine collections of Michael Booth and George Rowell were far in the future, and I had to rummage in the outside barrows of bookshops on Tottenham Court Road on my occasional visits to England, and pick up shabby copies for sixpence apiece. I have now, I may say, about twelve hundred of those forgotten, scorned plays in their original form, and I smile when university librarians inquire, with the utmost casualness, where I intend to bestow them when I can read them no more. In my own reading, and in my university courses, I had thrust myself deep into the drama that the academic world at that time considered worthy of study. I knew the Elizabethans and the Augustans, and the playwrights who were admired during the last of the nineteenth century and the first thirty years of this one. But in between I had fitted the plays that came between Sheridan—the last English dramatist endurable to the academic mind—and Shaw.

Why did I do it? Was it perversity or eccentricity? No, it was curiosity, and a conviction that those plays—superficially false and rhetorical in their language and mechanical in their plots—must have some content that had once given them life. I think I found what I was looking for. The language in some of them is of remarkable vivacity and strength, and modern productions of Boucicault and O'Keeffe have shown it again in its special gloss. No less a critic than Hazlitt called O'Keeffe "the English Molière." At the heart of so many of them is the ideal of Poetic Justice, which appealed so powerfully to an age where great social upheavals and their inevitable injustices were the stuff of daily experience. I even went so far as to decide that melodrama is as valid a mode of synthesizing human experience as tragedy or comedy, and that whereas few of us are so happy as to live our lives in terms of comedy, and fewer still move in the terrible world of tragedy, most of us live out our existence in that combination of cheerfulness, despair, coincidence, poetry, low comedy, and slapdash improvisation that is the shimmering fabric of melodrama.

One of the astounding successes of the recent theatrical season in London is a nine-hour dramatic presentation of Dickens's *Nicholas Nickleby*; Dickens, who longed for success on the stage, has it at last, and it is made manifest in the theatre that his work is in the melodramatic mode at its greatest, and that at its greatest it is a profoundly revealing vision of man's existence.

Every September I smile inwardly when a group of students assembles at my university to begin a seminar with me in the study of these plays which were so utterly neglected when I was their age. I am proud that I have had some part of putting those plays into perspective. And when I begin by saying that it is not necessary for a play to have obvious literary worth in order to reach far into the spirit of man, I seem to hear at my shoulder the gasps of my professors of forty-five years ago who would have burned their gowns rather than admit any such thing.

As a young man, I spent several years working as a book reviewer. There is little chance for rakishness there, because a reviewer has to do his best with what comes to his desk, and inevitably the popular books that everybody wants to hear about make first demands on him. But when I worked on *Saturday Night*—which I did, all told, for several years—I was able to give attention to some of the best books Canadian writers have produced, and I am proud to say that I welcomed the best with enthusiasm.

It was a principle with me to review, so far as possible, only what I could honestly praise; I have never seen much use, or found much satisfaction, in knocking a book. Praising the best of these Canadian books was easy and delightful work. Hugh MacLennan's *The Watch that Ends the Night*, Sinclair Ross's *As for Me and My House*, and Gabrielle Roy's *Where Nests the Water Hen*, to name only three that came my way, were fine books by international standards. I was particularly pleased to have the opportunity to praise the books of reminiscences that were published, late in her life, by Emily Carr. Canada has had more than enough of gaseous, self-justifying political reminiscence and biography; the distilled thoughts of an artist of fine and strongly individual perception have a value far beyond such nonsense, and I still think Emily Carr one of the finest writers this country has ever produced, although her great fame is as a painter.

A book reviewer has to read a great deal, and he is lucky if he is a fast reader. I have not that gift. I rank only slightly above those who move their lips and follow the lines with a careful finger. I read most of each day in an inner office, without daylight, in a constrained posture and heavily sedated by a pipe or a Dutch cigar. Did it take a heavy toll of my health? As you may see, I am not of a noticeably feeble frame, and my eyesight is decidedly better than it was when I was twenty-one. The Little Red Hen would not approve, but these are the facts.

Not only did I read most of each day, but I did some of my reading for review at night, and when I was tired of that I read for pleasure. What did I read? An incoherent mass of books, as I had done, and continue to do. I am one of those obsessed creatures who must read any print that comes within my range. I have told you that as a child I read anything and everything. When I visited my grandmother I read my grandmother's books, and that is how I came to be one of the few people I have met who have read *Lavender and Old Lace*. It was at my grandmother's that I made the acquaintance of an author nobody seems to read now, Charles Lever, whose *Charles O'Malley* and *Harry Lorrequer* exactly suited my romantic and melodramatic taste. I have read a lot of Charles Reade, Wilkie Collins, and Harrison Ainsworth. If some of you are saying, So have I, let me ask you this: How much have you read of Henry Cockton? I do not urge him upon you, for he is not third-rate, he is thirty-third rate, but he provides a special insight into the nineteenth century, because he was once a bestseller, and he is a startling example of what people will read by an author who has a reputation for being funny. It has long been a principle of mine that to understand the writing of any age, one must read not only the best, but what was most popular at the time. In Thomas Hardy's words—

> If way to the better there be
> It exacts a full look at the worst.

Cockton, a comic novelist, was part of the worst of nineteenth-century writing.

What any age thinks funny is a special key to its nature. That is what has led me, in my time, to read a great many old Jest Books. It is a salutary experience to read Jest Books from the seventeenth century, for they reveal what the ordinary man of that era thought uproariously funny, while the comedies of Farquhar, Vanbrugh, and Congreve were amusing the intelligentsia. A clerical friend of mine used to say that nothing is so dead as the last generation's books of theology: I dispute that—dead humour is not merely dead, but rotten, and only a literary ghoul like myself can feed on it with pleasure.

Do you ask for an example? Consider this from *The Pickwick Treasury of Wit*, the date of which is 1845—almost yesterday: "It having been proved on a trial at Guildhall that a man's name was really *Inch* who pretended it was *Linch*, I see said the judge, the old proverb is verified in this man, if we allow him an *Inch* he will take an L." Or do you prefer this: "A tailor who lived near a church yard in a large town, used to count the number of funerals by putting a stone into a pot, hung up in his shop for that purpose. On his death taking place, his house was shut; and on enquiry, it was observed by a next door neighbour, that the tailor himself was *gone to pot*."

In the course of time I became a writer myself, and of course that had a strong effect on my reading. In what way? I quickly found out that there was no advice better than that of Sir Walter Scott, who said that when he was writing, he read avidly, anything and everything, so long as it had no bearing on the subject of his book. A writer reads to distract the surface of his consciousness, while below the surface it is busy composing. He must be careful that he does not absorb, and unwittingly repeat, something that has been written by somebody else. With him, more than with most people, reading is a drug.

You might suppose that what is called "light reading" would be just the thing under these circumstances. I never found that to be the case. I have never been able to read detective stories with any satisfaction; they are puzzles, written, it seems to me, by people who are not in the least interested in the wellsprings of criminal thought and behaviour. I do not like travel books, because I have a poor visual imagination, and descriptions of foreign scenes baffle me. All my life I have refused to read any book whatever that attempts to explain politics or economics.

So, when I am writing—which is virtually all the time, nowadays— what do I read? Dickens, the great melodramatist, I have read and reread many times, and the more I read the more I find. I have often said that if you hope to come seriously to grips with a book, you should read it when you are at least the age the author was when he wrote it. Alas, I am now considerably older than Dickens was when he died, but he still has secrets for me. But one must read Dickens as a whale takes in its food, in vast gulps. The broad effect is everything, though many of the details are exquisite. But unless you attack the books as melodramas, they will not yield their splendid savour to you.

Too much unrelieved Dickens is bad for you, and as an antidote I recommend Anthony Trollope, one of the greatest of realistic novelists, though, as with all realism, his has, with the passing of years, taken on a romantic glow. Trollope called Dickens "Mr. Popular Sentiment," and it is true that Dickens would do extraordinary things, and sometimes unworthy things, to catch the crowd. But not even Trollope could be as realistic as he knew how; read his *Autobiography* and learn how much he had to falsify the love scenes in his novels to make them palatable to an age that dearly loved a long, eloquent, agonized proposal uttered by a young man to a girl who fully intended to accept him and would have been a fool if she had done otherwise. Of course, neither Dickens nor Trollope, nor any of their English or American contemporaries, was free to write what they knew about the sexual involvements of their characters.

If you want to know what they knew but dared not tell, you must read Balzac. There is a writer who fills me with extravagant delight, for he seems to deny himself nothing. If he wants to tell you in detail how the printing trade worked in the early nineteenth century he does so, because he knew a lot about printing and thought it interesting. We could do with less of this, but his enthusiasm is so great that he carries us along, protesting but yielding. About sex he knew everything, and whatever he knew, he wrote into a novel. There are sophistications of sexual involvement in Balzac that are beyond the range of any but a handful of writers. I particularly enjoy his descriptions of those very rich bourgeois who had to maintain a mistress because it was owing to their financial importance; furthermore, the mistress must be of transporting beauty and wit (by which was meant a gross and abusive impudence toward her protector) and she must have horses, carriages, and apartments equal to the finest in Paris. In return her protector was permitted to visit her often, if he gave sufficient notice that he was coming, and he was allowed to talk with her, be petted a little by her, and cheered by her slangy, guttersnipe conversation. He might sleep with her now and again, but this was a rare indulgence, and apparently it was not necessarily his right; indeed, he was jeered at so harshly that he might not feel like attempting it. But the final turn of the dagger in the wound was that he had to maintain her real, youthful lover, as well as the girl, give him an allowance, and pay his debts. An unenviable bargain, one might think, but fashion has its dreadful exactions, like any other addiction.

Balzac knew obsession as no other writer of my experience knew it. I mean obsession with money, and also with objects, as well as people. If you wish to know what the collector's mania can do to a man, read *Cousin Pons*, which is at once one of the funniest and most pathetic books known to me.

Balzac, however, writes of bourgeois life and I sometimes have a taste for dash of high life, and I find that in Proust. The world is full of people who talk about *À la recherche du temps perdu*, but they are more numerous than those who have read its full twelve volumes. Much of it is tough chewing, but it is enormously rewarding. It is a book within which one may live, and I have known people who seemed, for years at a time, to be subsumed in it. It has been described in many ways, but to me it is romantic and melodramatic. Perhaps those are qualities I bring to it, but certainly I find what I am looking for in its pages.

Proust's aristocrats are gold and silver plate, and Proust collects them as Cousin Pons collected objects of art. Real aristocrats are to be found in the novels of Tolstoy, that immense, dismaying genius. Here we find people who are not obsessed by society, which they do not notice any more than the air they breathe. I am not convinced by Tolstoy's peasants; he never knew them as, for instance, Thomas Hardy knew them. But his aristocrats ring true, and they are to Proust's people as the krugerrand is to those chocolate coins wrapped in gilt foil that children used to be given at Christmas. I called Tolstoy dismaying, because as I read him I cannot help but compare his people with the people I know, and the sort of person I am myself, and the comparison is not a comfortable one. Tolstoy is full of compassion, but I mistrust it because he has no humour, and I believe humour and compassion to be inseparable.

Not all these novelists who move on the heights put us to shame. I am happy, at any time, to enter into the world of Thomas Mann, labyrinthine though it often is. But with Mann there is always a saving irony; he has an extraordinary sense of humour that does not shake one with laughter, but possesses one with a mirth too deep for noisy expression. If you do not believe me, reread the passage in *Joseph and His Brothers* in which Joseph is set upon by Potiphar's wife. If you do not find it splendidly comic, I think you have missed the point. Mann is serious but he is not drowned in his own seriousness, as is, for instance, Dostoyevsky. In reading Dostoyevsky it is often useful to remind oneself that he considered himself a pupil of Dickens; he has the Dickensian eye, and the Dickensian instinct for the revealing detail, but the pull of his spirit is toward tragedy. What is really Dickensian about him is his revelation of the absurdity, the hilarity that stands so close to much tragedy, including the tragedy of Dostoyevsky's own life.

Don't you read anything but novels, I hear you say. I wish I could say that I really read novels. There are libraries full of novelists who are thought great whose work I have not read, or cannot read. I know some of Henry James, but not much, because I would rather read Powys. With the best will in the world I have never been able to get beyond the first few pages of *Moby Dick.* Of the novels of Virginia Woolf I forbear to speak, because although I have read them, nothing can make me read them again; too much acute sensibility affects me as if I were a deep-sea diver—I get the bends. And I have to keep my mouth shut about D.H. Lawrence. I do not deny these delights to those who are able to appreciate them, but I am too old to pretend that they are for me.

It was Oscar Wilde, I believe, who said that nobody appreciated all periods of art equally except an auctioneer. I am suspicious of people who love all the fashionable writers with an undiscriminating zeal, and talk about them all with equal enthusiasm.

To return to the question, however, I read a great deal outside the huge world of the novel. I read a great deal of poetry, old and new, but I mistrust my judgment of the new, so I do not consider myself a judge of poetry. I read many plays, old and new, but we have not the time to talk about that, for it is another address, and quite a different one. There, I am prepared to back my own judgment against anyone.

But in the time that is left, I should like to comment on seven books that I read and reread—books that I do not read from cover to cover, but into which I dip for refreshment and reassurance. They are an odd jumble, but if you attempted some such assemblage of the books that really mean much to you and which have done much to shape your life, you might arrive at an even odder list.

First comes a conventional choice, for it is the Bible, with which I link the Apocrypha and the Anglican Prayer Book. For many years I never read the Bible at all. I had too much of it in childhood, and it is not a child's book, and the children who appear in it are not attractive. My parents were drenched in the Bible, and I heard it quoted from my birth. Unhappily, my parents too had had too much Bible in youth, and their quotations were often of the kind that Bibliolaters would rather forget. I early became acquainted with the vomit quotations: "He hath swallowed down riches, and he shall vomit them up again: God shall cast them out of his belly." (That's from Job.) "As a dog returneth to his vomit, so a fool returneth to his folly." (That's Proverbs.) This dog was a close friend of the sow that was washed and returned to her wallowing in the mire. (That's Second Peter.) I knew about the Philistines who were smitten with "poignant emerods in their secret parts," and in my own battles with the Philistines I have often longed for the power to serve them in the same way. My parents had a deep loathing for anything they considered sanctimonious, and in their experience the Bible was often the weapon of the sanctimonious. So it took me some time to discover the book as a repository not only of salty, hardbitten wisdom, but as a never-failing book of wonders and inspiration that are timeless, and in the Prayer Book I discovered how much, for me at any rate, religious feeling is dependent on invocation, on splendour of language. The people who are always monkeying with these great books to make them fully comprehensive have no friend in me, for in their realm the fully comprehensible is not worth comprehending. It is to be felt, not worried and interpreted like a Blue Book. Poetry will carry us nearer to God than the unleavened bread of painstaking translation, for some things are beyond full comprehension but are not for that reason unapproachable.

About the religious approach of the Bible—because, despite its immense variety, it has a prevailing attitude—there is something rebuking, and there are often times when I want something nearer to my own frailty than that. I have said nothing about my long involvement with the work and thought of C.G. Jung, which I have studied and puzzled over for something like thirty years. I spoke earlier of my careful reading of Freud, and although I still reverence him as one of history's great liberators of the human spirit, I disagree with his idea that the human spirit is completed in each of us by the age, roughly speaking, of forty, and that after that we run downhill. Jung's insistence that intellectual and spiritual development continues as long as life lasts, and the convincing proof he provides in his own life, have won my allegiance. But it is not easy to follow Jung and be a strictly orthodox Christian; in much of Christianity there is a considerable measure of the spirit of the Little Red Hen, and indifference to the vagarious nature of the human soul. I determined, when composing this address, to be as honest with you as I could, and so I confess that there are times when I wonder whether polytheism has not a great deal to be said for it. And that is what leads me to frequent readings and browsings in a very great book from the pagan past; it is *The Golden Asse* by Apuleius. It reminds me of another great work that is often misunderstood—Mozart's opera, *The Magic Flute*—which blind people see simply as a splendid pantomime, but which contains enough wisdom to shape a life.

As you see, I am a great man for marvels, and I dearly love to read books that had a greater importance in the past than they have now, because they are a port of entry not merely to an age that has gone, but to the human mind, which changes its fashions, but not its body. So I frequently dip into *The Golden Legend* by Jacobus de Voráginé. This thirteenth-century compost heap of legend and belief has been described by the greatest of modern hagiologists, Hippolyte Delehaye, as a compilation not of careful, historically based lives of saints, but rather of legends which contain what people wanted to believe about the saints, at a time when saints were as near as, in our time, world figures in politics, or rock stars, or great athletes, about whom extraordinary accretions of legend deposit. What people greatly desire to believe is quite as interesting as truth, and generally it is more immediately influential. *The Golden Legend* is rich feeding for the reader whose mind has a Jungian bias. But this sort of thing needs a corrective.

I find my corrective in three books written by men who thought of themselves as clear-sighted, perhaps even as realists. Two were great humorists—among the greatest in literature. One is François Rabelais, and the other is James Joyce. Great humorists, certainly, and great humanists as well. Neither one, to me at any rate, is a man to be read from cover to cover every time one picks up *Gargantua and Pantagruel*, or *Ulysses*. I confess that though I wrestle with *Finnegans Wake* from time to time, I am not of the elect who exult over it. But dearer to me than Rabelais or Joyce is a man who never meant to be a humorist, but who has written a magnificent work of humanistic learning and reflection; I speak of Robert Burton and his *Anatomy of Melancholy*. He wrote the book, he said, to dispel his own melancholy, and since his day it has worked the same healing and lenitive art on thousands of others, among whom I count myself.

The last of these books to which I turn for refreshment when others fail may seem to you a surprising choice. It was once popular and ran through countless editions, but you do not find it now in many private libraries. It is *The Ingoldsby Legends, or Mirth and Marvels*, written, in the character of Thomas Ingoldsby, by a clergy-man of the nineteenth century, the Rev. Richard Harris Barham. It is, in its way, a sort of parody of *The Golden Legend*, and it is a reprehen-sibly prejudiced work by an Anglican parson, who wrote much of it in mockery of the revival of interest in saints and ritualism that troubled his church during the first part of the nineteenth century. I do not read it for the satire, which is absurd and often rooted in ignorance; I read it for its irrepressible gaiety of spirit and the magnificently ingen-ious comic verse in which most of it is couched. But I confess it is a cult book, and you might not like it. It seizes upon some people, and not long before he died the American critic Edmund Wilson confessed in an article in *The New Yorker* that he never felt happy in any house in which he lived, if there were not an Ingoldsby on the shelves. This is precisely my own situation; I loved it as a boy, and now

I find I have nine copies. I wrote to Mr. Wilson to say so, and received from him a letter in which he said that he knew of only one other addict, and he was the Bishop of Texas. I am sure there are others, but God forbid that we should ever form an association, and publish a newsletter, as is the modern trend.

I realize now how foolish and hopeful I was to embark on an address about the reading I have done in my lifetime. It sounds as if I were recommending books to you, which is quite the contrary of what I intend. No: I want you to find your own books. Which is another way of saying that I want your own books to find you.

That is not the tedious excursion into whimsicality that it might appear. If you were to question me now, you might reasonably ask: If you had your life to live again, would you read in the same way— wanderingly, capriciously, following your own nose? And I should reply, Certainly I should do so, without in the least expecting that I would read the same books. Another life means other reading. You might ask: Have the books you have read done anything to make you whatever it is you are? Of course they have, but that cuts two ways, because when you read a book, you are at least half of the totality of that experience; the reader makes something fresh of whatever it is he reads. A book is renewed every time it finds a perceptive reader, and no book is the same to every reader. If the books I have talked of have made me, in part, whatever I brought to them made something individual of them. Logan Pearsall Smith was wrong; reading is not a substitute for Life, because it is indivisible from life. Indeed, it is a reflection of the spirit of the reader, and I am truly convinced that we who are committed readers may appear to choose our books, but in an equally true sense our books choose us. By an agency that is not coincidence, but something much more powerful that Jungians call synchronicity, we find, and are found by, the books we need to enlarge and complete us. Reading is not escape, something done at random; it is directed unerringly toward the inner target. It is truly a turning inward. It is exploration, extension, and reflection of one's innermost self. If I have been a rake at reading, the caprice has been to the outward eye alone. The inward spirit, I am convinced, knew very well what it was doing.

3

Literature and Technology

"If democracy is not to prove a gigantic mistake, the many must have only the best, and that does not always mean the fastest or the easiest."

"I cannot understand how it is possible to neglect what a man is and the way he lives when one considers what his artistic work adds up to."

Insights like this abound when Davies tackles the subject of literature and technology. Beginning with a look at how new technology, such as the word processor, changes the way an author writes, in this speech he brings his thoughts to bear on wider topics, from *Vanity Fair* to the mystery of artistic creation and its relation to the unconscious.

The speech was given at the Ontario Science Centre in Toronto as part of the Tuzo Wilson Lecture Series. Wilson, a distinguished geologist best known for his work on tectonic plates, was not only a former Director General of the Science Centre but an old friend. Indeed, when Davies, the founding Master, was engaged in the task of establishing Massey College, he was delighted to have Tuzo Wilson become one of the original Senior Fellows in 1963.

On November 11, 1989, a significant period before the lecture date of November 26, Davies wrote in his diary a tribute to his wife: *Finish the Wilson Lecture and think it not bad. Read it to Brenda who likes it and makes some good criticisms, as usual. She is by far and away my best critic ...*

JP

I am going to talk to you, in part at least, about Literature and Technology, though how that will work out I cannot be sure, for, although I know something about literature, I am very much a novice in the whole world of technology. I am not even sure what it means. Of course I know what the dictionary says it is; it is the application of science to practical or industrial things. And I cannot pretend that it lies outside the sphere of my experience, because I live in a house that has a telephone and electrical power, and is heated by a sophisticated system activated by oil, and I drink cleansed water and am quite often in buildings where the air is circulated and its temperature controlled by technical devices. Technology touches me at every aspect of my physical life. But that is not the same thing as saying that I *understand* technology. Whenever something goes wrong with any of the things I just mentioned, I have to get somebody—referred to usually as "the man"—to put it right, and what he does and how he does it are mysteries to me.

I am happy to find that there is now a word for me as I relate to these things. I am a technomoron. I am a man of words and I glory in that splendid title. Technomoron; it has resonance.

When it comes to Literature and Technology I confess that I am more than usually puzzled, as I cannot really convince myself that the two things have any connection. Perhaps they have connections that I have not yet discovered. Let us see.

As a writer, I receive a great many letters, some of which are from schoolchildren. They are curious about what it means to be an author, and a question they always ask is: "Do you have a word processor?" Sometimes children come to see me, face to face, and when they ask this question I reply, "Why would I want a word processor?" They say: "It's the way everybody writes now," and they tell me about their own experiences with word processors, which they value greatly because the machine can spell, and it is easy to make corrections on its offprints, and it is quick and you can have as many copies as you like of what you have written.

If I am not in a particularly benign mood I reply that I am rather a good speller myself and my secretary is infallible, and that the machine cannot spell a lot of words I wish to use; the machine has a restricted and commonplace vocabulary. In my sort of work speed is not the most important thing, and writing done too quickly always has to be done again. As for having as many copies as you like, I never want more than one copy. My secretary urges me to use carbon paper to make at least one extra copy, and I have been warned by all sorts of people that if I ever lost my single copy I should be in great trouble. To which I can only reply, simpleton that I am, that I have never lost my single copy and I hate carbon paper, which is dirty.

I am not being completely honest with these children, because I use an electric typewriter, which is certainly a technological marvel, but I want to find out why they are so enthusiastic about word processors, which they think are wondrous and indispensable. I tell them the old story about Mr. Sam Goldwyn, who picked up a volume of the *Complete Works of Shakespeare* and said, in admiration, "And to think he wrote it all with a feather." I explain to the children that writing is not a technological process, and to rely on technology to do what you cannot do with a feather, or perhaps a lead pencil, is to fall into grievous error.

I assure you I am not a dinosaur. I do not wish to return to candlelight and the horse-drawn vehicle. I have investigated the question of word processors. I asked the man from whom I get typewriters, and who also sells word processors, what he thought about the matter. He is an honest man, and what he said was this: "The word processor is a marvel for everything connected with business, because it can do tabulations brilliantly, it allows for unlimited correction by the easiest possible means, and it produces as many duplicates of a document as you want. But you are not interested in speed; it would take you six months to master a word processor completely, although I can teach a secretary to do all she needs to do in two weeks. You live in the country and, knowing you, I am sure you would need a serviceman at least every two weeks, and that would be fifty dollars a call, exclusive of his cost of transportation. You are better off without one."

I listened to these words of wisdom and was grateful to my friend for his frankness. So I asked another question: "Does not the word processor tempt its user to overwrite, to say too much, because it is so easy?" "Oh yes," he replied; "they certainly encourage blather and many business documents are needlessly extended because they are so easy to make. Business people are very innocent and they are impressed by bulk."

That, again, was frank and I knew it to be true, for every week I throw away yards of stuff written on word processors that people have sent me. This is always marked, "For your information." But it is usually information I don't want and haven't asked for—speeches by politicians, reports about things I don't want to know, masses of figures in which I have trouble locating my bank balance, which is all I require. Word processors tempt people toward profusion, and my work is writing the best prose I can manage, in which profusion is almost the worst of sins. I want to say what I have to say in the clearest, briefest manner I can achieve, and you may take it from me that the work is slow.

I get letters that are obviously written on word processors, and they are always too long. I have read novels and essays written on word processors and they are always at least one-third too long. Anything that tempts me to write at self-indulgent length is the work of the Devil, and whatever word processors may be to the world of business, they are not for me. I must be slow. I must be deliberate, and I must not work with anything that gets between me and what I really want to say, the best way I can say it.

Of course, as an author, I rely heavily on technology, but the technology must be applied by somebody else, when I have done the best I can, in my own slow way.

For twenty years I worked as a journalist, and I left the world of journalism just before a gigantic application of a new technology in printing revolutionized the newspaper and magazine world.

You know what I mean. When I was a journalist the job of putting a newspaper together and printing it was a highly sophisticated application of techniques which were, in essence, the work of the blacksmith. Printers worked with metal. What I wrote went to men who converted it into lengths of metal on a machine called a Linotype, which was in its day a miracle of technology. When my father was a young man, learning the printing trade, everything that appeared in a newspaper had to be set up by hand, with movable type, one piece of metal for every letter, space, and mark of punctuation. It was a true craft. It was a slow process, even when the printers were quick and expert, and it employed a great many skilled compositors, as they were called. Modern technocrats called that "work-intensive." The Linotype could do rapidly in an hour what five hand-compositors could do, and it put a lot of men out of work, of course. And when the Linotype had done its job, all those trays of type had to be assembled on stone tables into newspaper pages, and then another process known as stereotyping came into play, which made moulds of those pages, again in hot metal, which were transferred to a large printing press, which in its turn printed the newspaper at great speed. We thought that technology had gone as far as it could. Those printers were highly skilled workmen, proud of their job, which demanded a four-year apprenticeship to master. Then came a technological revolution.

Nowadays newspapers are produced by what is really an elaborate system related to photography, and all the setting is done on miraculous machines which are often worked by women, as they do not demand the physical strength which used to be part of the qualification of a printer. Printing of this new sort produces not only newspapers but books and everything else that appears nowadays in printed form. This is one aspect of the new computer-based technology.

Much has been gained. Printing is now clean work, and in the old days of metals and oily, thick printer's ink it was dirty work, however skillful the men might be. It is very quick work, for several processes have been made redundant. But in the old days—not so very old, but now gone forever—a printer took pride in the aesthetic appearance of his work and he knew certain things that machines cannot be made to do. He knew, for instance, how to make all the lines on his page present an even appearance when printed; it was an art called "justifying." The machines cannot justify, and so the pages they present are often enough to turn an old-fashioned printer grey, for they are full of ugly gutters and cramped or loose lines. The machines do not speak English, or any other language, so they have no idea where a hyphen ought to appear in a word that comes at the end of a line. Consequently you are likely to find even the word *and* printed as *a* at the end of one line, followed by a hyphen, with the *nd* on the next line, which is ugly and illiterate, and unaesthetic. Maddeningly and confusingly, the word *the* may well appear as *t*—hyphen—*he*. Tee-hee—and that, of course, is laughable. Old-fashioned printing had still something of the art which was a necessity to printers from Gutenberg down to twenty years ago, and that has gone. And because it is so quick, the modern work is often careless, and even in an expensive modern book you will find errors of spelling which are there simply because the old, tedious art of the proofreader has been superseded by the slapdash bad manners of the machine, which has no mind.

There are things, of course, which the machines know, or think they know. They think they know how to punctuate, because a system of punctuation has been built into them. But they don't seem to know what a colon is, and as I use colons rather often, I conduct a running battle with machines and the people who own them, who assure me that the colon belongs to the past. This is nonsense. The colon is invaluable, and the machines will have to learn, just as they will have to learn about justification and the proper placing of hyphens.

They will also have to learn that when I quote from some old author who spelled differently from the machine, the wishes of the long-dead author must be respected, and the machine will have to mind its manners.

This is my complaint: These machines have no manners and no conscience, for these are human traits, and machines are not human yet, though only God knows what they may become with the passing of time.

I have another complaint against these machines, and some people think it a frivolous one. It is simply that they offer what they print in such hideous type. I was brought up in a printing family where typography was taken seriously as a minor art, which it is. The letters of the Roman alphabet which we use are all related, in some fashion, to the letters inscribed on Trajan's Column in Rome; the great typefaces designed and originated by the great type founders of the past, and which bear the names of Bodoni, Bembo, Caslon, and many others, are exquisitely proportioned to combine legibility and beauty so that the printed page is a thing to rejoice the eye, and a worthy interpreter of careful thought to the receptive mind, and sometimes of genius to the astonished and recreated mind. The hideous, deformed letters produced by the word processor or the computer are barbarous, and for no conceivable reason except that their designers wished them to be barbarous. All too often the word *technology* is synonymous with *ugly*. Self-conscious ugliness is bad morals and bad manners, and I want nothing to do with it. I forbear to speak of the disgusting paper which goes with these machines. They appear to be capable of working only on paper which is an offence against a great craft.

Am I making myself clear? I am no enemy of technology; I just want better technology, and if it is not available, I am happy to go on doing things the old way, even if it is the hard way.

I am sure that you have already grasped my point. Writing, either as an art or simply as a means of conveying necessary or desirable information, does not begin with technology. It is the job of technology to make such writing available to those who desire it, and at present it does that job with questionable literacy. Literacy is not just good manners: It is a guarantee of some measure of thought.

If this sounds obvious I must assure you that it is not so to the schoolchildren who are now made familiar with computers at school, and often with word processors at home. Children delight in complexity, for good reasons, they have the whole complex world before them to discover and master. It is not quickly apparent to them that good writing has its origin not in complexity but in simplicity, and that speed and rapid reproduction have nothing whatever to do with it. Good writing belongs to a world and a concept of life and art which were already old when printing—which was the technological revolution of five hundred years ago—came into being, and the former laborious method of reproducing books by careful hand-copying was outmoded. Printing was a powerful force in the spread of democracy and we all know that democracy means the rule of the many. But I will not be moved from my conviction that if democracy is not to prove a gigantic mistake, the many must have only the best, and that does not always mean the fastest or the easiest.

I must repeat: I am not an enemy of advanced technology, but technology touches what I do—which is to write books—only when the book has been given its form by the writer. And how is that done?

Nowadays the word *creativity* has become immensely popular. Everybody, beginning with the youngest child, is assured that something called creativity lies within his grasp, and that for his soul's good he must be as creative as he can manage. There is a good deal to be said for that idea, but when it is linked with democratic education, it can be mischievous. It is perfectly true that many people can draw and paint and make up tunes and write—after a fashion. Sometimes in children, quite interesting things result from this conviction. But it is an indisputable fact that as people grow older this creative ability wanes and usually disappears altogether. Believe me, I speak from long experience as an editor and also as a teacher. It is in the realm of writing that I have the most experience and the most claim to be a judge. I have been on panels which have considered writing by amateurs, who feel themselves possessed of some gift, more often than I now like to remember, and it has been my experience that the older the contestants are in these affairs, the less truly creative they become. They want to write, but unhappily they want to write like somebody else, whose work they admire; they do not offer anything which is indisputably their own.

This is not wholly bad. Many writers have begun by imitating established masters, but very soon they discover that they cannot say what they themselves have to say disguised as somebody else. They must find their own voice and their own way of looking at the world, and follow that even if it means failure. But there are very many aspiring writers who never proceed so far as making that discovery. They are discouraged because their imitations do not quickly win them the recognition they want. And therein lies an important truth. They want *recognition*, and if writing will not bring it, they stop writing. What they want and—I apologize for the obviousness of what I am about to say, but many truths are obvious—what they want is to be *recognized as writers*, far more than they truly want to write. If they are real writers nothing—not failure or obscurity or misunderstanding—will stop them, and often it is a long struggle before they win any sort of acceptance. Sometimes, indeed, acceptance never comes. It has been my melancholy duty to read manuscripts by people who were undoubtedly writers in this sense of total commitment, but who lacked enough gift or talent to win them any attention from the world.

These words—*talent* and *gift*—are bitter words, for the thing they describe is not common, and no amount of effort and certainly no word processor or other appurtenance of writing will bring it into being.

Let me tell you a sad story. I knew a man who wanted agonizingly to be a writer. There had been one writer who was a member of his family whose ability the world had acclaimed. This man—he was a Canadian, and indeed a Torontonian (and, of course, nobody is more unquestionably a Canadian than a Torontonian)—had the good fortune, or the ill fortune perhaps, to be quite rich. So he secured for himself a fine house, and in it he fitted up a study which contained everything he thought a writer could need or wish. It was a panelled room with a fireplace in it, and it was hung with excellent pictures. There were cases of reference books and dictionaries and thesauruses and of course the works of many esteemed modern writers. It had a desk which was in itself an invitation to brilliant writing, because it was a costly antique, polished to the highest lustre. But he also had all the technological equipment that the innocent heart could ask—a magnificent electric typewriter, and a dictaphone, and a Xerox machine, and God only knows what else, so that his inspiration could be caught on the fly, so to speak. Having assembled all this splendid equipment, he sat down to write. And he sat. And sat. And nothing came. Not long afterward he died. The doctors gave some scientific name to what killed him, but I have a powerful intuition that it was disappointment. You see, he wanted to be a writer, but that could not make him one. This is both a farcical and a sad story.

Let me tell you another, which is wholly farcical. I do not tell it simply to amuse you but because it contains several dreadful truths. I knew a man, knew him very well, who was a journalist, and a pretty good one. He could write acceptably about anything you gave him as a subject. This man had the mixed fortune to marry a woman who was extremely ambitious. I did not know her well, but she thought she knew me, and she was not impressed by what she knew. I wrote books. It could not, therefore, be beyond the power of an intelligent man with an ambitious wife to do the same. She said so, to several people. "If Rob Davies can write a book, Johnny can write a book," she declared; "I know he has a book in him." She was determined to get that book out of him, and she knew just how to do it. Every night she fed him, as well as her abilities as a cook made possible, and then she sent him to a room where there was a typewriter, and there he was to write his book, and when he was released at about ten o'clock, and rewarded with a bottle of beer, he was to show her what he had written. But after a few weeks the poor wretch could bear no more; he knew he was not writing a book, he was just spoiling paper, and he rebelled. He was too intelligent to deceive himself, though I think he might have deceived his wife. (There is more than one way of deceiving a wife.)

There is no use whatever trying to write a book unless you know that you must write that book or go mad, or perhaps die.

Let me explain at once that when I say *book*, I mean a work of fiction or poetry which has some claim to be regarded as a work of creation. I do not mean a travel book or a history book, or a biography, because although these books may be works of art if they are good enough, written with taste and elegance, they have their subject matter provided by travel, or world affairs, or somebody's completed life. Art may be manifested in the way they are written, but the original inspiration comes from somewhere outside the writer.

The kind of writing I am talking about was described in a short verse by Henrik Ibsen, that mighty, unforgiving genius who knew every sort of trouble and struggle that can come a writer's way. He wrote:

> To live—is a battle with troll-folk
> In the realms of heart and head:
> To write—is a man's self-judgement,
> As Doom shall judge the dead.

I have had those grim words always in my mind since I became a writer, and the older I grow the more I am awed by their terrible truth. Let us consider them for a few minutes.

The battle with troll-folk—what is it? It is impossible to make it really clear to people who have never experienced it, and they are many. The trolls are part of the dark forces of nature, and of mankind as a part of nature; they are the inadmissible parts of ourselves that we rarely face—if we ever face them—and of which we are ashamed, and by which we may be horrified. They are the parts of ourselves which suggest that we do mean things, dishonest things, grudging and vulgar things, even criminal things. They are the thoughts that suggest to us how convenient it would be if someone who complicates our life were out of the way—dead, perhaps. They are the thoughts that make us write a revengeful and destructive review of a book by a rival or someone we detest, making it seem that we have held the scales with the uttermost scrupulosity. They are the thoughts which make us deny promotion to a junior, simply because we do not like his table manners. And they are the thoughts of a rejected junior, who thinks he has been denied promotion because of his table manners, when everybody else knows that it is because he is not up to the job. They are the thoughts that make the judge find against the driver of the Rolls-Royce, when there has been a collision with a Ford, whatever the rights and wrongs of the case may be. It is the troll-folk who make mankind little and mean, and who also break up marriages, provoke murders, or cook the books of a charity to promote a political cause. It is the troll-folk who make us pretend that the worse is the better cause, and prove it with clever argument, for the trolls are greatly gifted in argument.

The troll-folk are everywhere and hard at work. In old mythology, they are misshapen dwarfs who work deep in the mines, and many of those mines are in our own hearts and heads. As I said, there are plenty of people who say they never see the troll-folk. Watch out for those, because they are innocent, and after a certain age innocence is a dangerous quality.

The troll-folk, I may say, are brilliant technologists, because they had their beginnings as ingenious mineworkers.

So there are the troll-folk, against whom we all have our deeply personal struggle. Now, what about writing, which Ibsen says is a man's self-judgment, as Doom shall judge the dead?

I am often asked if any of my books are autobiographical. To most of these inquirers I answer that they are not autobiographical at all, because they do not report the facts of any part of my life. That is not a wholly honest answer, because the true answer is not something which children or literal-minded people can understand. There are people to whom the complex truth is less comprehensible than the simple lie. To ask an author who hopes to be a serious writer if his work is autobiographical is like asking a spider where he buys his thread. The spider gets his thread right out of his own guts, and that is where the author gets his writing, and in that profound sense everything he writes is autobiographical. He could not write it if he had not seen it and felt it deeply. Sometimes letter writers tell me that the women in my books are wholly unreal, because they have never met any women like them. There is a rude answer to that sort of criticism, but the proper answer is: "Have you met women like Lady Macbeth, or Juliet, or Rosalind? When did you last meet a woman like Beatrice Esmond or Shaw's Saint Joan? Have you ever met a woman precisely like Becky Sharpe, or Lucy Ashton, of the Lammermoor Hills?" All of these women, who have become exemplars of many kinds of femininity, are the creations of men, and they seem to millions of readers to be as convincing as Jane Eyre or Mrs. Dalloway, who are the creations of women. Nor are women writers behind their masculine colleagues in their perceptions of masculine nature. Are there better portraits of a certain type of impotent self-honouring scholar than Mary Ann Evans's portrait of Mr. Casaubon, or of bull-headed masculinity than Tom Tulliver, from the same splendid hand, known to fame as George Eliot? The work of the best writers is bisexual: The man finds the women in himself, and the woman finds her men in the same creative womb.

I know that most of you are familiar with the story of the woman who said to Gustave Flaubert, "How could you possibly explore a certain kind of female nature as you have done in your character of Madame Bovary?" To which Flaubert replied, with total sincerity: "Madame Bovary, c'est moi." The real writer deals not with masculine or feminine, but with human nature, as he has observed it in life and as he finds it in himself.

He does not make these discoveries easily or without pain. This is the self-judgment of which Ibsen speaks in the terrifying four lines that I have quoted to you.

Does he do it with a word processor? I do not say that he could not do so, for that would be very stupid. I say only that in the examples I have quoted, he has done it by a slower method, which gives unlimited time for reflection, and does not tempt to easy, exuberant work.

When I was asked to speak to you today, several questions were put to me, as themes which I might explore. One was: "Does a word processor change the way we think and create?" I believe I have answered that one already. It depends on what you suppose thinking and creation is. If you think it is work that can be hurried up and made easy, the answer is Yes. But if you understand that thinking and creation are extremely difficult work, the answer is certainly No. If you will pardon an impudent generalization, I think that if Shakespeare had owned a word processor he might have written not 36 plays in his twenty-odd years of work, but 72 or perhaps—if he had really put on speed—he would have written 108. What they would have been like I leave it to some computer technologist to tell us.

I am not being wholly frivolous. Some of you may be acquainted with the name or even some of the works of Lope de Vega, the Spanish contemporary of Shakespeare who wrote something like 1,500 plays. He is said by his admirers to present a picture of unparalleled mental activity, but it is quite a while since one of his plays appeared on the world stage. What he might have done if he had owned a word processor I shudder to think.

I am not, you must understand, presenting a case for the writer whose output is small. That would be foolish, for most writers of great stature have written a good deal. But mere bulk is not the measure of a literary artist's capability. He does the best he can, and like a cow we judge him by his butterfat content and not by the number of pails he fills.

Again, I was asked to comment on "the synthesis of art and technology." I have done that; the art comes first, and then technology puts it in a form by means of which it reaches the public. It cannot be called a synthesis; the two processes are wholly different.

I am sure I need not labour the fact that with all technological devices they cannot do better than the human creature who puts them to work is able to understand and direct. I have been talking to you about a quotation from Henrik Ibsen, the great Norwegian dramatist. I quote him often, for he was a very wise man. Not long ago I quoted him in an address which was transferred from tape to word processor by a girl who had never heard of him, and I was astonished when my address came back to me to find that I had quoted somebody—a Scotsman, perhaps—named Henry Gibson. No technology is proof against human error and human ignorance.

To return to the questions I was asked to consider in this speech, one which is basic to the whole matter is, "Does a word processor change the way we think and create?" I can't see how it can possibly do so, unless we are so delighted with the machine itself that we allow it to dominate us. Anything the machine can do happens after the thinking and creating have taken place. Some consideration of what thinking and creating really are makes this abundantly clear.

It is possible to define thinking in elaborate terms, but perhaps you will allow me to define it as exercising the mind otherwise than by passive reception of somebody else's ideas. That covers a lot of ground. In the restaurant you say, "I think I'll have the salmon," when everybody else has chosen the roast beef. You have *thought*; you have made a personal choice; you have not tagged along after your friends. If you are a great philosopher, attempting to come to terms with the question of being, you may say, "I think, therefore I am," and immediately you have opened up a vast field of argument and speculation. It is this power of speculative thought which raises man to his preeminent place in nature. No other creature is so aware of itself in so many ways as we are. No other creature has knowledge of the remote past, or any power to influence the future. The higher animals possess some measure of choice, some ability to learn, some consciousness of themselves as separate from their fellows, but of our sort of thinking they are quite unaware. This power of thinking depends to a high degree on our possession of language—language of great flexibility and variety, which enables us to formulate our perceptions of the world with a consciousness of past and future, and of possibility.

What has a word processor to do with that? It can record, it can tabulate, it can assemble material of all kinds, but somebody must have thought of everything it does before it can do it. The word processor may speed things up, but as I have already said, speed is not always important to serious thought, and the necessity for speed—which the machine may impose upon a careless or innocent user—may reduce the value of what is thought. The machine is valuable only after the real work has been done.

As for creation, I do not think that a machine has any effectiveness whatever. For what is creation?

May we call it imaginative thought? That word *imaginative* opens up a world where no machine can intrude. What is imagination?

I do not want to get into a discussion of extreme complexity on this subject, though I cannot avoid the subject itself. I am not a philosopher, but I do work of a sort which is called creative, and I must confine myself to talking about what I know. And in order to do that I must talk of something which you may dispute, which is related not to philosophy but to psychology.

In this extraordinary century in which we live, we are all affected in some degree by what I may call the Freudian Revolution, which had its beginning exactly in the year 1900 when Sigmund Freud published his revolutionary book called *The Interpretation of Dreams.* Everything in that book rests on Freud's theory of the mind, which was not original with himself because it had always been familiar to artists of all kinds, writers included. But Freud put it on a scientific basis, and proved it scientifically by his work with hundreds of patients; it has been extended and refined by the subsequent work of thousands of psychologists and psychoanalysts, some of whom disagreed with Freud about matters of detail, but all of whom begin their work with his discoveries and formulations. The effect of the Freudian Revolution has been to enlarge to an immeasurable degree our ideas about how the mind works and what the mind is. One of the things we now know, unless we have neglected the subject altogether, is that the mind works on several levels and that the process we call thinking is only one of these and perhaps not the most important.

It was Bertrand Russell, a philosopher who surely knew what he was talking about, who said that "intellect, except at white heat, is apt to be trivial." And how many of us dare say that we have ever thought at white heat? And what does thinking at white heat mean? Freud asserted that it was not the often-superficial ratiocinative process, but something else which reached into another realm of the mind, which Freud and his followers call the unconscious mind.

What is the unconscious mind? It is that part of the mind which lies below the area of wholly conscious thought, in which there lies a mass of memory, recollection, emotion, and—this is what many people wish to reject—a great many things we did not know we knew but which may well up from the unconscious mind when it is working creatively. This sort of knowledge is most apt to assert itself suddenly, in a flash, and frequently surprises the person to whom it happens.

Creative people have always known this. Artists, poets, romancers, and also scientists know that they have always worked in this way. I included scientists because some of their most extraordinary revelations and perceptions of the nature of things have come to them in this way. Einstein of course worked out his revolutionary theory of relativity by long and exhausting thought; but the intuition that lay at its root came in a flash, and when it had come he did the hard work which proved that the flash was an overwhelming and scientifically defensible theory, and not just an illusion. We all know the story about Newton recognizing the theory of gravity when he saw an apple fall from a tree. The work by which he refined and asserted that astonishing insight is explained in his writing, and is plain for anybody to see, and it followed the fall of the apple. Both Newton and Einstein, of course, were ripe subjects for inspiration; they were certainly not scientific ignoramuses.

I once asked an eminent scientist—I will not name him but will content myself by saying that he was the last Canadian to be awarded a Nobel prize for his work—whether he got his best ideas in sudden intuitions, or by elaborate trains of speculative thought. He replied without hesitation that the intuition came first, and then the hard work was finding the intellectual means by which the intuition could be asserted as a truth, or at least a matter for careful discussion.

It is so also with writers, if they are writers of any considerable attainment. Frequently schoolchildren ask me, "Where do you get your ideas from?" The answer, which usually puzzles them is, "I don't get my ideas; they get me." That is the simple truth. Writers of many kinds have said the same thing, in different ways, for centuries.

I write novels, and a good novel is a work of art. How good my novels are it is not for me to say but I try to make them as good as I can. A very good critic has said, "A truly great novel is a tale to the simple, a parable to the wise, and a direct revelation of reality to a man who has made it a part of his being." That sort of novel does not make its influence felt because it arises from a simple job of invention, it is rooted in something much deeper, something which comes at least in part from the unconscious mind, and which says something more significant about the story it tells.

What kind of thing? Nobody will be content with a single example, but we have not time for an extended discussion of this matter. Let us look at something that teaches you without appearing to do so. There are countless examples, but the one I bring to your attention is a novel which I expect many of you have read, even if you have not looked at it recently. It is Thackeray's *Vanity Fair*.

What is it? Everything is contained in the title. It is a story about some not very remarkable people who live lives that are amusing to read about, but which in themselves are trivial and sometimes despicable. It is in part about a young adventuress called Becky Sharp who resents the humble station into which she is born and is determined to climb and claw her way into another kind of life where the world will have to take account of her. It seems to be about the surfaces of life and the pettiness and triviality of society. But every now and then in that book there is a sound like the tolling of a great bell, which reminds us that all this nonsense is played out against the march of history, against the fall of Napoleon, the making and breaking of nations and empires. And when we hear the bell we think: Is this sort of life really worthy of rational beings? Is this sort of struggle what life is really about? How can people devote their energies to such petty achievements and foolish ends? And we realize what a very moral novel *Vanity Fair* is.

From what does it spring? From the life of its author, who had cause to know, if ever a man did, what the costs and exactions of a society life can be. As a young man Thackeray had a fortune, and it seemed that his future was a glowing one. But he foolishly blew away his fortune, and had to face the task of supporting himself as best he could. He fell deeply in love and he brought two daughters into the world whom he loved very much. But his wife became mad and he had to bring up his daughters without her, at a time when girls sorely needed a wise mama to launch them in society and show them how to take their proper place in the carefully ordered world. Thackeray had to be both Victorian papa and a mama as well. In middle life he fell in love with a woman who encouraged him until his love became a nuisance to her, and then she made her husband reject Thackeray with great cruelty and self-righteousness. And all through his life he was plagued by a particularly exhausting form of ill health.

Do you find any of this described in *Vanity Fair*? No, you do not. But the distillation of that experience, and the promptings of the unconscious mind of a true artist, brought about the great novel which still rings true, although the sort of society it describes has almost vanished from the earth.

I have done something in the last few minutes which is supposed to be bad criticism. I have linked the life experience of a writer with his work. But I cannot understand how it is possible to neglect what the man is and the way he lives when one considers what his artistic work adds up to.

The time is near when I must draw to a close, so I would do well to go over some of the things I have said, and try to pull them together. I was to talk about literature and technology, was I not? And what I have been saying suggests that what is important in literature is not to be approached by technological means, which belong to quite a different kind of life and work. Now, you may object that so many of the writers I have mentioned lived long ago, and are thus irrelevant to our subject. I don't agree. All the writers of whom we have any intimate knowledge have worked in the same way, through a most careful and respectful solicitation of their own unconscious processes, and by building upon what they bring to the surface.

I suppose that at some point I am expected to make some comment about my own work, though I am reluctant to do so. My novels have been both praised and disliked because of elements of what people call the supernatural in them, which strain the credulity of readers who insist that a novel must be an uncompromising picture of life—by which they mean what they themselves can see of life. But I myself do not see life in tones of grey, nor do I believe that all human affairs are limited by what is called "realism," meaning a photographer's vision of what is obvious to the most limited inspection. I reject the term "supernatural." If I perceive something, surely it is natural? If there is anything unusual about it, it is the clarity of my vision. All my life I have been too much aware of the part that what we call chance, but which might also be called destiny, plays in everybody's affairs, and I have also been aware of the existence of ghosts where most people refuse to see them. I assure you that I do not mean spooks in white sheets; no, I mean the persistence after death of the influences of people who cannot be forgotten or discounted as influences in the lives of their children. Hamlet's father's ghost is no outmoded dramatic device in a play which is now nearly four hundred years old. It is a part of Hamlet's soul. There are many of you here who have not freed yourselves from the ghosts of your fathers, and perhaps more particularly of your mothers, and because they haunt you, they also haunt your children, your lovers, and sometimes even your friends. That is part of what heredity means, and it deserves careful attention. I try in my novels to come to terms with aspects of life which many people do not observe, or choose not to observe, but which I feel are determining elements in what we do with our lives. Need I emphasize that the promptings that move me to this sort of writing come from the unconscious, as well as from the most careful observation I can command of my daily life and the lives of the people about me? Life is not a movie show, projected flatly on a flat screen. It is a drama, in three or more dimensions, with some of the most important things happening offstage. I have described life as a World of Wonders, and my metaphor for that was a travelling show of freaks and cheats, and also of extraordinary people, capable of goodness and even on occasion of nobility. My novels are rooted in my own vision of life, and what gives them vitality comes as much from the unconscious mind as from unresting observation of the visible world.

Of course there is another element in the writer's work which I have not mentioned, because it is not immediately applicable to our theme. But I must speak of it now, because to neglect it entirely would be to give a lopsided picture of what literature is.

It is a form of art, and all artists must work in some medium or other, whether it is paint, or stone, or pure sound—as with musicians—or with words, as writers do. The way a writer uses words is one of the things that defines him. He may be an extremely careful, conscious artist, like James Joyce in our own century, who takes many years to complete a book of great complexity and variety of meaning. Or he may be a writer like Dickens, who works at lightning speed, and seems careless of the technicalities of language, but who achieves extraordinary effects apparently by the profusion and diffusion of his means. This technical variety, I suggest, is not so much a matter of conscious choice as of the unconscious process, from which the writing springs. This is why it is quite impossible to write in the style of another person. There is always a tinny sound about such writing, because it has its origin in the wrong place.

Nor is it by words alone that the writer produces his effects. It is by the form he gives his book. There are writers whose work we can analyze almost as we analyze music, showing how brilliantly he produces his effects by the use of recurrent thematic matter, or by the assembling of paragraphs and chapters which seem to move at different speeds, and of which the careful reader must be heedful if he is to feel the full effect of what is written. A modern example is afforded by Sylvia Townsend-Warner, whose exquisite novels and short stories are still seriously undervalued. The writer may disguise great seriousness of purpose beneath an appearance of frivolity, which deceives imperceptive readers into thinking that he is no more than a funnyman. And here Evelyn Waugh gives us a brilliant example. Or the writer may seem to deal in simplicities, like Ernest Hemingway, but the simplicities are anything but simple in the effects they produce.

I could go on at length, but I shall not do so because I am sure you have taken my point. Once he has dredged the depths of his unconscious, the writer must clothe what he has to say in the garments most suited to it, and that is the second most important aspect of his art.

Inspiration first: the promptings that cannot be faked, or compelled to arise from the depth where they have their being. The style second: and that may be a very elaborate and consciously sophisticated creation, or it may be a simplicity which, as I have said, is by no means simple.

Now, do you think either of these things can be assisted—not to say evoked—by technology of any kind? If you do, I have spoken here in vain.

4

Literature and Moral Purpose

Davies was back in New York again three years later, this time to give The Erasmus Lecture at the Institute of Religion and Public Life on April 15, 1990. The theme—"how far literature may be expected to discuss moral problems and what contribution it can make to their solution, without being untrue to itself"—is one that has engaged authors and critics, not to mention theologians and dictators, down through the centuries.

Davies tackles the theme with great imagination. He also leavens the high seriousness of the subject by dealing with "literature which is moral before it is artistic," and in the process devastates *Little Men*, *Beautiful Joe* ("Joe was a sort of Canine Christian, and what was more, a Total Abstainer"), *Little Lord Fauntleroy*, and their like. He also gives personal testimony about the creation of novels such as *Fifth Business*: "I assure you that as I wrote those books I had no sense of moral purpose whatever. I have never thought of myself as a moralist."

As a performer, however, Davies was a conscientious and thorough professional. He prepared this particular speech two months in advance, in time to incorporate, at his wife's suggestion, the paragraph that mentions Hemingway and Faulkner and other twentieth-century moralists. We notice that already, in February, he knows just how long the well-polished piece will take to read in performance in April: *Read the Erasmus to Brenda; she likes it but says that all the literary references are to nineteenth-century books and should say something about living or recently dead authors. Very sound criticism*

*and I insert a paragraph doing so, but explain that my chief references
will be to an earlier day, and to acknowledged classics. Speech runs fifty
minutes, without laughs or breaks; will be an hour in performance.*

❧

It is tedious when a speaker begins by protesting modestly that he is
inadequate to the task before him, that he is the last person who
should have been asked to discuss the theme of his address, and so on
and so forth. We are apt to dismiss such wincing disclaimers as
belonging to what Goldsmith called "The decorums of Stupidity." But
the fact is that speakers often do feel inadequate to their task, and I am
one of them at this moment. "Why, then, did you accept our invitation to speak?" you ask. I did it because I was intrigued by the theme
you proposed, and wanted to think about it. I may even have been so
vain as to suppose that I might say something illuminating about it.
But as I thought, and wrote, and wrote and thought, I was driven to
admit that I had bitten off a very large chaw, and that I could only
chew a part of it. I understand that there is to be a discussion arising
at least in part out of what I am about to say; perhaps you will be able
to take the subject farther than I can.

The subject is "Literature and Moral Purpose." It is not a particularly engaging title, but your Director and I were unable to come up
with anything better that was equally descriptive. What I am going to
talk about is how far literature may be expected to discuss moral
problems and what contribution it can make to their solution,
without being untrue to itself.

I suppose I had better make some attempt to define or to give
some general notion of what is meant by moral purpose. Is it not to
give some guidance toward whatever is good as opposed to what is
evil? At once we meet a difficulty, for in some parts of the world
things are considered to be good, or at least within the bounds of
reasonable conduct, which are condemned elsewhere. Consider
pederasty and sodomy, for instance, which were tolerated in the
pagan world, but which until about the middle of this century were
thought to be immoral in the Christian and Judaic world. But now

the Christian and Judaic world, or a considerable part of it, has done a moral U-turn and what was condemned is tolerated, if not countenanced, even among members of the clergy, who are expected to be moral exemplars.

Presumably this is because among the seven Virtues, the Natural Virtues are regarded as less needful to the good life than the Supernatural Virtues. If one has Faith, Hope, and Charity one may presumably manage with a smattering of Justice, Fortitude, Prudence, and Temperance. But these are very deep and stormy waters, and only subtle theologians can swim in them. As a literary man—specifically a novelist and a playwright—I must keep within the bounds of what I may be expected to know. And what I know is this: Virtually all novelists, playwrights, and poets of serious artistic purpose become inevitably involved in problems of morality, but such writers are on dangerous and artistically ruinous ground when they allow their work to be dominated by moral purpose.

I cannot think of an exception to this statement; perhaps you can, and you will have your chance to object to what I have said. And I must make it clear that when I speak of literature I mean poetry, fiction, and drama. Philosophy and avowedly moral disquisitions I cannot discuss, because it is about imaginative literature that I suppose you wish to think today. But when I speak of great works of imaginative literature which have an avowed moral purpose I think at once of *Paradise Lost*, in which Milton the artist so overreached Milton the theologian that Satan emerges as by far the most interesting character in the poem, and we are all drawn to admire him; in *Paradise Regained*, where Satan is reduced from the proud rebel to a much lesser tempter and schemer, the genius of Milton seems to be less happy. Or consider *The Pilgrim's Progress*, which is remorselessly and unanswerably moral, so far as it goes, but which lives by the beauty of its style and its succession of vivid portraits and pictures. When we were children, did we ever want to be Christian, as we read that book? Would we not have yearned more toward one of the lesser roles, even that of Giant Despair? Reprobate children that we were, we thought that Christian was rather a pill, and that the others were full of exciting life.

Literature which is moral before it is artistic is rarely on the level of Milton or Bunyan. When I was a boy I was a voracious reader. I would read anything even if it were only the directions on a bottle of medicine. My home had plenty of moral literature on its shelves, and I was urged to read it, for my betterment. There was lots of other literature, as well, but I was—not forbidden, but discouraged—from reading it as it was said to be "beyond me" which I quickly discovered meant that it dealt with life pretty much as life was, and not as the determinedly moral writers wanted me to think. My parents had both been brought up in uncompromisingly Christian homes, and so we had many books which they had won as Sunday School prizes—which meant that they had good memories, rather than aggressively contrite hearts.

How awful those prize books were! I shall not bore you with too much detail about them, but I must mention one which was called *Striving to Help*. It was about a noble boy whose father was a business failure, through no fault of his own, but because evil men worked against him. The boy possessed a boy's printing press, equipped with rubber type, and he single-handedly lifted his family out of despair by going into the printing business; he sought orders from temperance societies to print their notices, and thus he killed two moral birds with one stone, although evil boys often altered the bills he printed to give them a pro-alcohol bias. But he won through in the end, because right always triumphs. He was very decent to his father, and never rubbed it in that his father was a failure. To his mother, of course, he was an object of almost hysterical adoration. There was an Oedipal element in this story, which, at the time, I did not appreciate.

I have since wondered if some of those writers of moral tales for youth knew just what they were doing. Even Louisa May Alcott—unquestionably a writer of substantial gifts—included puzzling things in her books. Think of *Little Men*, which I read with avidity. One of the little men is a boy called Ned, and he is a boy of wavering moral character; but at Plumstead School he comes under the influence of Professor Bhaer, a German pedagogue, who had an unusual method of discipline. When Ned is naughty, the Professor does not punish him—oh, no—the Professor makes Ned strike *him* on the hands with the cane, as hard as he can, until Ned is reduced to tears, because he dearly loves and admires the Professor. Even as a boy I thought there was something decidedly kinky about the Professor. But did Louisa May Alcott know it? She was not wholly without kinks herself. But let us return to the noble boy in *Striving to Help*.

That boy made me feel very cheap indeed, for I too had a boy's printing press, and it produced the messiest, worst-spelled, and most despicable work that anybody had ever seen. The most abject temperance society would have scorned to employ me. Fortunately my father was not a failure, or my family would have sunk under the weight of my ineptitude.

Noble boys in fiction were the bane of my life. My family subscribed, on my behalf, to a journal called *The Youth's Companion*, which originated in Boston, and every month it arrived, heavy with tales of noble boys who imposed their moral superiority on everybody around them by much the same sort of admirable industry. In my dark heart I hated those boys. They were unfailingly noble in their behaviour toward girls, and I confess that there were times when my feelings about girls fell below their standard, because I knew quite a few girls, and they were divided between the voluptuously desirable, and beastly little sneaks and tattle-tales.

Only one thing saved me, I now believe. The boys in the Sunday School books were all English, and the boys in *The Youth's Companion* were all Americans—usually Bostonians. I was a Canadian, and grew up believing that Canadians were different—a lower order of being, incapable of morality in its highest reaches. One of the satisfactions of being a Canadian is that one is not expected to be a good example.

I gagged on tales of moral animals, like *Beautiful Joe*. You may not have encountered this powerfully moral dog, who met with much of the world's evil in the form of wicked and cruel masters. But Joe was a sort of Canine Christian, and what was more, a Total Abstainer; Joe's lips never touched alcohol. But I knew a few dogs in real life, most of whom were idiots, and whose moral behaviour was well below Joe's standard, for Joe lived a life of unwavering chastity, and the dogs I knew did not.

I could not stomach *Little Lord Fauntleroy*, who presented me with the political puzzle especially hard for a Canadian. What was that boy, and what did he do? He was an American, but by chance he inherited a title and went to England and became a Lord, and thereafter was remorselessly democratic toward anyone who kept it firmly in mind that he *was* a Lord, and behaved accordingly. The Little Lord existed to hammer home two things that were presented as mighty truths: We must be democratic and we must recognize the moral superiority that goes with poverty. It was easy, I thought, to be a democrat if everybody toadied to you, and I wished that the Little Lord could spend a few days at the school I went to, where to be known as a tireless reader (for I could not conceal it) was to be an outcast. Many of my persecutors enjoyed the blessing of poverty but it did not seem to improve their characters. They were savage, jealous, and without bowels of compassion.

My sanity was saved by the books I read on the sly. Dickens, where evil people were plentiful and often rich, successful, and attractive. Thackeray, where snobbery seemed to be the mainspring of much of the action. Thomas Hardy, where life was complicated by opposed moralities and the uncontrollable workings of Destiny, and where God was decidedly not a loving Father. I did not know it at the time, but of course these were the works of literary artists who observed life with keen eyes, and wrote about what they saw, as their widely varying temperaments enabled them to see. When I myself became a writer, it was these whom I chose to follow, as best I could, and not the aggressive moralists.

When I went to Oxford I fell in with a young man in my college who had already been ordained as a Presbyterian minister. He found out that I had ambitions as a playwright and he conceived of a great scheme: We would collaborate on a series of plays based on the great moral tales of the Bible—The Sacrifice of Isaac, Moses and the Golden Calf, Naboth's Vineyard, and the like. I would write the plays, and he would supply the theology, the moral fervour, and zeal and keep me from going astray. I pointed out to him that in the eighteenth century Mrs. Hannah More had produced, in 1782, four *Sacred Dramas*, and they were *Moses in the Bulrushes*, *David and Goliath*, *Belshazzar*, and *Daniel*. Even the authoress could not really like them. She wrote: "It would not be easy, I believe, to introduce Sacred

Dramas on the English Stage. The scrupulous would think it profane, while the profane would think it dull." My friend the young dominie was not daunted: We would succeed where Mrs. More had failed. But I was not convinced. In my childhood I had seen sacred dramas— *Queen Esther*, and *The Prodigal Son*—and even in such a stage-struck child as I they produced a profound ennui. I had a lot of trouble getting rid of that ambitious young parson, I may tell you.

It was because I had changed my personal definition of the word *moralist*. For me it meant not someone who imposes a moral system upon his art, but someone who sees as much of life as he can, and who draws what conclusions he may. What courses of action lead to what results? Are there absolute standards of good and evil? To what degree is what appears to be acceptable to society rooted in the truth of a particular man or woman? To what degree may the acceptance of a popular or socially approved code of conduct define or perhaps distort a character? Where do the springs of behaviour lie; to what degree may they be controlled; how far is a human creature account- able to his group, or his country, or his professed belief (or unbelief) for what he does? How far is it permissible to talk of what a human creature "makes" of his life, and to what degree does an element of which he may be unaware in himself "make" his life for him? How far may we accept the dictum that life is a dream, and that we are crea- tures in that dream, which is being dreamt by something of which we have no knowledge? These, it seems to me, are the concerns of the true moralist. He is an observer and a recorder; he *may* not permit himself to be a judge, except by indirection.

In what I am about to say it may seem to you that I dwell heavily on writers of the nineteenth century and earlier, to the neglect of writers of the century in which we live. Of course there are many writers of comparatively recent times who might be discussed; one thinks at once of Hemingway and Faulkner in the United States, and of Graham Greene, James Joyce, and that resounding moralist Evelyn Waugh in Great Britain; Marcel Proust's great novel is virtually a long disquisition on vanity, and much might be said of Thomas Mann, of Günter Grass. In the drama, one of the most deeply searching moral- ists of our time is Arthur Miller, and in Britain Alan Ayckbourn, under the cloak of sardonic comedy, presents us with some complex moral problems. But of these and of more recent writers I shall say nothing, because the nearer a writer is to us, the more varied debate and opinion become. Therefore I have stayed with writers of an earlier day, about whose work the dust of dispute has in some degree subsided.

It may appear to you that I have weighted the scales unfairly against books of avowed moral purpose by talking of Sunday School prizes, and publications for children. Certainly there have been widely accepted works of fiction and drama that are not so simple. I think of the famous play *George Barnwell, or the London Merchant* which was written in 1731 and enjoyed something like 150 years of popularity on the stage. It was often performed on holidays as a moral warning to apprentices who, like Barnwell, might fall into the company of evil women and—what was worse—rob their masters. One thinks of *Uncle Tom's Cabin*, powerful both as a play and a novel. There were books like *Danesbury House*, which Mrs. Henry Wood wrote in 1860, and which won a prize of one hundred pounds from the Scottish Temperance League because of its description of the evils of drink; this was the first of Mrs. Henry Wood's remarkable flow of novels, all of which were extremely popular—and all of which were of a determinedly moral tendency. But their morality has not been able to save them, for a simple reason: Morality changes from age to age and her morality was dictated by her society. The deeper truths about human nature, which form the foundations of great drama and fiction, are of more enduring stuff.

Compare, for instance, Mrs. Henry Wood's most famous novel, *East Lynne*, with Tolstoy's *Anna Karenina*. The theme is the same: A married woman falls hopelessly in love with a man who wearies of her, she destroys the peace of her husband, and is estranged from her beloved child; in the end, having ruined her life, she dies. But in *East Lynne* her infatuation is dealt with very heavily on the basis of what Mrs. Grundy might think. Who can forget the line from the play, spoken by the heroine's father: "O Isobel! you, an Earl's daughter! How utterly have you forgotten yourself!" Tolstoy treats Anna's defection as it reflects on the career of her husband, who is brilliantly portrayed as a wronged, if unsympathetic, man. But chiefly Tolstoy tells us of the moral destruction of Anna herself, of her abandonment to a passion which she finds overwhelming but which seems from the outside to be merely foolish. We see Anna's ruin and her final realization of what she is and what she has done, and her suicide. Anna Karenina is pitiable, and she is almost noble in her passion, but we cannot escape the realization that she is also something of a fool. Not so the heroine of *East Lynne*; she sins, and she is rapturously forgiven; much of her conduct must be described as sneaky, but nobody seems to care; she dies at last in a glow of virtue, mourned by her husband, whom she has treated badly, as if she had been an angel all her life. Anna dies because it is her fate. Lady Isobel dies, one suspects, to make all the other characters feel cheap.

Why has Anna Karenina lived, whereas Lady Isobel is forgotten by all except a few hobbyists like myself? Because in *East Lynne* the cards are all stacked to the benefit of the principal character, the repentant sinner, the woman whose sins are forgiven her chiefly because she is the heroine of a popular novel. But Anna Karenina is a human being, not a doll devised to perform in a doll's drama. Anna's faults are plain for all to see, and the morality of the novel dips far below the surface of what was considered moral in the Russian society of the 1870s. We read it now, in a very different moral climate, for its fine understanding of what may happen when passion overcomes prudence, which is a timeless theme, and the way in which Fate may intervene in an apparently ordinary life.

Of course not all fine fiction is written at the Tolstoy level. There are many literary artists who do their best to represent man in society, and man at odds with society, whose literary gift does not take them into the front rank of writers. A gift is not to be commanded. We know how grievously Tolstoy himself sank in the latter part of his career when he often wrote to prove a point and drive home a lesson, rather than to record what he saw and what he understood intuitively from what he saw. The genius of fiction seems to be always at war with orthodoxies, always resistant to established creeds because the literary artist is drawn toward those things which are exceptions to orthodoxy and which seem opposed to creeds. And this is not because literary artists are necessarily rebellious (though some have been so) but because they are wary and unrestingly observant. They are well aware of the sunlight, but they are driven also to examine the shadow that it inevitably creates.

If I seem to be talking as if writers have an orthodoxy of their own—an orthodoxy of unorthodoxy, so to speak—a determination to go against the grain of society, let me disclaim any such intention at once. Writers are not unrestingly intellectual in their approach to life; indeed, some acquaintance with the history of literature shows how far authors, in the main, fall below the determined intellectuals in their power of analyzing and theorizing. I once got myself into some trouble by saying that authors are not, as a rule, highly intelligent. People attacked me and contradicted me because they were certain that anyone who can create plots and characters must be a person of powerful intelligence. But I defend myself by saying that I do not take intellectuality, as it commonly appears in society, with entire seriousness. The power to argue strongly, and what I may call the puzzle-solving and examination-passing cast of mind, is often the possession of people of arid and limited perception and uneducated heart. In art, and in science as well, it is the power to see what other people do not see, to jump to conclusions *and to be right*, to see through a brick wall, in short to be creative, that counts. Intuition is an abused word, but if we define it as the power to apprehend things without the intervention of a reasoning or logical process, we are talking about something which is not intelligence in the accepted sense of the word. Anybody who has tried it knows what a poor tool logic is when it is applied to questions of human conduct. A very great logician defined intuition as "the perception of shadows" and it is the perception of shadows that is at the root of the greatest poetry, and fiction, and drama.

Because they are not unrestingly intellectual, writers may not be strongly aware of the intuitive impulse that drives. Consider a novel which has survived for almost four centuries, and is still regarded as one of the great masterpieces of world fiction. I speak of *Don Quixote*, by Cervantes.

Its story is of the adventures of a gentleman whose wits have been turned by reading old books of romance and chivalry; he equips himself absurdly with miserable armour and an old and wretched horse, and he rides forth in search of adventures. Their story is not told with tidy literary art; it is a rambling and often coarse tale of the foolishness of a mad old man who is mocked, beaten, and humiliated until, on his deathbed, he understands the folly of his delusion.

The book is often read superficially. More often it is not read at all, by people who are nevertheless aware of it, because the story is familiar from stage, film, and operatic versions, and has given our language the word *quixotic*, meaning actuated by impracticable ideals of honour. But if we read the book carefully and sympathetically we find the secret of its extraordinary power. It is the first example in popular literature of the profoundly religious theme of victory plucked from defeat, which has strong Christian implications. The Don, who is courteous and chivalrous toward those who ill-use him, and who is ready to help the distressed and attack tyranny or cruelty at whatever cost to himself, is manifestly a greater man than the dull-witted peasants and cruel nobles who torment and despise him. We love him because his folly is Christlike, and his victory is not of this world.

Is this what Cervantes meant? I cannot say, for I am not a Cervantist, but this is certainly what he wrote, and we know that such a book could not have been written except by a man of great spirit. This is the puzzle which has led some impetuous critics to assume that a writer is sometimes an *idiot savant* who writes better than he knows, and who, of course, needs critics to explain him to the world, and probably also to himself.

The theme of victory plucked from defeat, and the folly which is greater than conventional wisdom, is at the root of many novels. One of the best and most enduring is Charles Dickens's first success, *The Pickwick Papers.* When we first meet Mr. Pickwick he is an almost buffoonlike character, but when he is unjustly imprisoned his character deepens and he becomes aware of the misery and injustice which are part of the society in which he lives. By the end of the book Mr. Pickwick is a man of real worth. It is interesting and very important that Mr. Pickwick is dependent on his valet, Sam Weller, a streetwise youth who is to him what Sancho Panza is to Don Quixote; that is, an element of common sense and practical wisdom that is lacking in his master. When we think about it we see that the great virtues are exemplified in these four people: Don Quixote and Mr. Pickwick possess faith, hope, charity, justice, and fortitude, but they need their servants to supply prudence and temperance. A character who possessed all the seven great virtues would never do as the hero of a novel; he would be perfect, and in consequence unsympathetic, for we are impatient and suspicious of human perfection. But when a hero who has most of the virtues is partnered by a helper and server who has what he lacks, great and magical fiction may result.

Did Dickens know what he was doing? Here I am on safer ground than I am with Cervantes, for Dickens has been one of my lifelong studies, and I think he knew exactly what he was doing, in this and in all the novels that followed *Pickwick Papers*. Dickens's life showed him to be a man who was far from intellectual, and sadly astray in much of his personal conduct, but when he was at his desk he was in total command, and he knew very well that, after a shaky start, he was working with a great theme.

What, throughout his career, was Dickens doing? There are critics who insist that he was a great social reformer, a scourge of the society and laws of his time. So indeed he was, though a careful study of his work suggests that he was often *behind* reform rather than before it. His famous attack on the iniquitous Yorkshire schools that existed as places to conceal and forget illegitimate children, came after those schools had already been attacked and were in the process of being investigated. Certainly he attacked the Civil Service and the Court of Chancery savagely in *Bleak House*, but whether any changes resulted as a result is open to question. The world has a strong tendency to separate what it reads in novels from what it experiences in real life, and, although a reformer like Dickens may rouse public indignation, it is carrying things a little too far to attribute reforms to his interventions. Abraham Lincoln may indeed have said that Harriet Beecher Stowe's *Uncle Tom's Cabin* started the American Civil War, but one suspects that in his heart he knew better. So, was Charles Dickens moved by moral fervour when he wrote?

Yes, he was in part, but he was moved more strongly and effectively by something else, and that was the instinct of an author—a very great author—that worked within him. There were plenty of reforming writers in his time, and in some of them indignation burned more fiercely than it did in Dickens. There was one, Henry Cockton, who you may well be excused for not knowing, who wrote a very popular book called *Valentine Vox* (1840) which was a furious attack on the private asylums for the insane which, during the nineteenth century, served very often as prisons for inconvenient relatives. There is some reason to believe that *Valentine Vox* had its effect in provoking investigation, but who reads it now? Why? Because Cockton was no Dickens and except for eccentrics like myself his book is unreadable. So, what was it Dickens had which places him so high in the ranks of writers in English, that Henry Cockton lacked? It was the instinct, the nature of the author. Can it be defined. Let us try.

It was Plato who first said that we gain our knowledge of the world about us by means of four functions, which we may call Thinking, Feeling, Sensation, and Intuition. Thinking is reasoning untinged by emotion; Feeling is the forming of what are now called "value judgments" on the basis of emotion; Sensation is the quality which gives us the physical reality of things—of height, depth, softness, hardness, distance, temperature, and all such palpable things; and last is Intuition, which is the perception of possibilities. We all have these four functions in some measure, but one is likely to be dormant and thus determines our approach to life. Please do not ask me to defend this opinion. If you don't like it, argue with Plato. I bring it up because it is useful to the present discussion. The author is likely to be particularly strong in Intuition.

It is Intuition that enables the writer to see beyond the facts of a situation, to embroider and extend their scope, and to discover possibilities which do not appear to the Thinker, for instance, or the Sensation man. I used to tell my students that every Monday morning the story of *Othello* was reported in the morning papers, but it took a Shakespeare to see its possibilities. I reminded them also that Henrik Ibsen said that he read virtually nothing but the Bible and the newspapers, because it was there that he found all he needed for his dramas. Human experience is not illimitable; the same things tend to repeat themselves in all our lives; it is the individuality of our response that gives them their personal quality. Dickens encountered the same poverty, squalor, meanness, magnanimity and heroically endured pain in the London of his childhood that was met with by his boy companion, Bob Fagin, but it was his intuitive quality which enabled him to people the scene with Mr. and Mrs. Micawber, with Bill Sykes and Nancy, with Dick Swiveller and the Marchioness, with Uriah Heep and the grandiloquent Crummleses. I think it is superficial to say that he invented his characters; rather it should be said that he discerned them in the welter of life and experience that pressed upon him; he saw the gold in the ore, and he made the gold palpable to his readers, then and now.

The vitality of Dickens's work, I suggest, lay not in his indignation over long-dead abuses; there was plenty of indignation in Victorian England. It was in his extraordinary perception and illumination of the life that lay about him, inanimate as well as animate. He was not nearly so aroused about the incompetence and dishonesty of the hospital nurses of his time as he was fascinated by the incompetence and honesty of Sairey Gamp and her partner Betsey Prig; he did not care so much about the grinding slowness of the Court of Chancery as he cared about Miss Flyte, whom it had driven mad, and the Jarndyce family, whom it impoverished. When he looked at the Lord Chancellor seated in his court, wigged and gowned and attended by all the splendour of precedent and ritual, he was not a lawyer who had reached the top of his profession, but Old Krook who sat in his nearby junk shop surrounded, like the Lord Chancellor, by the dusty evidence of ruined households and broken lives.

It tells us nothing to say that Dickens was an artist. Why was he an artist, and what did his artistry incline him toward, as a writer? Not, I think, to causes far better pursued in Parliament and the newspapers, but to people and things and the raw stuff of life in which he saw wonders hidden from other eyes. If you want to find out what Dickens's opinions on social subjects were, apart from his novels, read what he wrote for the popular papers he edited; you will be astonished at how commonplace and un-Dickensian many of those articles are.

The editor was driven by moral purpose: The great author was driven by intuition.

Do not mistake me. I do not say that Dickens lacked moral purpose; he had as much as the next man and more than many. But it was not moral purpose that made him a great writer.

There have been writers, and good ones, who have rejected any suggestion of moral purpose in their work. Vladimir Nabokov wrote, in a letter to a friend, "Writers have no social responsibility," and certainly he admits of none in his own novels. But in the three published volumes of his lectures on Western Literature he has to recognize the powerful social responsibility of Tolstoy and Dostoyevsky, to name no others. Unless one writes extremely astringent novels, as Nabokov himself did, it is difficult to avoid some influence of social responsibility because it appears to be something deeply rooted in human nature. Ever since *Aesop's Fables* mankind has had a strong appetite for stories from which a moral is drawn directly, or in which some moral attitude is implied.

If you truly want to discover what people expect from what they read, forget about great writers and masterpieces for a while, and look at the bulk of popular novels—the kind of novels that sell in the hundreds of thousands in drugstores and airports, and which are never reviewed in the literary papers. G.K. Chesterton, a perceptive and unjustly neglected critic, wrote in 1905, "Men's basic assumptions and everlasting energies are to be found in penny dreadfuls and halfpenny novelettes." To rise above that level, but to deal still with a genre of literature that is hugely popular, consider the detective novels that sell in such astronomical numbers, and are eagerly passed from hand to hand by enthusiasts. I do not suppose that many of their readers ever give a thought to moral purpose, but their attitude could be summed up as "Vengeance is mine; I will repay, saith the Lord." Scores of detective novels are rooted in the words of Exodus: "And if any mischief follow, then thou shalt give life for life, eye for eye, tooth for tooth, hand for hand, foot for foot." And in these stories, so various in their form and so widely separated in the kind of society they depict, who is the instrument of the Lord's vengeance, who brings the thief or the murderer to his just reward? It is the Great Detective, of course. Perhaps, like

Sherlock Holmes, he is the Thinking Man, the cold reasoner. Or he may be the Man of Feeling, as in Chesterton's Father Brown. He may be the aristocratic Lord Peter Wimsey, or the immobile intellectual Nero Wolfe. In the work of Miss P.D. James, the acknowledged queen of the modern detective story, he may be Adam Dalgleish of New Scotland Yard, who is a poet when he is not on the trail of a murderer, and plainly a Man of Intuition. But whatever Platonic type he may belong to, anybody who has given even superficial attention to medieval religious drama recognizes in the Great Detective the figure called Divine Correction. He is the restorer of balance, and dispenser of justice, working on behalf of a higher authority.

What higher authority? The mass of readers might balk at calling that authority God, but they might agree to calling it Poetic Justice, desire deep in the human heart to see evil punished, however delightedly as readers they may have bathed in that evil for two-thirds of the book.

Even in the much-abused television series, and the movies where the villains wreak hideous punishment on the Good Guys, the Good Guys must triumph in the end, or there would be outraged protest from armies of viewers.

You may say that in this the public is having its cake and eating it too. I make no denial. That has always been the public's way, whenever it can be managed. It is neatly summed up in the story about the little boy who burst into his mother's drawing-room, crying: "Ma—I caught a toad, and I bashed him and jumped on him and ran over him with the lawn mower till—(suddenly seeing the parson, who has come to tea)—till God called him home." The moral attitudes of the majority of people are not intellectually reasoned but they are deeply rooted. Evil must be punished, one way or another. But while the Evil is going on we do not want to miss a gunshot, or a blow, or a drop of gore. As an English satirist wrote, a century ago:

> It's human natur, p'raps—if so,
> Oh, isn't human natur low!

Perhaps, in a more generous mood, we may say that human nature is not so much low, as unreflecting. It is people like ourselves who have determined to reflect on this theme of literature and moral purpose, and I have put forward my opinion that literature at its higher levels must beware of allowing moral purpose to assume a dominant place in its creation. Moral purpose, if it asserts itself as it has done in much of the finest literature we possess, will come unbidden from the place where literature of the serious kind has its origin, and it will be part of the fabric of the whole work, and not something that can be abstracted and discussed as an element in itself.

Consider a novel acknowledged to be great, from the French Literature of the nineteenth century. I speak of Gustave Flaubert's *Madame Bovary* (1857). In it we follow the brief life of Emma Bovary, who is fated to live in provincial dullness, with a dull if worthy husband; she is not a woman of strong character or intellect; she has been sentimentally educated, and what intelligence she has is poorly employed; she seeks a broader life through ill-fated romances with men of no greater intellectual or moral stature than herself, and in the end she dies wretchedly, a disappointed woman. It sounds a dismal theme but as Flaubert treats it, it is transfixing in its depth of understanding and its illumination of a kind of life that is led by millions of people. Is Emma treated by the author with compassion? No, she is treated with justice. Has the author no pity for Emma? It does not appear, but it is plain to the understanding reader that the author has great pity for mankind. It is not the pity that slops and gushes, nor would it be just to Flaubert to say that it attempts to be godlike. It is the pity of the observer, the recorder of things as they are, rather than as they should be.

It is significant that on a famous occasion when a lady said to him: "How could you write so profoundly about Emma Bovary? Where did you find your extraordinary understanding of woman's nature?" Flaubert replied: "Madame Bovary, c'est moi."

He spoke the simple truth. A writer finds his themes and his characters in the depth of his own being, and his understanding of them is an understanding of himself. This is not to say that Don Quixote is Miguel de Cervantes or that Mr. Pickwick is Charles Dickens in any simple sense. It is to say that Cervantes and Dickens are capable of the Don and Mr. Pickwick; they embrace the character, not because it is an obvious part of their own nature, but because it is a possibility which they are capable of seizing and bringing to a fictional life. They have intuitions of the Don and of Pickwick, as Flaubert had his intuition of Madame Bovary.

Incidentally, it is nonsense to say, as some extreme feminists say now, that a man is incapable of writing perceptively about a woman; nobody, so far as I know, has ever said that a woman is incapable of writing perceptively about a man. George Eliot, one of the truly great writers of the Victorian age, could draw men with a breathtaking verisimilitude and perception. It needs no genius from the genetic laboratories to tell us that in every man there lies a substantial, physical element which is feminine, and that in every woman there is a substantial genetic element of masculinity. Authors, it appears, have unusual access to this contra-sexual side of themselves, which is not only mental, but physical. Heavy books are written now to explain this androgynous element in human character, but great numbers of people of all sorts have always been aware of it, and artists of any significance have always been among their number. Perhaps we may say of the author what Walt Whitman said of himself: He is large, he contains multitudes.

You will expect me to develop this theme of intuition, and I shall do so, but it will be necessary for me to speak of personal experience, if I am to make what I say real to you. What I am about to say is not prompted by vanity, but by the fact that only by telling you what I know from my own experience to be true, can I hope to carry conviction.

When people speak of intuition they seem as a usual thing to mean some sudden leap in the dark, some instantaneous flash of enlightenment. Certainly that is intuition of one sort. But there is another kind of intuition, which is the slumbrous, slow-moving kind, and it is not so widely recognized.

Some years ago I wrote a book called *Fifth Business*, which attracted a flattering amount of attention. For six or seven years before I wrote it I was very busy about some work that demanded the best of my attention, it seemed, and all of my energy. I had been entrusted with the task of setting in motion a new college in my university, exclusively for graduate students. But however hard one works at a task, one is never totally absorbed in it. Personal matters, family matters, involvements of all kinds must be given their necessary attention. And in addition to these things, one is never free of one's fantasy life, or the life that asserts itself in dreams. During all the years that I was busy in the way I have described, I was visited from time to time by a scene which appeared in my fantasy life—when tired, or when dropping off to sleep, or when travelling in an airplane when a better-organized man would have had his lap full of papers and letters.

I have called it a scene, and that is what it was; the action in it was slight, but the picture was vivid. The picture was of a village street; it is six o'clock at night and as it is two or three days after Christmas it is dark; snow is everywhere. Two boys are in the street; one is hurrying home to his supper, and the other calls abuse after him and throws a snowball at him; I know that inside that snowball there is a stone and that it can hurt, and that it is meant to hurt; just as the snowball is about to find its mark, the first boy dodges suddenly in front of two people, a man and a woman, who are walking in the street, and the snowball hits the woman on the head; she falls to the ground.

There it is. An incident which takes about thirty seconds to act out. Does it mean anything? It recurred so often that I decided that it was stupid to ignore it any longer, so I called up the scene and invited my imagination to do what it could with that material. In a very short time I knew who all the people in the fantasy were, and what the outcome of the incident was. The book demanded to be written. And as I wrote, over a period of several months, the remainder of the story and its outcome appeared as they were needed. And not only did the story of *Fifth Business* appear, but other aspects of the same story which made up two subsequent novels, resulting in a trilogy.

I assure you that as I wrote those books I had no sense of moral purpose whatever. I have never thought of myself as a moralist. What I was writing about might be summed up in two themes: First, that the result of a single action may spread like the circles that expand when a stone is thrown into a pond, until they touch places and people unguessed at by the person who threw the stone; in my story it took sixty years for the flight of that stone-laden snowball to expend itself; second, I wanted to explore the matter of childhood culpability for evildoing—may a child be guilty of true evil? And what may be the outcome of deeply felt childhood guilt?

These, I protest, are a novelist's themes and it was as a novelist that I treated them. I was surprised when some critics decided that I was a moralist. Of course there were moral aspects of my story, but to me they were of far less importance than character and incident. Character and incident were the results of intuition, not of careful intellectual work, and when critics wrote about the book as if I had decided on a moral theme first and then cloaked it in fiction, I was at once amused and indignant.

This, I am sure, is the way that real books—I mean books which are not simply manufactured for the market from themes popular in the market—get themselves written. They have already formed themselves deep in the unconscious of the writer, from which they can be coaxed, or dragged, when they will not emerge gently and readily. Before a word was put on paper, the book existed as a possibility.

This accounts, I think, for the unsatisfactory nature of some very great books, when they are looked at from the viewpoint of the literary critic. Critics appear to have in their minds some sort of Platonic Ideal of what a novel should be, and any novel that does not conform to that ideal they declare to be "flawed." I once asked a member of this Druid circle if she could name any novel to me which was not flawed. After melancholy reflection she declared that she could not. Even Henry James, the high priest of the finely crafted novel, showed flaws, at points where outraged artistic instinct refused to be bullied in the name of academic excellence. We all know these great, flawed books. *War and Peace* is a horror to the literary critic, but it is a work of unquestioned greatness. So is *Moby Dick*, which seems at times as if it would exhaust the patience of the most besotted reader. Dostoyevsky and Balzac never know when enough is enough. But would we wish to be without any of the great, flawed masterpieces? No, we would not.

Nor would we say that we valued them first of all for the emphatic moral purpose that unquestionably appears in them. Again and again as we read the great works of fiction—and I apologize for the fact that I have almost wholly neglected poetry and drama, but our time is not without limit—again and again as we read the great works of fiction we hear voices afar crying, "God is not mocked: For whatsoever a man soweth, that shall he also reap"; "The dog is turned to his own vomit again; and the sow that was washed to her wallowing in the mire." But can we find any evidence that these things were written up over the desk of the great author? Why then, do they assert themselves in his work?

I have said that I am not a moralist. Nor am I a philosopher or a theologian. So when I suggest, or tentatively hint, that perhaps morality is part of the structure of man, that it has some archetypal root, I am not speaking as anything but a novelist. You are the experts on the subject, and it is for you to say your say.

I am all ears. But I do not imagine for a moment that anything you say will change the way I write, for you are theologians and moralists and I am that quite different creature, an artist, Neither the greatest nor the least of my kind, but still—an artist.

Having said that, let me hasten to add that I do not use the word *artist* in any grandiose sense, nor do I claim particular status because I apply it to myself. The word, traced to its origin, means simply "a maker," and not necessarily a superior being, though, as Aldous Huxley said more than sixty years ago, we live in a time when anybody who chooses to call himself an artist seems to imagine that the world owes him a living. Literature is unquestionably an art, but we must be cautious in whatever claims we make for it.

Everyone is aware of the sad plight of Salman Rushdie who has offended the world of Islam. I shall not say anything about the rights and wrongs of that matter, because I do not know enough about it to do so usefully. But I was sorry when, in a recent public address, Mr. Rushdie appealed to what he called "the sacredness of art" to justify what he had written in *The Satanic Verses*. An age that has often urged us to regard the Bible simply as literature is no time to throw a cloak of sanctity over a novel. Art has no overriding "sacredness" that lifts it above the other works of man. Some books, because of their splendour of conception and execution, are unquestionably art on the highest level, and are so valued. But their glory does not spill over onto the run-of-the-mill works of the journeymen of literature, and writers are on shaky ground when they think otherwise.

So, to sum up, I have given an opinion that literature may indeed have a moral purpose when the moral judgment rises naturally from the work of art and is answered by a strong inner conviction in the reader. Morality which is applied cosmetically to catch a particular taste is found in many books, but not in the best books. I have confined my remarks pretty well to fiction, and of fiction I may say that it is by its nature a secular form of art, taking the whole of life as its province, and impatient of bonds of any sort, including those of popular morality. But if, as I suspect, some moral purposes exist deep in the psyche of man, they are certain to rise to the surface in literature of the highest order.

Collecting

5

In Pursuit of Pornography

This selection should be included for the title alone! I have chosen it from *A Voice from the Attic* because it is about book collecting, and Davies was a keen collector. The information about reading and collecting pornography may be out of date in our very liberal society, but the plea that we should be allowed to read what we choose is as relevant today, which can be confirmed just by reading the newspaper.

When Davies was putting together the pornographic books he needed to read he applied, in some cases, to the local library. Mrs. Davies tells a story about going in to collect his selections and being glad that the librarian, Bob Porter, was a friend and knew of the project. I remember being on a trip that took me to Paris as a teenager and being asked by Davies to pick up a book for him in Paris and bring it home. I had no idea at the time that I was transporting a copy of *Lolita*. He was quite right in thinking that no one would look for such a book in a young girl's luggage.

When the book was reprinted in 1990, Davies added this Preface:

This book was first published in 1960 and reprinted in 1971; I do not think that much in it needs bringing up to date, excepting the comments on pornography. The past quarter century has seen a revolution in this sort of publishing, and writers now enjoy a freedom that would have roused the astonishment and envy of some of the greatest Victorians, and perhaps of Joyce and Lawrence. Whether the arts of the novel and the play have been correspondingly enlarged we cannot yet know, but it is plain that pornography as a genre in itself has entered on a new life. If I were to rewrite Chapter

VII, I do not think I would strike anything out; rather, I should add some additional comment, but as I make no claim to being an expert in this realm, and write of pornography rather as an area for the collector than as a genre in itself, the reader will be just as well off without any extension of my opinions. There are references, also, to writers who were *avante-garde* when the book was written and who are so no longer, though I do not think their work has lost much in value for that reason. Books of the *avante-garde* either establish themselves as books of lasting value, or they slip from the rear guard into the discard, and I believe the writers I mentioned have not proven trivial. This is, after all, a book about reading, and the kind of reader I am addressing does not care primarily about being in fashion.

♫

It is with reluctance that I begin this chapter with some comment on book collecting, for I do not know how I shall avoid the many pitfalls which lie in the path of all who approach that subject. Hobbyists are likely to be bores to those who do not share their madness, and I am not writing this for other collectors, nor am I trying to make converts. But it is a plain fact that anyone who has ten books on a shelf which he has bought and kept because he likes them is a collector on the humblest level, and his books are, in a special sense, a reflection of himself. It is of collections of books as reflections of their owners that I wish to write. But the temptation to wallow and disport myself in the purple prose of the doting collector is strong, and it will need all my vigilance to resist it.

The trouble is that books have always been what the jargon of the sociologist calls "status lenders." Books are likely to lay bare unsuspected foolishness, even in people who do not read them. "It's an education just to look at all those books," said a man who came to hang curtains in my library; he was sincere, he was awed, he wished to pay tribute to something which he believed to be good, and he also wanted to show that, though not a reader himself, he was a fellow of fine feelings. "Books are my husband's one vice," said a woman to me, pleased as Punch—as she might well have been had her statement been true. "Why don't you read a book?"

say parents to their troublesome children, as who might say: "Why don't you take a tranquilizer?" There are great numbers of people to whom the act of reading a book—any sort of book—is wondrous; they speak of the reader in the tone of warm approbation which they use otherwise when referring to pregnant women, or the newly dead. And how often do we meet the man who prefaces his remarks with: "I was reading a book last night …" in the too loud, overenunciated fashion of one who might be saying: "I keep a hippogryph in my basement." Reading confers status.

BOOKS FOR PRESTIGE

How much more, then, does the acquirement of rare books add to the prestige of the collector! They need not be very rare; a shelf of first editions of the better sort of modern novelist is quite enough, though it is even better to have some books by reputable dead authors, preferably bound in leather. What matter if the edges be trimmed so that the margins are destroyed, and the binding a tasteless horror? Plenty of people will be impressed.

Another collector, a little higher up the ladder, will not be impressed, however, and it is at this point that the real dog fight for status begins. He takes down the first edition of *Vanity Fair*, for which his host paid $130 at Ladrone's in New York, and remarks brusquely that two of the plates are substitutions, and that the trimming and rebinding have robbed it of all bibliographical interest. "A good reading copy, of course—if that's all you want," he says, and leaves his host a prey to rage and envy, demoted to the ranks of those who collect books merely to read.

Thus it goes, up and up the ladder until those dizzy heights are reached where rich collectors vie for Gutenbergs or First Folios, and where a single note from Lewis Carroll saying "In my heart of hearts I have always detested that little prig *Alice*" can command a sum equivalent to the annual salary of a union executive.

The world of book collectors is a curious mingling of dreamy charm, poison-fanged competition, and snobbery. It reveals itself in the books they write. How winning they are as they confess their lifelong passion for the gentle Elia (they mean Charles Lamb) or Miss Austen (they mean Jane, but they are so courtly that they cannot bring themselves to use her first name). How polysyllabically rude they become when writing of Samuel Johnson, and when they tackle Gibbon, how their prose squirms and undulates as they struggle to catch the rhythm of his splendid music! But behind all this posthumous courtship of the literary great we are conscious of another and very different spirit; it is that of the junkman with his wretched cart and his gloomy howl of "any ol' rags, any ol' bones, any ol' bottles?" They write gleefully of the "finds"—meaning books which they have acquired for ridiculously less than their value to collectors. Nobody would grudge them the reward of expert knowledge and long searching if only they were less unctuous about it, if only they could refrain from rubbing their hands in print. But always in these books the haggling, overreaching sharper is at war with the self-honouring book lover, and the struggle is a disquieting one to the non-collector, who wishes that they would come down flatly on one side or the other.

The collector, however, must haggle, must boast, must croon over his treasures, because it is his nature. And a very peculiar nature, too. Time and again book lovers have written of their libraries as harems and of themselves as sultans, holding captive the beauties who exist for their pleasure alone. It is not in the least inappropriate that Casanova ended his days as librarian to Count Waldstein at Dux; he, who knew every art of seduction, thus became guardian of another man's zenana. The eroticism, snobbery, and shameless greed of book collectors can be shocking if we are so naive as to suppose, like my decorator, that books are, in their influence, solely educative—which is usually taken by simple minds to mean emasculating.

COLLECTING CONDEMNED

Doubtless it was this mania of collectors which drove Edmund Wilson to write in 1926, when the trade in rare books was at one of its occasional peaks: "There is no special virtue in first editions: one would usually prefer to read a later one in which the printing is up to date, the paper has not faded and the author has corrected the errors. All this trade is as deeply boring to people who are interested in literature as it seems to be fascinating to those others who, incapable of literary culture, try to buy the distinction of letters by paying unusual prices for bibliographical rarities.... It may be necessary for a critic or a student—unless he has within reach a large library—to accumulate a considerable number of books; but it is doubtful whether any first-rate man of letters has ever gone in for collecting books except on some special subject in which he might happen to be interested ... it is easier for a camel to pass through the eye of a needle than for a collector of first editions to enter the Kingdom of Literature."

Disgust has forced Mr. Wilson to take an extreme position, and I do not think that what he says is true. There *is* a special virtue in first editions, they are the form in which the author first saw his work, the form in which it was acclaimed or neglected by his contemporaries, the form very often with the best claim to be considered authentic. To prefer a modern reprint, unless for some very good reason, is bibliographic puritanism, and like all unnecessary austerity, it suggests that its professor is making a virtue of his lack of taste. There are also people, no doubt, who like the meals served on airplanes, eaten out of compartmented trays with plastic knives and forks; such people might assert that their victuals are as nutritious as those served on china and silver, but we should not be likely to heed them to the extent of providing our houses with such nasty things; we eat for pleasure as well as to stoke our fires. We read for pleasure, too, and the desires of hand and eye, though inferior to those of the mind, ask for some occasional gratification. First editions, old editions, and handsome books are aesthetically gratifying.

A PLEA FOR PRIVATE LIBRARIES

It is not necessary to be a lunatic collector, either, to object to the suggestion of Mr. Wilson—one in which Bernard Shaw also concurred—that the existence of a public library makes a private one unnecessary. If we admire a book, we like to own it, and we like to have it at hand whenever we want it. Furthermore, there is about public books a public feel, and even a public smell, which some people dislike. Strive as they may, librarians cannot keep books from being marked and dirtied by some of their borrowers. It has long been so, and one of the oldest books in praise of collecting bears witness to it. I speak of the *Philobiblon* of the good Bishop Richard de Bury, written in 1345, from which this passage comes:

You may happen to see some headstrong youth lazily lounging over his studies, and when the winter's frost is sharp, his nose running from the nipping cold drips down, nor does he think of wiping it with his pocket-handkerchief until he has bedewed the book before him with the ugly moisture. Would that he had before him no book, but a cobbler's apron! His nails are stuffed with fetid filth as black as jet, with which he marks any passage that pleases him. He distributes a multitude of straws, which he inserts to stick out in different places, so that the halm may remind him of what his memory cannot retain. These straws, because the book has no stomach to digest them, and no one takes them out, first distend the book from its wonted closing, and at length, being carelessly abandoned to oblivion, go to decay. He does not fear to eat fruit or cheese over an open book, or carelessly to carry a cup to and from his mouth; and because he has no wallet at hand he drops into books the fragments that are left. Continually chattering, he is never weary of disputing with his companions, and while he alleges a crowd of senseless arguments, he wets the book lying half open on his lap with sputtering showers. Aye, and then hastily folding his arms he leans forward on the book, and by a brief spell of study he invites a prolonged nap; and then, by way of mending the wrinkles, he folds back the margin of the leaves, to the no small injury of the book. Now the rain is over and gone, and the flowers have appeared in our land. Then the scholar we are speaking of, a neglecter rather than an inspecter of books, will stuff his volume with violets, and primroses, with roses and quatrefoil. Then he will use his wet and perspiring hands to turn over the volumes; then he will thump the white vellum with gloves covered with all kinds of dust, and with his finger clad in long-used leather will hunt line by line through the page; then at the sting of the biting flea the sacred book is flung aside, and is hardly shut for another month, until it is so full of dust that has found its way within, that it resists the effort to close it.

The Bishop was no book miser, but the founder of a great library, and the passage above comes from the chapter which tells how he wants his books to be used. He is also severe against those who write opinions of their own in margins. His complaints have a modern ring because the faults he abuses persist. Flowers, straws, and unpleasing stains are to be found in public-library books to this day, and I have more than once found a used pipe cleaner in their pages. Librarians say, very properly, that they would rather have books read to pieces than preserved untouched, and we must all, when we need many books, use public collections. But if we truly love books, or indeed if we merely like and respect them, we shall want as many as we can get for our private possession.

Mr. Wilson's protest, however, is against the nonsensical side of book collecting, which is a very prominent side. To me, at any rate, there is a perversity in collecting books without meaning to read them, and it is maddening to meet people who regard books as a form of decoration or a substitute for insulation; I once knew a young woman who would own a book only if it had a white binding, and quite recently I heard a man say that a wall of books was the best fire-break a house could have because they burn so slowly.

The moderate collector is likely to be a book lover of moderate means; he values what books can say to him too much to overvalue their age, their rarity, or their appearance, and because he has no money for such pomps, the temptations of books too valuable to be read (and perhaps unreadable) do not torture him. But he may still have a fine library, and to people who know something of books, it will be a partial index to his character.

PRIVATE-PRESS BOOKS

Books need not be old or particularly rare to have beauty and value. Modern craftsmen can produce them, and if you want to know how and why, *The Gregynog Press* by Thomas Jones gives an account of one of the finest private presses of our time. Perhaps the most famous of the private presses was that which Horace Walpole directed for his own pleasure at Strawberry Hill from 1757; the books and pamphlets he produced are rare enough and fine enough to have been worth forgery after his death. He purposely created rarities; of *Hieroglyphic Tales*, for instance, which he produced in 1785, there were only six copies. But it was in the nineteenth century that private presses began to flourish; there were great presses before that time, such as those of Aldus Manutius and Louis Elzevir, but these men were themselves commercial printers, and not, as were the private presses of our own day and the last century, attempting to produce books which commercial printers could not, for economic reasons, attempt.

The names of the private presses are familiar to lovers of books. Kelmscott, Ashdene, Doves, Golden Cockerel, Corvinus, Eragny, Fanfrolico, Gregynog, Nonesuch, Cuala, Grabhorn—they are well represented in the catalogues of sellers of fine books. They are not extremely rare, but they are rare enough; the handsome Nonesuch editions of the Restoration dramatists—Rochester, Otway, Congreve, Farquhar, Wycherley, Vanbrugh, and Dryden—run from 900 to 1,350 copies each, and the Nonesuch Milton is confined to 1,450 copies in two volumes and 90 copies with the two volumes bound as one, printed on a special paper. The Golden Cockerel edition of Colley Cibber's *Autobiography* runs to 450 copies; *Covent Garden Drollery*, from the Fortune Press, 575 copies; the Gregynog *Elia and the Last Essays of Elia*, 260 copies. To own any of these books is to have a thing of beauty, and the prices, though not trifling, are very much below the millionaire level.

Not all books in this category are equally worthy of the collector's attention. About the directors and workers of the private presses there was necessarily a strong individuality, which sometimes became eccentricity, and fashionable books were brought out which are merely ugly now. Some presses were long on taste but short on crafts-manship, and their books do not stand up well. An example is *The Paintings of D.H. Lawrence* brought out by the Mandrake Press in 1929 in an edition of 510 copies. The quality of reproduction of the paintings is poor, and the pretentious binding is hardly likely to last a century. The book appeals, however, to the pious zeal of Lawrentians, and if they have luck and twenty pounds, they can get one of the 510 copies; presumably it would suffer the usual sea change before it appeared in a New York shop, and would cost more than the equivalent—say sixty dollars—there.

Another fault of many private presses, in my eyes, at least, was that they were more interested in books as objects to be prized than as volumes to be read, and they chose to bring out in handsome form books which very few people care about. If one wanted to read the *Idyls of Theocritus, Bion and Moschus*, would one choose to do so in the prose translation of Andrew Lang? The Riccardi Press thought so. Does someone pine for fourteen poems by James Elroy Flecker, at eighteen guineas? Darantière of Dijon thought they did. Do you famish for *The Parlement of Pratlers* by John Eliot? The Fanfrolico Press thought that at least 625 bibliophiles were aching for it. I cannot escape a disagreeable impression that these books were chosen because someone thought he could do a pretty job with them, rather than because the books were wanted for themselves.

PRIVATE PRESSES CRUDELY IMITATED

The private presses had other unfortunate consequences. In the books produced under the influence of Elbert Hubbard we see what Kelmscott mannerism can sink to when not controlled by Kelmscott taste. Thick paper, queer type, lavish ornament, and ragged edges will not make a fine book, though they will make a book odd enough to impress people who know nothing of books and perhaps do not greatly like them. The assurance given in a fancy colophon that the object has been "done into a printed book by the handicraftsmen of the Roycroft Shops at East Aurora" does not make up for the fact that the thing is inconvenient to read and that the binding creates the same disagreeable feeling in the hand as wearing cheap suede gloves. Any book lover would much rather have a decent job done by a commercial printer. The only justification of the private presses is that they can design books of unusual beauty and make them at least as well as the trade publishers; if they fail in this they should give up. Hubbard cheapened the craft he thought to elevate.

The snobbery attaching to the products of private presses has given rise at various times during the past fifty years to clubs or associations which produce and distribute supposedly fine books. They have existed in the United States, and at least one exists in England now. Their books are of uneven merit (as indeed were those of the private presses), but they have always some confession of economy about them, of pinching and corner cutting. The gold on the bindings is not good enough, and it comes off in powder after a time; the books do not open well, the illustrations—usually called "decorations," for it is beneath the dignity of artists to illustrate any more—may be four scratchy etchings which bear no relation to the text, or woodcuts of a determined and self-conscious naïveté. About them is an air of not being quite first-rate, either as commercial books made by a decent publisher, or yet as examples of fine printing; sometimes they are refined to the point of being epicene, and if they are meant to be robust—as when a novel by Fielding or Defoe is offered—they exhibit the false and excessive manliness of the tough homosexual. They are not honest books.

THE INSCRUTABLE PORTRAIT

When I write of a collection of books as a portrait of its owner I must hasten to make several qualifications. The idea was first suggested to my mind many years ago, when a university lecturer solemnly assured the class of which I was a member that it was so. He was urging us to become buyers of books, and he was eager that we should spend our money only on good books. He spoke exultantly of the joys of collecting a library as an extension of one's personality. I took him at his word then, but during the intervening years I have seen so many collections of books which did not seem to square with what I knew about their owners that I cannot think of his dictum now without overtones of travesty. There was a time when I fancied myself capable of studying a man's books as I might study his portrait, but I have dismissed such prideful nonsense long since. There is no art to find the mind's construction in the books, as Shakespeare would doubtless have written if he had thought of it.

What are we told by the presence of those pretentious, unreadable, complete sets of Balzac and Daudet, which were sold in the early years of this century to people who had never heard of Balzac or Daudet, but who were persuaded by book agents that they needed such culti-vated trappings? Showy but tasteless in binding, and illustrated with dingy engravings "guarded" by bits of tissue, they still turn up at country auctions in Canada—pathetic witnesses of man's desire to be learned without taking the trouble to learn.

What are we told by the rich man's collection, glowing with bibli-ographical rarities? Perhaps only that he has a long purse and a good adviser, but we must beware of hasty conclusions. Edmund Wilson's strictures on the collector are too severe; a man is not precluded from taste and literary enthusiasm merely because he is rich; that belief is to be classed with the foolish notion that the real lovers of opera are all to be found in the cheapest seats; it is naive and uncharitable to dislike the rich merely because they are rich. The wealthy collector may be a mere hobbyist, or he may be of the strain of Richard de Bury, or, in our own time, of Arthur Houghton. And if, as sometimes happens, he is both, with the courtier to the dead, the rag and bone man, and the benefactor of mankind all mingled in one creature, we must be shrewd indeed to read his portrait in his books.

HIDDEN BOOKS

Nor should we attempt to do so unless we have seen *all* his books—not only those which are on the shelves, but those which are locked in his desk, or hidden behind the shelves, or tucked beneath the winter underwear in his bureau. Even collectors on a modest scale have something of this sort—a surreptitious *Lady Chatterley* purchased years ago on a visit to Paris, a *Ulysses* bought before it became legal and still smelling a little of brimstone, or a *Tropic of Capricorn* concealed from the children or even perhaps from that guardian of the purity of the hearth, The Wife. What a man considers indecent is an important clue to his character, and although there are exceptions, it has been my experience that book collectors have strange opinions on this subject, and few of them lack a book or two which they think they should conceal.

Books are status lenders, but they are something much older and stranger; they retain a quality of magic for people who are deeply concerned with them, as well as for those who know little about them. Books are often burned; as I write this the fires are cooling in Fort William, Ontario, where all local copies of *Lady Chatterley's Lover* were thrown into the flames at the urgency of a female mayor. But when did we last hear of a picture being burned? What angry mayor has recently smashed a statue? It is the hated book which alone suffers the fate of the witch. The fearful are ready to declare that the young will be perverted by suggestive books, but they rarely turn their attention to the contents of art galleries. Books are thought to have a power not granted to other works of art, not only by the simple but by the learned. Among collectors the possession of a few volumes of doubtful character seems to be a fearful yet irresistible necessity.

It is when we discover what these volumes are that we gape and pop our eyes. A man once favoured me with a sight of his unholy treasure, which proved to be a first edition of Cabell's *Jurgen*; perhaps tactlessly I told him that it could be bought half a mile away, in a very good bookshop, with illustrations *à la* Beardsley; the information made no impression on his belief that it was a dreadful yet beautiful book, which must be kept at all costs from the eyes of his womenfolk. Another collector, a wealthy Canadian, appealed to his bookseller in despair; his physician had warned him that he might die suddenly, and locked in his desk was a copy of Cleland's *Fanny Hill, or the Memoirs of a Woman of Pleasure*; he had paid one hundred dollars for it (though it was a modern reprint and of no bibliographical interest), and the notion that his lubricity might be exposed to his daughters after his death was pushing him toward the heart attack he feared. From *Jurgen* to *Fanny Hill* is a far cry, and between are all sorts of books which apparently sensible people consider heinous.

A concept of obscenity appears to be as necessary to one's view of life as a concept of purity. If we seek to encompass all that we can of the spectrum of human intellect and feeling, we cannot confine ourselves to the reds and oranges; we must know the violets and indigos as well. Which is the wiser course—to attempt to suppress a large part of what occupies the human mind, or to examine and cultivate everything in the mind that can be reached? "Vice loses half its evil by losing all its grossness," said Edmund Burke. Book collectors who are, as I have said above, usually men of strong and mingled emotions offer evidence to support Burke's opinion.

MY SEARCH FOR PORNOGRAPHY

Simple pornography has little appeal for them. When I undertook the writing of this book and planned the present chapter, I attempted to find out something about the trade in pornography, but without much success. I asked a good many booksellers about it, and sometimes my reception was amusing; a few of them thought that I had disguised myself as a pedant in order to gratify the literary passions of a voluptuary, and our conversation proceeded, on their side with "strange *oeillades* and most speaking looks" and on mine with mounting embarrassment; they had heard of pornographic books, ha ha, but they never dealt in them—no, never. They had heard of collectors who sought out pornographic books, but they got them in New York, or in London, or in Brussels, or obtained them from Japan—the market was anywhere, it appeared, except where I happened to be. Other booksellers were less jocose and more helpful. One, in an English university city, had handled three large collections of pornography in a lifetime of bookselling.

What he told me about these collections was interesting and pathetic. The mania for completeness had possessed the collectors; if they heard of an item in Port Said, they must have it; if a little book of pictures was popular among sailors in Cape Town, they must include an example in the collection. The result was that when the collections were disposed of, there were a few hundred volumes which might be considered saleable, and thousands of pamphlets, booklets, and broadsides which could only be burned; nobody, however eager for pornography, could bother with so much repetitious, ill-printed, crudely illustrated trash. One of these collectors was a clergyman of the Church of England who spent all his fortune on his accumulation; his heirs were lucky to get two or three hundred pounds out of a large library which had cost many thousands.

Another bookseller told me that the pornographic market was a closed and special one, with its own scale of prices. This information complemented what I had been told before about the avidity of collectors in this realm; they have a compulsion toward completeness, and as they seem rarely to be the kind of people who can, or will, go to the places where the cheapest pornography is retailed, they must depend on agents. All pornography, it appears, costs more than any other sort of publication in relation to the expense of producing it; nevertheless, some of it sells quite cheaply in, for example, the ports of the Near East. But by the time these chapbooks or pamphlets have been purchased by agents and sent to buyers in Britain or North America, the original price has been multiplied by five, by ten, perhaps by a hundred. And the collector, to satisfy his mania for completeness, pays.

Several booksellers spoke with admiration of the books—perhaps pornography is not the right word for them—of erotic content which are produced in Japan; I was told that they are often of great beauty and delicacy of illustration. The Western market for them seems to be Brussels, with Amsterdam a close rival.

Commercial booksellers, either of new books or collector's books, have no connection with the pornographic market. Some of those to whom I spoke tried to help me by producing volumes which they considered, for one reason or another, fell within the forbidden category. One was the book of D.H. Lawrence's paintings already described; because the original exhibition of these pictures was closed by the police in 1929, the book could not be freely offered for sale. There is not a picture in it which appears to me to be pornographic, if it is admitted that the nude human body is a permissible subject for a painter. Another bookseller showed me some French copies of

Rabelais and Baudelaire, illustrated by modern French artists; on his shelves were many books with equally lively illustrations, but they were not French, and thus were free of suspicion. He also showed me a copy of *The Golden Asse*, with illustrations much milder in tone than those in the Bodley Head limited edition of 1923, which sells without hindrance.

A number of helpful booksellers urged me to make myself known at the British Museum, which has the second-largest collection of erotica and pornography in the world, the only superior one being in the library of the Vatican. But they mistook my purpose; I did not want to examine pornography, I wanted to find out how the trade in it works, and in this I failed. Had I been a more dedicated scholar, I suppose I would have taken greater pains. I would have disguised myself as a sailor, a dissolute parson, or a gandermooner, and lurked in the places where such people congregate, waiting to be approached. Adolescents, I was told, bought pornography of a particular kind, and I might have tried to impose myself upon a shady bookseller as a wanton adolescent—the half-baked in pursuit of the wholly raw. But I had no confidence in my ability to assume any of these characters convincingly, or yet to pass myself off as a jaded worldling to whom the costly erotica of Japan might be offered. Neither was I successful in discovering a Fred Hankey to assist me.

DON QUICHOTTE OR DIRTY HANKEY?

Frederick Hankey took pains to surround himself with mystery, and facts about him are not easily come by. He was an Englishman of good family who lived in Paris in the middle decades of the nineteenth century, devoting his energies to the collection of pornographic books, pictures, and images. His austerity and dedication to his work was commended by several of his distinguished clients, and in particular by Richard Monckton Milnes (1809–85), Baron Houghton, politician and poet, best remembered as the earliest biographer of Keats. Milnes's library at Fryston (which he sometimes called "Aphrodisiopolis") contained six principal sections, including English poetry, studies of the French Revolution, theology, magic and witch-craft, crime and punishment, and erotica; Hankey supplied the erotica, and it was at Milnes's house that Swinburne made his acquaintance with the works of the Marquis de Sade. The collection was open to Milnes's guests, and many of them made ample use of it. Richard Burton, translator of *Arabian Nights*, was an amateur of erotica and a guest at Fryston at one time; he referred to the Paris buyer as "poor old Hankey." But to other people Frederick Hankey was a sinister figure; it was the Goncourts who named him *"le Don Quichotte des obscènes."*

Hankey and Burton exemplify two opposed attitudes toward erotica. To Burton it was a subject for study, a part of the comedy of life, but it was not an obsession and it had no mystical overtones. To Hankey it was a reason for being, a support for his own ruling passion (which was Sadism), and probably the source of the deepest emotions of which he was capable. Burton's own great translation and edition of *Arabian Nights* gained the reputation of a pornographic book prin-cipally because of one section of the Terminal Essay in which he discusses the Arab attitude toward sex; he was a fearless man and unaccommodating toward the prudery of society in his time. He paid heavily for his frankness, for it was at least as hard a century ago as it is now for people of conventional mind to recognize that a man can be interested in the vagaries of sexual behaviour without wishing to practise them himself.

Milnes's library included most of the classics of erotica; some books were included under that heading which do not seem to modern taste to belong there. Voltaire's *La Pucelle* is not a very dread-ful book, and Choderlos de Laclos's *Les Liaisons dangereuses* enjoys a special regard nowadays for its psychological insight. Aretino's *Sonnetti Lussuriosi* are certainly erotic, but the famous engravings which gave rise to them are so little pornographic that one of them is reproduced in Dr. Richard Lewinsohn's *A History of Sexual Customs*. Milnes had the works of Sade, of course, who was a novelty in England in the nineteenth century, and whose influence on Swinburne and Rossetti is described in a letter which the former wrote to Milnes after a reading of *Justine*. "I really thought I must have died or split open and choked with laughing.... I literally doubled up and fell down with laughter.... I read it out and the auditors rolled and roared ... screams of laughter." It is a pity we cannot hear that laughter. Was it hysterical? Was it caused simply by the Marquis's rather odd sense of drollery? Or was some of it snob laughter, the amusement of sensitive but not notably mature Englishmen enjoying a book which added to the pleasure of being outrageous the tickle of being outrageous in French?

It is extraordinary to what a degree French culture has dominated some aspects of English literary taste. It cannot very successfully be argued that there is an intellectual sympathy between the two nations. But for more than a century Englishmen of cultivation have felt it necessary to have at least a nodding acquaintance with French literature, although there has been no corresponding impulse to know anything at all about what was doing in Germany or Italy. When Thomas Mann died, several English critics admitted without a blush that they knew little of his work and found it unsympathetic; there was some suggestion that he was a rude American enthusiasm, rather than one of the masters of our time. But not to be acquainted with what is happening in literary France is to feel disgraced, and in the pecking order of literary criticism a Frenchman can humiliate an Englishman just as readily as an Englishman can humiliate an American, and an American a Canadian. One of Canada's most serious literary needs at present is some lesser nation to domineer over and shame by displays of superior taste.

This is not said to belittle French culture, even if it lay in the power of any words of mine to do so. It is said, rather, to suggest that for Swinburne and Rossetti at least some of the pleasure of Sade lay in the snobbery of being smutty in the tongue which they so much admired and to which they attributed exquisite nuance and piquancy.

To those who admire French literature but are not beglamoured by it the romances of Sade can become a bore. We read of the Duke of Blangis in the ecstasy of love that "horrible shrieks and dreadful oaths escaped his heaving breast; flames seemed to dart from his eyes; he frothed at the mouth; he whinnied ..." and we feel that the Duke must have been a tiresome lover for any woman of taste. The selection published by the Grove Press in 1953, with Simone de Beauvoir's essay, gives us a taste of Sade, and there are many for whom a taste is enough. He is sometimes very entertaining, even though we do not roll on the floor and fear that we may split, like Swinburne. But it is overstrained, without achieving the kind of magnitude we find in tragedy or comedy of the first order, and in the end it proves wearisome.

PORNOGRAPHIC TEDIUM

Indeed, boredom is the effect of any prolonged application to erotic writing, and the most ingenious literary art is hardly able to keep ennui at bay. Boredom is inherent in the very nature of the subject. Sex is not a bore, but books about sex can be. The climax of such books is, necessarily, the same, and repetition lessens impact. Consider such an admired classic of erotica as *Le Sofa*, by Crébillon *fils*. It is a beautifully written book and, as Bonamy Dobrée points out, it has the characteristic of the best French erotic books in that it deals with the body but never forgets the soul. In it a courtier named Amanzei diverts his Sultan, a grandson of Scheherazade, with the story of his adventures; his spirit was for a time confined by Brahma in a sofa, from which he could only escape if a couple rendered to each other the first fruits of mutual affection, using his sofa self as a bed. This is an admirable beginning, but we know at once how it must end, and all the entertainment lies in the deferment of the completion. Every skill is brought to the narrative, but it is possible to feel that the book is too fine-drawn. In William Blake's phrase, one can be connoisseured to death by this sort of thing.

It might be said that any long work in the erotic or pornographic line invites failure The sturdy favourites are such brief things as *The Bride's Letter*, which persistent tradition attributes to Byron, and Mark Twain's *Conversation at the Social Fireside as It Was in Ye Time of Ye Tudors*. This last work was solemnly produced by a New York bookseller when I asked him about pornography, bound up in baby-blue morocco with *The Old Backhouse* by James Whitcomb Riley and *When Willie Wet the Bed* by Eugene Field; such is one interpretation of the bookseller's term "erotica" on Fifth Avenue.

Again and again I asked myself, as I trudged about looking for some clue to the origin and distribution of pornography, why anybody troubled with a secret trade when so much was plainly for sale which was demonstrably erotica. The trade in pictures—moving, still, coloured, and in monochrome—is understandable, for these things are not ordinarily obtainable; but a secret trade in pornographic books—was such a thing really necessary?

WHAT IS OBSCENITY?

I struggled, as must everyone who concerns himself with this matter, with the question of nomenclature. When does what booksellers call "erotica" become pornography? Why does the use of common words for sexual acts and objects in *Lady Chatterley's Lover* disgust people who apparently feel no repugnance from novels far less serious in tone, which describe the same things in frivolous euphemisms? But I was no more able to decide these matters than most people who think about them, and was compelled to turn to the professional moralists for definitions.

Those among them who are honest admit the great difficulty of defining what is obscene and separating it from what may have literary value. Only Havelock Ellis makes the obvious point that obscenity is a type of pleasure which mankind has always wanted, and which mankind has always somehow contrived to get, and which mankind may need for the good of its soul. Some degree of earthiness is greatly to be preferred to a wincing daintiness, and the enantiodromia which operates in human affairs will see that we get obscenity, whether we like it or not; we are wise, then, to choose rather than to be forced to accept what fate brings. An international Conference at Geneva, to discuss the suppression of the circulation and traffic in pornography, attempted a definition of obscenity but could not arrive at one, recognizing that emotion and also fashion play so great a part in any idea of the obscene that no single definition can be valid, even in all parts of the Western world, at any given time. Levels of education and income also exert an influence. As the old painter Northcote so wisely said to Hazlitt, concerning some supposed offensive matter in a stage play: "The common people sought for refinement as a *treat*; people in high life were fond of grossness and ribaldry as a relief to their overstrained affectation of gentility." Often when discussions of public morality are in progress, we receive the impression that refinement is still sought as a treat by some of the disputants, and that the form the treat takes is a particular kind of prestige, or status. Erotic literature is a species of erotic play, and as the investigations of Dr. Kinsey and his associates have shown us, erotic play is disapproved by people below the college level of education, as a general thing. Reformers and self-appointed civic censors very often belong to the group which does not care for erotic play in private, and is shocked by erotic literature, which is not so private. In any public discussion of this matter somebody's liberty is certain to be abridged, and zealous morality usually wins—for a time.

Even where liberality of thought on this subject would be expected, there are oddities of opinion. D.H. Lawrence, for instance, expressed a high regard for the *Decameron* and would allow it free circulation, but he had strong reservations about *Jane Eyre*, and thought that presentation of Wagner's *Tristan und Isolde* should be restricted because of its powerful eroticism. If Lawrence finds offence in *Jane Eyre*, we can have no quarrel with those people who have, at various times, wanted to ban *Madame Bovary*, *Trilby*, *Nana*, *Leaves of Grass*, and Cellini's *Autobiography*.

The best, because the frankest, definition of obscenity I found was in *Catholic Viewpoint on Censorship* by Harold C. Gardiner, S.J. It consists, says Father Gardiner, "in the intrinsic tendency or bent of the work to arouse sexual passion, or, to put it more concretely, the motions of the genital apparatus which are preparatory to the complete act of sexual union." He adds the qualification that this does not apply to abnormal people, who might be sexually aroused by references to shoes, the hair of the head, the ear, and all the rest of the curious catalogue of the fetishists.

Father Gardiner deserves our thanks for saying unequivocally what he means, but his definition still leaves the matter of obscenity in doubt. Those who find that a book affects them in the way he describes should, he says, put it aside. This recalls a friend of mine, by no means of lewd mind, the son of a Presbyterian minister, who told me that the first book to stir him in the manner described in Father Gardiner's definition was *Quo Vadis*, which he read when he was twelve. This book still enjoys a reputation as a novel of Christian moral force, though it is written in a manner far from the namby-pamby and ignorant style of some later examples of the genre. What was it that aroused sexual feeling in my friend? It was not, as you might suppose, the scene in which the slave girl Eunice presses her white body to the statue of her master, Petronius, and kisses the cold marble; that seems to me to be an erotic scene, but a young reader might miss its significance. No, what troubled him was this passage: "Nigidea, stripping herself to the waist, dropped her drunken childlike head on the breast of Lucan, who, drunk in like degree, fell to blowing the golden powder from her hair, and raising his eyes with immense delight." The description of Nero's homosexual attraction toward the Greek youth, Pythagoras, which is part of the same scene, was not even noticed by this reader at twelve. Here we have a moral puzzle: Should he have put the book aside, banishing the vision of the half-naked Nigidea, to return to it when he was sixteen and might have understood the passion of Nero, or until he was twenty-five and could have sensed the perversity of Eunice? And what importance are we to give to the fact that Henryk Sienkiewicz drew the dark side of Roman degeneracy with all his considerable skill in order to throw Christian virtue into greater relief? All definitions of obscenity run quickly upon such rocks as these because the supposedly obscene book is only obscene if it provokes a lewd response in the reader. What legislation or definition is possible in a matter so subjective? As Father Gardiner suggests, a reader may feel a book to be obscene for himself, but he is on shaky ground as soon as he asserts that it is, therefore, obscene reading for anyone else.

THRILL OF THE FORBIDDEN

What if the reader feels the enjoyment of obscenity to be his right and a legitimate pleasure? Such readers are not, however, all of those who buy the kind of book which is to be found in so many of the lesser book-shops in Great Britain and the Continent. (If I seem to neglect the United States in this discussion, it is because bookshops of the small, unfashionable, hidden kind which are so common in Europe are not common there; bookselling in the United States seems to be a less complex and perhaps less interesting form of business than it is in older lands.) Many buyers of books which could be classed as obscene appear to count the thrill of the forbidden or the morally questionable as part of their pleasure. The dubious bookshops of London offer the strangest assortment, to suit as many tastes as possible. Some works of Aristotle jostle a novel by Jean-Paul Sartre; the novels of Paul de Kock, which I would have thought unreadable, still have their public; I was amused to see Edmund Wilson's *Memoirs of Hecate County* in a window between Balzac's *Contes drolatiques* and that dull compilation, *The Heptameron*; nearby were two favourites of such shops—*History of Capital Punishment* and *History of the Torture Chamber*, both by George Ryley Scott. In such shops a few years ago a novel was being offered which had as its theme a supposed homosexual relation among the Twelve Apostles and their Master; this is in a very old pornographic tradition, where a strong whiff of blasphemy is used to give extra zest to indecency.

To me, the books which describe acts of cruelty are especially repugnant, for they seem to be aimed at a taste which has nothing to do with ribaldry or legitimate sexual appetite. One old favourite in this realm is *A History of the Rod in All Countries* by the Reverend William M. Cooper, B.A. It describes every kind of flogging, from that which might kill a sailor or a Russian serf to the whipping of high-bred English girls in boarding schools; it is extraordinary that a man should be able to write 530 pages on such a theme, but Mr. Cooper never seems to flag, and his style is one in which an unconvincing disapproval is mingled with grisly jocosity. He speaks of the "romantic and comic side" of flogging, and he is fond of the word *curious* in the sense which dictionaries now mark as archaic. His book is designed to please those who get a thrill out of reading about flogging. They must surely be an odd lot, and as one who went to a school where caning was the regular punishment for serious misdemeanour, I can only marvel at them.

PRURIENT AND PORNOGRAPHIC

As for blasphemy, it is harder to achieve than might be supposed, but apparently many people are content with something less—a mingling of religious prejudice and prurient detail. An old favourite in this class is *Awful Disclosures of Maria Monk, or the Hidden Secrets of a Nun's Life in a Convent Exposed*, which was first published in New York in 1836. When I asked a bookseller in Leeds how it sold today, he replied: "One of our steadiest; we reckon a gross a month. It sells mostly to mill girls; they hand me a shilling and take the book. They're ashamed to name it, but they all read it." The *Awful Disclosures* is to be found in all the lesser bookshops in the large towns of England, though I have been told it is harder to come by in the United States, and I have never seen it on sale there. It is of interest to the student of literature as an example of the pathology of romanticism; it is intended to produce the same sensations as M.G. Lewis's Gothic novel *The Monk*, but it is designed for a puritanical and ignorant readership, and thus is presented as a true tale. It is axiomatic that if a thing is supposed to be true, it can be immeasurably more lurid and crude than if it is labelled as fiction.

Maria Monk was a girl who appeared in New York in 1835 and ingratiated herself with two clergymen who published a paper called *The Protestant Vindicator*, the Reverend George Bourne and the Reverend W.C. Brownlee; she said that she had escaped from the Hôtel Dieu nunnery in Montreal, and that the child she was shortly to bear had been fathered in that institution by a priest. She told hair-raising tales of wicked goings-on in the nunnery, of infanticide on a large scale, of subterranean passages, of the murder of insubordinate nuns. She dictated her revelations to one Theodore Dwight, and as neither of them was blessed with any skill as a writer, the book is without form, style, or climax. When Bishop Lartigue of Montreal granted permission to a committee to inspect the nunnery, the imposture was exposed, but the fight continued for some time; it had reached the point where mere truth was powerless to quell bigotry, and facts had less appeal than malignant fantasy. Maria Monk appears to have been a paranoid young person, and after her notoriety, she disappeared until her death on Welfare Island in 1849; she had been living as a prostitute for some time. But her book enjoys a popularity which better authors might envy, and I think it is because it combines sexual misdeeds with a religious atmosphere in a way which very simple readers can comprehend.

Maria Monk deserves, in my opinion, to be classed as pornography, for although it is not so extravagant in sexual detail as many books which are not so called, there is about it a low and disgusting atmosphere, and an obvious determination to appeal to base passions which the author knows to be base, which is calculatedly pornographic. Not all pornography is so. Consider, for instance, what is one of the most popular of all pornographic novels, *Fanny Hill.*

FANNY HILL AND MALE VANITY

Its author was John Cleland, who published it in 1750, when he was forty-one. Cleland was the son of a talented soldier and poet, and he received an excellent education, which fitted him for the consular service; but he could not get on as a consul, nor yet as an official of the East India Company, and when he was down on his luck, he wrote his famous novel and sold it to Griffiths the bookseller for twenty guineas; Griffiths is reported to have made a profit of ten thousand pounds on it. The book attracted the unfavourable attention of the Privy Council, who summoned Cleland and, after a rebuke, gave him a yearly pension of one hundred pounds in order that he might be able to make better use of his talents. Whether he did so or not is a matter of individual opinion; he became a journalist, a playwright, and at last a philologist, a scholarly profession for which he was pitifully ill-equipped.

Fanny Hill is not a classic for nothing. It is a pornographic book because it sets out determinedly to excite the passions of its readers; in the phrase of Fowler the Phrenologist, it is calculated to Inflame the Propensities. The story is simple, and is told in letters. Fanny is a lovely country girl of fifteen who goes to London when her parents die. She falls into bad company and is debauched, but she finds a lover named Charles, from whom she is separated by the malignity of fate.

During this separation Fanny engages in every sort of sexual misbehaviour that Cleland could think of, and he was, as I have said, a man of education and talent. But at last Charles returns, the lovers are united, and Fanny settles down in happy domesticity. What merry evenings she and her Charles must have had, talking over old times by the fireside!

Two things about *Fanny Hill* deserve attention. The first is that it is written in a simple, graceful prose, which has not a coarse word in it, and which is so charmingly turned that we can forgive the heroine anything; a girl who wrote so could not be really bad. Truly, this is an instance where vice loses half its evil by losing all its grossness. The other point to be noted is that it is the work of a man, although it purports to be told by a girl, and from time to time we catch a glimpse of an inordinate male vanity in the amorous descriptions. Fanny describes her Charles, not as a girl might speak of the man she loves, but as a very vain man might wish to be spoken of. The ecstasies which Fanny experiences in the arms of some of the magnificently endowed men she meets are not convincingly those of a girl; they are those of a man worshipping the glory of man. They describe the effect a man might wish to have on a woman. Psychologically there is much for reflection in *Fanny Hill*, and women, when they read it—for they do read it—must smile at a man's extravagant notion of the pleasure he can give.

The book is as different from *Maria Monk* as daylight is from dark. The one presents real evil and corruption, not in its story, but in the mind that lies behind the story; when Maria died, she was a ruin not only in body but in spirit. *Fanny Hill*, frankly sexual in its matter, is so candid and healthy in its revelation of the mind behind the story that we cannot seriously condemn it. To adapt a Victorian phrase to a Georgian book, we laugh and think that it is only pretty Fanny's way!

PURPOSE OF PORNOGRAPHY

Why do readers want pornographic and obscene books, ask the moralists, expecting, as is their wont, that every decent and responsible person will agree that only perverse minds could harbour such a taste. The answer is plain: Such books deal with one of the subjects, like war and religion, about which mankind can never hear enough. Taste governs our choice of such books, as it does in all literature; the man who likes *Mademoiselle de Maupin* is not usually the man who delights in *Eskimo Nell*. The public for *Lady Chatterley* is not the same as for Mark Twain's *Fireside Conversation*, though both use the same forbidden words; the one is the novel of a philosopher and the other is unmistakably the diversion of a river pilot. Nor does the outhouse humor of Eugene Field or James Whitcomb Riley appeal to readers whose interest is sexual rather than excremental; no Freudian needs to be told why. These works, of whatever category, supply an element which is lacking in the lives of most men and women. The demanding and inexorable tension of modern life, especially in North America, and the countless duties which are imposed by getting a living and maintaining the type of domesticity now fashionable, do not bring the satisfaction of some of the heart's deepest desires. These desires are not necessarily reprehensible, but they are at odds with much of our democratic slavery. Our modern way of life has not created the need for erotica, but it has perhaps increased it, and has made possible such a phenomenon as the publication, by a reputable house, of *A Treasury of Ribaldry*, edited by a respected man of letters, Louis Untermeyer, and sold freely in all bookshops. Ribaldry and erotica are safety valves for people who feel the weight of modern life heavily upon them; those whose ideal of civilized man approximates to the ox or the gelding, toiling to drag the plow, do not approve, and this is not the place to try to persuade them that their attitude is a dangerous one for the future of civilization.

Erotic books feed a part of that fantasy life without which man cannot exist. Contrary to the belief of the fearful, this fantasy life rarely has any manifestation in the outer world; it is a private realm of gratification, where its possessor is supreme and where he enjoys those sweets which real life has denied him—including forbidden sweets. Those who starve the fantasy life in the name of morality do so at their peril; reading has for the past century been the principal ministrant to it, offering, in Carlyle's phrase, "phantasmagoria and dream-grotto" which enlarges life in directions where external and daily living cannot approach. The fantasy life is not an end in itself, but a long road by which we travel toward the deepest truth about ourselves; to close that road is to deny much of the best life has to give.

It is recognition of this need in modern life which has brought so much liberty to the modern novel—liberty which may well be temporary and which, certainly, some writers have abused. The filthier a modern novel is, the better it sells, cry the moralists. This is not quite true; it is only a part of a much wider truth. And why does it never occur to the moralists to ask themselves why there should be such a need today for the kind of book which they call filthy, and which critics untroubled by their preoccupation describe very differently?

Those who complain about erotic books should confine themselves to *Amadis de Gaule*, that old romance whose author, when a man and a woman are left together, writes: "And nothing shall be here related; for these and suchlike things which are conformable neither to good conscience nor nature, man ought in reason lightly to pass over, holding them in slight esteem as they deserve." For the majority of readers the touchstone is one of taste; if an author offends you, do not read him. But it will not occur to any true book lover, I think, to take another man's book from him.

My search for the sources of pornographic publishing was not altogether a failure, for I discovered where a good deal of it came from, in a general sort of way. What really astonished me was that so many of the books which form the backbone of the lists of the pornographic houses were classics which could be bought anywhere, legitimately and at a fair dealer's price. There are, of course, a few great rarities, most of them illustrated books, but the unaccustomed buyer, unless he has a very long purse, will not be able to get them. The market in such things is a special and artificial one, and certainly I received the impression that secrecy and condemnation formed part of its charm for the initiates.

BOOKS ARE FOR READING

As I said at the beginning, if you have ten books which you have acquired because you truly want them, you are a collector and your library is in some degree a portrait of you. But few people with the book mania reckon their books in tens; they count them in hundreds and thousands. If you read a great deal you will almost certainly want some books which are out of the ordinary, because of their rarity or beauty. It is at this point that I beg you to be careful. You will be tempted to think of books as objects, not to be read, but to be possessed for show, and when that happens, you are easy prey to those booksellers who deal in harlot volumes, tricked out in pretty skins (which will not last because the leather is not well prepared) and bedizened with gold ornament which resembles nothing so much as the gold paint that used to be daubed on steam-heating coils. All the arts of the horse dealer will be exercised to make old books which are of slight value look like treasures. And if you fall for this trash, you will at last have an accumulation which looks like the background for one of those advertisement pictures in which a model is impersonating an advertising man's notion of a gentleman and a scholar drinking Somebody's whisky. It will not be a library at all, but an adjunct of that pompous buffoonery which is called, by its dupes, "gracious living." You will be surrounded by a bad stage setting, and its effect will be to turn you into a bad actor. You will have committed the great sin of our time, which is to put ends before means, and striving and competition will become more important to you than reading. Be ambitious, rather, to be able to say as a reader what Hilaire Belloc said as a writer:

When I am dead, I hope it may be said:
"His sins were scarlet, but his books were read."

6

Painting, Fiction, and Faking

Many readers of his novels are enchanted by the arcane knowledge that flows so effortlessly from Davies's pen. Clearly, his mind was unusually well stocked, but in many cases that encyclopedic knowledge was hard won. He researched many of these topics tirelessly, expending great effort to give the proper effect of ease.

For example, *What's Bred in the Bone* (published in 1985) involves Francis Cornish in the mysteries of art restoration and art faking. As Judith Skelton Grant puts it in her invaluable biography, *Robertson Davies: Man of Myth*, it was not that the author knew nothing of art, but that his knowledge of painting fell "far short of his grasp of music, literature or drama, and so he did a great deal of research to underpin what he did know and to avoid errors." Before writing the book Davies made himself thoroughly conversant with art fakery both through wide reading and direct consultation with authorities in the art world, including his brother-in-law Sir Russell Drysdale, the well-known Australian artist.

Three years after *What's Bred in the Bone* appeared, Davies was invited to speak at the Metropolitan Museum of Art, on April 7, 1988, and he made good use of the wide knowledge he had gained. One point he did not make when describing Bronzino's *Allegory of Love* to the New York audience is worth noting here. Judith Skelton Grant points out that Davies hung a reproduction of this painting in his rooms at Oxford in 1935. Exactly fifty years later when visiting the original in London he recalled an unhappy youthful love affair. His diary notes: *Impressed as always by the facial resemblance of the figure of Fraude with a girl I loved when I first met her when she was seventeen. And Fraude she was to me, with the honeycomb and the sting.*

Dealing with the speech at the Metropolitan and its agreeable aftermath, his description of his performance ("not too bad") is quintessentially Canadian: *The auditorium where I speak is big—750 seats—and sold out; pretty good speaking arrangements but as so often the lectern is not the right height, so I have to hold my manuscript above it or disappear below it. But I do my best, though not as good as I wish, not too bad, and the reception is very friendly and prolonged. As the reception was so good I cut the text hardly at all and it ran one hour and ten minutes. Went to the Lures' apartment after the speech. A wonderful supper—I was reminded of the late-night suppers in Balzac and other nineteenth-century writers—and the kind of conversation one so much wants and so rarely gets—sophisticated but not sharp-edged, informed but not pedantic, witty but not wise-cracking—and we enjoyed it hugely.*

☙

It would have been of inestimable help to me when I was preparing this address if I had known who you would be—you who are gathered here tonight to hear me talk about Painting, Fiction, and Faking. Are you a group of connoisseurs of art? If so, what could I say that might interest you? Is it the word *Fiction* that draws you? I may claim to know a little bit about fiction, especially in its primary meaning of "the action or product of fashioning or imitating"; fiction, looked at in that light, has a strong underground link with painting. As for Faking, are we not all fascinated by it? Are we not at once drawn and repelled by those people who produce works of art—sometimes very fine ones—and pass them off as the work of someone the world has agreed to think of as a man far greater than the faker? At the name of Rembrandt every knee shall bow. But at the name of Tom Keating, who, during a career of twenty-five years, produced over two thousand fakes, and successfully passed them off as Rembrandts, Paul Potters, Fragonards, Bouchers, Goyas, Degas, Renoirs, and Turners, our knees do not actually bow, but certainly they shake, partly in awe of his astonishing effrontery, and partly with laughter. I confess to a fascination with fakers. They carry into the world of art the spirit of the god Mercury, who was the special protector of both artists and thieves, and to whose heart both Rembrandt and Tom Keating must have been dear. Without the intervention of Mercury in human affairs, what pompous asses we should surely be!

I do not say that I know nothing about art, but I approach painting simply for refreshment of spirit, and not with any aesthetic theory to help me. All my life I have been a gallery visitor—this gallery, among many others. I have favourite paintings, to which I return again and again; one—an obvious choice—is Vermeer's *The Painter in his Studio*; but another, not so obvious, is Bronzino's *An Allegory of Love*—you have doubtless seen it in the National Gallery in London—about which I have puzzled my head for over sixty years, and I never visit it without having some new idea about it. I like Mannerist painting, and I think my wife and I must be among the few people whose kitchen walls are hung with hill-size reproductions of Arcimboldo's refreshing and evocative picture of The Seasons. Do we collect? Yes, we have some very good Novgorod School icons, which we bought before they became so popular as they are now. We have some of the work of my brother-in-law, an Australian painter of great attainment. And we have an extensive collection of pictures—paintings, prints, and odd things done in tinsel, which illustrate the theatre of the eighteenth and nineteenth centuries in all its immensely energetic variety. We have this ill-assorted assembly of things for a reason that would surely bring a frown to the face of the art expert, and a patronizing smirk to the face of a dealer.

I am not going to say we have them because we like them. That is what everybody, including some of the most informed and wealthy collectors, say. Of course we *like* them—but why? Because they speak to us of enormous energy and spiritual insight. The theatre things tell of the dreams and ideals of a past age, to whom the theatre meant something that it means no longer. And the theatre, I need not remind you, is the very home and temple of illusion, in which some of the most important truths known to man are given form and body by means of the most elaborate and sophisticated arts of—fakery. The icons speak resonantly and without illusion of faith and the shackles of the flesh, and the nobility that triumphs over death. So, you see, we have the world of illusion and the word of truth constantly before us.

When we lived in university surroundings, students who came to our house would say, "It must be like living in a museum." But it isn't. It is living in a place where everything on the walls has something important to say. Suppose for an instant that I am at home, and I am looking at a watercolour of a very pretty girl dressed in green velvet; she has decorated her charming face with a saucy little moustache and a tiny beard; she is showing rather a lot of leg. To you it might not call for a second glance, but to me it is the beautiful Miss Louisa Fairbrother, dressed to play the part of Little John in a pantomime about Robin Hood. The time? Oh, about 1845. I know a lot about her, including the surprising fact that she became the morganatic wife of one of the sons of King George III, and that she lived a long and very respectable life under the name of Mrs. Fitzgeorge. You smile the superior smile of the art lover; this information has nothing to do with the artistic quality of the picture. Ah, but when I look at Miss Fairbrother's beautiful eyes, I know that those eyes once rested on this picture, and obviously approved of it. I know what a lot of pleasure Miss Fairbrother gave when she appeared in that guise on the stage. I know also that she lived long and died rich, and was loved by a duke and respected by a fashionable circle, thereby giving the lie to the notion that all such girls died in poverty and of the pox. Indeed, you understand, I am *reading* the picture; I am not admiring its planes, and its composition and its coloration—though they are all there. And when I look at our icon of St. Paraskeva I am reminded of a life of noble renunciation and purity of spirit. It is a very good icon, but to me it is first and foremost a saint.

This is not, you see, the art expert's approach. But it is very much the approach of the man whose life is preoccupied with fiction and whose desire is not merely to look *at*, but *through*, objects and situations. The question is not: "What is this object that I see before me and how does it conform to the aesthetic principles I have made my own?" No, the question is: "What does this *say* to me?" That may not be the most artistically pure approach to a picture, but I venture to think that it is the approach of a very great number of people, by no means all of whom are simple-minded.

It is the question that is asked by the public of every new school of art as it presents itself, and until the question is answered the new school is greeted with rejection and often with mockery. This is as true today as it ever was, and perhaps the mockery is uglier than it has been in the past, because so much new art is deeply confusing.

All art, I think we may agree, is created in the hope that it will say something to interested people. The purpose of all art is to give delight, whether it be painting or sculpture or music or literature. The special problem of the modern artist, who offers us arrangements of colour and form, is that he has—along with the rest of the world— abandoned the language which every cultivated person used to understand, and which has now become almost a dead language. I speak of the language of faith and mythology; to great numbers of people, even when the language is carefully translated, it carries little conviction. In the jargon of our time, it has ceased to be "relevant."

I want to speak of that language for a while, because we cannot walk through any great gallery and not be aware of it, even when it says little to us. It is a language that tells us a great deal about what painters are saying. I do not for a moment suggest that the great painters of the past were simply illustrators, offering us scenes of the Old and New Testaments, or from the Lives of the Saints, or from Classical Mythology. Not at all. But it was through such subjects that they spoke to us of what was most significant to themselves, because all art of the highest quality rises from the depths of the artist's personal perception of the great mysteries of the spirit, which may not have a great deal to do, directly, with religion or mythology but which could be made known to the world through those means.

Let us consider a picture which has recently been acquired by the Detroit Institute of Arts; it is called *Madonna and Child with St. John the Baptist* and it was painted in 1540 by a painter whom I particularly admire, Agnolo Bronzino. I choose it because it is not extremely familiar, and it is not the work of an artist who is put in the very first rank by most experts, though he is an admired Old Master. Therefore no overwhelming mystique attaches to it; we are not hypnotized by the reputation of the artist or by centuries of admiring description by literary artists like, for instance, Ruskin, who could make you believe that a kitten playing with a ball of string had extraordinary spiritual resonance. Allow me to quote to you some words in which one of the experts in Detroit describes it:

The painting illustrates many features characteristic of Bronzino's mature style and of Florentine mannerism in general. The figures are placed close to the foreground plane and occupy much of the surface of the picture; their features are highly refined, conforming to a preconceived, formal, and even abstract idea of beauty, rather than deriving from the observation of real individuals. The serenely perfect and delicate features of the Madonna reflect an ideal of divine beauty, while the infant Christ and John the Baptist seem more like angelic than human types. The Virgin's head is proportionally small compared with her body while her torso appears unnaturally elongated. Such features conform precisely to the highly artificial mannerist ideal of beauty, which emphasized extremely attenuated proportions and anatomically difficult yet apparently effortless and graceful poses. In the twisting postures of both the Virgin and the Christ Child, the mannerist love of complicated and contorted but nonetheless elegant movement is expressed. Complex torsions are harmoniously resolved and all sense of strain or struggle has been drained from the figures.

Excellent. Not a thing wrong with that. But is that what you think when you look at the picture? If you are a trained critic and art historian these things are apparent at a glance, but I do not think that is why Bronzino painted it. After all, there are innumerable pictures of the Virgin with Christ and St John, and if the painter had wanted to exemplify what the critic calls "his typically mannerist, flame-like posture of the Madonna" he could have painted something else. But he painted this subject. Why?

As I have told you, I am particularly interested in Bronzino, and among other reasons it is because he has so much to say about women. Art critics tend to be patronizing in their references to him. They speak of "elegant posturing, empty of religious feeling," and of "a secular, court style," of "icy fascination" and "insolent assurance." Of course I am respectful of these learned men, but I am skeptical of their pretensions to be experts about depth of religious feeling. That cannot be confined to the peasant Christs and Apostles of Rembrandt. Certainly Bronzino conveys a kind of religious feeling that has much to say to me, and in the Detroit picture he paints an idealized Madonna, who is indeed idealized womanhood, just as the Christ and St. John are idealized children. The love in the face of all three figures is perhaps cool, but nonetheless real for that. What I see in this picture is a thrilling realization of two great archetypes: Our Lady Soul and the Miraculous Child. If they are refined in appearance, what about it? Surely we are not so naive as to equate squalor and ugliness with sincerity? The holy figures of Bronzino appear to me just as evocative of religious belief as the most hideous, decaying Christs of Grunewald or the haloed Flemish runts of Rembrandt; it is simply that they do it in a different way and the belief they provoke is of a different quality. Beauty is just as devout as ugliness.

In this fine Bronzino which is now in the Detroit collection we see one aspect of womanhood superbly depicted. In Christian faith it is called the Divine Mother; in other beliefs it may be the Great Mother; whatever the form of belief, this aspect of femininity—the sustaining, protective, uplifting, and ennobling element in the human spirit is deep in the heart of mankind. It seems to me that in this picture Bronzino looks forward 410 years to the declaration by the Pope of the bodily Assumption of Mary to Heaven, to sit with the otherwise male Trinity in the highest seat of splendour and power. This is woman as God. Bronzino's Mary looks down with delight upon her Divine Child, who is playing with—with what? With a globe of the world of which he is Saviour and King. But the observer may very well see in this picture of the Christian goddess her predecessors Isis and Semele, for this is a truly religious, and not simply a sectarian, picture of womanhood in its aspects of love, wisdom, and mercy.

Now I invite you to consider another Bronzino which I mentioned earlier. It is in the National Gallery in London and it is usually called *An Allegory of Love*. Let me recall it to you. The central figure is a nude woman, wearing a coronet of jewels; in one hand she holds an apple, in the other an arrow. This is clearly Venus, and she is playing with her son Cupid, shown as a boy of perhaps fourteen. And how is she playing? He is caressing her left breast, the nipple between his fingers as if exciting it. They are kissing, and since the picture was cleaned, we can see that she is putting her tongue into his mouth. Interesting play for mother and son, is it not? A naked child, laughing at them, is pelting them with rose leaves, and at the feet of this child are masks of cheating and dissimulation, mixed with the thorns from the roses. Behind the principal figures are one of a woman, in agony, apparently Jealousy, if we understand her expression rightly; the other is a monster, for a rich gown conceals a body with lion's feet and a stinging tail, and we notice these things after we have seen her exquisite, dissembling woman's face and the honeycomb which she is offering to the principal players in the scene. We do not have to be great iconographers to recognize this as Fraude, the Cheat. The whole scene is displayed against a blue cloak, which is either being drawn aside or thrown over the love affair, by a bearded figure and a woman, whose face may—we must not be too eager to read meanings into expressions—reveal either dismay or astonishment. Who are these two? Plainly they are Time and his daughter Truth.

May I pause for a moment to tell you about the last time I saw this picture? I found a group of schoolchildren, with their teacher, sitting on the floor in front of it. The children were filling in some sort of questionnaire. I asked the teacher what was going on and she said, shortly, that the children were learning Art Appreciation. I looked over the shoulder of one little girl—about ten, I suppose—to see what the questions were and was astonished that one of them was "Is this picture rude?" What on earth could it mean? The little girl had ticked the box which showed that, in her opinion, the picture was "rude." "Why do you think it is rude?" I asked. "Because that Lidy is niked," said the child, indicating Venus. I looked at some of the other papers filled in by the other children and found that they were all agreed that the naked human body, however beautiful, was "rude." Such is Art Appreciation in our day.

What do we make of this remarkable, arresting composition? It is another aspect of womanhood. This is not the divine love of the Madonna in the Detroit picture; it is erotic in the highest degree, and the mother is tempting her son to something not usually regarded as maternal. And yet—is it something we do not care to acknowledge? These days the papers are full of horror stories about the fathers who debauch their young daughters. But what is sauce for the gander is sauce for the goose, and I foresee that it will not be long before we are reading of mothers who debauch their sons, and any social worker or experienced magistrate has stories to tell about that kind of involvement. Are Time and Truth revealing or concealing this form of sexual passion? We shall see. Meanwhile, we all know plenty of mother's boys, and many households where the presence of the father seems almost to serve as a cloak of respectability cast over a lively affair—not overtly sexual, but certainly powerfully emotional, between a mother and her son. I suggest to you that Bronzino was not only a Mannerist, but in a comprehensive sense a moralist, as well. He knew the facts of life, including some that modern morality still does not choose to admit. The Fraud and Jealousy that play their part in many love affairs seem to have been strongly present in his consciousness. There is a fine Bronzino in the Museum of Fine Arts in Budapest in which once again we see Venus and her enamoured son; and once again a figure called Jealousy, but who might also be called Terror, or Horror, is prominent in the composition. The innocent, tempting figures of rose-crowned children are here as well. Are these not two aspects of the same love? This is what the literary man sees in these pictures— love in its divine and its all-too-fleshy aspects. The art critic sees the splendid technical accomplishment in composition and colour, but he makes no mention of what the pictures are saying to us. Speaking for myself, I am not greatly concerned that Bronzino was a Mannerist—which at the moment seems to be a bad kind of painter to be—but I am fascinated by him as a Moralist, which does not mean somebody who codifies and dictates what the behaviour of mankind should be, but someone who sees what the behaviour of mankind really is, and shows it to us.

Mannerism has been defined as a degenerate form of High Renaissance Classicism, which flourished between 1530 and 1590. But the most recent Mannerist picture to come to my notice was painted in 1977 by an American artist, Audrey Flack, and it leapt off the wall at me in the art gallery of the university in Tucson, Arizona. We can sometimes identify the models of Renaissance artists; do we not see the superb Simonetta Vespucci in several of the finest canvases of Botticelli, whose Madonna and whose Venus she was? And in Audrey Flack's picture we know at once whose life, and beauty, and unhappy fate, is displayed before us, because the picture is called *Marilyn* and two unmistakable faces of Marilyn appear in it, in a composition which includes some unmistakable moral symbols—cut and decaying fruit, grapes (always a fruit associated with the highest luxury), a rose in full bloom, a photograph of Marilyn as a child, luxurious drapery, and two reminders of the cruel passing of time—a watch and a burning candle. Over the whole picture broods an air of cheap, fleeting, sweet, and pathetic beauty. I am told that this is one of three pictures in a series, which includes one of the Wheel of Fortune and another of World War II, and in all three the symbol of the burning candle appears.

Don't tell me that Mannerism is dead. It is not a technical style of painting; it is a way of feeling and thinking about life, the way of the moralist who sees and records and reminds, but who does not insistently judge. Bronzino uses the symbols of faith and mythology to say what he has to say. Audrey Flack is addressing another audience and she uses symbols of today but the fruit, the roses, the candle, and the timepiece would have been familiar to Bronzino. But if she had chosen to show us Marilyn's fate in, for instance, a picture of Susanna and the Elders, or perhaps Danae in the Tower of Brass—Danae, you recall, was destroyed by an overwhelming love which visited her in the form of a shower of gold—how many of her viewers would have understood what she was saying? Because, I repeat, painters are always saying something, and in our time, when religion and knowledge of the Bible have sunk into a heavy eclipse—once, in a class of graduate students I met with a young man who did not know who Noah was!—and mythology where it exists at all has become an incomprehensible tangle, the language which painters once used with such eloquence is almost forgotten.

Do I regret it? Yes, I do, because faith and mythology summed up in themselves vast wisdom which we neglect at our peril. Yet, among what we assume to be educated and sophisticated people today this classicism of the Bible and mythology is a matter of ignorance and sometimes of downright hostility; I make no apology for quoting the very familiar words of Santayana, who might have been described as a Mannerist philosopher. He said: "Progress, far from consisting in change, depends on retentiveness ... Those who cannot remember the past are condemned to fulfil it." The Bible, which has now sunk to the level of a book of admonition and law in the hands of people who profess to take it literally, remains perhaps the greatest compendium of history, philosophy, and fruitful reflection available to us, and as lately as our parents' time it was possible for public speakers to make allusions to it, in the confidence that virtually all of their hearers, highly educated or not, would understand them. And mythology, which was familiar to generations whose education included a good deal of Latin and probably some Greek, was a constant reminder of the ambition, downfall, and suffering to which mankind is liable. And where the Bible insisted that God is not mocked, mythology made it equally clear that the gods are not mocked. They were ever-present reminders that pride, and the stupidity that is inseparable from pride, goes before a fall; reminders that God, and the gods, are within us and must be cherished and listened to; reminders that we are not a glorious completion of the history of mankind, but beads on a string, which extends from the cloudy beginnings of life to whatever may be its conclusion. I must leave this theme or I shall begin to sound like a prophet, whereas I constantly remind myself that as a writer of fiction I am a moralist, an observer, and a recorder.

As an observer I have, of course, been aware of the remarkable increase in tension in the art world during the past few years. Suddenly, art news is big news and people who are not in the least interested in the picture itself are in some way thrilled to learn that Van Gogh's picture of some irises has sold for $59.9 million, and the fact that the artist himself lived and died in poverty gives a savour of commonplace romance to the affair. People love to think of artists as innocent sufferers and poor while with the stroke of a brush they are creating riches. When it is revealed that in 1987 Sotheby's turnover amounted to $699 million the most abject philistines are forced to admit that there must be something in this art stuff after all. When I agreed to come here to talk to you tonight I began to take more than my usual interest in the art news in the London *Times*, and read about the Chardin that fetched $192,000 and the Modigliani that fetched £2 million. A newly found and perhaps not entirely authentic Mantegna has an expected price of £600,000 put on it by Sotheby's, which is modest when one considers that in 1987 an unquestionably genuine Mantegna sold for £8.1 million. A Tiepolo has turned up for which £2.5 million have been offered, and for another Tiepolo £10 million have been realized. A Chardin goes at $192,000 and a head of a child by Greuze brings £125,000.

The reputations of painters have changed radically. In 1939 I could have bought a large canvas by Fuseli in London for five pounds, and I didn't buy it, though I coveted it, because I did not have a spare five pounds or a big wall. Today a good Fuseli will, as they say, set you back a few hundred thousand. Pictures which have what is called "association interest" by Winston Churchill or Noël Coward fetch handsome prices, though they are undistinguished as paintings. Two painters of association interest whose high prices give me special pleasure are Richard Dadd and Thomas Griffiths Wainwright. Dadd's dates are 1817 to 1886, and from his twenty-fourth year until his death he lived first in Bedlam—yes, the old hospital of St. Mary of Bethlehem for lunatics—and the greater part of his last forty years in Broadmoor prison for the criminally insane. On August 28, 1843, he went for a walk with his father, and cut his father's throat with a razor. He was otherwise an amiable man; fond of his father, but moody. In prison he had plenty of time to paint, and his wonderfully fantastic pictures have been, until recently, available at substantial but not amazing prices. But in 1983 his masterpiece, a picture of Oberon and Titania and attendant fairies, was sold at Sotheby's for just under three hundred thousand pounds. I would love to own a Dadd—not because he was a murderer but because his pictures appeal to me—but I came too late upon the scene.

As for Wainwright, he did his best work in Australia, where he had been transported in 1837 for forgery. He was not an amiable man, but he was a handsome one, and as well as forging he was suspected and tried for poisoning his mother-in-law, his uncle, and his sister-in-law.

He was an art critic by profession, and he made one uncommonly perceptive statement in that capacity. He said: "I hold that no work of art can be tried otherwise than by laws deduced from itself: whether or not it be consistent with itself is the question." But he carried criticism too far for his own good; when he was accused of murdering his sister-in-law the murder could not be proven, but he so far forgot himself as to offer, as part of his defence, that she had very thick ankles. It was assumed by the court that there was only one place for a man so dead to all decency, and it was Australia. So off to Van Dieman's Land he was packed, and because of his talent he was allowed a good deal of leeway there, and painted a number of portraits of Australian citizens of means, who were not of the criminal class. Today, in Australia, to have a portrait of an ancestor painted by Wainwright confers a wholly understandable distinction. But if he had not been a gentleman-crook one wonders if it would be so.

May I pause for a moment in the logical progress of what I am saying for a few words in praise of Henry Fuseli, a painter who has only recently begun to attract the attention which I think was always his due. When we speak of Surrealism we are apt to think of it as a movement of this century, coming into being between the two World Wars. Some perceptive critics have indeed seen hints of it in the past, in the work of Hieronymus Bosch, and Arcimboldo, and indeed Goya, who used grotesquerie of subject and treatment to make statements that could not be made in any other way. But Fuseli is a greater figure in this group than is generally admitted. It was Thomas Griffiths Wainwright, the poisoner—who was, as I told you, an art critic—who explained his own great admiration for Fuseli when he said, "The little Swiss does not consider that an artist should paint only what he sees." Sees, that is to say, with the physical eye. Fuseli was one of those who painted what appeared to the mind's eye, and there is about his pictures a fascination of the sort we find in the wonderful stories of E.T.A. Hoffmann.

While we are pausing thus, I should like to confess my own strong interest in portraits and my admiration for portrait-painters, who are not a class of artists as highly considered in our day as I think they should be. But their art, when they are artists of high attainment, is perceptive and critical in a degree that other painters—even when they are masterly in their achievement—may not possess. I think of the words of a literary man, Thomas Carlyle, who said: "Often I have found a portrait superior in real instruction to half a dozen biographies ... I have found that the portrait was a small lighted candle by which the biographies could for the first time be read, and some human interpretation made of them." That is a writer's opinion, and I have spent many happy hours in the National Portrait Gallery in London, in full agreement with Thomas Carlyle.

Now, to resume our thread of thought. We were talking of painters who are notable through their association rather than their demonstrable talent—politicians, playwrights, and poisoners. As well as these oddities, we have all seen the return to popularity of painters who dropped out of fashion, like the marvellously observant Tissot, and the ebullient, strongly flavoured Bouguereau. Pre-Raphaelites, once laughed at, have made a strong comeback, and for a good Burne-Jones you must dip deep into your pocket. Victorian narrative pictures, of the kind exemplified by *The Old Shepherd's Faithful Mourner* in the Victoria and Albert Museum, where the body of the dead shepherd is seen receiving the tearful tribute of his dog, now sell at substantial prices. Animal pictures of all kinds are eagerly collected, even dismayingly sentimental canvases of kittens or puppies playing with balls of wool, or their master's slippers. Indeed, there is hardly anything that cannot be sold today, if it exhibits some workmanlike command of paint.

The enthusiasm is unbounded, and many countries that were, until recently, indifferent to what their artists had done make a great clamour about what they call their Heritage. Scotland has begun to pay huge prices, not for Raeburns, but for quite undistinguished work, which can be shown to have some historical association. Indeed, the word *Heritage* has achieved new and unaccountable meanings. I visited a museum in Canada a while ago, in which I was assured that the splendours of my Heritage would be made visible. It proved to be filled with Red Indian artifacts, and although I can claim some Red Indian blood—about a teaspoonful, it would be, I suppose, after 150 years—I did not find my bosom swelling with anthropological pride.

But the word *Heritage* has become magical. Phillips, the auction-eer, says: "We have seen amazing prices paid for golfing and cricket memorabilia. Tennis and football have started to rake off in a big way, and now it's the turn of boxing." Phillips is expecting £150 for a bust of Tom Sayers, the last of the bare-knuckle boxers, and they are offer-ing an inestimable treasure—a baseball signed by Babe Ruth. Art connoisseurs, of course, are scornful of this stuff, and refer to it as "sporting tat." But what do you make of £5,000 which was recently paid for a lock of Lord Nelson's hair? Or several hundred pounds for an authentic cigar butt, flung away long ago by the great Franz Liszt? I recall that in the early fifties a Liszt cigar butt, complete with a bell jar to display it, fetched only $25. Never before has Oscar Wilde's remark that the only person who admires all schools of art with equal fervour is an auctioneer, been so true.

One of the many magazines devoted to art and the world of the saleroom has published for the last four years a list of America's Top One Hundred Collectors. That means that there must now be 400 top collectors and one wonders how far the list can be extended. The magazine says: "Our research has been as extensive as ever—we've talked to dealers, auction-house experts, curators, art-world journal-ists and, in all but a handful of cases, the collectors themselves." It is significant that on this list of persons consulted, dealers and auction-eers come first. That disturbs me because however admirable and honourable these people may be, they are still essentially tradesmen, and in their words about what the top hundred have bought they write and speak in what, as a writer, I consider a very unchaste prose. They exult, they bombinate, they scream in print, and however tactful they try to be it is always the prices that fascinate them. And what do these giants among collectors collect? Pictures, of course, and usually by living artists. But they are not above Fabergé eggs, presidential manuscripts (I hope they really mean manuscripts and not merely typescripts), toy soldiers—one hundred thousand of these in one collection!—and vintage photographs. I was amazed to discover that somebody collects work from the Roycrofters, that group of handi-craftsmen assembled by Elbert Hubbard at East Aurora near Buffalo, where they tried to work in the spirit of William Morris and fell desperately short of their aim. Have you ever heard of Elbert Hubbard? One should not speak ill of the dead, but before he died in the sinking of the *Lusitania* in 1915 he spread pernicious views about art and filled the living rooms of aspiring American homes with much shocking junk, which a few people are now collecting. American Indian art, we learn, is "going through the roof." *Art nouveau* is very popular, as well as art deco and Tiffany lamps, which we used to think of as expensive trade goods. One top collector has the middle portion of a drip painting which Jackson Pollock once chopped into three when he was drunk; if you have either of the other portions, he is certainly your man. Of course many of the hundred collect unquestioned fine art, and what they think about being lumped with these other hysterical enthusiasts the magazine does not record. The compiler of this list assures us that the old adage "Buy what you love" is as true today as ever. We can only comment that love is a many-splendoured thing.

Why do they do it? Why are there more collectors of art and artifacts today than ever before in history? I have a theory—a literary man's theory—and it has to do with Time. By acquiring objects from the past and the immediate present these collectors are trying to stop the clock, and to seize, so far as they can, a portion of the past and make it their own until, with their names attached to it, the collection goes into a museum and they are assured of a kind of immortality. Religion, as I have already said, has lost its grip on a very large part—perhaps a majority—of people in the modern world. The body of knowledge of the Scriptures and of the classics and mythology has ceased to be a common *lingua franca* of educated people; that splendid link with our cultural past has vanished except among scholars, who can rarely afford to be collectors. You must not suppose that I am grieving uncontrollably, because this loss to the educated and wealthy portion of mankind is simply an historical fact, and I do not suppose anything can be done about it. But in art hundreds of millions of people seek a sense of assurance about the past, and a link with the past. Those who can afford to do so make collections of their own, and the rest of us frequent museums and collections to refresh ourselves at the deep well of the past, even when we understand only in the most general terms what the artists of the past were saying and, as I have suggested, saying through a language once common to educated people. For the language of faith and classical literature, and mythology, the art critics have substituted, with some success, a language of their own, and the people who follow them look no longer at the *Madonna and Child with St. John the Baptist* or *An Allegory of Love* as portrayals of the Great and Divine Mother, or the Mother as Seducer and Devourer, but as handsome assemblies of planes and composition, and arrangements in tones of colour. Personally I suspect that they understand the pictures in the old way to a greater extent than they are willing to admit, because none of us wants to seem naive. But they look and look and look in extraordinary numbers. I read in *The New York Times* a few months ago—I am sorry that I have lost the clipping and cannot give you the exact date—that more people visit art museums in the course of a year than attend all the sports events held in the United States during the same year. That is an awesome statement, but it appears in *The Times* and if we begin to doubt *The Times* surely the heavens will fall.

What are all these people looking for? Some come for curiosity, but vastly more for beauty, for an enrichment and fulfillment that they cannot find anywhere else. It is for this reason, I think, that the galleries which confine themselves to modern art, though they are crowded, are not so popular as those galleries that show pictures of the past, arranged in some order, usually chronological. There is no difficulty in understanding why this is so. Modern art is demanding in a way the art of the past is not, or seems not to be to the unreflecting observer. Modern art does not speak the language of faith or the classical world; what it has to say is expressed by the painter as it arises from his unconscious, creative centre, and this may take the widest possible variety of forms. As with much modern poetry the forms and the symbols the modern painter employs are his alone, and they may not be readily understood by other people unless they bring a sophistication and a knowledge of an uncommon kind to the task. The language of modern painting is thus far a secret language, and it must be learned anew for each painter.

For this reason a special and subtle temptation assails the modern painter, if he does not happen to be quite first-rate, either as a painter or a person. It is the temptation to fake the secret language, and to paint mysteriously where there is no real mystery. Perhaps *fake* is too harsh a term. I doubt if many modern painters set out deliberately to hoodwink themselves, believing that what arises most readily from within is not therefore the real stuff. I know that this happens in literature, and the remainder tables of the bookshops are heavy with novels and books of verse written by people who demand that the public find a key to their secret language or climate of feeling. But with them the desire to write is greater than any genuine necessity, any overwhelming impulse, to write, and what emerges is showy but really feeble stuff.

A painter in a past age—in the seventeenth century, let us say— could not embark on a painting with a muddled and incoherent idea of what he was going to express. He could not depend on variable inspiration to carry him through. The language painters used was prescribed, and anybody who lost himself in it was judged incompetent. There was also a level of technical skill that was expected, and those who could not rise to it were simply village daubers, who painted clumsy pictures of burgomasters, or ill-contrived Virgins and saints. Now you must not suppose that I am so stupid as to suggest that modern painters of the first rank have abandoned technique; they have adapted the traditional painter's technique to their manner without having much command of their matter.

I think that is why many gallery visitors are leery of ultra-modern pictures. They cannot judge them by any standards they know, and they are very much afraid of being taken in by a confident second- or third-rater.

That is why painters of the humblest order—the people who exhibit their pictures in the street—usually paint in the best imitation they can achieve of some bygone style. The people who buy a picture for twenty-five or a hundred dollars want something about which they can be confident. They are investing just as much of their capital, proportionately, as the Hundred Top Collectors.

Don't laugh at them. Many of us also want something about which we can feel confident before we admire it. A great name and an indisputable history of informed ownership assure us that what we are looking at is the real thing, before we permit ourselves to—to do what? Here is where I approach a realm more congenial to the literary man than to the gallery-goer.

I think that what so many of us want is a picture in which we can invest something of ourselves, which I can only call soul. I know *soul* is a dirty word to many people; it is one of the four-letter words that even the people who write dirty words in spray paint on walls hesitate to use. But how else can I define that quality of trust and humble acceptance with which we approach the great unknown things of life? There are not many among us who have been so irredeemably coarsened and battered by the vicissitudes of life that there is not, deep within us, something that cries out for belief and unquestioning trust. What we bring with us to a great gallery like this one is not, as a usual thing, the simple piety of the confessedly religious man or woman, nor is it the complex tapestry of understanding that makes scenes from mythology or classical learning evocative and enriching to us. But the yearning which was satisfied and enabled by that common language of the past—the language of belief and acceptance—is still there, and these pictures from the past give us an assurance of the continuity and value of life. People in past ages, we say, lived and felt to some degree in the mode of these wonderful pictures, and when we look at the pictures we can do so too. We reach out a hand to the past, and we feel a responding touch.

I must repeat that I do not undervalue the sheer beauty of the great pictures of past ages. But beauty is not an element that can be divorced from the thing that it illumines. The professors of aesthetics can haggle as much as they please about what beauty is, and there can be no doubt that we have to be taught to see it. But once we have learned our lesson, beauty seizes us and blesses us, and enslaves us.

There. You may think I have been speaking in a high fashion of ineffable things and matters for which there is no indisputable proof. But I have another string to my bow. It is a psychological string, and some of you may think it a rather dirty string, but I am unrepentant. In the human psyche the ineffable, the elegant, and the praiseworthy are inextricably mingled with the grubby, the commonplace, and the reputedly inadmissible. That is what keeps us sane. I want to talk now about money.

People are apt to talk stupidly about money, as though it were something shameful, or simply a means to an end. Not at all. Money is one of the aspects in which the soul manifests itself in mankind. It is adventure, it is aspiration, and an important means through which we invite the Goddess of Fortune to enter our lives. If I were the president of a bank I would have a fine statue of the Goddess of Fortune standing in the middle of every branch and I would have Cicero's great dictum "Man's life is ruled by Fortune, not by wisdom" embossed on all the bank's stationery. I suppose I am explaining to you why I am not the president of a bank. I doubt if many bank presidents would agree with me that money enables our souls to manifest themselves. When I say *soul* I hope you understand that I am not speaking of an intoxicating gas, rather like ether but pleasanter, which is the peculiar property of saints and girls who are still virgins. What I mean by soul is that mysterious element which nobody has ever been able to define that separates a living creature from a corpse. Soul is a lot of things; it is energy, of course, and it is also the secrecy and obsession that live in all of us, unless we are too near the corpse. And soul must have expression. It does not exist by itself. It is something that we invest in those things that can enlarge our lives, and one of the greatest of these is money.

Because this line of thought may be strange to you, and perhaps disagreeable, allow me to support what I am saying with a quotation from a Jungian analyst, Dr. Adolf Güggenbuhl-Craig. He writes: "Wherever soul appears there is secrecy, a secrecy that is expressed through many symbols. Initiation rituals designed to connect us to soul are shrouded in secrecy. The soul is often depicted as a hidden treasure in the woods, guarded by dragons in caves, etc. Second, fascination. Being concerned with one's soul is the greatest aim in life; losing it the greatest calamity. Third, strength and energy. The loss of soul results in weakness, while being in touch with the soul produces boundless energy." But, as I said before, soul has to have a habitation. In psychological terms, we have to project it on something. In the past many people projected their souls, understandably, on religion. In the present time, you have only to read the daily papers to see that great numbers of people have projected their souls on sex, and for some of them it appears as if the orgasm were a unit of currency, the new, unshakeable gold standard. But for many, the soul is projected on money, and I want to repeat that this does not mean that the soul is degraded by money, but rather that money is exalted by soul.

What do we do with our money? Even if we prudently tuck away a good deal of it, we spend most of it, and what we spend it on shows the nature of our souls. It shows what we are doing with an external, exchangeable symbol of the soul. All those collectors we were talking about earlier, the serious ones and the merely solemn ones, are projecting their souls into their collections, they are seeking to possess some portion of what was best in the past, and one might almost say that by so doing they are trying to slow down the flight of Time, or they may wish to stop Time altogether.

We are particularly concerned with Time nowadays because we are approaching the end of a millennium, and for some reason which I cannot begin to explain, mankind is fascinated by these millennial completions. When the last one was approaching, and the year 1000 A.D. was almost at hand, all sorts of extraordinary predictions were made, all sorts of monsters and portents were reported to have appeared, great wars were declared to be inevitable, and above all it was assumed that Christ would come again to earth, to judge the quick and the dead at a great Last Judgment. It was widely agreed that the Last Judgment would take place at Jerusalem, and years before the actual date, thousands of pilgrims from all over Europe set out toward Jerusalem on foot or, if they could afford it, on horses. They wanted to be there in plenty of time, presumably so that they could get good seats for the great occasion. It was altogether a most unhappy and ill-judged pilgrimage. Some of the travellers were killed by robbers; some were captured and sold into slavery among the heathen; some just never made it, and were lost somewhere on the way. Many, of course, did complete the journey, and hung around like discontented tourists, waiting for something to happen, and indulging in elaborate calculations designed to show that Christ was not really late, but that the pilgrims were early.

Now we approach another millennium, and I am sure that we shall hear of extraordinary things, and morbid or apocalyptic expectations. Indeed there has already been a lot of talk about the progression from the Platonic Month of Pisces to the Platonic Month of Aquarius, which will bring great changes in the character of human life. I take no sides in these matters. I merely point them out as evidence of the tendency of mankind to think along such lines, and understandably to dread the great changes that are thought to be imminent, because we always assume that change will be for the worse, and we fear it. What is more natural, then, than to seek out those things that do not change, that have abiding value and give an assurance of a great past, and to get them into our own collections if we can, or to visit them where they are already collected, if we cannot.

The modern enthusiasm for painting, I suggest, is in part linked to the human yearning for certainty at a time when uncertainty seems imminent; for links with a great past when the future seems menacing; for tradition when society is in flux; and, in short, for a means of slowing, if we cannot stop, the world clock. And the vast amounts of money which in one way or another are invested in this yearning, are, in fact, investments of soul, of life energy, of what is deepest and most prized. And one of the things we demand is the assurance of value, of tradition, of association with the great men of an earlier day.

What happens then, when it is discovered, as it so often is, that some great painting is not the work of the Master to whom it has been attributed—that it is by a lesser man, or a pupil? Even worse what happens when—horror of horrors!—it is shown to be a fake, painted within the last fifty years by some clever fellow, and palmed off on the credulous as the genuine article?

Faking goes on all the time and it operates on many levels. When a tourist goes to Paris and buys a Corot for one hundred dollars we do not waste pity on him. But when a serious collector, or a museum, buys a picture for hundreds of thousands, or millions, and it is shown to be a fake, what then?

The faker is regarded as a criminal of the worst kind. He has made the experts look foolish, which is unendurable, because experts of all kinds are our modern priests and we want to think them infallible. He has exacted from the public praise and high esteem for his painting which is not justified by the passage of time, and by association with a great Master whom we unquestioningly revere; he has dared to tinker with the World Clock. And high among his enormities is that he has made fun of money, and as money is a bearer of the projection of the soul he has blasphemed against the gods, which is to say against something very precious in every one of us.

Consider the case of that unhappy man, Henricus Van Meegeren, who was discovered in 1947 to have been forging Old Masters. He had been accused of selling art treasures to the Germans during the years when his country was occupied by the Nazis, and he sought to clear himself by revealing that the pictures were fakes, painted by himself. But before the war, in 1937, he had pretended to discover a large painting of *The Supper at Ammaus*, which he declared was by Vermeer. Great numbers of experts examined it and declared without reserve that it was indeed by Vermeer. But after his exposure in 1947 other experts, and some who were the same, sneered at the idea that the picture could have been by Vermeer. They even asserted that the model for the face of Christ was one of the most highly revered countenances of our own day—that of Greta Garbo. Poor Van Meegeren was in very bad trouble; he was tried and sentenced to imprisonment, but he died before he could serve his term. The public obloquy which attended his unmasking was extraordinary, but he maintained great dignity at his trial. And he asked a question which nobody attempted to answer; later, a play was written about him in which his question took this form: "Yesterday, this picture was worth millions of guilders, and experts and art lovers would come from all over the world and pay money to see it. Today, it is worth nothing, and nobody would cross the street to see it free. But the picture has not changed. What has?"

Since then a variety of art critics have been attempting to answer that question, and some of them reach heights of indignation that give us the measure of their spirits. The only honest one of the lot, so far as I know, is Denis Dutton, who says simply, "The magic has gone out of it." Magic. That's the word. Length of time, association with a great name—these are magical elements, unbecoming the austerity of an art critic.

In the course of Van Meegeren's trial it came out that he had been hurt because his own paintings had not gained him substantial recognition. If you look at them, they are modern in subject and technique and they have little to say for themselves. But when Van Meegeren began to paint in the Old Language of art, and counterfeited the saintly innocence of Vermeer, he was acclaimed as great. The more sophisticated we are the more reluctant we are to admit that we are open to the magic of past time, and the greatness of Masters long dead. It seems simple-minded, somehow. It is when the faker exposes us, and especially the art experts, as simple-minded that the roof falls in.

Consider the case of Tom Keating, whom I mentioned earlier, and, who died on February 12, 1984. He was an Englishman of humble origins, who had been a sign painter, then became a picture restorer, and found that he could paint like almost anybody you care to name. And he did. He painted a lot of pictures simply as Tom Keating, but they were not very interesting; competent but not remarkable. Then Tom Keating, who was a man of refreshingly irreverent mind, began, as he said, to flood the market with fakes, to show up the art experts and, as he said, "as a protest against merchants who make capital out of those I am proud to call my brother artists, both living and dead."

He was a true son of Mercurius. He said that his fakes could be detected by anybody with half an eye, and furthermore he inserted clues into his fakes—things that could not historically have been there, or things that should have leapt to the instructed eye, as when he used eighteenth-century paper for his Rembrandt drawings. These Rembrandt drawings, by the way, he did with quills and a special ink he made himself out of apple juice and Nescafé. If you are ever offered a Rembrandt drawing that somehow reminds you of breakfast it is probably a Tom Keating. He went farther. Before doing a fake he would write his name, or the word Fake, or perhaps a ruder word of about the same length, on the canvas with white lead paint; this meant that if the picture were X-rayed it would be shown at once as a fake. He lived to be sixty-six, and painted, as I said earlier, rather more than two thousand fakes. In 1977 he was arrested on charges of conspiracy and criminal deception but it took many months to reach the courts, and in 1979 the charges were dropped because Keating was in very bad health. But the indignation against him is undying, and in some art circles to laugh about what Tom Keating did is a grave offence. Yet can we help laughing? We must be dull of soul if we are not amused by these convulsions in the ultra-solemn world of art.

A few years ago, in London, I visited an exhibition of fakes at the Tate Gallery. It was very refreshing, dispelling a lot of the smoke of incense from art. Without exception the pictures had great charm and quality as art. But they were fakes. Ought I to have been ashamed?

Are we too solemn about art? I think perhaps we are when Dr Gilberto Algranti can set up a gallery in London from which you can rent any one of 250 Old Masters, to brighten up your house for a cocktail party, or your daughter's wedding. A Canaletto will run you about £17,000 for a week. Dr. Algranti says: "This is not an activity for social climbers, but rather those concerned with beauty in the home." Yes, doctor. We hear you.

I am speaking to you not as a critic, or someone primarily concerned with painting, but as a writer, and understandably my perspective on the whole business of faking is different. First of all, of course, it makes such a very good story. Second, and more important, is the alarm it causes in the world of dealership, of extraordinary prices, of competitive connoisseurship. But most interesting, I think, are the reflections it arouses on the nature of Time, and Time's ability to create magic, and to cast a palpable but inexplicable wonder over pictures that were once simply the last to leave the atelier of some notable artist-craftsman, working for a patron with definite ideas of what he wanted. This is the magic which allows us to link ourselves with the past, and in one way or another to project, or invest something of our souls into the past. It is not impossible to describe, but it is rather difficult to explain.

The Daughter of Time, as you know, is Truth, and when we ask Truth for an explanation, she smiles and is silent. Sometimes, when confronted by a Van Meegeren, or a Tom Keating, she winks.

7

How to Be a Collector

Late in his life Robertson Davies was invited to become an Honorary Fellow of the Pierpont Morgan Library in New York, an honour he accepted with alacrity. He attended the Board Meeting of the Library on May 9, 1995, to accept the Fellowship and then made this speech before a dinner given at the Library. Wishing to respond to the great honour the Library had done him, he presented the Board with two handwritten, unpublished poems by Max Beerbohm which he had in his collection.

On April 23 Davies wrote: *Finish the Morgan piece and read it to Brenda; she thinks it first-rate and funny, which is odd as it was born of fatigue and despair* ... On May 9 he writes: *Brenda goes shopping and I to Doubleday, but feel unwell and tottery and am displeased with myself therefore* ... *We lunch at the Club and rest; I am plagued with nerves. The Pierces pick us up, and we go to the Library and to the reception* ... *Then I give my speech which goes well but demands a great deal of effort from me as I am under par.*

ℐℛ

The title of my speech is "How to Be a Collector Without Having the Wealth of a J.P. Morgan." I must make it plain at once that I did not choose this title; your Director did so and it was not until later that I realized how deeply embarrassing it was. The suggestion that my personal fortune falls short of that achieved by J.P. Morgan I find humiliating and hasten at once to assure you that I am a man of

155

substantial means. I have never in my life gone without a meal or owned less than two pairs of shoes; I change my shirt according to a program which I have perfected over the years, which ensures that I always give the appearance of wearing a *clean* shirt but not always a truly *virginal* shirt. I frequently ride in taxis—not, I assure you, for pleasure, because nobody crawls into those dirty moving prisons for pleasure—but to show the world that I am a man of means. A man above the subway, indeed. Could Mr. Morgan, for all his vast wealth, say more? Could he sit in more than one chair at a time, eat more than one meal at a time, wear more than one suit of clothes at a time? There is a limit to the privilege that wealth brings. Mr. Morgan and I are more alike than we are unlike and if Fortune had decreed that we should meet I am sure we should have found much to say to one another.

Mr. Morgan was a collector, and I am a collector, and that establishes a bond between us and explains why I am now talking to you about my humble collection in the midst of Mr. Morgan's immense and splendid collection.

My collection is not like Mr. Morgan's. Our tastes were different. But did his collection give him any greater pleasure than mine gives me? It is possible that it did so; he was a bulkier man than I am and there was more of him to be pleased. But mine gives me all the pleasure I can contain.

Like Mr. Morgan, books are the things I collect, and to be perfectly honest with you, it was not until a few years ago that I realized that what I possessed was indeed a collection; up until that time I had simply thought of it as an accumulation. But if an accumulation is truly the mirror of a mind, it will end up being a collection. My collection is a mirror of my mind, or a large part of it, and sometimes I think what a sorry, frivolous mess it is. But then I remember that French priest who, early in this century, began saving a weekly supplement of the paper, *L'Illustration*, in which a play currently appearing in Paris was printed. Because he was a priest and lived far from Paris he could not attend the theatre, but through those printed texts he could indulge his love of it. And behold, after thirty years or so, he had on his shelves an enviable assemblage of all that had delighted the playgoers of the capital—a collection, in fact. My enthusiasm, the theme of my collection, is the theatre.

I did not begin in this frivolous vein. My ideas about collecting were from an impeccable source, nothing less than the *Philobiblon* of Richard de Bury, who was Bishop of Durham in the fourteenth century. He was a very great collector. He owned more books than all the other English bishops put together; his bedroom was full of books and he could not walk or stand without treading on them. How do I know about him? Because some of his books are in the library of Balliol College in Oxford, and that is my own college, and when I read his confession that "in books I find the dead as if they were alive" I knew that this was the man for me. And I loved him when I read that "no dearness of price ought to hinder a man from buying books ... how shall the bargain be shown to be dear when an infinite good is being bought?" I sometimes had to speak eloquently to persuade my father of this truth, for he thought my book bills rather high. But fathers can be indulgent. Some years ago Arthur Houghton, who presented his very great library to Harvard, told me that when he was an undergraduate, his father visited him one January and found that he had no overcoat. Somewhat shamefaced, he confessed that he had sold his overcoat in order to buy a book he coveted. His father laughed and bought him another coat. We fathers are a very fine and greatly misunderstood class of society.

The Bishop of Durham and I saw eye to eye on many things. He hated people who were dirty or neglectful of books. He would have loathed Samuel Johnson, who would break a large book into several pieces in order to read it more comfortably. As a boy I sometimes made use of a library which was also used by uncommonly dirty people; many of the books were heavily thumbed, and others showed evidence of bread and butter—even peanut butter; I remember one volume in which a reader had used a dirty pipe cleaner as a bookmark. Later in life, when I was the head of a college in a large university, and thereby the custodian of a very good library, I used to be driven to fury by students who cut whole articles out of expensive books of reference, with no thought for others who might need them. To be frank with you, I have never much liked public collections and of late years have avoided them totally. If I want a book, I buy it, and if it cannot be bought, I find a way of doing without. There is a joy known only to collectors in possessing the physical form of a book, quite apart from its contents. A library is a personal possession, not a brothel open to all comers. Of course we honour the names of the great collectors who have left their darlings to be enjoyed by others, but we collectors are also a jealous, miserly lot, and while we live, what is our own, remains our own. Collectors are rarely lenders. Remember what happened to David Garrick, who lent precious volumes to his friend Dr. Samuel Johnson—who promptly broke their backs and, in a word, strumpeted them, and was reluctant to return them.

I don't think that the great Bishop of Durham would have approved of the direction my love of books took very early in my life. But then, in his time the theatre was in a very primitive condition. I had always been in love with the theatre, as were my parents before me, and I could not resist books which fed and assuaged that passion. Many which I saw when I was a student I could not hope to buy.

How I remember them! My special study was Shakespeare, and I had to find out all I could about Shakespeare's theatre. It was always a good plan when you want to investigate some matter buried in the past to take a look at what its enemies said about it. One of the great enemies of the theatre, not precisely in Shakespeare's time but not long after—it was seventeen years after Shakespeare's death—was one William Prynne, a rancorous Puritan, who wrote a book called *Histriomastix, The Players Scourge or Actors Tragaedie*, in which he flails the stage through 1,006 pages of vituperative hate. I dutifully read that awful book as it was important to my subject, which was the circumstance that in Shakespeare's day all the female roles in his plays were acted by youths, often described as boys, but rather too old for that category. They were probably between fifteen and twenty years old and in that time more experienced than their counterparts today. I wished that I might have *Histriomastix* for myself, having read it in the Bodleian Library. I never thought to achieve my ambition, but at least twenty-five years later I was snooping through the antiquarian collection in Brentano's on Fifth Avenue in this very city, and there it was—an enviable copy. Faint with desire and dread, I looked for the price: Obviously nobody at Brentano's knew anything about the book, which is of considerable rarity, or else they judged that *Histriomastix* would not move quickly off their shelves. I sought the price, and could not believe my eyes: Brentano's wanted—what? could it be?—they wanted ten dollars for that book! Trembling like a thief and gloating like a collector I laid down my money, expecting somebody to rush forward and demand a revision of the price. But no. I escaped into the street, bathed in that unholy glow that suffuses a collector who has, for once in a way, got the best of a bookseller. What was ten dollars to Brentano's was priceless to me.

In my student days I found bargains, too, but in the main the Oxford booksellers were well aware of the value of what they had. I knew what I wanted, and often viewed it covetously on Blackwell's shelves. *Bell's British Theatre* in thirty-two volumes, published in 1791; beyond my reach. And the great collections of Mrs. Elizabeth Inchbald, herself a dramatist and editor of the twenty-five volumes of her *British Theatre*, ten volumes of her *Modern Theatre* (modern in 1811, that is to say), and the seven volumes of her *British Farces*. I knew quite a lot about Mrs. Inchbald, who was celebrated for her beauty and her charm—though one critic records that she had no bosom, not a hint of any such thing; how he knew I shudder to think. But Mrs. Inchbald was out of my welkin. The prices asked in those days were trivial compared with what I have had to pay for those collections in later years, and I did not at that time have the wealth of a J.P. Morgan, nor did my father. But I have them now and am happy that my finances have at last pulled even with my desires.

Without being very strongly aware of it, I had established the confines of my collection; it would contain anything I could find that related to the theatre between 1660, when the Puritan ban on the playhouses was lifted by the restored King, Charles II, and the age in which I was living. I was especially attracted to the nineteenth century, which was the last great inclusive age of theatre. In our century, the movies and television have taken over a huge area of entertainment which used to be occupied by the live theatre; for us, the theatre has become almost a coterie art, aimed at highbrows. I do not speak of course of the giant musicals that dominate so much of our theatre; they are a phenomenon in themselves. But for us, the theatre has drifted toward being a socially conscious concern, attacking modern problems with a seriousness which appears to excuse a want of what would once have been thought of as theatrical art. We go to the theatre to be harassed about the agonies of abused children, or battered wives, or people with AIDS. Comedies are rare and sometimes it is hard to recognize them as comedies. But in the nineteenth century the theatre had to satisfy a huge audience eager for entertainment, and every theatre offered a night's pleasure that included a tragedy, and also a comedy, and after that a farce, to conclude an evening's entertainment that extended from half past six until midnight. A big theatre, like Covent Garden or Drury Lane, might have a staff of performers that included not simply actors and actresses, but musicians, singers, dancers, and the large crew of stagehands and gasmen necessary to provide stage spectacles that were by no means simple—were, indeed, ingenious and beautiful on a scale that the modern theatre has not surpassed. And what did they offer?

It was not hard to find out, if one had patience, because all of those melodramas, farces, comedies, and whatnot had been printed, and the printed booklets, cheap and shabby, with orange paper covers and small, broken type within, could be found on the barrows outside the second-hand bookshops on Tottenham Court Road in London. I spent hours grubbing through those barrows, getting dirtier and dirtier and in my own terms richer and richer as I pieced out the repertoire of the nineteenth-century theatre in England. I early decided that I could not cope with the American theatre, for that would have extended my range far beyond what I could manage. Those little playbooks cost, as a usual thing, sixpence, and that meant that for a pound I could get forty of them, and a pound on each hunt was about what I could afford. My mother used to wonder what I wanted with so many grubby, tattered, often smelly, little books, but I knew. I was studying the popular entertainment, and therefore the taste, of a bygone age.

Because that is what the theatre is, you see. When Shakespeare said that its purpose was to hold the mirror up to nature I am sure he included popular taste in the category of nature. What does society admire? What does society fear? What are people thinking about, worrying about, laughing about? The theatre will tell you and tell you honestly. The theatre has told me a great deal about the nineteenth century.

But did you do it a play at a time, you ask? Well, no. I did what I could when I was young, but later in life I had a chance to secure a very large collection of those nineteenth-century playbooks, and I was able to snatch it from under the nose of a great library that took too long making up its mind. So now I have rather more than a thousand of those little playbooks, and in addition about 2,500 which various enthusiasts had, for one reason or another, caused to be bound up, sometimes very handsomely.

Was it a determined search, attempting to complete some precise catalogue of popular theatre? Not at all. It was whatever I could find, it was always exciting, and sometimes it was hilarious. Because, you see, it led to a study of fashion in humour. What did people think was funny, three hundred, two hundred, one hundred years ago? Frequently now people complain of the jokes in Shakespeare; they don't seem like jokes at all. Did people ever laugh at such stuff? Of course they did. And all through my four hundred years people have laughed heartily at things which now don't seem funny at all. Those of you whose memories extend back to the days of vaudeville can remember jokes that would not do on the stage today, and when you go to the modern theatre you hear jokes which would have caused a theatre to be closed fifty years ago. In our solemn day we have wrapped a cloak of seriousness about a great many subjects which our parents found irresistibly funny. Indeed, it sometimes seems to be a miracle that we have anything at all left to laugh at and are not smothered under a wet blanket of Political Correctness.

Do I laugh at the ancient jokes I find in my old plays? Yes, I do, but not as the original audience laughed. What makes me laugh is the change in ideas of humour. And it supports my long-held belief that very few people have any real sense of humour, any deep appreciation of the ludicrous, any acquaintance with that elusive essence that is called comedy. What they have is a carefully circumscribed idea of what it is fashionable to think funny, and that idea is changing all the time. If you doubt me, leaf through some of the first years of *The New Yorker* and compare it with the latest copy you have received. What has happened to all the jokes about Bella Gross and her family, who aspired to move to a district they called "The Concuss." What happened to that Hollywood agent Benny Greenspan, whose English was all his own—who searched "every nook and granny" and who called anybody who was stupid about money "an incomepoop." What has happened to that feature called "Letters from Coloured Maids"? What has happened to the world of Peter Arno, and those richly moustached elderly gentle-men who seemed always to be accompanied by pretty but cripplingly stupid chorus girls? Compare them now with the jokes about the sophisticated man and woman who converse, it appears, in incomprehensible monosyllables. Why are they funny and to whom?

What did people laugh at in the theatre of the past? Well—they laughed at sex, of course, and the way in which sex is dealt with, from age to age, is utterly fascinating. To begin in my period—that is to say, in 1660 when Charles Stuart had been returned to the throne as Charles II—sex was almost the only joke. That was a reaction against the Puritan rule which had been overthrown and which was savage in its condemnation of what Puritans called "the more than Solomitical uncleanness of the players." The great comedies of the Restoration are well-known—the works of Congreve, Wycherley, and Vanbrugh—and they are funny about sex with an elegance that still makes us laugh. But read some of the plays by the lesser playwrights of the period—Thomas Shadwell, for instance—and it will wipe the smile off your face. A lot of the plays that Samuel Pepys, for instance, enjoyed, were simply dirty. We seem to be making a return to what is simply dirty, in our time. In London, recently, I was taken to a play called *Dead Funny*, which might have been written by Shadwell, except that Shadwell did have a certain sense of humour.

In the eighteenth century sentimentality became the fashionable mode, and the jokes about sex began to be less explicit. But it is in the nineteenth century that we find a theatre where sex was virtually excluded from the range of permissible subjects for comedy. Not entirely; it was still permitted to make harsh fun of old maids, and to attribute to them an unappeasable sexual appetite. But jokes about marriage, about courtship, and about anything that might involve an unmarried girl had to be managed with the greatest circumspection. As the nineteenth century retreated, a greater freedom in dealing with sexual matters was regarded as passable material for stage comedy, but it was still very mild by the standards of today. Such rib-ticklers as *Getting Gertie's Garter* and *Up in Mabel's Room* are not likely to raise any blushes now. What, indeed, does raise a blush now?

How did the nineteenth-century theatre manage without sex? By a very curious device; it concentrated on puns and wordplay. It delighted in "insider" jokes, as for instance in one comedy; the scene was ancient Greece, and a picnic basket appeared onstage and on its side was printed the name of the most famous of London food shops, Fortnum and Mason. But the name was printed in Greek letters and so only those in the audience who knew Greek got the joke. Indeed, Greek jokes had quite a vogue. I recall one comedy about ancient Greece in which two ruffians were called Ragtagaides and Bobtailos. That made me laugh for I am quite enough of a snob to enjoy a joke that not everybody sees.

As for puns, nineteenth-century burlesque and burletta—as it was called—abounded with them. Nineteenth-century audiences must have had very quick ears and quick wits. I am tempted to give you a lot of examples, but I shall content myself with one exchange between a pair of girls discussing suitors. Once again the scene is ancient Greece:

ACTACA: There's young Cockeyes; choose him.
PARTHENIA: That I shan't

He *squints!*—the man pretends to see as can't.
ACTACA: He's well off.
PARTHENIA: But if Fortune him forsook

You'd find he didn't know *which way to look*.

Grim stuff, I think you will admit.

What do you say to a pantomime of *Little Red Riding Hood* in which Jack the Woodcutter rescues the heroine from the Wolf "quite by axey-dent," when the Wolf is paying his "devoirs" to the pretty girl. Red Riding Hood's mother, Dame Margery, is described as a "crusty rôle, and very ill-bread." The Fairy Felicia who is the good spirit of the pantomime is said to be "quite *au fay* in magic." As the puns pile up the mind grows dizzy and one is haunted by the fear that one has missed something—as puns always remind us is likely to happen. Many of these puns involve Greek, Latin, and French. What quick wits the children must have had who laughed at such stuff. Or perhaps the children were laughing because their parents laughed. Perhaps the parents laughed because they saw their betters laughing; humour is no stranger to snobbery. But not all the laughter can have been imitative. The Victorians were quick-witted in ways we are not.

Not plays alone engaged my rapt attention. I delighted in theatrical reminiscence, such as Tate Wilkinson's *Memoirs*. I have two copies of that not easily accessible book; for one I paid a pretty penny at Quaritch's in London, and the other I bought for ten dollars from a Canadian bookseller who didn't know what it was, but who thought as it was bound in leather it should bring an easy ten. The autobiographies of nineteenth-century actors are good fun, because they are so wondrously grandiloquent. When John Ryder, for instance, writes "I utter valediction to the author of my being," he means simply that he said goodbye to his mother. Reminiscences of triumphs, though charming, are not such good fun as descriptions of performances that went wrong, actors who were drunk, and similar disasters. One of my favourites is from the diary of Rev. R.H. Barham, who will be familiar to some of you as the author of the *Ingoldsby Legends*. He was a jolly fellow—the nineteenth century seems to have abounded with jolly clergymen—and he writes of a dinner party he gave. It tells of what must surely have been the strangest presentation of a very popular tragedy, called *Douglas*. It was popular because it was gloomy and it was Scotch, and both gloom and Scotland were very popular at the end of the eighteenth century and the beginning of the nineteenth. It was widely quoted, especially such lines as—

He seldom errs
Who thinks the worst he can of womankind.

That was accepted as great poetry and was extravagantly praised in Scotland itself. Indeed, the story goes that when *Douglas* was first presented in Edinburgh, an excitable patriot bawled from the gallery—

Whaur's your Wullie Shakespeare now?

The hero of *Douglas* is a young shepherd called Norval, and of course he isn't a shepherd but a great nobleman who has been brought up by peasants, for reasons highly melodramatic. He first appears, nobility outshining his simple shepherd's dress, and his introductory speech is this:

My name is Norval: on the Grampian hills
My father feeds his flocks; a frugal swain,
Whose constant cares were to increase his store
And to keep me, his only son, at home.

There's noble simplicity for you! Little boys were taught to spout those lines in the nursery. But it was possible for things to go wrong even in *Douglas*. Hear what Barham writes in his diary for March 18, 1828—

Lord W. Lennox, Sir Andrew Barnard, Theodore Hood, Mr. Price, Captain E. Smart and Cannon dined here. The last [that was Cannon] told a story of a manager at a country theatre who, having given out the play of *Douglas*, found the whole entertainment nearly put to a stop by the arrest of Young Norval for debt as he was entering the theatre. In this dilemma, no other performer of the company being able to take the part, he dressed up a tall, gawky lad who snuffed the candles, in a plaid and a philabeg, and pushing him on the stage, advanced himself to the footlights with the book in his hand, and addressed the audience "Ladies and Gentlemen—

This young gentleman's name is Norval. On the Grampian hills
His father feeds his flock, a frugal swain
Whose constant care was to increase his store,
And keep his only son (this young gentleman) at home.
For this young gentleman had heard of battles, and he long'd
To follow to the field some warlike lord;
And Heaven soon granted what—this young gentleman's sire denied.
The moon which rose last night, round as this gentleman's shield
Had not yet filled her horns," etc.

And so on through the whole play, much to the delectation of the audience.

As every collector knows, one thing leads to another and it is often difficult to know where to stop. Not only the plays, and the reminiscences of the players, but the history of the drama became an absorbing concern of mine, and I greatly desired a rare book in ten volumes called *The History of the Drama and Stage in England from 1660 to 1830*. It was printed in Bath in 1832, and the title pages modestly give no name for the author. But it was a clergyman called the Reverend John Genest, who became an invalid—I believe his illness was tuberculosis—and retired to Bath where, to employ his time, he did the enormous research involved in the book I have mentioned. It is a marvel, because subsequent investigation by armies of scholars equipped with every sort of research assistance has revealed very few errors in it, and Genest corrects innumerable errors in books written before his time. He read and annotated every play, and his literary style is a constant delight, as he describes the plots of the plays of which he writes. He is just, and gentle; perhaps the most damning comment he makes upon a play is "This Tragedy may be considered more apt for perusal than for performance." I honour John Genest, and I used to hold him up to the graduate students whose theses it was my duty to supervise as a model of scholarship, for he did all the work himself, and as the *Dictionary of National Biography* says, "Few books of reference are equally trust-worthy." Trustworthy, yes, and wonderfully good reading, a feast for the browser.

Did I say that one thing led to another? Yes, and I am afraid that in my enthusiasm I may dodge hither and thither in my collection until you are thoroughly weary of the subject and of me. Because there seems to be no end to it, and in my enthusiasm for books relating to the theatre, and in my pursuit of rarities, some of which I happened on by luck, and some of which I had to pay for in grievous sums, I found myself also involved in the pursuit of those little pictures of popular actors in their most successful roles, which were sold for a penny to theatre enthusiasts between roughly 1800 and 1830. The penny pictures were uncoloured; for tuppence you could get them beautifully adorned with the richest reds, greens, and purples. There is a story that William Blake, during a time when his fortunes were at a low ebb, earned a pittance by such colouring, and every time I buy one if the date is right I think that I may have acquired an original Blake.

That is one of the byways into which my collecting has led me. Another lies in the direction that I have never known to be taken by another collector, and this is children's drama, for in those days when the children of affluent parents had large nurseries and governesses who were eager to find amusement for them, quite a few plays were written for nursery performance before, one presumes, audiences of parents, friends, and nannies. In *Little Plays for Little Players*, *Dick Whittington and His Cat* and *Cinderella* and *Beauty and the Beast* are all given a thoroughly moral treatment, which was not always the case with plays written for adult amateurs. I have several collections of *those*, and although they made a pretence of innocence they provide plenty of opportunities for flirting, and one imagines that the rehearsals must have been very enjoyable. Some of these are what might be called "potted Shakespeare," in which the more demanding works of the Bard are adapted for the use of amateurs in the drawing room. It is noteworthy that in all of these the costumes of the ladies are described in detail. In one, for instance, the scene is that in which Romeo and Juliet part, after their marriage and which we are now accustomed to see in Juliet's bedroom, with both lovers as near naked as the most rigorous realist could desire. Not so the Victorian amateurs; "The stage represents a nicely furnished room, with a small table and chair on the left side, near the front, a large armchair on the right, and a small stand, with a vase of flowers upon it." Just the thing for the wedding night. It is suggested that the love duet from Faust might be played (offstage, presumably, by the governess). It is all very touching and determinedly chaste, and it must have been great fun to see and to do.

Amateurs also acted innumerable charades, for which books of directions exist and some of them seem to have demanded almost as much trouble as a full-scale theatrical performance. How, for instance, would you act out the word *Surgeon*? Would it occur to you to set some of the action in the Middle Ages? Perhaps you do not amuse yourself with charades? But they must have been such fun that I am sure they will enjoy a revival at some future period.

Some of the most attractive things that have come my way are actual promptbooks of stage productions of an earlier day. Have you ever seen one of those? They are interleaved copies of the play, in which the prompter has carefully marked all the action and stage business of the actors, all the properties needed, details of the stage setting, and everything that related to a stage mounting. By chance I came upon one prepared for a production of *She Stoops to Conquer*, late in the eighteenth century; another is a prompt copy of Lord Byron's play *Werner* which was immensely popular in the repertoire of the great tragedian Macready after 1830; my copy was prepared by Macready's prompter. But such treasures are hard to find, and book-sellers are now alive to their value. Mine cost me a trifle because they looked like spoiled copies.

I am aware that one person's enthusiasm quickly becomes another person's boredom, and the time has come for me to hold my peace. I could go on until you were all fainting from hunger and ennui. I could tell you about my collection of failed plays written by great writers who proved to have no talent for the theatre; some very great names are in that group—Dickens, Browning, Henry James, and many more. One of the worst playwrights among great authors was Sir Walter Scott; I have all his stage works in first editions—there do not seem to have been any second editions—and I cherish also first editions of the plays of Matthew Gregory Lewis, who might be called the father of the vampire-and-monster dramas that now abound on the screen. I promised not to speak of these, and as you see, I have not done so.

But have I explained why I collect the books—not beautiful on the shelf, not delightful in the hand—that have absorbed so much of my leisure and my income—my income which is somewhat less than that of J.P. Morgan? Did I not at the beginning quote the great Bishop of Durham, Richard de Bury, who said "in books I find the dead as if they were alive"? In my collection, to me at least, the theatre of the past lives again and those long-dead playwrights and actors have in me an enthralled audience of one, and I applaud them across the centuries.

Ghost Stories

8

Harper of the Stones

This unusual piece is a ghost story with music and was written in November 1986. Davies produced it at the request of Chamber Concerts and it was set to music by Louis Applebaum, one of Canada's most prodigious composers. The ghost story was staged at the Young People's Theatre in Toronto for the "Musical Mondays Series" and Davies narrated the tale at the first performances on May 1, 1987.

He recorded in his diary: *By 10:15 at the Children's Theatre. Rehearse with Lou and the orchestra until twelve; the orchestra are a very nice group and the violinist proved to be the concert master of the Hamilton orchestra ... Jenny comes with Brenda to rehearsal and we eat a picnic in our car on the street, then I go back for the performance at 1:30. Full house of children from seven and eight to sixteen; attentive, and applaud generously but do not laugh or show any sign of involvement while the thing is going on. It was very well received, and I exerted myself to put a spell on them ... Rest and a light dinner, then back for the performance at eight. House chiefly adults, and the piece goes much better and received with laughs, also with some dread. A little girl behind Brenda clung to her mother and whispered "I'm frightened." Good questions afterward. None of the "How much money do you make?" order ... Enjoyed this departure from routine, though it cost me a good deal, as public performance always does, but I greatly enjoy working with Lou, a fine composer and a delightful man.*

♫♪

I live in the country because I need quiet for my work. Not that one gets complete quiet in the country; it is full of sound. For instance:
The natural sounds of birds. (MUSIC)
The sound of a farmer in a field far away cutting hay. (MUSIC)
The sound of a jet plane passing overhead. (MUSIC)
On Sunday night there is the wavering hum of traffic on the highway, as the city folk hurry back to be ready for work and school on Monday morning. How I pity them! (MUSIC)
And sometimes there are unhappy sounds. They come in the night when the animals we call brush wolves capture something. The brush wolves will not attack a man, but they are terrible to rabbits, raccoons, and even an animal as big as a deer. Then we hear the sound of Nature in her harsh mood, for Nature is not the dear old lady that foolish people think she is. (MUSIC)

What I do not hear in the country is music, and that is why, when I heard the harp last Halloween, I went out at once to see what was happening. (MUSIC)

I live on the slope of a hill, and I have a fine view. There, looking at my view, and sitting on one of my stones, meditatively playing a large harp, was an old man.

"Good day," I said.

"Good day to you," said he, but not in a friendly tone. He was a very dirty old man, dressed in clothes so worn and stained I could not tell whether they were of cloth or leather. He wore a huge hat and had a dirty bandage over his right eye. An evil-looking old man, I thought. But I had the right of proprietorship.

"I must inform you that you are trespassing," I said.

"Must you inform me of that? Well, now!" he said. "And what if I asked you who you are?"

A hard case, I decided. "I am the owner of this property," said I. "I live here because I need quiet for my work."

"And what work would that be?" he said.

"I write stories," said I.

For the first time he showed something other than contempt for me.

"Do you so?" he said. "Then maybe there's some good in you after all. Maybe you and I have something to say to one another."

"What I have to say to you," said I, "is that you are trespassing on my land, and you must go. I can see that life has not used you generously, so I should be glad to give you something to help you on your way. But you cannot stay here."

"Can I not?" said he. "You'd better believe I can't go anywhere else."

Did I mention that it was a rather foggy day? That it was Halloween? As I looked at him I understood that I was seeing a ghost. (MUSIC)

I know a good deal about ghosts. They are part of my profession. When you meet a ghost, there is one question you must always ask.

"What have you come for?" I said.

"Because it is what you call Halloween, but it's rightly called Samhain [pronounced Sawen] in the Old Language. I come here every year on this day to play for the stones."

He touched his harp. Oh, it was easily seen that he was a fine harper! We have all heard harps, the graceful gold-plated concert harps that give so much beauty to every orchestra. But this harp was taller and thinner than those, and it was made of wood, and on the front of it was carved a woman's head. This was none of your French-made orchestral harps and I saw now that it was one of those harps with three rows of strings, such as harps had before the invention of pedals. The strings were made of gut, and some of them were very thick. And the sound that came from them! It was the sound of a harp, but it was not—I don't know how to describe it—it was not a concert-hall sound at all. Not what you would think of as a civilized sound. I can best describe it as a very ancient sound. (MUSIC)

"Tell me," I said, "why do you play to the stones?"

"I didn't say I played *to* them. I said I played *for* them," he said.

"What is the difference?"

"What a fool you are! But that's to be expected in a man of your time," said he. "Maybe you're not as big a fool as you look."

I did not take offence. As I told you, I am a writer, and every time I write something a few critics tell me what a fool I am. But even though he was very cross in his speech, this old man did not seem to be a critic. And what he said next proved it.

"Stay here by me, and you'll see why I play for the stones."

"I don't want to seem inquisitive, but after all I live here. Are you telling me that this is a magic place?"

"All places are magic places, though fools everywhere pretend otherwise," said he. "But there are some places where the foolishness is thinner than others, and this is one of them. Have you such a thing as a drop of drink about you?"

He was becoming friendlier. I went into the house and got something to drink and hurried back to him.

"That's more like it," said he. "Gimme aholt of that bottle."

He snatched the bottle out of my hand and without troubling about the glass I had brought he took a great swig out of it.

"Not bad," said he. "Not good, because it has a kind of a government taste about it, but I've drunk worse."

I managed to get the bottle away from him long enough to pour a heartening drop for myself. It was the best straight malt whisky, and I had been saving it for a special occasion. I knew that this was certainly a special occasion. The drink had made the old man talkative.

"Is this a magic place, you said. Well, boy, that's just what it is, and I knew it the first time I set eyes on it."

"When was that?" I asked.

"Nor long ago. About 170 years ago, I suppose it was. I come here from the Old Land to make my fortune, and it was here I settled."

"And made your fortune?" said I.

"Not what the world calls a fortune. But what I knew was a fortune, because I knew at once that the Old People had been here, and were still here, for people like myself with the gift to see it," said he.

"I suppose you mean Indians," I said.

"There were Indians, sure enough, but they're not the Old People. Oh, there's been lots of people here, you know. Before me and my life there were some Frenchmen—just passing through. Great explorers, the French. (MUSIC)

"And before the French there were some fellas from just across the water. Norsemen, they called 'em. A very rough lot they were, but brave—Oh, they were very brave. (MUSIC)

"But before any of them, there were Indians, the people of the lightest step you ever knew. The French cut their way through the forest. The Norsemen just burst their way through the forest. But the Indians glided through the forest with never a sound to say where they were. (MUSIC)

"But before the Indians—long, long before them—were the quietest people of all. They were the fishes."

"Fishes?" I said in astonishment.

"Aw, sure the fishes," said the old man. "How ignorant you are! Did you not know that where we are now used to be under the water? That was when Lake Ontario, as they now call it, was a great inland sea, and this was the farthest shore of it. Have you never digged up any fossils, as they call 'em, in your garden? Those were the fish folk. And very quiet folk they would have seemed if there had been any men around to listen out for them. But they were not quiet to themselves, you see. They had a sound of their own. Have you never heard fish talking? (MUSIC)

"But even before the great sea was the ice, and the great sea came when the ice melted. Now the ice had a very queer sound, let me tell you. (MUSIC)

"When the ice went away, it left the stones behind. Because, you see, the ice had brought the stones with it down, down, down from the farthest north, from what you must call Ultima Thule. And these very great stones that you see all around this land that you say was yours, came from Ultima Thule."

I began to remember some things I had been told by my neighbours as local history. "Then you must be Old MacLir, who tried to make a farm in these stony fields and broke his heart doing it," I said—and at once I knew I had made a mistake, for he looked scornfully at me and spat a ghostly gobbet on the grass.

"You've been listening to fool talk," he said. "I did not break my heart and I made a very good farm, around the stones. I was a popular man, let me tell you. A very popular character, I was. I was the only musician of note in this whole Irish settlement. Of course there were others—inconsiderable bosthoons who could do well enough at a wedding or a hooly—that's what we called a social evening, if you don't know the word. There was a fella played the tin whistle, and another one who could manage a fiddle. They were good enough for a hooly of the cheapest quality. (MUSIC)

"But for music—for real music—there was nobody to touch me. Ah, boy, you should have heard me at a wake! Solemn and lamenting to begin with, then wild and merry as the drink took hold. That was music for you! (MUSIC)

"But for the great music I came here where we are sitting now, and I played for the stones."

"I am afraid I don't understand," I said. "Why did you play for the stones? Did you imagine the stones could hear you?"

"I imagined nothing at all," said Old MacLir. "They heard me, right enough. To begin with I had to guess what music they would like. So I began very gently. (MUSIC)

"Nothing happened, but I knew they were listening, so I grew bolder, and played louder. (MUSIC)

"I knew they were pleased. You see, boy, fools never heed a stone. The farmers around here thought the stones were just nuisances. They put chains on them and dragged them to the boundaries of their fields, to make rough fences to keep their cows from straying. The stones didn't like that, not at all. They knew they were hated, and treated with scorn. Never hate a stone, boy. The stone may decide to hate you. There were terrible accidents, when stones rolled on a man's leg, or knocked down a horse so there was nothing to do but shoot it. But I respected the stones, and never moved one of them, and the other farmers said I had a poor farm, no better than a stone heap. They said I was lazy. But I knew what I was doing. Do you know what I was doing?"

I thought I knew, but it would have been tactless to say so, so I shook my head.

"No, of course you don't know. But I'll tell you. I was wooing the stones, boy. I was seeking their trust and their favour. And at last I had it. They taught me their music."

I thought the time had come to speak boldly. "Could you give me just a hint—just a few measures—so that I may know what their music was like?"

"Ah, you're like all the rest of the people nowadays," he said, "You want to know in a few minutes what it took me years to learn. You want all the gain, and none of the pain. It was slow—slow. For years I played to them, and nothing could be seen, but much could be felt. I felt I was getting nearer and nearer. Then one day I knew I had hit it, fair and square. I played my best, I can tell you, and then I knew I had learned their music."

"How did you know?"

"I knew it when the stones began to dance."

I knew he was mad. I looked all around us, and there were great stones—huge boulders of granite, some grey and some pink, scattered about the fields in front of us. A friend of mine, who is a great geophysicist, once told me that those stones were not less than a billion years old, belonging to a time long before man was on the earth—or in this part of the earth, at any rate.

I told you I know something about ghosts. I have met a few, but never before had I met a ghost who was mad. It was an astonishing experience. He heard my thought.

"You think I'm a madman," said Old MacLir.

I did not answer.

"I'll show you how mad I am," said he. And then he struck a great chord on his harp. (MUSIC)

He played, and I believe it was some sort of Irish jig, but enlarged and elevated beyond anything you might hear at a hooly. I looked around me at the stones. They did not budge. Of course the old man was mad, but his music was great. (MUSIC)

"I know what you're thinking," he said, and once again I knew he had heard my thought—because ghosts can do that, and you should keep it in mind when you meet one. "You're thinking I'm mad, and the stones aren't dancing at all.

"They're not dancing because they want to make me wait. They want to humiliate me, to put shame on me because of something I once did when I was young and foolish.

"I might as well tell you what it was. The first time I succeeded, the first time the stones danced, I was wild with joy and pride. 'O amn't I the marvellous fella!' I thought. 'O amn't I the greatest harper in the world.' And I began to dance myself and left my harp and pranced around like the proud goat I was, and bowed to the stones and grinned at them as if I was at a military ball. I thought how obliged to me they were. I even thought they were my servants, to do what I wanted. I went up to a big stone and I put out my hands as if it were a lady who would dance with me. And sure enough the stone took a lurch, and though I sprang back as sharp as I could, it fell on my leg, and crushed it, and though I lay there all the night through calling and calling it wasn't until the next morning that a boy heard me and fetched help and it took four strong men with crowbars and chains and horses to get that stone off my leg, and then the doctor came and cut it down to a stump, and left me as you see."

True enough, I saw then that he had only one leg, and a wooden peg that was held in place by straps that went over his shoulder.

"That taught me not to try to dance with my betters," he said. "The stones are very proud and high, you see. What you call aristocratic, because they are so old and have been in the country so long. And now they always make me play a while before they begin to dance, to show me that they don't do it because of me, but because it is their wish. But now I think the fine lords and ladies are ready."

He grabbed the bottle from me and drained it to the dregs. A heroic swallow that would stagger any drinker who was not a ghost. Then he smashed the bottle, as if to give a signal. Again he struck the harp, and began the jig. But this time it was such music as never came from a harp. It was the wildest, strangest music you ever heard, full of the sound of birds and the cries of animals and the wind and the rain, and the thunder and the lightning, and the dashing of huge waves against the shores of a great cold ocean that was formed from ice that had made its way slowly down from Ultima Thule. It was the sound of a world before mankind. It was the sound of the great merriment God must have known during the long days of Creation. (MUSIC)

The stones were dancing now. O yes, they were dancing! But it was not hopping and skipping like jigs or reels, nor was it the dismal revolving of a ballroom.

Not a stone moved from its place, but they rocked and turned, slowly and with the greatest dignity, as if to say: "We are the lords of the earth and of the water. We shall stand when all has gone. We shall endure until better things come. But what can be better than we? So we shall endure forever." (MUSIC)

177

I watched for as long as I could bear it. How long that was I cannot tell, but night came, and the stars broke out of the sky, and the moon shone down on the strange dancing. It seemed to me as if the stones sang, in the strangest voices, in the language of Ultima Thule.

When at last dawn began to appear the music ceased, and the stones were immovable in their places.

And Old MacLir was gone. Gone, I suppose, until the next Samhain, when the stones would dance again. (MUSIC)

9

A Ghost Story

From 1963 to 1981 Davies was the Master of Massey College, the graduate residential college at the University of Toronto. For most people, to conjure a university community out of thin air and to leave it with its traditions proudly established would mark the culmination of a life's work. Though not without achievements in other fields, Davies was justifiably proud of what he had done, and of the legacy left to later generations of scholars.

One of the happiest traditions established in these early years was Gaudy Night, a concert staged by the College community for its friends shortly before Christmas. The Gaudy incorporated another tradition, the annual ghost story told by Davies. (These stories have been collected and published under the title *High Spirits.*)

On December 10, 1988, in the Gaudy that celebrated the twenty-fifth anniversary of the College, Davies took the opportunity to pay tribute not only to the college, but to Vincent Massey, the remote, rather distant figure whose family fortune established it. The former Canadian diplomat, for many years Canada's High Commissioner in London, was reputed to be so urbane and polished that a British peer once complained that Massey made him "feel like a bit of a savage." Here Davies shows a different, more relaxed side of the man. Appropriately we find Davies remembering, at the end, his laughter.

His diary records the events of the Gaudy: *College Gaudy Night and a considerable success, for the Hall was full and the audience appeared to enjoy themselves. The student choir sang a few carols; LePan read several poems. Robert Finch read some occasional verse about the College; read well, verse admirably suited to the evening, witty and accomplished; warm applause. My Ghost Story went well, and afterward several people said how much they liked hearing somebody speak well of Vincent. After spiced wine and cake a group did Lister Sinclair's* We All Hate Toronto *very well, to deserved applause.*

❧

When I was master of this College it was haunted, not just by a single apparition, but by a new ghost, or group of ghosts, at least once a year. I do not attribute this fact in any way to my own presence here; I have never had any reason to think myself particularly attractive to ghosts. Therefore I assumed that when I had retired the hauntings would continue, and I presume they did so, though I heard nothing of it. My successor was a scientist, and scientists do not hold with ghosts. I had not expected ever to meet with a Massey College Ghost again. But this is the twenty-fifth anniversary of the founding of the College, and it was my luck to be the one, in this special year, to see the ghost.

No, I should say, the ghosts, for there were two of them. Were they ghosts? Not precisely, but—let me explain. It happened one night in the late autumn—the Eve of All Souls, to be precise. I had been dining with the Master, and any of you who have had that splendid experience know that the Master not only provides an excellent dinner, but rather a lot to drink. I have frequently observed this in women who occupy official and ceremonial positions; they are astonishingly brisk and generous with the decanter—much more so than their male counterparts. Thus it was that, midnight having struck, and having dined very well, I picked up my coat in my own room, at the end of the quadrangle, and was making my way toward the gate, when I observed an extraordinary figure standing beside the pool. It was a young woman, stark naked, and so far as I could judge in the darkness and seeing only her back, of remarkable beauty. She seemed to be dipping a toe in the water, as if to test the temperature.

Who could she be? Since the College decided to include women among its Junior Fellows such apparitions are not utterly unheard of, but there was something about this young woman—rather a lot about her, in fact—which made it unlikely that she was a female academic. Some member of the Toronto Polar Bear Club, I wondered, training for the New Year's Day swim in Lake Ontario? But no. I do not know how to phrase this without seeming ungallant, but about the Female Polar Bears there is a want of spiritual quality, which this young woman evinced very strongly. She was no mere pretty girl, nor even a very beautiful girl; she was goddesslike, and I felt a strong sense of awe as I approached her. Because, you see, I had to pass her quite closely to reach the gate, and what with the stillness of the night, and the late autumn chill which had raised a slight mist, and it must be confessed the Master's generous drinks, I was not sure how I could do so without seeming to brush past her.

I had an unhappy inspiration: I would sing, or rather hum, thus displaying goodwill combined with nonchalance, and she might move out of my path. So I hummed the first thing that came into my head, and as it proved I could not have made a worse choice.

What I hummed was a round, the sort of round one learns as a child, and in which one takes an innocent delight because it is such an easy way of producing what sounds like fairly complicated harmony.

> Youth is brief;
> Hours of glee,
> Time's a thief
> And steals from me.

That was what I hummed, in a rollicking, carefree, but very musical manner.

The girl snatched her foot out of the water, and rounded on me. Her eyes were blazing, her nostrils dilated and contracted rapidly, and fierce indignation seemed to well out of her like heat from a fire.

"What did you say?" she demanded, in a voice that was indeed goddesslike, imperious and terrible.

Taken aback I hummed again:

Youth is brief;
Hours of glee,
Time's a thief—

"You wretch!" she said in low thrilling tones. "How dare you speak so? You shall be punished for your presumption. Into the pool with you!"

She seized me and began to push me toward the edge. I struggled, but I am no wrestler, and in any case she was a good fifty years younger than I, and in the pink of condition. I, after all, am no chicken—and I *had* been dining with the Master.

I was a gone goose, it seemed. Within seconds I would have been floundering in the icy water, but from behind me came a protesting voice.

"No, no, Verry! He meant no harm! Let the poor old soul alone. He might catch a dreadful cold."

"Didn't you hear what he said, Daddy?" cried the girl, or the goddess, or whatever she was. "'Time's a thief,' he sang. Am I to stand by and hear you spoken of in that way? Let me give him a good dowsing! Teach him a lesson."

I had escaped her clutch, but my umbrella was now floating in the pool, and I was astonished and frightened. My days of wrestling with girls, even clothed girls, are long past. But now the source of the protesting voice came within my view.

He seemed to be very old indeed, but he was a muscular, robust old man, to judge from the one bronzed arm with which he steadied me on my feet.

"Now, now, Verry. How often have I urged you not to make hasty judgments. You must excuse my daughter, sir," he said, very courteously. "She means well but she is dreadfully impulsive. Allow me to introduce myself: I am Time, as you may see from my hourglass and scythe, and this is my daughter Veritas. I call her Verry, for reasons of affection. Truth, the Daughter of Time. You fetch the gentleman's umbrella, Verry, and mind your manners."

"Shan't," said Veritas, pouting.

"Verry," said Time sternly, "just you do what Daddy tells you, and none of your nonsense."

Still pouting, but cowed, Truth stepped into the pool, and after a good deal of splashing about she found my umbrella, which had sunk to the bottom. She clambered wetly ashore, and thrust it at me. It was soaking.

I was greatly surprised. I shall go further, I was amazed, taken aback, flabbergasted, and totally overthrown. These were not *ghosts*, of which I have considerable experience, but mythological figures, whom I have never met before except in the pages of books, or represented in ormolu on the tops of those old-fashioned French clocks which insensitive relatives thought suitable as wedding presents. I accepted my dripping umbrella with a slight bow.

"I am much obliged," said I.

"No you're not. You're as mad as a wet hen, and so am I," said Truth, crossly.

"Verry, where are your manners?" said Time.

"But Daddy, he spoke an Untruth, and you know that if there is one thing I can't stand, it is an Untruth," said the girl.

"Don't tempt me, my daughter, to teach you that Truth is relative," said Time, looking threateningly at her.

I attempted to be a peacemaker in this family spat. "And a splendid young relative she is, sir," I said. "You have obviously given her a truly moral upbringing, and you may be proud of her. A fine figure of a goddess," I said, looking at her admiringly.

Mythological manners are not ordinary manners. Truth, who was still wet from the pool, shook herself like a large dog, and drenched me with water.

"Do you mind if we walk?" said Time. "You know, no doubt, that I never stand still. Let us promenade gently around this handsome quadrangle." And, taking me by the arm, he set out on what proved to be rather a long trek around our paths.

"Better put on your robe, Verry," said he; "we all know that truth is naked and unashamed, but Truth can also be embarrassing, and you may attract the wrong sort of attention. Not everybody recognizes mythology when they see it."

Truth picked up a splendid robe which I had not noticed at the poolside, and threw it about herself in a classical but not totally concealing manner.

We walked. Oh, how we walked! I have often walked around our College quadrangle, happy in its peace and retirement, but this was walking of a different sort. This was walking with Time. There was a disturbing inevitability about it, a lack of any occasional pause or stepping backward. I know that some poets and philosophers talk about Man being the prisoner of Time, but I had never understood the sinister overtone of the expression until now. But I tried to be agreeable.

"You are a formidable walker, sir," said I. "And I quite understand that you have to keep on the move. But did we not stand still for a moment or two beside the pool while your daughter was recovering my umbrella?"

Time laughed; a quiet, old man's laugh like the rustling of leaves. "That's because of your College clock," he said.

"You mean it's stopped? My dear Father Time, it would be more correct to say that it has never gone. It's a very modern clock, you see. The very latest thing—state of the art, and all that. So it's always been out of order. Sorry."

"You disappoint me," he said, chuckling deeper than ever. "I thought you kept it like that to signify that learning is eternal and outside time. I love stopped clocks, and wrong clocks, and clocks that have lost their hands; they give me a fleeting sensation of choice—as if I might stop for a bit and rest myself. That's part of the reason why I came here tonight; to refresh myself with a peep at your wonderful, computerized, solenoid-controlled, ineffectual modern clock."

"Indeed?" said I. "I had ventured to hope you were adding a little something special to our twenty-fifth anniversary. Not that twenty-five years means much in university life. Nevertheless, it has seen great changes in this place."

"Massey College looks as if it had been here much longer than a quarter of a century," said Time.

"Yes, but you know how fast Time flies in universities," said I. "Three years is a student generation. Twenty-five years ago, when this College was brand new, everybody hated it: The architecture was ugly, the concept of the place was an insult to democracy, the peaceful structure of the life within these walls was an absurdity in the feverish modern world. But now, eight student generations later, it seems to the freshmen to have been here forever. They peep reverentially through the gate, hoping to catch a glimpse of Northrop Frye. As for the second- and third-year students, they have new buildings to hate, and new insults to deplore. You spoke a moment ago as if Time stood still in the world of learning, and, although that may be true, it is also a fact that Time flies here, as well." And carried away by the situation, I began to sing—

> Youth is sweet;
> Hours of glee—

"That's enough of that," said Truth, nudging me rudely and painfully in the ribs. "You keep a civil tongue in your head."

"Don't be intolerant, Verry," said Father Time. "He means no harm. He is a musical person, you see, and musical people never pay any attention to the words they are singing. They just like the noise. He doesn't really mean that I am a thief. Of course, I am a collector, but that is quite another thing. For instance, I have collected quite a lot of the past of this College."

"The best of it, I hope," said I.

"The most interesting," said Time. "Which is not the same thing. I have a fine collection relating to the Student Revolt of the sixties, when this College came into being. What lively times they were!"

"Pretty well forgotten, now," said I. "Modern students are very placid, on the whole."

'Yes, the revolutionary group have moved on," said Time. "Several who once were student leaders are now in politics. What nostalgia it arouses to see them in Opposition in the Legislature as they wave their accusing fingers across the House at the Government benches, uttering the same old cries, denouncing the same old enormities, and threatening the same old vengeances. Dear, good souls, they are growing grey in the cause of Reform, which is a very durable cause, but demands terrible personal sacrifices. The pickings are very poor in the Reform parties, so they have to find their satisfaction in virtue."

"You are a cynic, Father Time," said I.

"Not in the least. I think of myself as a realist because, placed as I am, I am able to see behind things, and know significant facts that escape the historians. For instance, you didn't have much trouble with student revolt here, did you?"

"Some slight protests," said I, "but nothing to speak of. I put it down to the fact that our Junior Fellows were graduate students, and had more serious things to do than raise Cain."

"Oh, but some of the most ensanguined student revolutionaries were graduate students," said Time. "No: what saved you from trouble here is a simple but powerful truth. It was regular meals."

"And that's a *very* powerful truth," said Truth.

"You were wise when this College was founded to establish a series of regular mealtimes. Sit-down meals nicely served are irresistible arguments against disorder," said Time. "The keenest revolutionary fervour has to pause when the bell rings for dinner. Consider the history of all revolutions: They are implemented by hungry crowds raging through the streets, and without any idea where or when their next meal is going to appear. Think of the French Revolution: People who were angry because they were hungry. Think of the American Revolution, begun by a people eager to initiate the Age of Fast Food. But here in Massey College dinner was always a certainty. Though the sky fell, dinner would be on the table. It is very hard to eat and feel indignant at the same time."

"And wine on guest nights," said Truth. "That was a clincher. Revolutions have been floated on gin, but never on good wine."

"How true all that is," said I. "It reminds me of one of my favourite Massey stories. In our very first month we were picketed by a group of girls carrying placards, demanding that they should be admitted to the College as Junior Fellows. They stalked up and down outside the gate, shrieking with fury. I had no idea what to do. But my wife and I were at lunch, and she said, 'Let me deal with this,' and she picked up a large loaf of gingerbread from the table and walked out to the protesting mob. 'Have you girls had any lunch?' she asked. The noise of the protest abated; indeed, it became almost pathetic. 'No,' said the girls. 'We haven't had a bite since breakfast and we won't get anything now. The seniors said we had to picket Massey for an hour, and when the hour has gone the seniors will have eaten everything. It's because we're freshies, you see.' Thereupon my wife, with Napoleonic éclat, unveiled and divided the gingerbread among them, and the atmosphere became positively genial. It was a lesson to me, I can tell you."

"I don't suppose you are going to pretend that you bought off all the ill will toward the College with gingerbread, are you?" said Truth. She was a disagreeable girl; always bringing everything down to rock-bottom.

"No," I hastened to assure her. "Gingerbread would have been powerless against the students at Devonshire House, who were great wits, and thought it wildly funny to poison the goldfish in our ponds. Nor would gingerbread have prevented the cunning thieves who stole one of our bells right out of the tower, which must have been a dangerous and difficult thing to do. I often wonder where that bell is," I mused.

"I know where it is," said Truth, "and it has not brought much happiness to the people who took it. A bell is a noisy, embarrassing piece of booty. Hard to dispose of a hot bell."

"But aren't we becoming rather solemn?" I said. "You are visitors to the College. As one of its oldest members I should not like to think that we had dwelt too much on unhappy memories. We had some first-rate jokes. Of course you remember the lamb and the rabbits that appeared in the Quad our first Easter Sunday? Our College chronicle is really rather a happy one. You, Father Time, the great chronicler, know that very well."

"Oh indeed, I do," said Time. "But it is beginning to rain quite heavily and you seem rather wet. Wouldn't you like to come under my mantle? You'll be very snug there."

I was tempted, for I was indeed very wet. That miserable girl Truth, who had shaken a lot of pool water over me, had wetted me thoroughly, and the sleety downpour of the November night—All Souls' Eve, as I told you—had completed a terrible drenching. Could I avoid a cold by huddling under Father Time's ample blue cloak?

He lifted his arm invitingly, and I stepped forward—but only to recoil at once, in horror. For under Time's cloak I saw the faces of all the Massey people who were no longer with us: my dear friend Bill

Broughall, the college lawyer; Austin Thompson, who was the most genial of financial advisers; Lionel Massey, who took such delight in the College and who died so early in its history; Vincent Bladen, dean of arts and sciences and a strong College friend; Gordon Wry, who used to arrange delightful music for us on such occasions as this; Ron Thom, our architect, who believed so devoutly and so truly that architectural surroundings influenced the people who lived in his buildings, either for good or evil, and who built so strongly for the good. There was Peter Lapajne, one of our best Porters, with a squirrel perched on his shoulder. And several faces I saw there, of Junior Fellows who had died untimely; there were young Africans there, who had been killed in the bloody disputes of Nigeria, and whom I remembered with respect and affection; some who had died of what are so strangely called natural causes, but which seem so unnatural in the young; and there was one who had died, unhappily, by his own hand. Many others; too many.

"Come along," said Time. "I have them all safely in my cloak, and there is plenty of room for you."

"Not yet," said I. "The wet and the cold are not so bad as I had thought."

"You never spoke a truer word than that," said his daughter. "And never forget it when you think you have cause to complain."

"Have it your own way," said all-devouring Time, and dropped his cloak.

"But Father Time," said I: "There was one face I missed, which I should dearly like to see again. Wasn't Vincent Massey somewhere beneath your cloak?"

"Indeed he was," said Time. "Didn't you see him?"

"I did not," said I. "But—no, no, the request is too bold—still, let me ask: Could you, do you think, allow him to revisit this College that meant so much to him? It was here, I think, that he was most truly himself. It would give him so much pleasure to walk these paths again."

"What a fool you are," said Truth. "Do you suppose he is ever absent from it?"

"You mean that?" said I.

"Of course I mean it," said she; "I mean every word I say. Don't you remember that he used to talk about the *Genius Loci* of the College?"

"Indeed I do," I said. "The Genius Loci: the guardian of the Place."

"The atmosphere, the presiding spirit," said Time.

"That is what Vincent Massey is here," said Truth. "And so long as he is remembered by the College, it will continue to be so."

"How do you remember him?" said Time.

"Ah, well," said I; "I remember him as few people do, I think, because I knew him in a very special way. You see, he was not a man to whom everybody warmed, when they met him. They said he was austere, and forbidding, and he made them feel inferior. That wasn't what he wanted, of course, but he aroused that feeling in many people who are unsure of themselves. Canadians are like photographers: They think everybody smiles all the time. They knew that he was a friend of royalty, that he had known great statesmen and world figures intimately, that he was impatient of fools and people who took refuge in what was second-best so that they could not be accused of elitism. Jealous people told rather derogatory stories about him. They said that he had built this College as a monument to himself. But he was a wise, shrewd, and ironic man; he used to laugh when high schools were named after him, and he cherished a headline about a high school hockey game that read: 'Vincent Massey Lambastes Sacred Heart.' If perpetuating the ideals that were dearest to him makes this College his monument, let it be so."

"You do not paint an especially endearing picture," said Time.

"But I haven't finished," said I, "and I want your daughter, Truth, to understand that in what I am going to say I am very much aware of the quality she exemplifies and desires in others. His outward man could be chilling, but the inner man was a romantic and an artist, and he desired fiercely that romance and art should touch as many lives as possible. I understood that he was, in his heart, an artist, and I treated him like one."

"Being rather in that line yourself," said Time.

"Pooh! A concocter of complicated lies to amuse idle people," said Truth.

"You must excuse Verry," said Time. "I can never get it through her head that Art and Truth are not enemies but near relations."

"Exactly what Vincent Massey thought!" said I. "And so he found an artist to design and build this College for him, and he hoped earnestly that it would touch the lives of all who were associated with it in a special way, and give their lives an enduring truth. Because that is what colleges can do, you know. And whatever political and diplomatic concerns may have occupied a part of his life, he was first, last, and always a university man, and he believed in universities as places that could touch their children with fire, and light a flame that they would carry with them through the whole of their lives. You have seen the flames on the bordure that surrounds the College Arms. If, as you tell me, he is truly the Genius Loci of this place, he must be a very happy man, infusing the place that was dearest to his heart."

"What do you remember most clearly about him?" said Truth.

"I must say, his laughter," said I. "I always remember him as laughing, not because it was frequent but because it was so characteristic. He loved a joke—a real joke and not simply a wisecrack or a silly anecdote; he loved a real joke, that echoed and recurred and fed the fire I spoke of. He never forgot that one of the principal values of a college to the world around it is that it creates and fosters such jokes. Sometimes the jokes raise a laugh; sometimes they provoke a smile that is a signal of quiet enjoyment; sometimes they do not show themselves outwardly at all, but sink down into the heart, and nourish it. I have heard him, in the Common Room here, yes, and in the Master's Lodging, produce jokes of all three kinds, and the students and the Seniors who heard him were enlarged and enriched, and were encouraged to seek jokes of their own, so that a splendid spirit of Humour was created. A spirit which never wholly dies, and which can be evoked and enlarged at any time when the Genius Loci is felt to be at work."

"If that is what you feel about him, why do you ask to see him?" said Truth. "What is deeply felt does not need to be seen, surely?"

"Quite true, Verry," said Father Time. "She has you there. But you know, we must be going. Time marches on, as people say, and time flies, and time hangs heavy, and all that nonsense. But Time must move. We have rested long enough under your ineffective clock—there's a joke for you. We shall say goodnight, sir, and ask you to present our compliments to the Master of this College, and beg her never to forget the Genius Loci, for without it your College is no more than a heap of brick, inhabited by students who are no more than lodgers, untouched by the hopes of the Founder."

Time shouldered his scythe, took a firmer grip of his hourglass, and began his walk to the gate. And much to my astonishment, as he walked he sang, and what he sang was a different version of the round by the singing of which I had fallen foul of Truth.

> Youth is brief;
> Hours of glee;
> But no happy hour
> Is lost to me.

Thus he sang, and Truth took up the second voice, and I the third, and so we carolled happily until Time and Truth reached the gate and—as one would expect of mythological creatures—walked right through the iron bars and into Devonshire Place, where they vanished.

I did not leave the College at once. I looked about at the quadrangle, which was still wet, though the rain had ceased, and a shy moon was peeping tentatively through some ragged cloud. The College looked very fine, I thought. All set for another twenty-five years of doing what, from the beginning, it had been meant to do. And as I left I thought I heard, faintly but clearly, a well-remembered laugh.

10

Ghost Story Begun for Massey College, Gaudy, December 9, 1995

In 1995, John Fraser was elected the new master of the College, and he asked Davies if he would write a ghost story for his first Gaudy. Davies accepted, though he was not well at the time. He started the outline for the story on September 30, and wrote the first two pages on October 1st and 5th. I have included the fragment here because it is so exciting. It is fun to speculate on where it might have gone.

જી&

How, or why this College came to be so extensively haunted I have no idea. I only know that during my period of Mastership there were eighteen ghostly visitations, to my knowledge, and who can say how many there were of which I heard nothing. Because, you know, there are people who will not admit that they have seen a ghost; they think it reveals an unhealthy state of mind; they have their suspicions about Hamlet. Since I retired I have heard nothing of College ghosts. Were Professors Hume and Saddlemeyer utterly free of them? Of course their minds were in the peak of professorial condition; if a ghost visited them, they probably shooed it away. But I was never so enviably strong-minded; when I meet a ghost I compose myself to hear what it has to say. Because, you know, ghosts always come to tell you something and it is supernatural etiquette that you must speak to them first.

The Ghosts tend to come at Christmas, and I have not been near the College at Christmas for some years. But this year I happened to be working late in my room on All Souls' Eve, which you know is November the first. The time was close to midnight, and I found that I wanted to look something up in one of the reference books in the Library, so I made my way down there through the underground passages, and as I drew near the Library I became aware of a kind of light that I have come to know well: ghost light. The electric light had been extinguished, but that eerie bluish light filled the reference room.

"Filled the room" did I say? Yes, and something else, something unaccustomed, filled a good part of it. It was something that looked like a guillotine, but which I slowly identified as a printing-press. Nothing extraordinary about that; the Library is famous for its collection of antique printing presses and Marie Corey is tireless in acquiring more. But this was no simple old press; it seemed almost to have the mass and proportion of a guillotine.

It looked strangely familiar, and slowly I identified it. How many of you, I wonder, have noticed that in our Library there is a small case which contains a delightful miniature, the work of that fine craftsman, Norbert Iwanski; it is, in very small proportion, the printing-press of the sort that was used by that great, great, immeasurably great-grandfather of all printers, Johannes Gutenberg. And before my astonished eyes it stood at full size, and beside it, in the dress of a master-craftsman of the fifteenth century stood a tall, solemn bearded figure who I knew—because in the company of ghosts introductions are wholly unnecessary—to be Johannes Gutenberg himself and in his left hand he held a proof page which I had no difficulty in recognizing as a page from the great Mazarin Bible, the superb forty-two line Bible, the Bible which is known to all the learned world as the Gutenberg Bible.

The Bible which, by the way, if you should happen to want one, now sells—on the very rare occasions when one changes hands—at something like—well the last one brought $4,900,000.00 for the first volume alone. So you had better wait for the paperback.

Printer's ink runs in my veins and I know my place in the hierarchy of the typographical art; I sank to my knees. "Master," I cried, "say that you have brought this treasure to Massey College, to make us the greatest bibliographical centre in this country's academic world. That treasure—that miracle—" I was becoming incoherent.

"Trash!" cried Gutenberg. "Rubbish! Filth!" and to my astonishment he tore the precious page in two

Dickens

11

A Christmas Carol Re-harmonized

In the early 1980s Davies wrote an updated version of the Christmas Carol story. Bound up in seasonal red binders, signed photocopies were sent out as a Christmas greeting to twenty-five fortunate friends. Since then, its fame has spread. Around Christmas 1982, *The Washington Post* printed the story in its Book World. Later, when the Penguin publishing group in the United Kingdom wanted a story for their sixtieth-anniversary celebration in 1995, Davies was happy to oblige with this tale of Dr. Scrooge, the Great Museum, and another villain named Croucher.

∿

Once upon a time—of all the good days in the year, on Christmas Eve, Dr. Fred Scrooge sat in his office from which, as its Director, he attempted to guide the fortunes of the Great Museum. It was cold, bleak, biting weather outside, but in Scrooge's room and in the adjoining room where his secretary Miss Cratchit worked, all was comfort, culture, and amenity. They even had roaring wood fires, a whim of Dr. Scrooge's. It was just upon five o'clock.

"Unless you have something further, I'll go now," said Miss Cratchit; "I've a few details of Christmas shopping to finish."

"A very merry Christmas to you, Roberta," said Dr. Scrooge, rising and pressing upon her an expensive phial of perfume. Where would she wear it? At dinner with her large and loving tribe of nephews and nieces; no husband, no lover, but Miss Cratchit nevertheless liked being treated as a woman of incalculable allure.

"Oh, Dr. Scrooge, you are always so kind," said Roberta; "how I wish that all the staff wished you a merry Christmas! But I do! *I* do"— and she hurried out, in an emotional flutter, for she admired Dr. Scrooge, in an entirely nice way.

But of course the staff did not wish Dr. Scrooge a merry Christmas, for they were professional museologists, hard and sharp as flint from which no steel had ever struck out generous fire and, although, in the tradition of their profession, they were jealous and intolerant of one another, they were exceptionally intolerant and jealous of the Director, who was, by virtue of his office, their enemy.

This was Dr. Scrooge's great sorrow, for he came of a long line of philanthropists, and wished to love all men and be loved in his turn. Had not his great-great-grandfather been that very Fred Scrooge, nephew of the Great Ebenezer Scrooge, from whom the family wealth and the family disposition toward broad philanthropy descended? Dr. Scrooge had never quite cursed his wealth, which he had used so well on behalf of the arts and sciences, but sometimes he had heartily cursed the family inheritance of benevolence and the desire to be loved. It was that weakness in his nature which was now driving him toward crime—or what his colleagues would certainly regard as crime.

He opened a concealed panel in his office wall, revealing an illumi-nated screen, upon which was a plan to the Great Museum; little red lights were appearing in every gallery, and as he watched, a pattern was completed, and he knew that all the staff had left the building, and the alarm system was in action—that very expensive system which was designed to defeat even the remarkably cunning thieves who made museums their prey. He touched a combination of buttons, and the red lights went off in the foyer, the Medieval Galleries, the Gallery of Musical Instruments, and the Near Eastern Galleries.

Quite needlessly on tiptoe, Dr. Scrooge ran downstairs, through the foyer, the Armour Hall, the Gallery of Musical Instruments, and into the Near Eastern Section, and stopped by showcase Number 333. Yes, there it was! Of course it was there, for who but himself and the

Curator, Dr. Dagon Croucher, had access to that case? There it was, the thorn in his flesh, the bone of contention!

So small a thing to cause such a mighty row! Just a small flask of smoky glass, with a nicely wrought silver stopper, but unquestionably Persian, unquestionably twelfth century, and unlike any of the other ancient glass objects in the case. Last summer, during his travels, Dr. Scrooge had found it in the shop of a dealer in Istanbul, and had bought it for a substantial sum of his own money. He had presented it to Dr. Croucher with glee, as an addition to the Great Museum's splendid collection of Near Eastern glass objects, hoping that Croucher would be pleased. But Croucher had been furious, and was furious still.

How dared the Director interfere with Dr. Croucher's careful plan of acquisitions? How dared he buy such an object without consulting Croucher beforehand? Even though he had bought it with his own money, the Director had no right—this was outright abuse of the directorial supervisory mandate—was Croucher to be patronized and taught his job by someone whose own area was Renaissance Carved Gems—a dabbler who wouldn't know a twelfth-century flask from a Coke bottle—Dr. Croucher's rage made him incoherent. He wrote a memo to the Governors, protesting intemperately. He roused his curatorial colleagues, Drs. Katt, Grout, and Eisel, against the Director, and gained power by so doing, for though Katt, Grout, and Eisel hated Croucher, they hated the Director even more. Dr. Croucher raised hell, and was raising it still.

Of course the Curator put the flask on exhibition, for in his black heart he knew it was a good piece, but he put it in a position of disadvantage, and attached to it a description that knowing readers could tell threw doubt on its authenticity. The description said it was a Gift, but named no Donor. Dr. Croucher had not enjoyed himself so much in years—not, in fact, since he had discredited a book which was the life work of his greatest rival; the rival had died of rage and mortification. Maybe Dr. Croucher could hound the Director out of his job, thereby crowning his own career as a learned malcontent.

Dr. Scrooge, however, was not a man whose soul was entirely defined by Renaissance Carved Gems, and he suspected something that would never have occurred to Dr. Croucher. He opened the display case with his master key, removed the flask, and looked carefully at the stopper.

Nobody had been able to open it, though if Dr. Croucher had been less malignant and scornful, the preparatorial staff might have found out how to do so. Pulling and twisting had been of no avail, but Dr. Scrooge suspected that the stopper worked like that of one of those modern medicine bottles that are for the protection of children; you pushed it inward, then gave it a quarter turn to the left. The Gallery was as dark as five o'clock on Christmas Eve can be, but the Director had a flashlight, and now he tried his theory. It worked like a charm.

Like a charm indeed, for there was a flash, a roar, a gust of wind that threw Dr. Scrooge back against a neighbouring case, and towering above him stood a huge, naked Jinni of surpassing ugliness, who roared, "Speak, Master. What is your will? I hear and obey."

Dr. Scrooge had been expecting something of the sort, so although he was startled, he was neither dismayed nor afraid. Aware that his voice was a lyric tenor, as contrasted with the basso roar of the Jinni, he fluted authoritatively: "First, I must return this bottle to its case, lock the case, and get away as fast as possible. Meet me in my office at once, and I should be glad if you would put on some clothes, and perhaps assume a less extraordinary appearance."

There was a very rapid whirlwind, and Dr. Scrooge was seated in his office, with the transformed Jinni in the visitor's chair.

"*Inshallah*, you are a cool one," said the Jinni, smiling broadly. He was now an Oriental gentleman of impeccable elegance; he wore a pearl-grey morning suit, and shoes of patent leather, with pearl-grey buttoned tops. Upon his head was a most beautiful rose turban, his complexion was coppery, and his beard and moustache were splendidly in order. "How do I look?" said he; "quite the modern museum curator, I think. Don't you feel the pearl in the tie inspires confidence?"

Dr. Scrooge, who was himself a good dresser, thought of the terrible garments affected by Croucher, Katt, and Eisel (though not Grout) and did not answer. Instead he came to the point.

"My problem is this," said he, "and I want your most carefully considered advice and help in solving it."

When he had finished his explanation, which took about half an hour and was perhaps rather emotional, the Jinni, who had never ceased smiling, spoke.

"If I have understood you correctly, O Master, your colleagues detest you for professional reasons, and you wish to sweeten their dispositions, to change their characters; as the character of your great ancestor, Ebenezer Scrooge, was changed in a single Christmas Eve experience. You want them to have a merry Christmas."

"But nothing Dickensian, please," said Dr. Scrooge. "No big turkeys, no dancing Sir Roger de Coverley. These are people of today, you understand."

And Dr. Scrooge looked mistrustfully at the Jinni's patent-leather shoes with the buttoned cloth tops, which hinted to him that the Jinni was not fully aware of the modern era. He looked rather pre-First World War. But the Jinni was full of assurance and spoke laughingly.

"No, no, of course nothing Dickensian," he said. "But human nature does not really change much. Every man has his price, what?"

"Don't forget that Dr. Katt is a woman," said the Director.

"No, of course not. Do they really call her Pussy Katt? How awful! But a Pussy Katt must have a price, too. A nice mousie, do you think?" And the Jinni laughed merrily.

"Everything is now in your hands," said Dr. Scrooge. "The Museum is closed on Boxing Day, but I shall be here at five o'clock in the evening, and I shall expect your report then."

"Master, I hear and obey," said the Jinni and vanished, fancy shoes and all.

AFTER A CHRISTMAS DAY and a Boxing Day in which he vacillated between hope and doubt, Dr. Scrooge was prompt to the minute in his Museum office. A glance at the Jinni's face confirmed his worst fears. The Jinni was greenish, rather than a ruddy copper in complexion, and his clothes did not fit so well as before. There was even— could it be?—a splash of salty slush on the toe of one of the splendid shoes, and his expression was almost hangdog.

"Let me know the worst," said Dr. Scrooge.

"Alas, Master, these are such people as I have never met before. My principle is the age-old one of my kind: All men desire Gold, Earthly Power, or the Joys of Sex. But in the past thousand years much has happened to complicate such work as mine. Listen, and you shall hear.

"Dr. Dagon Croucher is obviously a man whose soul yearns for earthly power. What would give such a man a merry Christmas? My device was a subtle one. I discovered that for the past six months he had been intriguing against the scheme that brings thousands of children to visit the Museum. He says they are too young to understand, that they are noisy and disruptive, and that their teachers do it simply in order to spare themselves the trouble of teaching. All these things are true, but they go against the beliefs of the present time. Recently, in a television interview, Dr. Croucher won a brief notoriety by confessing, in answer to a direct question, that he hated children. Surely therein lies the seed of a merry Christmas for Dr. Croucher.

"On the festive day he watches TV for many hours, because it is his pleasure to sneer at the seasonable programs. So I devised one, visible on his set alone, at which he would not sneer—at which indeed he could rejoice, and be deeply happy. I arranged that the Slaughter of the Innocents should be played before him by the original cast, beginning with Herod the Great himself. Herod, as everybody knows, decreed that all children under two years old should be slain, and there was great lamentation and weeping in consequence. What St. Matthew fails to record is how the slaughter was accomplished, and it has been assumed for centuries that it was done by soldiers. With reprehensible carelessness I had assumed this myself. Alas, what appeared on Dr. Croucher's screen was different.

"It seems that Herod's soldiers had many duties at the time, and only a few could be spared for infanticide. So the palace eunuchs were marshalled, and not being fighting men they devised a rapid, effective, but inglorious means of carrying out their orders. They divided themselves into groups of three, in which one eunuch seized the child, another restrained the mother, and the third and fattest eunuch placed the child beneath a cushion and sat on it as hard as he could. It was lacking in tragic dignity.

"Did it delight Dr. Croucher? It did not. He was soon on the telephone to the president of the broadcasting system which he believed, quite erroneously, to be screening my special program; the president, when at last he was found, was outraged and he and Dr. Croucher exchanged ugly words. Then Dr. Croucher called the Human Rights people—another frustrating search for anyone in authority—to complain that the program brought eunuchs into disrepute and derision, and that eunuchs were discriminated against as a minority, and what was going to be done about it?

"I fear it was a day of total frustration for Dr. Croucher. He has a new outrage to deplore—society's indefensible refusal to accept eunuchry as one of the Alternative Lifestyles. He is even more immovably the man he was. Not a merry Christmas at all."

Dr. Scrooge felt sorry for the Jinni. He said, kindly, "Well, well don't be downhearted. I'm sure you managed beautifully with the others."

"Alas, Master," said the Jinni, "women have changed greatly since last I left the happy obscurity of my bottle. What was I to do for Dr. Pussy Katt? I knew but one solution to the problem, and on Christmas Eve I placed in her bed a young man of surpassing beauty. His hair hung in ringlets scented with ambergris, his eyes were as pools of cream in which two perfect amethysts float, his teeth were like new ivory, his limbs were like old ivory, his armpits gave out gusts of musk and cinnamon, and his sexual power was inexhaustible. When Dr. Katt returned from her bath he turned to her and cried musically, 'O thou garden of a thousand unexplored delights, hasten to embrace me, my sister, my spouse.'

"At first everything seemed to be going according to plan. Urged by a spirit of inquiry and three hearty Scotches she had had during the evening, Dr. Katt allowed herself to be drawn into the bed, where my young assistant linked the poetry of speech with the poetry of physical action until Dr. Katt stood—or rather lay—upon the threshold of an experience hitherto unknown to her life. But my young man failed—a poetical failure.

"'O queen among women,' he breathed, 'when has the world seen your like? Your hair—so rich an auburn and yet, like the mystery lying in the heart of a beautiful flower, with a thumb's breadth of dark green at the roots—'

"It was then that Dr. Katt gave a squawk which aroused her companion in life, a lady of much her own stature and sort, who professes Household Science at the University; she appeared with a rolling pin which she kept always on her bedside table for just such emergencies, and stunned my young man with a heavy blow. Confusion! A call to the police. My young man, wrapped in an eider-down, was whisked off to the police station, where I let him undergo interrogation for a bruising half-hour, to teach him a lesson. Then I spirited him away, and the police, who are entirely accustomed to the inexplicable disappearances of people under charge, promptly forgot all about him.

"Not so Dr. Katt and her companion. 'To think what might have happened,' said Pussy, half in awe of herself as an enchantress, half indignant; 'a rapist!' Her companion was half firm in her natural austerity, half jealous; 'Tush, Puss,' said she; 'just a crazy burglar. You were never in the least danger, so don't give yourself airs.'

"The complexity of hurt feelings, jealousy, and unfocused indigna-tion rages still in the dwelling of Dr. Katt and her friend, and I fear it will never be wholly subdued. Not at all a merry Christmas, I fear."

"You must comfort yourself with the reflection that you did your best," said Dr. Scrooge, and immediately regretted it.

"My best belongs to another age, another concept of life," the Jinni grieved. "The intrusive modern state has made such magic as mine wholly ineffective. Oh, what a mess of things I made with Dr. Ernst Eisel, third on your list, and a man who never stops whining about money, as well you know. So I gave him money.

"You have never been in the Eisels' house—or rather, their stuffy apartment, which might well be in their native Prague, so firmly does it keep the New World outside its door. Twenty-five years here have done nothing to change them in any serious respect. Childless people, they make children of each other, and on Christmas Eve they hang up stockings, and secretly fill them. Pitiable, if they were not so nasty.

"The stockings made my task simple—so I thought. When they were fast asleep, huddled together like withered children, I emptied

Ernst's stocking of the candies and cookies and toys that Anna had provided, and instead tucked in one thousand bills each of one thousand dollars' value; it made quite a swollen stocking.

"Christmas morning came, and when Ernst unpacked his stocking he fainted dead away. Anna waited until she had counted the money, then she elected for hysterics instead of a faint. Slowly, I came to understand their problem. How could they possibly present notes of such a denomination in any shop, how deposit them in their bank, how, in fact, conceal what they had? For if it became known that they had a million dollars, how could they explain where it had come from? They had no papers establishing an inheritance, no numbered account in which it could be concealed.

"Their pitiable state slowly became clear to me. There was much talk of a mysterious body called They, to whom such a fortune would have to be explained, and They seemed to be a muddle of tax authorities and public opinion. Their fear went even deeper. I understood, as they chattered in pain, that Ernst and Anna were wedded to what they regarded as their poverty—meaning the by no means trivial salary he received as your Curator of Paleontology and some money he gets from his publications and a handful of widow-and-orphan investments. I had robbed them of their poverty, and they were stricken.

"Where to hide the money—for it was quite out of their moral power to destroy it. It could not be buried, for they had not even a window box. As I left them, deeply cast down by my failure, Ernst was wrapping the money in small packages and sticking it in the back of their freezer, while Anna peeped from beneath drawn blinds to watch for the approach of the Secret Police, who were Jinni greater even than I in their terrible world. They still sit, trembling, unable even to dress themselves, waiting for something awful to happen. A failure, but not my greatest, Master. O, Master, not my greatest!

"For my greatest, I confess in tears of grief, was with the fourth of your colleagues, Dr. Dirk Grout, your elegant Curator of Fine Art.

"Grout lives, as I am sure you know, with a man younger than himself, an interior decorator ravenous in his yearning to turn their condominium—which Grout paid for but which is now, lock, stock, and barrel, in the name of his young friend—into something so exquisite that even the heart of this inordinate youth could crave nothing finer. So, hopeful of pleasing Grout by appeasing the companion, I hastened on Christmas Eve to cram the condominium with what decorators call 'palace pieces'—boiseries, cloisonné, silken carpets, rare tapestries, Buhl and intarsias; paintings of the quattro-cento and tables and chairs of the dixhuitième, all finer than any to be found even in your Great Museum. I took special care to include many articles made of scented woods, so that the condominium smelled like the very Garden of Paradise.

"But—O wretched creature that I am!—when Grout and his companion woke on Christmas morning, what a scene of jealousy and madness! The companion—jealous because Grout seemed to have dared to acquire these things without seeking his approval and the seal of his impeccable taste! Grout—insane because he had invited the Chairman of the Museum Board for dinner on this very day, hoping to poison the Chairman's mind against you, O Master!

"And now—what would the Chairman think? Here there came into the uproar of lamentation and reproach an element utterly unknown to me, called Conflict of Interest. The Chairman, seeing the splendours of Grout's condominium, would at once assume that Grout had been obtaining for himself, at a heavy discount, objects which, as a matter of professional honour, he should have bought on behalf of the Great Museum.

"Grout rushed to the bathroom—now a wonder of gold taps and marble fittings—intent on suicide, but the elegant étagère I had substituted for the medicine cabinet offered nothing more noxious than a roll of Tums. In his distraction he began to rave of a garage sale on a scale of hitherto undreamed-of magnificence. But the companion, having had his fill of insult and affront, began to turn his mind to practicalities, and recalled an uncle who had solved a difficult financial problem with the aid of a fire. He rushed down-stairs, siphoned all the gasoline out of the Bugatti Grout had given him last Christmas, and was back in an instant, flinging the stuff hither and thither, like a bishop aspersing his congregation, while Grout heaped any precious thing he could lift into a pile on the living-room floor.

"Alas; they were but children in arson, and they overdid things disastrously. Five minutes after they had left the condominium, flinging a lighted match behind them, the whole building was ablaze, and it was twenty-four hours before the Fire Department could bring it under control.

"Eighty families are now homeless, four firemen are in hospital suffering from smoke inhalation, and the Chief has declared that the blaze must have been caused by a Christmas tree lighted with candles. The companion took an early plane to Florida; Grout is in a padded cell in the psychiatric ward. And I, O Master—if death lay within my power, I would beg to die, but of course I can't. Do with me as you will."

The Jinni, by this time, had shrunk in stature, his fine Edwardian clothes were rumpled and shabby, his beard was grey, and several buttons had burst from his splendid boots and hung by threads, like doll's eyes. Even his rose turban was dishevelled, and one end hung forward over his blubbered face. Grovelling on the carpet, he whined, over and over—"And you commanded me to give these people a merry Christmas! Another chance, Master, I beg you—another chance. Let me accustom myself to this strange new world, so tangled in rules, restrictions, and complexities of scruple, and then permit your slave to try again. I am sure I can learn."

Dr. Scrooge had no such certainty. He wanted time to reflect, and he gestured the Jinni to silence.

What was to be done? He reached behind him to the shelf where stood the twenty-four elegantly bound volumes of *Sermons of the Reverend Timothy Cratchit*. Surely Tiny Tim, who had become an enormously popular Victorian evangelist, would have some words of guidance? By chance, however, his hand fell upon a book by a great, but now neglected, American sage and it opened, from long use, at a passage he had forgotten. It began, "Happiness is impossible, and even inconceivable, to a mind without scope and without pause, a mind driven by craving, pleasure or fear." Of course, Santayana knew what he was talking about. What a fool he was to think that Croucher, Katt, Eisel, and Grout could be made happy by anything. But—but—

He was interrupted by the Jinni, who was capering about the room in a transport of delight. "O Master, it has just come to me! I can make them all happy! Why did I not think of it before! When I looked into their minds—dark caverns filled with serpents as they were—they shared but a single desire. It was that you should resign. O Master, I entreat you to resign! Let me carry you to a castle, East of the Sun and West of the Moon, where a hundred slave girls, every one with sound teeth and totally free from superfluous hair, await your pleasure! O Master, let me inscribe your resignation in letters of purple on parchment made from the skin of an unborn lamb, and bear it at once to the Chairman of the Board!"

"Shut up, idiot!" said Dr. Scrooge. "Now listen to me—"

"O Prince of the Compassionate Word!" cried the Jinni. "O fairest child of the Angel of Mercy!"

"Shh! I want to think. Now, see here: no more of this Arabian Nights business, do you hear? And no more tinkering with people to whom happiness is impossible, because inconceivable. You are to do something for me. And this time, if you don't get it right, I shall send you somewhere that you will dislike very much. Are you ready? Are you listening?"

The Jinni was once more coppery, bright-eyed, and smiling "O Master, I hear and obey," and his voice might have roused envy in Chaliapin.

"You are to give *me* a merry Christmas. To hell with merry Christmas for those who are without faith and therefore without joy. Be very careful because it is with my mind, my personality, indeed with my very soul, that you will be working. I command you, in the name of Allah, who alone is great, who sits throned in Eternity above the shifts of Time, to give me a mind freed of craving, pleasure, and fear. And watch your step."

The Jinni resumed his true guise, naked, splendid, and awesome. "I hear and obey," said he.

DR. SCROOGE DID NOT RESIGN, but remained Director until his mandatory retirement, at which he received a handsome pension and left the Great Museum regretted by all, for Croucher, Katt, Eisel, and Grout, unable now to touch him, had become biddable and almost civil.

Why? Because their Director had outsoared the shadow of their malignity. He seemed to want nothing, and yet everything he might have wanted came to him without his bidding. He pursued no satisfactions, and for that very reason he seemed to be fulfilled and happy. He feared no one and nothing, and perhaps because of that he was never forced into situations where he had to display obvious courage. Although his associates could not have known it, this was the most extraordinary transformation of character since his great-great-great-uncle Ebenezer encountered the Three Spirits in a single night.

Above everything else, it was seen even by the most unobservant that he knew how to keep Christmas well, if ever man alive possessed the knowledge. Would that that might be truly said of us, and all of us!

And so, as Tiny Tim would have observed, if he had had the wits to do so, to Hell with those who are in the grip of craving, pleasure, and fear, and being thus without faith, cannot know happiness.

12

An Unlikely Masterpiece

When the Pierpont Morgan Library in New York, holder of Charles Dickens's original manuscript of *A Christmas Carol*, wished to celebrate the 150th anniversary of the book's publication, Robertson Davies was a natural choice as speaker. To the task he brought not only a love of Dickens's work but also a deep knowledge of "the theatre of his time," which so greatly influenced the book Davies calls "one of the most powerfully theatrical creations in the whole of English literature." To go through the book with Davies as a guide pointing out stage effects is an extraordinary experience.

His account of the November 1993 event to a friend makes clear how much he relished it: *The other affair, which I enjoyed greatly, was in New York where the Morgan Library asked me to speak about Dickens's* A Christmas Carol. *It is a book I have loved since childhood and I was happy to say my say about it. The Morgan Library has Dickens's original manuscript of the book, which was the reason to celebrate the 150th anniversary. I spoke twice, and had large audiences, and loved every minute of it. Part of the fun was a Dickensian Christmas Dinner, at which we ate fried oysters, turkey with chestnut stuffing, and plum pudding with brandy, all washed down with some splendid wines and ending with hot spiced wine—which I avoided as I learned long ago that it is for younger drinkers than I.*

∽

That Dickens's novella A *Christmas Carol* is a masterpiece there can be no doubt. But I have given my address the title "An Unlikely Masterpiece," and you may very well wonder why. It is because the little book offends against every canon of conventional criticism, and if it were to be published today we can imagine the harsh terms with which it would be greeted. "Ill-constructed"; "absurd extravagances of character"; "maudlin sentimentality"; "total failure to find and adhere to a single tone of the authorial voice"; "unmistakable signs of haste in wrapping up the plot"; "vulgarity of diction interspersed with rhetorical wooden thunder"; "total failure to comprehend the economic infrastructure of the modern world"; "an affront equally to labour and management"; "dependent on a world outlook long abandoned by the majority of readers"; "though rooted in Christmas is chary of Christian forthrightness"; "an absurd and psychologically impossible resolution." And so on. You can hear the heavy newspaper reviewers, the wits of the glossy magazines, and the deep voices of the academic quarterlies—those Rhadamanthine judges of the quick and the dead in the world of literature—searching their hearts for condemnation bitter enough to reflect the greatest possible credit upon themselves.

Nevertheless, the book remains a masterpiece. The latest of Dickens's biographers, Mr. Peter Ackroyd, calls it "this powerful Christmas tale, which has achieved a kind of immortality, born out of the very conditions of the time." Of Dickens's time, and of our time, and of any time, for hardness of heart, avarice, human misery and degradation are not passing things that can be banished by legislation. Dickens, as so often, seemed to be writing about his own time, but it was one of the splendours of his genius that he wrote for all time, and the abuses he attacked, and the virtues he extolled, have not vanished, but only found new shapes.

The book has been praised extravagantly, and sometimes in terms that quite reasonably arouse the enmity of critics, who are, of course, the most even-handed and moderate of men. Everybody is acquainted with the exuberant judgment of A. Edward Newton who declared that it was "the greatest little book in the world," adding, with genuine belligerence, "if you think that rather a large order, name a greater!" A. Edward Newton was not a critic; he was merely a very distinguished collector of books and an ebullient enthusiast for literature of all sorts. Some of the warmest praise has come from contemporaries and fellow writers who might be expected to be jealous of Dickens. But it was Thackeray who said, with the generosity which was characteristic of him, "It seems to me a national benefit, and to every man or woman who reads it a personal kindness." It is even on record that Carlyle, though a Scot and a philosopher, rushed out after reading it and—bought a turkey!

So, a masterpiece it is. And what is a masterpiece? The production, surely, of a master in his art working at the height of his powers. If it appears to run counter to accepted standards of excellence, may it not be that those standards are not applicable to *A Christmas Carol*? Should we not judge it by other standards, by no means high-flown or contradictory of critical opinion, but simply different from those we have been talking about? That is what I want to talk about tonight.

It is my opinion that in discussing the works of Charles Dickens we should never forget the theatre of his time, to which he was devoted, and in which he first of all hoped to make his career, and whose techniques and characteristics, however he may have seemed from time to time to mock them, determined the form of much of his work and indeed may be discerned even in the later novels, in which his earlier extravagances of plot and character have been moderated.

I come to this opinion as a consequence of sixty years that I have spent in intermittent study of that theatre, and many years in which I have talked to generations of students about it. Much of the popular literature of the nineteenth century leans on this theatrical tradition, but none so plainly or so successfully as Dickens.

It was a theatre, we must remember, that combined in itself all that is shared nowadays among theatre, film, and television. It was popular entertainment ranging between the highest and the lowest taste, incorporating all I have named, and also generous portions of circus and ballet. It was peopled by artists of the highest order, like Dickens's friend Macready, by Edmund Kean (of whom Coleridge said that to see him act was like reading Shakespeare by flashes of lightning), by Samuel Phelps who did the almost impossible task at that time of presenting all but five of Shakespeare's plays, without a penny of subsidy, by the scholarly Charles Kean, and still within Dickens's lifetime, Henry Irving, who compelled the British government to accept the theatre as an art when it knighted him. Below this level were serious artists who brought to the stage qualities of intelligence combined with theatrical insight, who won and held the affection of a huge middle-class audience. And lower still, there were the actors of lesser talent but no less enthusiasm whose rich theatricality delighted Dickens and which he made immortal in Vincent Crummles and his company. Bernard Shaw, who devoted so much of his life to changing this richly emotional theatre into a theatre of ideas and intellect, nevertheless declared that it had been, in its own way, a great theatre, which he had seen when he was a young playgoer, before Dickens died.

The nineteenth century was an age of great acting, and it was Lord Byron—a playwright whose work would be admirably suited to television—who said, "I am acquainted with no immaterial sensuality so delightful as good acting."

We must not think of the nineteenth-century theatre as visually crude or impoverished; at its best it commanded the work of designers and painters of a high order and it had a system of changing scenes which was so rapid that it was done before the eyes of the audience, one scene melting into another with a swiftness that suggests the films rather than the time-consuming scene changes of the early part of this century. It had not our fine versatility of lighting, but it had gaslight which threw upon the scene a magic that was all its own. In those days of painted scenery, many of the effects which are now achieved by lighting were, in fact, painted into the background.

This was the theatre to which Dickens was devoted, and not Dickens alone but such of his contemporaries as George Eliot, Thackeray, Tennyson, and even so stern a critic as Matthew Arnold, who were regular attendants and generous in their praise of what they saw.

What did they see? This is where I have to moderate my enthusiasm for this theatre of the past. There were very few playwrights of even mediocre stature and the repertoire of contemporary plays often makes sad reading. I can speak with knowledge and with feeling because I have waded through scores of plays which seem to have been written by the same hand, repeating tried-and-true situations and putting in the mouths of the characters such language as has never been uttered elsewhere by human tongue.

If Dickens sometimes makes his theatrical characters speak in this extraordinary language he does not exaggerate. Consider the memoirs of John Ryder, a popular actor of the time who, when he is leaving home as a youth, writes—"I utter valedictory to the author of my being." He means he said goodbye to his mother. There were lots of actors who talked like that. Lines from plays became popular sayings, by no means reverently used. Such a line was "O God, put back thy universe and give me yesterday," from *The Silver King*; another was, "Once aboard the lugger and the girl is mine," from a play called *My Jack and Dorothy*. Many splendid lines are handed down in families where they took on a personal ring; I instance a line from a French Revolution play called *Jacques the Spy*, which became a catchphrase in my wife's family—"She who bathed in milk, and spent a fortune on a single pear." People liked verbal splendour in the nineteenth century, and often I wish it would return. As of course it will; in the theatre, nothing dies.

Nevertheless, verbal splendour divorced from any sort of original thought very soon degenerates into rant, and its intellectual poverty shows through the tinsel. Nineteenth-century theatre delighted in violent incident, improbable confrontations, absurd misunderstandings, and indeed anything at all which provided what was then called "a strong situation." It was the kind of thing we associate with the libretti of operas, but in opera the baldness of the plot and the arbitrary nature of the psychology is disguised, or given another dimension, by the music. Such a popular opera is *Lucia di Lammermoor*, for instance; the musical evocation of the sweetness of youth and the wretchedness of thwarted love conceals from us the violence that the libretto does to Walter Scott's finely psychological novel. The theatre of the nineteenth century was a theatre of feeling, of strong emotion, and it is not always easy for us, who live in an era where that sort of thing has been given over to the movies and to television, to sympathize with it. Our theatre has become almost a coterie entertainment, where we demand intellectual stress, or some reasonable facsimile thereof, and reject naked passion as improbable unless it is cloaked in some Freudian complexity.

It was an accident that Dickens did not join the vivid, rather brainless theatre of his time as an actor. That was his ambition, but Fate determined otherwise, for when he secured an audition with the influential manager Bartley, he was unable to attend because of a disabling cold in the head and deferred his audition for a year—by which time he was too successfully launched as a shorthand reporter to be able to pursue his earlier goal. What we know about his powers as an actor suggests that he would have had a fine career on the stage as a comedian, for he possessed brilliant comic invention, extraordinary powers of impersonation, and a hawklike eye for detail. He did, of course, take the keenest pleasure in amateur theatricals all his life, and scored successes in such dissimilar roles as Captain Bobadil in Ben Jonson's *Every Man in His Humour* and Justice Shallow in Shakespeare's *Merry Wives of Windsor*. It appears also that he could, at need, play tragedy—or at least pathos—with good effect. When he appeared as Richard Wardour in Wilkie Collins's drama of Arctic exploration, *The Frozen Deep*, his death scene brought tears not only from the audience but from the actress who was on the stage with him. But his greatest triumphs as an actor were in the readings from his own work with which he occupied so much of his time during the later years of his life. We know that he gave, in all, 444 of these readings to packed audiences in England and in America and there are abundant records of the effect he produced in both comedy and pathos. *The Trial from Pickwick* was apparently irresistible in its evocation of the sleepy, stupid judge, the garrulous Mrs. Cluppins, the ill-prepared but rhetorically overwhelming Sergeant Buzfuz, the irreverent witness Sam Weller, and the deeply affronted Mr. Pickwick. He filled the stage with people, changing from one to another with the uttermost rapidity and yet never scamping a characterization or a contrast.

From the descriptions that have survived of his readings we learn much about his technique. He had an astonishing range of voice; he could whisper horribly as the surly Creakle in *David Copperfield*, and he could be light, high, and twittering as Mrs. Nickleby; he could be winningly feminine, he could be shrewish, he could be wondrously drink-sodden as Sairey Gamp and her friend Betsy Prig; he could be sonorous and rhetorical as Mr. Micawber and he could be ignorantly pretentious as Wackford Squeers; as socially pretentious characters he was inimitable in his folly, and he could be ironically derisive as Sam Weller. There was nothing, apparently, that he could not do. In the reading which was his greatest success as a piece of sheer sensation, the murder of the harlot Nancy by the brutal Bill Sikes, his screams as the woman who was being beaten to death alternated with the blasphemous roars of her murderer so rapidly that it seemed almost as if they were heard at the same time. This same extraordinary rapidity and variation in what actors call "picking up his cues" was remarked upon in the scene where the reluctant Nicholas Nickleby is being subjected to the enchantments of Miss Fanny Squeers; people swore that both characters seemed to speak at once, in two wholly different voices.

His brilliance as an actor was not confined to vocal dexterity. As Mr. Pickwick he seemed innocent and portly, when his companion Mr. Nathaniel Winkle was slight and notably weak at the knees. The distinction he drew among the three spirits that visited Scrooge—the silvery Ghost of Christmas Past, the ebullient Ghost of Christmas Present, and the veiled Spectre of Christmas Yet to Come—was one of the many wonders of his always-popular reading of the *Carol*. In the *Carol*, too, many among his audience commented on the short but important scene where the reformed Scrooge leans from his bedroom window and orders an incredulous small boy to hasten to the poulterer's and buy the prize turkey. The boy has very little to say, but he appeared as a vivid personality to those who saw and heard that reading. Oh yes, Dickens was a very great actor, but great acting does not come simply. How did he do it?

We know from his letters how hard he worked to perfect all his impersonations. It was nothing to him to rehearse a reading two hundred times, in the privacy of his workroom. If that does not astonish you, I suggest that you might try reading a short passage from one of his books *five* successive times, trying to do it as well as you can, and I think you will discover what taxing, wearisome, tedious work it is. Dickens was a mighty man for detail and among actors whom we have seen he seems to me to resemble most the late Laurence Olivier, who was also a great man for detail, leaving nothing whatever to chance, and regarding no trifle of stage work as too trivial for his understanding and his study. I am not vapourizing about that; my wife worked with Olivier and saw what an insatiably curious artist he was in everything that went to make up the totality of a stage production. That was how Dickens worked, and when he appeared on a public platform to read, without any appurtenances except the book he held—but obviously did not need—and occasionally a paper knife with which he could extend a very few gestures—wearing only conventional evening dress, he was ready to people the stage with the creations of his own fancy, and to make them palpable to audiences of twenty-five hundred people, some of whom on occasions, sat on the platform at his feet. But never, be it noted, behind him.

What he read was not precisely what appeared in the printed texts of his books. He edited, he deleted, he strengthened a passage now and then, he occasionally wrote in a new joke, or an extension of a particularly telling piece of description. But he was able, at need, to do without description. In the *Carol*, for instance, he comes very early to the description of Scrooge: "Oh, but he was a tight-fisted hand at the grindstone, Scrooge; a squeezing, wrenching, grasping, scraping, clutching covetous old sinner." But in the reading all the latter part of that sentence was omitted. Why? Because, as many people have attested, and his manager Dolby, who heard him read the *Carol* scores of times, makes clear, the squeezing, wrenching, covetous old sinner stood before his audience, and the words were superfluous in comparison with the physical presentment.

He could, as it were, conjure up music. When Scrooge goes after his reformation to the house of his nephew Fred to humbly beg pardon for his earlier bearishness and to ask if he may join in the festivities, we are aware that a dance has been in progress—what the Victorians called a "carpet-hop" when the guests simply danced on the tight-stretched carpet to the music of a single piano-player, who might also be a talented guest. Dickens suggested that music by tapping lightly with his fingers on his reading desk, and that was all that was wanted to call up the simple, domestic music and the happiness that went with it. To explain how he did this is impossible without employing that now seriously overworked word *charisma*; people use it now to mean a particularly attractive personality, but it really means a gift of God not vouchsafed to everyone; a quality which may be refined and enhanced by indefatigable rehearsal, but which cannot be brought into being by any amount of effort.

The story of Dickens's travels and adventures as a reader are of the greatest interest. Undoubtedly he hastened his death by undertaking such efforts at a time when he was oppressed by fears that his creative powers were waning, by the failure of his marriage and the unsatisfactory nature of his relationship with the young woman who became his mistress, but who seems to have taken uncommonly little pleasure in that capacity; by the demands of his large family who must be launched in the world and in the case of the girls whose future must be assured; and by the anxiety of a man who had reached the top of a very high tree and was fearful of a fall. Those 427 nights of extraordinary exertion, achieved after heroic travel, were dearly bought and there were nights when the faithful manager Dolby feared that Dickens might not be able to complete his announced program. But Dickens always came up to scratch; he rallied magnificently when the time came to perform and there is no record of an audience going away disappointed.

Some of the details of how he did it are in themselves Dickensian, in their extravagance and strangeness. All through the nineteenth century actors seem to have recruited their powers during performances by eating and drinking. I am sure some of you know theatrical people, and are aware of their refusal to eat when a performance is near and, in most cases, to drink anything intoxicating. Not so the great ones of the nineteenth century. Edmund Kean, of course, had recourse to the brandy bottle and was sometimes almost incapable of carrying out his evening's work. Not so Dickens's friend Macready, who took his profession with the uttermost seriousness, and always consumed the lean of a mutton chop just before he went on the stage as he was convinced that it lent mellowness and unction to his voice. Not so Henry Irving, who, late in the century, relied on Bovril laced with brandy. But Dickens—well, in the interval in an evening's reading, he regularly ate a dozen oysters and drank a bottle of champagne, and this at times when otherwise he could hardly bring himself to eat at all. Have you ever eaten a dozen oysters and drunk, let us say, three glasses of champagne? Did it put you in form to do a heavy evening's work? But then, you are not a Victorian. They seem in many ways to have been an heroic race.

On Dickens struggled with the readings. He had his reward. In money, of course, they were very satisfactory. When he died his estate was reckoned at ninety-three thousand pounds, of which about half had been gained by the readings. What that estate is worth in modern terms I cannot tell, but in 1820 an English pound sterling was worth seven American dollars, and that would bring it up to substantially more than half a million dollars. What would it be today? Perhaps Miss Jackie Collins could tell us. His readings were packed, and at one Liverpool performance alone over three thousand people were turned away. One significant fact we must bear in mind, when we think of the effort the readings involved, is that this was long before the era of sound amplification. Yet nobody ever complained that they could not hear, even when he spoke in New York's Carnegie Hall. That demands of an actor a vocal technique in no way inferior to that of a great singer.

A notion of the quality and effect of the readings may have been experienced by some of you when the late Emlyn Williams toured the world, reading, in the character of Dickens, what Dickens had read. He enjoyed great success, and was by no means deficient in ranging from the pathetic weakness of little Paul Dombey to the noisy exuberance of Mr. Bob Sawyer. I saw and heard him several times, and I never failed to be deeply moved when, at the end of his performance, he acknowledged the ample applause of his audience and then turned and bowed in appropriate reverence to his reading desk, which was an exact replica of that which Dickens used. It was a fine acknowledgment, by an artist of distinguished gifts, of the genius to which those gifts had been applied.

But what, you may ask, has this excursion into the nature of the nineteenth-century theatre to do with the novelist and particularly with *A Christmas Carol*? Quite simply, everything, and I want to talk about that now.

If Dickens was so mad for the theatre, you may say, why did he not write plays? Ah, but he did, and of all the keen Dickensians I know, I am myself the only one who has read them. I claim some credit for it. It is not a pleasure. His farces, *The Strange Gentleman* and *Is She His Wife?*, might have been written by any one of a score of Victorian playwrights who turned out such formula work for theatres which were as demanding of material then as television is today. His dramas, *No Thoroughfare* and *The Battle of Life*, are once again without distinction—without indeed a trace of the Dickens touch. As a young man he wrote the libretto for a little operetta called *The Village Coquettes* and I had the experience of inspiring and assisting at a performance of it—I do not think there have been many performances during this century. The music, by John Pike Hullah, was pleasant, but the libretto was clumsy, and any comedy that emerged was provided by the actors. Why do you suppose a man so keen about the theatre failed so utterly when he tried to write for it?

In part I think it was because Dickens, though an original genius in his deployment of traditional forms, was no innovator. His novels are in the great tradition he inherited from his childhood reading of Defoe, Fielding, and Smollett, and even in his mature work he does not stray far from it, though he richly expands it. Now to be a traditionalist in the theatre in his time was to be committed to a worn-out conception of drama, composed of stock situations and mechanical fun, or else tearful pathos straining to achieve the dignity of tragedy. The successful playwrights were hacks whose names have not survived, except in the antiquarian enthusiasm of theatre historians like myself. Great acting could persuade the public that the plays of Sheridan Knowles or John Westland Marston were worthy of attendance, but there is no dramatic vitality in them and they have not lived.

Until late in the century, and after Dickens's death, the nineteenth century stage did not attract writers of first-rate ability. The reaso

was simple: The payment was ridiculous. A playwright sold his play outright to a manager, and thereby relinquished all rights to it. Royalties were unheard of. Douglas Jerrold's immensely popular drama *Black-Eyed Susan* brought the author fifty pounds, but made a fortune for a variety of managers and actors afterward. I do not know what Dickens got for his farces, but as a beginner it was probably twenty pounds. The rewards of authorship lay in the writing of novels and Dickens was strongly aware of it. Writing plays was a luxury he could not afford, and he was too intelligent a man not to realize that he had little talent for it, working under the restrictions of the theatre as it was during his youth.

Restriction—that is the word. He could not work in such fetters as the theatre put on its writers, though he could, and did, find room for his talent in the restrictions that were involved in publishing his works in monthly parts.

This system of publication involved Dickens with theatre in a way which was of considerable interest, but which is rarely discussed. We are so awed, nowadays, by the immensity of Dickens's genius that we are inclined to forget the keen man of business, who was eager to extract the last shilling from his work. He gained little money from the theatre but he was clever enough to exploit it as a tremendous source of advertisement.

As I have said, the theatre of his time was as greedy for material as modern television, and it was the custom of the day to adapt the popular novels which were appearing in monthly parts for stage presentations. These were often of a crudity that we now regard with astonishment, and many of them preyed upon a popular novel that was not yet completed. We know that Dickens's creating of Mr. Micawber offered such a chance for actors that versions of *David Copperfield* were on the stage before the novel had been finished; indeed, there were versions in which actors who desired to show their versatility "doubled" the roles of Micawber, the richly comic creation, with that of Dan'l Peggotty, the noble and much-wronged uncle of the wayward heroine, Little Emily. It has been recorded that Dickens attended one such version of Copperfield with some friends, and that his anguish at what had been done to his work was so intense that he

lay upon the floor of his box and writhed in agony. This was an early, and reversed, version of "rolling in the aisles." But Dickens was a man who could turn misfortune to account during his early days, and that is what he did.

We know now that he made available to playwrights and adapters whom he could trust, advance proofs of his books, revealing the conclusions, so that these favoured adapters could steal an important march on their competitors. Of course it goes without saying that the original author of a novel which had been adapted for the stage received no recompense, but we know that in exchange for these advance proofs money changed hands. And the advertisement value was incalculable.

This was not the case with *A Christmas Carol*, because it was published as a unity. The details of its publishing are, to the modern mind, astonishing: Dickens wrote it in late October and early November of 1843, delivered it to his publishers, Chapman and Hall, by mid-November and by the nineteenth of December this pretty little book, with its gilt edges and hand-coloured illustrations, was on sale at the price of five shillings, and by December 24 six thousand copies had been sold, and it has sold pretty briskly ever since. The modern author, who thinks himself lucky if his publisher gets his book before the public in six or seven months, is left with his mouth hanging open. As early as possible in 1844, there were four dramatizations on the London stage. One of these, called *The Miser's Warning*, was the work of C.Z. Burnett, and it was advertised as being sanctioned by Dickens; whether he received any money for that sanctioning we do not know, but certainly he did so for later works. Burnett's *Carol*, which is a clumsy and impudently altered version of the book, offered the celebrated actor O. Smith as Scrooge; Smith was the most famous "villain" of his time, and was the first actor of the Monster in *Frankenstein* when it was adapted for the stage. We have records of his performance, which was criticized as being too gloomy and villainous.

This is interesting. The public has never been ready to accept Scrooge as a villain. He is essentially a comic character, and the exuberance of his avarice is positively refreshing. His cries of "Bah" and "Humbug" sometimes find an echo in our own hearts when we are battered with demands for charities at Christmas. We are repelled by his oppression of his clerk, Bob Cratchit, but we never doubt for an instant that Scrooge is the greater man, and that Bob—decent, good fellow that he is—nevertheless must be reckoned as one of Nature's losers. It takes ghosts and disembodied spirits to get the better of Scrooge; he is in the most powerful sense an active agent in the story, not a passive one, and his conversion is brought about by apparitions that are, when we look at them carefully, elements of himself.

Now we come to my point. We cannot really know the essence of Scrooge, or the magic of his story, unless we meet it in Dickens's book, and that is because the book is in its deepest bones a theatrically conceived, theatrically written story. It is in this and in his other novels that Dickens shows himself to be not only a very great novelist but immeasurably the greatest dramatist of his time, and one might well say the greatest dramatic author in English since Shakespeare.

Drama, yes. But drama is what is left of great theatre when you have drained all the fun out of it. Drama is what serious people are ready to accept as worthy of their distinguished consideration. Theatre is the exuberance, the exaggeration, the invention, the breathtaking, rib-tickling zest of theatrical performance at its peak. There is plenty of theatre in Shakespeare as well as the dramatic essence. There is theatre in all the great playwrights, including even such unlikely figures as Ibsen. When the drama domineers, or drives the theatrical element out altogether you get the plays of Goethe—always excepting *Faust* in which he spoke most truly—and the plays of Schiller, of Racine—plays which we regard with profound respect but which perhaps we do not rush to see when deeply serious companies offer them.

The powerful theatrical element in Dickens's writing has been deplored by critics. Edmund Wilson writes disparagingly of what he calls the ham element in Dickens. But what is ham? May not a great ham still be a great artist? Is it not an element of excess, of—no, not too much, but more than the rest of us are able to rise to in our lives and our creations? My dictionary gives as one definition of excess "overstepping due limits." But whose due limits? Those of critics, who are always afraid of excess because they are at best classically restrained minds, and on the average crotch-bound, frightened people who fear that if they abandon themselves to the Dionysian excess of a great artist they may never again be able to retreat to their cozy nests? Do they not fear excess because it makes nonsense of their confined world? But the general public loves excess because it feeds upon the energy and invention of the great man, and thus it makes heroes of excessive characters, some worthy and many, it is to be feared, unworthy.

Dickens's excess was an abundance of theatrical device in his writing. His books, and especially the early ones before adulation and misfortune had combined to sadden him, vibrate with his excess. He infects us as readers with his marvellous excess; he even infected his early illustrators, Cruikshank and Leech. Have you ever noticed how theatrical the light is in their illustrations? How it seems to come almost entirely from the front and often from below, as if from foot-lights? That was how nineteenth-century stage light was. His books—the *Carol* as much as any—are full of effective touches of the kind that actors call "business." Consider the appearance of Marley's face in the knocker of Scrooge's house, illumined with a ghostly radiance like a bad lobster in a dark cellar; have you observed how, when he has opened the door, Scrooge looks to see if Marley's pigtail is sticking backward through the wood? Sheer theatre. Do you recall how, when the Ghost presents himself in Scrooge's chamber, the light flares up in the fire, as if to say "Marley's Ghost!" Now why do you think that was? I think it was because actors of the era of the *Carol* had a trick of stamping on the stage at crucial moments, because the stamp made the gaslights in the footlights flare up, giving a special emphasis, and that is what an actor playing the Ghost—and the actor was Dickens, don't forget—would have done. And when the Ghost retreats toward the window, and at every step the window rises a little higher—what an effective piece of stage management! You can go through the book looking for these stage effects, and you will find plenty of them. And from the nineteenth-century stage derives also the Ghost's elaborate rhetoric—"O captive, bound and double-ironed," it begins in its culminating address to Scrooge, and he, with brilliant comic utter-ance, undercuts the rhetoric as a great comedian might, saying, "Don't be flowery Jacob, pray." The mingling of pathos and terror is extraordinary, but the interjection of comedy is no less powerful, and it is achieved by means that Dickens had seen in the theatre, given fresh lustre by the splendour of his own invention.

I began by calling *A Christmas Carol* "an unlikely masterpiece." I have shown you, I hope, how unlikely it is as being one of the most powerfully *theatrical* creations in the whole of English literature. It invites us to take part in its nineteenth-century theatricality, becoming ourselves actors, directors, scene painters, gaslight controllers, and also audience as the play unfolds. It is unusual for a book to require this of us; most often a book allows us to sit back, as it were, as the story unfolds, and to judge it by the experience we bring to it. We agree with the new insights the author reveals, and we take pleasure in the characters he describes and the plot in which they are displayed. But how often are we asked so compellingly to be participators in what happens as we are asked to do by Dickens?

I think this is why stage and film versions of Dickens's books are so rarely completely satisfactory. I have seen many of them, ranging from the innocent adaptations of Dickens Fellowship groups to elaborate musical shows in which Dickens's verve and breadth of spirit is supposed to be offered in a musical form—and isn't. Mr. Pickwick singing is not Mr. Pickwick. Films have been more successful, though my gorge rises when I am asked to accept the archetypal con man W.C. Fields as the high-minded Wilkins Micawber. Many films have been made of *A Christmas Carol*, and one of them, in which the part of Scrooge is played by the great Alistair Sim, comes commendably near to the mark. But to know the *Carol* in its essence you must read it, abandon yourself to it, and personally body it forth with whatever theatrical skill you may command.

That surely is what makes the *Carol* unusual. But—a masterpiece? Why?

In his observations on literature the late Vladimir Nabokov put the matter succinctly. He says: "An original author always invents an original world, and if a character or action fits into the pattern of that world, then we experience the pleasurable shock of artistic truth, no matter how unlikely the person or thing may seem if transferred into what book reviewers, poor hacks, call 'real life.' There is no such thing as real life for the author of genius; he must create it himself and then create the consequences."

The author of genius who brings us artistic truth. Is that not Charles Dickens, and is it not its artistic truth, as opposed to the kind of truth that stands up in a court of law, that makes *A Christmas Carol*, however unlikely, an undoubted masterpiece?

13

Dickens and Music

In 1995 when the Penguin publishing group in the United Kingdom wanted a story for their sixtieth-anniversary celebration, Davies gave them a story he had in hand called "A Christmas Carol Re-harmonized." As it was a little short for Penguin's purposes, he offered to write an additional article or short epilogue about Charles Dickens and the music mentioned in his novels.

When Davies sent the original story to Penguin U.K. he wrote his editor, Mr. Peter Carson: *Here is the story. I am concerned that it may be somewhat short for your purpose, so if you agreed I thought that I could produce a short epilogue about Dickens and Music, which, so far as I know, is a subject that nobody has written about. The songs he mentions in his books are an interesting study and I must be one of the very few people in the world who knows the music for his operetta,* The Village Coquettes. *It may interest you to know that the music for this piece was written by John Pyke Hullah, whose name I borrowed for the hero of* The Cunning Man.

On March 1 Davies wrote: *To the College to do some research in the library for the piece on Dickens and Music to flesh out the "Carol Reharmonized."* On March 3: *Finished the Dickens "coda" and it is not bad but I would have liked to make it longer.*

❧

Anyone who has read widely in Dickens knows how often he refers to music and how plain it is that he took great pleasure in the kind

of music he knew. But what was it? His sister Fanny was an accomplished musician and received her education at the Royal College,
so Charles must have been aware of what was considered the best
music of the time. But his own taste seems to have been for the
popular music of the genial, domestic world in which he grew up—
not quite street and pub music, but the songs and ballads sung at
dinners for journalists and theatre people, and at such gatherings as
Scrooge's nephew offered their friends on that famous Christmas
night.

Even the music of Fanny's world was not demanding in modern
terms. Incidental pieces of trivial quality were interposed at concerts
between the movements of symphonies and concerti, so that the
hearers might not be too heavily taxed. The great virtuoso Paganini,
who enchanted England when Dickens was a youth, was greeted in
the press with such comment as—

> Who are these who pay five guineas
> To hear those tunes of Paganinis?
> Echo answers: *pack o' ninnies.*

—and the feat of Paganini's that attracted the greatest applause from
the general public was his imitation of farmyard noises on his fine
Guarnerius. The music of England in Dickens's formative years was
the music of ballads (not always sentimental but always strong in
sentiment) and comic songs. As a child little Charles sang comic songs
for the delight of his father's friends.

Comic songs! They seem to have vanished from our world. They
were the vessels through which high spirits were shared and
encouraged during most of the nineteenth century. It appears that
virtually everybody sang—so very unlike the age in which we live
when nobody sings except for money—and in Dickens's pages the
most unlikely people *do* sing. The villainous dwarf Quilp sings; his
attorney Sampson Brass sings, and in a moment of high glee
declares that "the still small voice" is a-singing comic songs *within*
him. How comic were these songs? In *Great Expectations* we are
given the first verse of what might have passed as a comic song in a
remote village.

When I went to Lunnon town, sirs,
   Too rul loo rul!
   Too rul loo rul!
Wasn't I done up very brown, sirs?
   Too rul loo rul!
   Too rul loo rul!

and the hero of that book tells us that though he did not question its merit, he thought that the amount of Too rul was somewhat in excess of the poetry. But in London things were brisker and a song like "Sich A-gittin' Upstairs" enjoyed a long popularity. There were indecent songs, too, and in *The Newcomes* Colonel Newcome is deeply offended when a singer in a London tavern strikes up such a song in the presence of his schoolboy son. But Thackeray was by no means caught up with the music of his time; for Dickens it was one of the elements in which he lived.

Its range is wide. Songs by Dibdin like "The Waterman," "Tom Tough," and "Tom Bowling" were immensely popular in an age when the British Navy was the greatest seaforce in the world and the memory of Nelson was still alive. The songs of Tom Moore were Dickens's favourites, and in particular "The Woodpecker," charmingly set to music by Michael Kelly.

I knew by the smoke that so gracefully curl'd
Above the green elms that a cottage was near,
And I said "If there's peace to be found in the world
A heart that was humble might hope for it here."

Ev'ry leaf was at rest
And I heard not a sound
But the woodpecker tapping the hollow beech tree

—and the woodpecker goes on tapping through a charming variety of musical phrases. Rollicking songs and pathetic songs were numerous, and we recall that Mr. Micawber confided to David Copperfield that when first he met the lady who became his wife she was famous both for "The Dashing White Sergeant" (a rollicker) and "Little Tafflin" (a weeper) and that when he heard her sing the first one she attracted his attention in an extraordinary degree but when it came to "Little Tafflin" he resolved to win that woman or perish in the attempt.

What was the manner of performance? Of course it varied with the ability of the singer, but there was a style toward which even undistinguished amateurs aspired and it had been set by the great Charles Incledon whose tenor singing was amplified by ten charming notes in falsetto, with which he ornamented his renditions, we are assured, with volubility and sweetness. His "shake" (which we should now call a trill) was especially admired. Not every guest at a literary dinner who was called on for a song sang like Incledon; some we know were roarers and some were not in tune, but they did their best, unaccompanied but encouraged, in all probability, by drink. Sometimes the company sang together, and a favourite for such choruses was "Away with Melancholy," adapted from a tune in Mozart's *Magic Flute*; this was the air that Dick Swiveller played so sadly on *his* flute.

Dickens's most ambitious musical venture was a "burletta" called *The Village Coquettes*, with music by John Hullah, written in 1836 when *Pickwick* was becoming the rage. It is sad stuff; Hullah was a conventional composer, and although Dickens could extrude lengths of technically correct verse he was no poet, and the songs in this little work are pleasing but nothing more. I have myself heard it well performed, but little lingers in the memory. Later in life Dickens disowned it. Several of his songs, such as "The Ivy Green," were set to music and sold respectably during his lifetime, but he took no pleasure in them.

Perhaps he realized that his musical vein, though deep, was not broad: was indeed *sui generis*. It is observable that in the later books the musical references are less frequent. He knew little of music of any complexity, and in *Edwin Drood*, where a cathedral and its choirmaster are vital to the plot, he tells us nothing of what music was sung. John Jasper, a musician of considerable accomplishment, plays the accompaniment while Rosa Bud sings. But what does she sing? Something characteristic of the time, doubtless; perhaps "'Tis but a Little Faded Flower" would do very well, but we would greatly like to know for a certainty.

Dickens was not the only Victorian novelist to refuse to take this fence. In *The Warden* Trollope assures us that the Reverend Septimus Harding played the cello admirably, and was devoted to his instrument, but we are not told what music he plays.

A number of Dickens's novels have been turned into "musicals" in the twentieth century and one, *Oliver!*, has been a great success. But it must be considered on its own terms; it is not Dickensian in feeling. Its rowdy geniality throws harsh light into a dark book. Other works, of which *Great Expectations* and *Pickwick* have had some success, have been brought to the musical stage but the same criticism applies. It seems odd that so fragile a story as *The Cricket on the Hearth* was chosen for full operatic treatment by two composers, Carl Goldmark and Alexander Mackenzie. Neither work has held the stage. Dickens's music is very deeply inherent in his prose and resists attempts to drag it to the surface. For, after all, only Ulysses can draw the bow of Ulysses.

Masks of Satan

14

The Devil's Burning Throne

These lectures were written during the summer of 1976, starting in June. They were ready by the end of September and then, as always, Davies practised reading them shortly before the event to time them, and then again the afternoon of the speech.

After the fourth lecture in this series he noted in his diary: ... *P.M. I rehearse and go for a walk and skip a meeting of the Theatre History gang ... Eve my 4th lecture; virtually a full house; the audience has grown every night. Lecture listened to with glittering attention and received with enthusiasm. I think I have really done something worth while with these performances* ... The next day he noted: *greatly relieved to have the lectures done, and well done. Before the next spring, I want a breather* ...

In his introduction to the lectures in *One Half of Robertson Davies,* Davies said:

The four lectures that follow were the result of an invitation from Trinity College, Toronto, to give their Larkin-Stuart Lectures in November 1976. The problem of Evil in Literature had engaged me for some years, and I knew from personal experience that to make Evil palpable and acceptable in fiction was not simply a matter of inventing horrors and displaying them through the agency of characters who had been labeled as bad. Why bad? and who determines what badness is? I do not pretend that I met and defeated the problem, but I think I gave it a tussle, in terms of what public lectures may do.

ↀ

It is not uncommon for the lecturer on such occasions as this to say that he approaches his task with a sense of his own inadequacy, and I ask your forgiveness for such a commonplace. However, in my case it is not meant as a ritual cringe, but as a statement of truth. If I had known what I was getting into when I accepted the invitation of your Provost to be this year's lecturer in this distinguished series, I would have had the common sense to decline. But you know how persuasive the Provost is, and it was only after I had accepted and set about the task of preparing my lectures that I realized that I had bitten off more than I could ever hope to chew. As I recall our conversation he put it to me like this: "Won't you come to Trinity in the autumn and talk about anything you like; the only condition is that whatever your subject may be, you should give it a mildly theological flavour." I agreed, and he said, "What do you suppose you might like to talk about?" As I had, for about five years, been busy with some writing which made me think a good deal about what Evil is, and how it works, and even where it comes from, I said, "How would it be if I talked about ideas of Evil as they appear in literature?" "Just the thing," said he, "and you'll have no difficulty in popping in a little theology here and there." Lightheartedly I agreed to pop in any amount of theology, and we turned our conversation to other things.

Now the day of reckoning has arrived, and you cannot imagine what troubles I have had in the interval. I am not going to tell you about them; other people's troubles are the dullest sort of topic. But I realized as soon as I set to work that I would have to set some limits to my subject, so I decided that I would confine it to the literature of the nineteenth and twentieth centuries. I decided that I would say nothing about poetry. As for theology, I soon recognized with horror that I did not know enough about it.

Theology, like politics, is a subject on which every human creature, male and female, has some sort of opinion. Real theologians, however, are subtle fellows who very properly scorn amateur intruders into what they call the Queen of Sciences. I know that there are theologians among you, ready to explain the difference between a Principality and a Throne, and all the intricacies of Prevenient Grace. What I say will probably seem like baby talk to them, but perhaps they will not be displeased that someone who is not professionally one of their number is nevertheless concerned about some of the problems that are their special concern.

Do I hear you say: If you don't know anything about your subject, what are you wasting our time for? But you see, I do know something about the literature of the nineteenth and twentieth centuries, and I do know something about the way in which Evil has been depicted and defined in it by writers who, like myself, are not theologians but who are seriously concerned by the problem of Evil. They look at it from a point of view which is not that of the theologians, but of the recorders, the analysts, the synthesizers of human experience. Their concern is principally to describe life, to experience human problems, and to feel deeply, though not always sympathetically, about them. They are fascinated by Evil, in the true sense of that much misused word *fascination*, and in the main they agree with Thomas Hardy that

> If way to the better there be
> It exacts a full look at the worst.

But the full look at the worst may not leave the looker able to define the principle behind what he has seen. What is Evil? Can it be conquered or avoided? Where does it come from? Why is it so often more attractive than Good? Some writers have tried to answer these questions, and it is the answers they have given that I want to discuss with you in these lectures. The answers may not satisfy theologians, because the answers are not usually expressed in terms of philosophical clarity, and they are in every case tainted, or infected, or whatever word you want to use to say that they are coloured by the intense personal feeling of the literary artist.

Nevertheless, these literary answers have satisfied, or partly satisfied, millions of people whom theology does not reach. Theology is a discipline and it must retain a scholarly calm. Literature is not a discipline, but an art, and when it is calm it is easily overlooked. It is the heated, sometimes rowdy approach of literature to the problem of Evil that is my theme.

How do I propose to approach it? In the first of these lectures I want to talk about Melodrama. That is tonight's lecture, and its title is

"The Devil's Burning Throne." A luridly dramatic title, is it not, quite in the nineteenth-century melodramatic mode? It comes from that supreme melo-dramatist Shakespeare. It is in *Measure for Measure* that he makes the Duke say

> —let the Devil
> Be sometime honoured for his burning throne.

And in the drama of the century past the Devil was given his full meed of respect, as I hope to show in a few minutes.

My second lecture, tomorrow night, is called "Phantasmagoria and Dream Grotto"; the phrase is from Carlyle, and it is also highly melo-dramatic, as was Carlyle's approach to history. Under that general heading I want to talk about the nineteenth-century novel, with a good deal of emphasis, but not exclusive emphasis, on the work of Charles Dickens.

My third lecture will be called "Gleams and Glooms." Whose phrase is that? It comes from Henry James, that great master of the ghost story and the uncanny story, and it is about ghost stories and uncanny stories I shall speak then. I offer no excuse for doing so. Ghost stories, as a *genre*, are somewhat neglected by literary critics, partly because so many of them are bad, but partly also, I think, because they tempt critics into quagmires and morasses in which critics fear to tread. The ghost story is above all things a story of feeling, and critics, for reasons we need not examine, are not particularly happy with feeling on this level. Tragedy—ah, with tragedy they are perfectly content, because you can discuss tragedy without becoming personally involved. But the ghost story is not tragedy; its light is moonlight, and there is an old belief that too much moonlight may make you mad. Critics, who prize their reason above all else, are understandably shy of it.

My final lecture is called "Thunder Without Rain"; that is T.S. Eliot's phrase. In it I shall talk about the novel of the twentieth century which seems to us so often to be rooted in the horror of life without any mitigation of whatever may be evoked of despair. Threat without blessing—that is, thunder without rain. Why are so many modern literary artists despairing? With some, of course, it is a fashionable pose. But what makes it fashionable? Why do so many readers hunger for this Dead Sea fruit? With our finest literary artists, however, it is far beyond any question of fashion: It is deep concern with the plight of man, to which there seems no solution. But I must confide to you that I am an optimist—not an idiot optimist, I hope, not a shallow-minded Pollyanna—and I think there is a solution, and in my final lecture I shall attempt to persuade you that it is an answer of a kind, though I dare not pretend that it is a complete answer.

There you are. That is what I am going to do, and I shall turn at once to the matter of Melodrama.

The word is often used now in a condescending manner, to suggest a bygone vulgar form of theatre art in which violent appeals to the emotions and sensational incidents were used to body forth a simple-minded morality. There are plenty of people—some of you may be of this class—to whom the word *melodrama* suggests a story about an innocent village maiden whose virtue is assailed by an evil squire, and who is rescued in the nick of time by her sailor-lover, whose nature is all courage, goodness, and devotion. Certainly there were melodramas of that sort, but they make up only a modest part of the whole melodramatic theatre. Similarly there are people who suppose that melodrama was always coarsely and vulgarly acted, and appealed only to humble and simple people. And there are many who cherish a few phrases from popular melodrama, such as "Once aboard the lugger, and the girl is mine!" or "Rags are royal raiment when worn for virtue's sake"; they suppose that all melodramatic writing was on that level. Consider this: Melodrama was the most powerful and widespread dramatic mode of the nineteenth century, and it included all kinds of theatre except comedies and farces. Shakespeare, as the nineteenth century knew him, was a melodramatic writer. If you had gone to *The Merchant of Venice* a century ago, you would have seen a play about the thwarting of a bloody-minded villain seeking revenge on his tormentors, and everything in the play that diverted your attention from that theme—including the whole of the lyrically comic Fifth Act—would have been omitted. So also with *Hamlet*, in which virtually everything that makes the King, the Queen, and Laertes psychologically interesting was cut, to throw into prominence the character of Hamlet, who was represented as a poetical young man, too good for the surroundings in which he found himself.

Let us not be patronizing about this approach to Shakespeare. Nowadays we see productions of A *Midsummer Night's Dream* in which extraordinary pains are taken to show that all rulers and courtiers are rotten, that all people of humble station and limited education are good, and that fairies are malicious and sometimes dirty goblins.

We see *The Merchant of Venice* performed in a style that suggests that a principal theme is the struggle for Bassanio between Portia and his homosexual friend Antonio. We see *The Merry Wives of Windsor* with a corrupt aristocrat, Falstaff, at odds with some middle-class social climbers. Every age gets the Shakespeare it wants, and if the nineteenth century seemed to want it sweet and hot, our age seems to want it sour and cold. Melodrama dominated the stage of the nineteenth century, and brought everything to a pitch of passion that was sometimes irrational: Our time, with its psychological and sociological bias, reduces whatever it can to psychology and sociology. We may say that, within certain limits, there is a correct and classical way to perform the music of Mozart or Beethoven, but we have not yet reached any agreement about a correct classical way in which to act Shakespeare and we put the stamp of our age upon him, however resistant his plays may be to that process.

The stamp of the nineteenth century was melodramatic. Emotion, the hottest and most violent that could be evoked, was what the public wanted. Why was it so?

In the nineteenth century in both Britain and the United States, hundreds of thousands of people moved from farms and villages to big cities, and changed from rural work to industrial work. These multitudes of uprooted people became aware of social inequality in a way that had not affected them before. More than that: They became aware of human inequality of the sort which is not subject to remedy by legislation and taxation in quite a new way. They found that some people were cleverer than others, more inventive and industrious than others, more adaptable than others, and—it must be said and it is relevant to our main theme—luckier than others. It was no longer a world in which

God bless the Squire and his relations
And keep us in our proper stations

was a possible prayer. It was a world of new opportunities, where a factory hand might see a man born in the same village as himself rise to extraordinary wealth and influence, and send his sons to Eton; understandably the unsuccessful man wondered what had gone wrong with the scheme of things. His strong back and biddable nature, which were all the capital he had, brought him less in town than it had in the country, and in town he had no Squire, who might be an easygoing gentleman with a kindly wife, who would feel an obligation toward him and perhaps take pity on his misfortunes, when they came.

What about this man's womenfolk? If they were lucky, they might escape factory work, and get into domestic service. And what was that? Very often it was slavery and wretchedness, psychological dwarfism and spiritual deformity. Frequently it was sexual exploitation. Maidservants in a badly conducted household were fair game for the footmen, who were great idle fellows with an inordinate opinion of themselves, of the kind made familiar to us in the writings of Thackeray. Sometimes also the girls were fair game for the sons of the household, or the master. And when a girl became pregnant, she lost her place, for who wants a pregnant housemaid, or her tedious bastard when it is born? So it was the street for her, and immediately the street became what Victorians called "the streets." It is an extraordinary fact that there were vastly more prostitutes in the great cities of the world in the nineteenth century than there are today. What then? Prostitution is not a calling which suits all those who take it up. One girl in a hundred might make a marriage of some sort; one girl in a thousand might do well at her trade; most ended up as prematurely old thieves, or prostitutes of the lowest grade, descriptively known as "tuppenny uprights"—as distinguished, one assumes, from the "grand horizontals."

The respectable female servant might marry a footman and keep a pub; that was success. Or she might shrivel in service, only one in hundreds having the luck to be settled in a good place with a kind mistress. In either case, sexual denial was obligatory.

What has this to do with melodrama? Much indeed, for the theatre was the popular entertainment of the time, filling the place now occupied by the films and television, and providing the most acceptable night out for people who might not be able to read, and to whom a supper at an oyster bar, followed by five or six hours in a popular theatre, was bliss, and spiritual refreshment, and a glimpse of the world as they wished it to be, and as perhaps they believed it really was, if only a few things could be set right.

What was it like, a night out in one of these nine nineteenth-century theatres that played so important a part in the inner life— and I must emphasize that it was the inner life that these robust entertainments nourished—of the city dwellers of that time? We know from a great amount of evidence how popular they were, and how faithful a local audience might be to a neighbourhood theatre. Because we must not think of London, let us say, in 1827, as having a "theatrical district" like the present West End. Officially the theatrical life of London was very much what it had been in 1660, when Charles II was restored to his throne, and very quickly licensed the building of two theatres, Covent Garden and Drury Lane. Until 1843 these two theatres were the only "legitimate" playhouses in London; there were others, of course, but they laboured under certain legal disadvantages: They might not present the plays of Shakespeare or indeed any of the classical repertoire, and they were officially regarded as music halls. To escape legal trouble, they had to provide some music at every performance, and the result was a series of productions of Shakespeare into which quite a lot of music was interpolated, making them for legal purposes, melodramas. For our purpose the most interesting development was that a new style of play, which combined music and drama, and was called "melodrama," came into being. At first the melodramas were performed in mime, with musical accompaniment, but very soon this gave way to a type of play in which there were plenty of songs, and a considerable amount of musical accompaniment from an orchestra which supported and heightened the dramatic impact of the plot. Any of you who have seen silent films with a musical accompaniment know how effective such drama can be. Even today, considerable numbers of filmgoers are almost unaware of the music that accompanies what they see, even though the musical scores are of a high degree of sophistication, and are sometimes music of a high order. Anybody who has seen *Scott of the Antarctic* (1948) with music by the late Vaughan Williams knows how splendidly the music enlarged the emotional quality of the film.

There were many melodrama theatres; in 1827 there were twelve of them, and by 1880 the number had grown to fifty-two. Actors who played at Covent Garden and Drury Lane were not above taking a profitable engagement at a melodrama house, several of which were across the Thames, on the Surrey side of the water. Edmund Kean often played on the Surrey side, and one of the theatres in which he did so is still in existence and some of you doubtless have visited it, for until very recently it was the home of the National Theatre. But in Kean's day it was known as the Royal Coburg, and after the accession of Queen Victoria, in 1837, it became the Royal Victoria, and subsequently the Old Vic. When you are in that beautiful old auditorium you see, despite substantial changes, what the size and general appearance of an early nineteenth-century theatre was.

What would you have seen if you had gone to the Coburg or one of the other melodrama theatres in, let us say, 1827? That would depend somewhat on your place in society; if you were poor, and sat in the Gallery, you would have been on hand not later than half past five in the evening, because the Gallery door opened between then and six o'clock. When the doors opened, you rushed in a pelting, shoving, eager mob up the stone stairs and snatched the best seats you could get in a cramped, steep gallery, equipped with hard, backless benches. The elderly and infirm were often crushed, squeezed, and pummelled unless they were so lucky as to go with young friends, who used them as battering rams in the scramble up the very long stairs. But once you were in your place, there you stayed, because if you left it unguarded somebody would snatch it. However, you had providently brought a basket with you, and throughout the long evening you refreshed yourself with bottled beer and porter, sausages and fruit, and anything else that pleased your fancy. If you were so infirm as to need a retiring room between six and midnight, you had to clamber over other people to the door, and make your way outside to a convenient alley, because the theatres made no provision for such needs.

If you were more affluent, you sat on the ground floor of the theatre, in the Pit. Competition here was not so strenuous, and you did not need to go so early, though you still sat on a backless bench. You might arrive any time up to eight o'clock, if you did not mind missing part of the entertainment. But you knew that at nine o'clock the Pit would be opened for half-price, and a horde of young men— City clerks, young lawyers, medical students, and the like—would come rushing in at that time and might jostle you uncomfortably, because they were a notoriously rude part of the audience.

If you had money, you sat in a box on a chair, because boxes surrounded the auditorium in two tiers, separating the Pit from the Gallery. You came when you pleased, and sat in comparative comfort. You left early. You were fashionably dressed, and a good deal of fan waving and flirting was usual among box-holders.

You may see what it was like in a delightful drawing by the great George Cruikshank, which is called *Pit, Boxes, and Gallery*, which was published in 1836. The Pit: solid people, not in their first youth, some with their hats on and some bare-headed. Children are to be seen, but pretty girls are few. The Boxes: lots of pretty girls, with their parents, and the kind of young men who habitually sucked the knobs of their walking sticks; there is a great show of bosom and wealth, and because cloakrooms were rare, many gentlemen are wearing their hats. It is observable that nobody in the Pit seems to be eating, but in the boxes there are what look like elegant little packets of sweets. The Gallery: Everybody wears a hat, a man who looks like a coal heaver is waving his cudgel at the stage, a woman with a black eye seems to be wooing a stolidly indifferent man, and a chimney sweep is peeling an apple and dropping the peelings into the boxes. We know from countless records that anyone in the Gallery who recognized a friend in the Pit gained his attention either by shouting or, if that failed, by spitting deftly on his hat.

If you can't find the Cruikshank drawing, you doubtless have access to an edition of Dickens that contains the original illustrations. Look in *The Old Curiosity Shop*, at the picture called "At Astley's"; it is opposite page 376 in the Penguin edition; it shows you the gallery at one of the favourite melodrama theatres of that time—which was 1840—where one of the characters in the book—the boy Kit—is giving his mother and his little brother Jacob, and his girl Barbara, and her mother, and a baby, a night at the theatre. They have been lucky and strong; they are in the front row; the two older ladies have hung their bonnets over the rail, and the baby is sucking an orange; Barbara's mother has a basket containing oranges and apples, and we know that Kit hit a man on the head with a handkerchief filled with apples as they were coming up the stairs because he was "scrowdging" his mother. Behind this happy group are women drinking porter, a man smoking a pipe, a man eating something out of his hat, and a man flourishing a cudgel. Cudgels seem to have been a common part of the dress of the humbler population.

What did they see, this happy family party? "Then the play itself! The horses which little Jacob believed from the first to be alive, and the ladies and gentlemen of whose reality he could by no means be persuaded, having never seen or heard any thing at all like them— the firing, which made Barbara wink—the forlorn lady, who made her cry—the tyrant who made her tremble—the man who sang a song with the lady's-maid and danced the chorus, who made her laugh—the pony who reared upon his hind legs when he saw the murderer, and wouldn't hear of walking on all-fours again until he was taken into custody—the clown who ventured on such familiar- ities with the military man in boots—the lady who jumped over the nine-and-twenty ribbons and came down safe on the horse's back— everything was delightful, splendid and surprising! Little Jacob applauded till his hands were sore; Kit cried 'an-kor' at the end of everything, the three-act piece included; and Barbara's mother beat her umbrella on the floor, in her ecstasies, until it was nearly worn down to the gingham."

These were long theatre evenings, for the hardy. They began with a full-length comedy, which played from six until half past seven or so; then followed the melodrama, which was the main fare of the evening; but when it was over there might be an extravaganza, or a harlequinade, or something light and fanciful with lots of music and dancing in it, and the curtain came down for the last time at about midnight. A big night out, for Kit and his party.

I find that modern students are often puzzled by the fact that so few melodramas are plays of protest—cries for the redress of wrongs. The answer to that, as to all such questions, is complex, but there is one important aspect of it that is simple: The masses in the nineteenth century did not think of themselves as masses, or mobs, or unions, or pressure groups, but as individuals. Melodramas are about individuals—single people who suffer wrongs and at last either get the better of their enemies in this world, or triumph over their enemies by going to an assured reward in the next world. There are melodramas about strikes, and about mutinies in the army or navy, but the hero is always well-defined, and he is a single man; if there is any sociological assumption behind such plays, it is that if the hero triumphs, all his lesser comrades will triumph with him, but to a lesser degree. It is important also that the wrongs he suffers are not solely or even primarily economic; they are wrongs to his self-esteem. He has been unjustly deprived of his job, or his superior officer has beaten him without cause, or—and this is psychologically significant—his superior has seduced or attempted to seduce his wife or his sweetheart.

In the world of melodrama, the wife or the sweetheart is not an autonomous human being; she is very plainly a psychological appendage of the hero. She is the Vessel of his Honour, or in a term used by anthropologists, she is the External Image of His Soul. A wrong to her is the most grievous wrong he can sustain and if it is not avenged, he has lost his soul, and he is no longer a man. Absurd? I don't think so. Read your morning paper any Monday in the year, and you will probably find a report of two or three fights over the weekend, sometimes ending in murder, because somebody in this city has seduced or attempted to seduce the External Soul of somebody who cannot bear it, and behaves very much like a character in melodrama. That is to say, he takes matters into his own hands and seeks redress on the personal level.

It is this intensely personal quality of melodrama that concerns us in our discussion of Evil and the way it is represented in literary art.

The path I mean to take in discussing this theme may be familiar to some of you, and if that is so I beg your pardon for labouring matters which you may consider obvious. I must explain my grounds, because I know that there will be many of you to whom the ideas I set forth are unfamiliar, and certainly at the beginning unacceptable.

To put my initial proposal as clearly as possible, I am convinced that the essential character of much literature—poetry, the novel, and drama—is that of the dream. I have said "much literature" though I really mean "all literature," but if I say that I shall not have time to make any convincing argument as to how—for instance—the novels of E.M. Forster are dreamlike. But if you will permit me to employ some shorthand to put forward my belief, here it is:

The dream world is the area of human experience in which the Conscious Mind and the Unconscious Mind meet and the elements of the dream come from both realms in varying proportions.

Literature—poetry, novel, and drama—is a product of its creator that draws upon conscious experience and reflection, but important elements in it come from the Unconscious realm.

The reader, or the playgoer, is powerfully affected by the elements of the poem, the novel, or the play that arise from the writer's Unconscious, and anyone who is at all sensitive to literature is sensitive to this dreamlike aspect which speaks to the dreamer in himself, and the more powerful this dreamlike aspect is the more powerfully it will affect him.

The application of this way of looking at literature to drama is special, because in the theatre an audience, large or small, encounters the play at one time, and insofar as the play they encounter is a dream, they may be said to dream it together. Among primitive peoples the great dreams of the race are common property, and are thought to contain great lessons and great riches of spirit for all the tribe. The great dreams of our tribe may be said to be the epics of Homer, the Greek tragedies, the Bible, the plays of Shakespeare, the novels of Cervantes and Dickens, a mass of poetry, and much, much more. But in the theatre we dream together, and the sense of community gives special power to our dream.

You see at once the bias of my mind and my approach to literature. It is certainly not the only approach, but I think it is a fruitful approach, and particularly appropriate to a study of Ideas of Evil in Literature. Of course it is a psychological approach, and that may put some of you against it because so much that is advanced as being of psychological orientation is repugnant to you. Well, let me go on and narrow my psychological focus, perhaps with the effect of clearing the hall: I attempt to consider literature in accordance with the psychological thinking of the late Carl Gustav Jung.

Let me tell you a story which may quiet some of your misgivings. Not long before his death, which took place in 1961, a young interviewer, not very well versed in any psychological thinking and certainly not in that of Jung, gained an interview with the old Doctor, and they talked for a considerable time. At last the young man, somewhat baffled, but fascinated, said: "Dr. Jung, do you realize that we have talked for an hour, and in all that time you have not said anything that wasn't complete common sense?" Jung was celebrated for his very loud laugh, and on this occasion he almost brought down the roof. When he could speak he said, "And what had you supposed that psychology was?" Jungianism is not a system of dogma, and it is no enemy to common sense. It does, however, try to persuade common sense to venture into paths which are not commonly explored, though they are not new, and many people before Jung called attention to them.

One of these paths is the dream path. From Biblical times and doubtless before then, mankind has had a feeling that dreams have a significance, but dream interpretation was always regarded with suspicion for the excellent reason that if you tell someone your dream you put yourself, to some extent, into his hands: You have given him a secret about yourself. It was at the very beginning of this century, in 1900, that the pioneer of psychoanalysis, Sigmund Freud, published his remarkable book *The Interpretation of Dreams*, in which he attempted to give scientific relevance to the age-old, dubious art. Freudian dream interpretation has been a powerful instrument in psychoanalysis as Freud conceived it, but his method is chiefly useful in dealing with the dreams of neurotics and sometimes of psychotics. It was left to his great pupil, Jung, to take heed of the fact that most people are not neurotic or psychotic, and to look at dreams as universal human experience. And universal not simply in terms of people now living, but allied to the dreams of the past, which were dreamt by people long dead, but in their essential human experience very much like ourselves. At the risk of labouring what is already known to many of you, I must point out that both Freud and Jung were empirical in their scientific method: What they asserted they derived from experience of their patients—in Freud's case neurotic patients, but in Jung's case very frequently people in good mental health who wished to enlarge the realm of their understanding.

One of the things Jung emphasized, and you will quickly see its relevance both to melodrama and to our larger theme, was that in a dream all the elements—all the characters, including the evil ones, the terrifying monsters, and the benign spirits, and even including the landscape of the dream, or its stage setting—were aspects of the psyche of the dreamer. He was indeed an observer of his inner theatre, in which the full company of actors, the scene designer, the director, and the author were included in himself.

Now, back to melodrama. Who are the invariable characters, the people without whom a melodrama cannot be constructed? Everybody knows the answer. They are the Hero, the Heroine, the Hero's Friend (usually a comic character, but nonetheless faithful and ingenious for all that), and the Villain. There were others, of course. The Heroine is usually equipped with a Faithful Friend of her own, who is her confidante and comforter; there may be a Mysterious Stranger, who bears a fateful secret; there may be Elderly Parents, who are tyrants or perhaps pitiful and deserving victims of ill fortune. But without a Hero, a Heroine, a Friend, and a Villain you cannot have a melodrama.

Have these people dream counterparts? Indeed they have and I must describe them baldly, for we have not time to talk of the thousands of dreams, docketed and filed by analysts, in which they show their infinite variety. The Hero is the dreamer's self as he conceives of himself in his innermost heart, and in melodrama he is the Great-

Hearted Sailor, or Soldier, the Wronged Sufferer, the man at the very centre of his life drama. The Heroine is the figure sometimes called in medieval morality plays Lady Soul, and she is the treasure protected by the Hero and threatened by external forces. The Friend is, quite simply, the Friend who sometimes appears in dreams as a dog or—in the case of Dick Whittington—a cat, who will befriend the Hero under all circumstances and make his interests his own. And the Villain—who is he? He looks so utterly unlike the Hero; he seeks to drag the Hero down into disgrace and even to death. He is more than merely ill luck, which has a quality of impersonality; the Villain is whole-souledly determined to destroy the Hero and destroy Lady Soul in the process. The Villain is Contrary Destiny, summing up in himself all that the Villain, and Lady Soul, and the Friend know to be hateful, inimical, and remorseless. But if our argument has any worth at all, can we doubt that the Villain is also a portion of the Hero's composition—a rejected and despised portion, a portion which is recognized in consciousness only on the rarest occasions, but a psychological fact nonetheless? The tension and fascination of melodrama lies here; the Villain is inescapable, because he is very, very near.

Of course melodramas are optimistic plays, in which the Villain is worsted. If he is not worsted, spiritually if not physically, our melodrama draws very close to tragedy.

What are the characteristics of the Villain? He is very often someone of a station and fortune above that of the Hero, and he has power in the world that seems extraordinary in anyone. Frequently he is witty and he is invariably eloquent, whereas the Hero, though often a great talker, is quick to declare himself a simple, downright chap with no rhetorical airs about him. The Villain is a thoroughgoing crook, who sticks at nothing to gain his ends. His ends are dishonourable, but almost always productive of pleasure—he covets the fortune, he lusts after the body of Lady Soul, and he eats and drinks uncommonly well: He is, if we permit ourselves a flying psychological leap—the Hero with the lid off. He is what the Hero would be if the Hero were not one of Nature's Noblemen, heavily laden with principle, greatness of heart, and—yes, it must be said—an invincible self-esteem. But as he appears in the play, he is Evil Incarnate.

To talk to you about melodrama without giving some examples of melodramatic rhetoric would be inexcusable, for it is by rhetoric that melodrama lives. But the subject demands a lecture to itself, and I can do no more than hint at the power of language that distinguishes the best of these plays. Very often the drama of the nineteenth century is condemned as of no literary value. That is not quite true. It is rarely poetic, and it is rarely philosophical, but it is vivid and racy and memorable. Those of us whose parents were born before the First World War may recall them as quoting often from melodramas, usually with humorous intent. But who quotes from a modern play, humorously or otherwise? I recall elders who, in moments of stress— not extreme stress, but when, for instance, the car broke down— would utter that poignant cry of William Danvers from *The Silver King*—"Oh, God! put back Thy Universe, and give me Yesterday!" But example is worth any amount of description. Listen to this brief scene from *Black-Eyed Susan*, one of the most popular of melodramas. The sailor hero, William, has returned from a voyage, and his dear wife Susan has not greeted him. He hails a former friend, a countryman named Ploughshare, who says

PLOUGHSHARE: What—William! William that married Susan!
WILLIAM: Avast there! hang it—that name, spoke by another, has brought the salt water up; I can feel one tear standing in either eye, like a marine at each gangway; but come, let's send them below. (*Wipes his eyes.*) Now, don't pay away your line till I pipe. I have been three years at sea; all that time I have heard but once from Susan—she has been to me a mainstay in all weathers. I have been piped up, roused from my hammock, dreaming of her—for the cold black middle watch. I have walked the deck, the surf beating in my face, but Susan was at my side, and I did not feel it. I have been reeling on the yards, in cold and darkness, when I could hardly see the hand of my next messmate—but Susan's eyes were on me, and there was light. I have heard the boatswain pipe to quarters—a voice in my heart whispered "Susan" and I strode like a lion. The first broadside was given—shipmates whose words were hardly off their lips, lay torn and mangled about me—their groans were in my ears, and their blood hot on my face—I whispered "Susan." It was

a word that seemed to turn the balls aside, and keep me safe. When land was cried at the mast-head, I seized the glass—my shipmates saw England—I, I could see but Susan! I leap upon the beach; my shipmates find hands to grasp and lips to press—I find not Susan's.

Ploughshare breaks it to this loving sailor that Susan is in great trouble, because her cruel landlord, who is also her uncle, has driven her from her cottage. William cries:

I see it! Damn it, I'll overhaul him—I'll bring him on his beam ends. Heave a-head shipmate! Now for my dear Susan, and no quarter for her uncle.

But worse than financial trouble afflicts Susan. William's superior officer, Captain Crosstree, has cast a roving eye on her, and he says

The wife of a sailor! wife of a common seaman! why, she's fit for an admiral. I know it is wrong, but I will see her—and come what may I must and will possess her.

Of course not all melodrama dealt with humble life, and not every Hero was a lover. So restricted a drama would not have drawn audiences that included many people of middle age, of education and position in the world. What they wanted were plays about an idealized version of themselves. One of the most successful in this realm was Edward Bulwer-Lytton's *Richelieu*, which first appeared in 1839, and held the stage for ninety years. It is a romantic piece about the great Cardinal and the courtiers who plot against him; one of their schemes is to secure his beautiful niece as a mistress of the King. Is there anyone here, except myself, I wonder, who suffered as a youth from hearing his elders quote these words at him:

In the lexicon of youth, which Fate reserves
For a bright manhood, there is no such word
As—FAIL.

That was from Richelieu, spoken to his adoring Page, François. It was this same François who, at a critical moment, brings the Cardinal his sword, which he can no longer wield, and the old man says:

You see, a child could
Slay Richelieu now.

The admiring youth says:

But now, at your command
Are other weapons, my good Lord.

Richelieu replies—picking up his pen—

True, this!
Beneath the rule of men entirely great
The pen is mightier than the sword. Behold
The arch-enchanter's wand: itself a nothing,
But taking sorcery from the master-hand
To paralyse the Caesars—and to strike
The loud earth breathless! Take away the sword,
States can be saved without it.

Now that is good stage rhetoric, and our great-grandfathers responded to it, just as they did to Richelieu's final words, as the play ends:

No—let us own it—there is One above who
Sways the harmonious mystery of the world
Ev'n better than prime ministers!

What about Villains? Let me quote to you a speech by a favourite Villain of mine from *The Vampire, or the Bride of the Isles;* the date is 1820. The speaker appears to the other characters in the play to be the noble Ruthven, Earl of Marsden, but we know that he is also a Vampire, and that he is going to take some very disagreeable freedoms with his fiancée, Lady Margaret, who is daughter of Ronald, the Baron of the Isles. Ruthven explains himself thus:

Demon as I am, that walk the earth to slaughter and devour, the little of heart that remains within this wizard frame, sustained alone by human blood, shrinks from the appalling act of planting misery in the bosom of this veteran chieftain. Still must the fearful sacrifice be made, and suddenly, for the approaching night

will find my wretched frame exhausted, and darkness, worse than death, anni-
hilation is my lot! Margaret, unhappy maid, thou art my destined prey! Thy
blood must feed a Vampire's life, and prove the food of his disgusting banquet.

You see that Ruthven is in the grip of Remorse, an ailment from which
Villains occasionally suffer, but from which they always make a quick
recovery.

Villains enjoyed a very special sort of popularity, because in spite
of their detestable morals a great part of every audience felt a sneaking sympathy and measure of envy toward them—because they spoke
what was, for every decent person, the unspeakable, and almost
managed to achieve the unthinkable.

Have we solved our problem, then? Is Evil no more than uninhib-
ited, self-seeking Man? No, that answer will not do because the world
of melodrama, though a large and vivid world, is still too limited to
serve as a mirror of life in general, or even of a sufficiently large part
of life. Melodrama is a form of art in which the Hero—that is to say,
every observer of the play—stands right in the middle of the action
and everything relates to him; melodrama casts a wide net, and tells
us something that is relevant to our study of the forms of Evil, but
there is much yet to be explored.

Nevertheless, melodrama offers its audiences one of the sweetest
rewards that art has to give, and that is Poetic Justice. It ministers to
that furtively acknowledged feeling in us all that we have, in some
respects at least, had a raw deal, that inferior people have triumphed
where we have been cheated, and that our true worth—our Finest
Self—has not been sufficiently appreciated. To the working classes of
the nineteenth century, and to many above that level, melodrama was,
in Isaiah's words, "as when a hungry man dreameth, and behold, he
eateth." Vicariously he received his due, he was recognized for what he
was. And indeed it is still so.

For melodrama lives, splendidly and to immense applause, on the
opera stage, and to a very great extent in ballet, as well. True, music
has supplanted language as the principal means of expression, but
melodrama is not tied to language, and music expresses emotion with
a fullness and directness that only the language of great literary artists

can rival. *Rigoletto, Pagliacci, The Flying Dutchman, La Bohème, The Magic Flute, Peter Grimes, Tosca*, all of Verdi, and a substantial portion of Wagner—this is the world of melodrama as we have it today, and who doubts its power? And in it—particularly in somewhat naive opera, like Gounod's *Faust*—we see Evil set forth as the Contrary Destiny, the Opponent, and the Villain, as one in whom "every imagination of the thoughts of his heart is only evil continually."

It may be that you wonder why I have chosen to begin this discussion of Evil in Literature with an examination of the roots of melodrama. Perhaps you are reminded of the story of the traveller in Ireland who stopped a native on a country road and asked him if he were going in the right direction for Ballyragget; "Ballyragget, is it?" said the Irishman, much amazed; "sure, if I wanted to get there I wouldn't start from here at all." But it seems to me that melodrama is a very good place to start, because it shows clearly one or two things that are less obvious in more complex literary works. First, it shows us Evil as a requirement—indeed, a necessity—for a plot that will hold our attention and provoke our concern. Without Evil there is no tension, and without tension there is no drama. One of the things that makes the usual descriptions of Heaven so repulsive is that it is shown as a place utterly wanting in tension. Similarly, Hell is unbearable to contemplate because it is imagined as a place of unrelenting and agonizing tension. Our conception of human life is of a varying degree of tension between opposites. In melodrama this tension of opposites is displayed in a manner that is simplified, but not therefore falsified. In its simplified form it is a reflection, not of the surface of life, but of its underlying structure, and thus it satisfies us as a form of art. And thus, also, it resembles our dreams—those dreams that arise from a realm within us not otherwise attainable, and understandable only from these symbolic messages. The modern forms of melodrama of which I have spoken—ballet and opera—are nearer to dreams than to photographic realism.

If these works of art are essentially dreams, whose Evil is this? It is our own. But is it all the Evil that exists? Is Evil entirely subjective? Has it no external reality? That is a question we must examine in the lectures that follow.

15

Phantasmagoria and Dream Grotto

The transition from our subject of last night—the melodrama theatre of the nineteenth century—to our theme for this evening—the novel in the nineteenth century—is by no means a complex or difficult one. It is the manner of the novel, rather than its matter, which is unlike the nineteenth-century play. The drama was so wanting in the qualities that literary critics value that it presented criticism then, and presents it still, with a state of affairs that critics find deeply disturbing: The drama of the nineteenth century was naked proof that drama is not necessarily a branch of literature, and that a vivid and satisfying drama and a lively theatre can exist almost without literary values.

Only literary critics, however, would be either surprised or disquieted. When we look at the long history of human culture we find that three elements are of great antiquity; they are Prophecy, the Epic, and Drama. Although language is the medium in which they express themselves, and sometimes express themselves magnificently, the subtlety of what we generally call literature is not necessary to them. Of the three, Prophecy and the Epic are somewhat in eclipse at present, but Drama has flourished for several centuries and flourishes still, and it undeniably flourished in the nineteenth century. I suggested that much of its strength lies in its quality of dreamlikeness; a drama is a dream which we dream as one of a group. The Novel, which reached great peaks of achievement in the nineteenth century, has dreamlike qualities as well, but as we encounter it alone, and interpret it much more personally than we interpret a play, it partakes more powerfully of purely literary qualities and appeals in a different way. I will not suggest that it is a better way, for any such judgment is so hedged around by exceptions and qualifications that it is really valueless.

What lies behind the Novel and the Drama, however, is somebody's desire to impart feeling and a measure of thought that is of great importance to him. The novel may be a medium for thought, and be valued chiefly for that reason, but woe betide the play which relies on thought before all else. When too much is said, and too little is done, a play will not last long. It was this plain fact that made *Hamlet* and *Othello* great favourites with nineteenth-century audiences, who thought of them as melodramas, and were unconcerned with the fact that they are also great poems. Whereas Byron's *Marino Faliero*—the only one of his plays to be presented in his lifetime—did not please at all, because Byron was first a poet and secondarily a dramatist. It is interesting, though not relevant to our purpose, that when he had died, and practical men of the theatre had hacked and reshaped his plays, he had a lively, posthumous theatre success. Byron, however, would not have liked what happened to such a play, for instance, as his *Werner*, when Macready had made it acceptable to a nineteenth-century public. Indeed, I should not be surprised to see Byron have a new life as a playwright in our own day, for theatre audiences have changed greatly in their character; the people who simply want action and sensation now go to the films and the television for it; not very long ago Byron's play *Cain*, which I personally admire very much, and think a splendid melodrama of the soul, had a strikingly successful production, in the most modern manner, in Switzerland. Perhaps Byron the dramatist was ahead of his time.

In talking about the nineteenth-century novel I shall have a good deal to say about Charles Dickens, because he suits my theme, and I have spent much time over many years reading his books, and reading them again, and thinking about them. One of the things that has worked against Dickens's reputation, until recent years, is that he is so easily and immediately comprehensible, on a simple level. We have all met those people who make no pretension to literary taste but who like "a good read" and who exult, somewhat embarrassingly, over

Dickens. I say their enthusiasm is embarrassing, because the things they like about him are so obvious and reveal so slight a depth of penetration.

They seem to care so little for his plots, and are so sentimental about his characters; they repeat over and over the assertion (which is open to debate) that he was a great social reformer, and that he loved the common people; what he actually said, or implied, about society and people generally, they have missed. But oh! how they exult in his inordinate and grotesque characterization! They do not examine or discuss; they simply name names. "Mrs. Gamp!" they cry, and look at you with a gloating enthusiasm which invites you to join them in a huge laugh about Sairey Gamp. Of course Mrs. Gamp is a very great comic creation, but she is also a criticism of society, and of humanity which, if you think about her, makes your flesh creep. Or they go into ecstasy about Mr. Pickwick, regardless of the fact that for the greater part of a very long book Mr. Pickwick is a fool who, like another great creation, Bertie Wooster, is saved from disaster by his valet, who is a cheerful cynic. Pickwick is endearing, as so many fools are, but he is also an acidulated portrait of what a private fortune, linked with intellectual pretension, may do to a man. These sentimentalists love the Dickensian villains; Uriah Heep and Fagin are as dear to them as the obviously good people, though Dickens makes it clear to any careful reader that Heeps and Fagins are caterpillars of society.

Much of this unthinking enthusiasm arises from the fact that its possessors have read some Dickens when they were very young, and have understood him as very young people may. But it has long been a contention of mine that if you truly value a book you should read it when you are the age the author was when he wrote it. If he is a great author you may well read him again at a much later time. I am older now than Dickens was when he died, and I am still reading his novels, and still find in them things I missed the first few times, and things that no very young reader could possibly hope to comprehend.

It is characteristic of the people who speak of Dickens with unthinking adoration that they do not like his later books as well as his earlier ones, and may not really have read them at all. I have, in my lifetime, had the disappointing experience of addressing several

Dickens societies, and have done so assuming that the members had at least read all of his major works. This was naive of me. They had read little and that poorly. But although I may be naive in my tendency to overestimate the extent of other people's reading, and the acuity of their comprehension, I can learn something when it is thrust right under my nose. And what I learned from these Dickens enthusiasts was of value; I discerned that it was not Dickens's books they loved, but Dickens's World as it appeared to them, and that one of the characteristics that makes Charles Dickens a great writer—a writer perhaps second only to Shakespeare in English—is that he brought forth from within himself a world complete in itself, into which other people can penetrate—even if they do not venture very far—and which seems as real as the world of everyday, and in some respects vastly more attractive. How many writers can do that?

There are several, and I cannot hope to give you anything approaching a complete list, because there are vast tracts of literature that are unknown to me. (Let me say, parenthetically, that I was once naive enough to believe those people who give the impression that they have read everything; they haven't, and they are faking, sometimes very cleverly, but faking nonetheless.) But who are the writers who have created worlds of their own, with laws that seem to apply to their own characters in ways that are improbable in real life, and weather, and architecture, and turns of fate that are supreme within their books, but not applicable elsewhere? Tolstoy was such a writer. Dostoevsky, who declared himself to be Dickens's pupil, and who wrote what he thought were Dickensian novels, but aren't, was such a writer. Marcel Proust was one of this special category of great novelists. It is a small and awe-inspiring group to which many writers of extraordinary powers do not belong. There are borderline cases, some of whom are favourites of mine. One among them is Anthony Trollope, who has certainly never yet received his full due, although he attracts many admirers. The people who love Trollope because he seems so calm, so much at ease in Zion in the world of Victorian politics and the Victorian church, are usually people who have read the Palliser novels or the Barchester novels, in search of a special quality of well-bred nullity, relieved by intrigue. That is all they seek and all they find. A very popular writer of our time, Mrs. Angela Thirkell, based a substantial reputation on her development of this tiny corner of Trollope, slightly enlivened with some of the lime juice of her own personality. But Trollope the stern judge of society, who wrote *The Way We Live Now*, and *The Eustace Diamonds*, and *Orley Farm*, has eluded such readers, and the world we find in these and several others among his great output, is the Victorian world with its skin off, and the Trollopian world is a disquieting place, when you really explore it. I never cease to be surprised that Victorian fathers and the fussy Puritans who controlled Victorian circulating libraries allowed Trollope to fall into the hands of innocent young women; a girl with her head screwed on straight could learn more about the kid-glove evil of the world—about selfishness, money madness, sexual manipulation, and cold-hearted social climbing—from Trollope than from any other Victorian, and it was all presented with a manner which seemed to say: This is how it is; what do you make of it? There is extraordinary understanding of Evil in Trollope.

The Evil, however, is presented in a manner that robs it of much of its sting. All the Seven Deadly Sins are paraded in this long series of novels, and they are all condemned. Condemned not as a moralist condemns, but as an artist condemns. But Trollope's kingdom is unquestionably a Kingdom of This World. If his people are evil, they either get away with it or they don't; their lives may be blighted by it, but they are frequently so worldly and stupid that the life they get is as good as any they can conceive. They know no sanction but the sanction of man. It is an irreligious world.

Trollope irreligious, you may say? How then, did he write so much about churchmen? Read him and see. His churchmen are not bad men, and one assumes that they are not irreligious men, but religion is not the first concern of their lives: personal ambition, or learning, or politics, or society are the affairs to which we see them giving their best efforts. Do they ever pray? Oh, indeed, they do. In my opinion the finest chapter Trollope ever wrote is the first of *Barchester Towers*. The Bishop of Barchester is dying; his son, the archdeacon, sits by his bedside and reflects that if the death comes before the fall of the ministry in London he himself is likely to be the new bishop, because he is of the right political party. Time presses. Does he wish his father dead? Ashamed of himself, he kneels by the old man's bedside and prays: prays that his father may live? No, he prays that his own sins may be forgiven. Then his father does die. What does Trollope say?

The archdeacon's mind had already travelled from the death chamber to the closet of the prime minister. He had brought himself to pray for his father's life, but now that that life was done, minutes were too precious to be lost. It was now useless to dally with the fact of the bishop's death—useless to lose perhaps everything for pretence of a foolish sentiment.

This is the perfection of a certain sort of novelist's art. Did you observe that the archdeacon prayed for forgiveness for his contemplation of his father's death; nowhere are we told that he prayed for the continuance of his father's life; yet when his father was dead, that was what he remembered himself as doing. Do we judge him severely? I can imagine a young reader doing so, and setting down Archdeacon Grantly as a hypocrite. But would any reader over thirty-five be able to do so?

Why do I say that Trollope is irreligious? I use the word in a particular sense: I mean that his people live in the light of this world, and do not refer their actions to any judgment that is not that of the law or their Victorian society.

What then do I mean by a religious novelist? Somebody who writes as if his characters were responsible to law and society but, *above all else*, to a divine ruling power, and were in danger also of falling under the sway of the constant and implacable enemy of that power. In short, a novelist who is conscious of God and the Devil.

Such an attitude is capable of producing the greatest art, and also the most trashy, sentimental, and tendentious art. To make things easier, let us look at painting; religious belief can produce Van Eyck's *Adoration of the Lamb* and the ceiling of the Sistine Chapel, and it can also produce all the silly statues and crude pictures of the Sacred Heart and of Guardian Angels that one sees in the *bondieuserie* shops. In the novel it may give you *War and Peace* or *The Brothers Karamazov*, or *Uncle Tom's Cabin* or *Oliver Twist*, or whole libraries of pious rubbish. It may give you a book for boys like Dean Farrar's *Eric*, or *Little by Little*, the name of which always raises a laugh, especially from people who have not read it; but I read it last year, and it is a book of considerable power with a highly developed idea of Evil as part of the machinery behind it.

What a religious attitude will not give you is a shrewd, worldly-wise novel by Trollope or Thackeray. Do not for an instant suppose that I underrate their art. It is the restriction on their range of feeling and apprehension I refer to. Where will you find the art of the novelist so brilliantly employed as in the final words of Chapter 32 of *Vanity Fair*; it is the chapter that refers to the Battle of Waterloo, at which, Thackeray tells us, both nations served "the Devil's code of honour." This is how it ends:

No more firing was heard at Brussels—the pursuit rolled miles away. Darkness came on the field and city; and Amelia was praying for George, who was lying on his face, dead, with a bullet through his heart.

Pathetic? Yes. Moving? Yes. The work of a novelist deeply imbued with religious feeling? No. Thackeray has made us too much aware that he thinks Amelia a charming simpleton, and George a commonplace, vain young man for us to feel anything other than the compassion that human folly and human limitation call forth. That is a noble feeling, certainly, but it is a cool feeling—as cool as, for instance, Thackeray's depiction in the same great novel of his villain, Lord Steyne, who is not a villain at all, but merely a man of privilege and wealth, who does not see why he should not have anything money can buy—including other men's wives. Thackeray is often called a cynic; if he was one, he was a cynic with a very tender heart. But a religious novelist he was not.

The novelists whose Kingdom is of This World may be artists of subtlety and depth of perception, and they often touch our hearts (if I may be permitted to speak of such an indecency to a modern audience). But they do not sound the deepest or the highest strings. Those are reserved for the writers whose own gamut of feeling extends both above and below the Kingdom of This World.

A subtle and profound artist in the greater realm—yet for all that not the subtlest or most profound—is George Eliot. She brings her people and her themes under the sway of a divine ruling power and its opposite, though she is a good deal weaker on the Devil than she is on God. This makes her curiously modern, and of late years her reputation has soared immensely. Now, as I told you when we began these lectures, I am no theologian, and I do not know how to put my beliefs about these things into theological or philosophical terms. So let me say crudely that I do not believe very much in the God of somebody who hasn't a first-class Devil as well. We have all seen during the past fifty years what happens to God when you try to pretend there is no Devil; God develops rheumatoid arthritis and senile dementia and rumours of his death are heard everywhere, including some of the very advanced church groups. Justice is vitiated by compassion, and compassion melts into a sticky sentimentality. And as the invitations are being issued to God's funeral, the Devil is laughing so hard that he can hardly cope with his extraordinary flow of business.

Am I a vile Nestorian? Am I a hateful Manichee? It seems very likely. But let me assure you that I became so by reading English and other literatures, and trying to make up my mind which works of art within them were of the highest quality. Art, I am utterly convinced, is one of the principal roads by which we find our way to such knowledge of this world and the Universe to which it belongs as may be possible to us. If art makes me a Nestorian, a Manichee, a dualist, and probably a Gnostic—so be it. I shall present myself in the world to come carrying those credit cards, and will have to take whatever accommodation is coming to me.

Let us look for a few minutes at what is probably George Eliot's best-known novel, *The Mill on the Floss*. What is it about? In a sense it is about the love of a brother and a sister which ends with the death of both. It is set in the English countryside, and the village of St. Ogg's, where it takes place, has usually been identified as Gainsborough, in Lincolnshire, so that the Floss must be the river Trent. The period is the first thirty years of the nineteenth century. What kind of place was it? The author tells us:

Observing these people narrowly, even when the iron hand of misfortune has shaken them from their unquestioning hold on the world, one sees little trace of religion, still less of a distinctively Christian creed. Their belief in the Unseen, so far as it manifests itself at all, seems to be rather of a pagan kind.

Yet conventional Christianity is as much a part of their accepted world as the weather, and the author tells us we should not be surprised when Tulliver the Miller, having suffered a terrible wrong from his enemy, Lawyer Wakem, records his curse and his wish that evil may befall him on the fly-leaf of his Bible. We are assured by the author, "Mr. Tulliver did not want spiritual consolation—he wanted to shake off the degradation of debt, and to have his revenge." Revenge is certainly unchristian but it is not unhuman; the Devil is very fond of it, and has coated it in an undeniable sweetness.

Evil, as it exists in this story, is shown as want of human kindness, of having succumbed to the heartlessness of a conventional provincial society and the cult of success, of *having*, of possessions. When Miller Tulliver is brought low his relatives, the Gleggs and the Pullets, are as hard as nails; they cannot relinquish any of their wealth to save him from disgrace, and they are crabbed about helping his wife, sister to the women of these two families, to save the linen and china on which she sets great store. With this slavery to possessions goes pride. The Miller speaks of life as a ladder and assures his son that you'll maybe see the day when Wakem and his son'll be a round or two below you." Tom Tulliver, the hero, is described as "proud as Lucifer"; he is untouched by religion, and his education, which his father was determined he should have, is worthless. What does the author say? "Tom, like every one of us, was imprisoned within the limits of his own nature, and his education had simply glided over him, leaving a slight deposit of polish." And so, when Tom thinks his sister Maggie has run off with a man to whom she is not married he has no kindly thought toward her at all. We are told, "Would the news be that she was married—or what? Probably that she was not married: Tom's mind was set to the expectation of the worst that could happen—not death, but disgrace."

This is certainly a world where the Devil is at work. George Eliot mentions him. When Maggie is a child one of the books she reads is Daniel Defoe's *History of the Devil*; her father bought it in a job lot at a sale. Maggie explains to a guest: "the devil takes the shape of wicked men, and walks about and sets people doing wicked things, and he's oftener in the shape of a bad man than any other because, you know, if people saw he was the devil, and he roared at 'em, they'd run away, and he couldn't make 'em do what he pleased." But when Maggie meets the Devil, he has taken the pallid disguise of a heartless woman- izer, and rather a fool. Her real Devil, I suspect, is her brother Tom. Surprising, but then, as Miller Tulliver says, "this is a puzzling world, and Old Harry's got a finger in it."

The world in which these people live is not an evil world; there is a great deal of conventional probity and sense of business honour. But it is a mean world, where people rarely lift their heads above provin- cial concerns. Maggie Tulliver does so, and much of her unhappy fate has its origin in her impulse to go beyond what is permitted by the society to which she belongs. Little people, little concerns, paganism without any of the freedom which sentimental people think goes with paganism; this is a world where almost everyone ignores the beauty of nature which surrounds St. Ogg's and gives it whatever dignity it possesses.

But it most decidedly is not a world in which everyone is without feeling. Maggie Tulliver is dominated by feeling; we can see how she comes by it, for her father is a man of deep passion, even though the outlet of that passion is restricted; her pudding of a mother feels little and understands less. George Eliot is particularly adept at drawing portraits of female fools and she has small pity for them. The fact that Mrs. Tulliver had once been a pretty, desirable girl cuts no ice with this writer, as it might do with a male author. A fool is a fool is a fool, and George Eliot is one of the writers in English who, though without rancour, never forgets it.

The edition of *The Mill on the Floss* which is most generally avail- able to students is that which has an introduction by Walter Allen. Everything he says demands respect, but I cannot myself agree with his notion that at the end of the book Maggie has "refused sexual passion." Maggie dies when she and her brother Tom are swept away in a flood on the Floss, and drown locked in each other's arms. It seems to me that this is the direction in which Maggie has been heading since the beginning of the book, and this is a love death. Tom is her strongest attachment. I do not imply any trivial incestuous element in the novel; incest is, after all, a form of love, and it may therefore be noble or ignoble. It need not be the sort of thing that gets simple and usually rather stupid people into the police courts. Maggie has sought sexual fulfillment with two men, neither of whom was the right man for her, because there was only one right man in her life, and it was her brother Tom. Tom, unhappily, is a selfish egotist who takes Maggie for granted, as a responsibility, a chattel. Her death with him, when they are symbolically overwhelmed by the river which has been one of the dominant elements in their lives, is, I think, meant to be a happy ending, though it is not happiness as conventional and sentimental novels provide it. Not happiness, perhaps, but fulfillment, is what we find here, and fulfillment may be vastly greater, and less obviously pleasurable, than happiness.

Mr. Allen does not think so. He writes of "the distressing sentimentality of the last paragraphs of the novel." I don't agree. Sentimentality is a flaw in a work of art, certainly, but the word is often thrown at great and overpowering works of art that embarrass critics who live, emotionally, in St. Ogg's, though intellectually they have journeyed south as far as Cambridge. The ending of *The Mill on the Floss* moves me to tears, though I am not an easy weeper. It is not the immediate pathos of the death of Maggie and Tom that thus affects me: It is rather that a genuine completion of a human involvement has been attained, but attained only through Death. A happiness beyond mere delight has been experienced—a happiness as blasting and destroying as an encounter with the gods.

To my mind, this is anything but sentimental. People who prate of sentimentality are very often people who hate being made to feel, and who hate anything that cannot be intellectually manipulated. But the purgation through pity and terror which is said to be the effect of tragedy is not the only kind of purgation that art can bring. The tempest in the heart that great novels can evoke is rarely tragic in the strict sense, but it is an arousal of feelings of wonder at the strangeness of life, and desolation at the implacability of life, and dread of the capriciousness of life which for a few minutes overwhelms all our calculations and certainties and leaves us naked in a turmoil from which cleverness cannot save us. Sentimentality is sometimes used by critics as a term to rebuke artists who seek to sound this terrifying note; if the artist fails, he is probably merely sentimental, but if he succeeds, the critic would be wise to slink back into his kennel and whimper till the storm passes. The critic knows that something great has been attempted, and that the chaos it brings is deeply disturbing to the heart. If it is a St. Ogg's heart—and St. Ogg's is a very large parish indeed—the critic will mock and rebuke.

No great novelist has been so bethumped with mockery and rebuke for his sentimentality as Charles Dickens. And of course he was often sentimental, because that is what sentiment becomes when it is pumped up, and does not arise naturally from a situation. Now I fully agree with the critical dictum that a man should be judged on his best work, rather than on his lesser achievements, and if I were to follow that path I should talk to you about *Great Expectations*, *Bleak House*, and *Our Mutual Friend*—the creations of Dickens's artistic maturity. But because I am talking to you about Evil as it asserts itself in books I shall talk instead about two of Dickens's novels that are most often reproached with sentimentality—*Oliver Twist* and *The Old Curiosity Shop*. Have you read them recently? I have—or rather I have not long ago completed the most recent of several rereadings. In them the barometer needle waggles distractingly between Sentiment and Sentimentality. But they are also written in the clear light of heaven and the lurid light of hell, and are therefore much to our purpose. Let us take a look at them.

First, however, let me speak once again about the structure of these lectures. Are you wondering why I gave one of our hours, last night, to a consideration of melodrama? I said, did I not, that melodrama was the prevailing weather of art during the nineteenth century, and attempted to persuade you that the melodramatic way of life is a good and a revealing way—just as good and revealing as the gifts of the artist who employs it. In the theatre the artists were not very good, but they met the needs of playgoers, not all of whom were critically sophisticated. In the novel, the artists were some of the best who have ever written in English. One of them of whom we have just spoken,

George Eliot, is rarely called melodramatic, because the word is still so often tinged with contempt, but *The Mill on the Floss* in my opinion is highly melodramatic; if you agree with me that melodrama may well mean a way of dealing with artistic material that reveals the wonder and caprice of life, as well as its undeniable tragedy, you will agree with me about that book. Melodrama is art in which not an implacable and malign Fate dominates the life of man, but art in which Good and Evil contend, and in which the dividing line between Good and Evil may often be blurred, and in which Good may often be the winner.

Did I say that in melodrama the Humble Friend is a character to be reckoned with, and that the Humble Friend may often be an animal, as it often is in fairy tale? In *The Mill on the Floss* there are three of these animal friends, and I have never seen any comment on them by a critic. One is Maggie's dog, Yap, who is all that Maggie is herself, but with the freedom of an animal. Devoted, emotional, sadly undisciplined, Yap is very much Maggie's dog. Then consider the dog who is the pet of the girl who is the belle of St. Ogg's, Lucy Deane; this is Minny, a lap spaniel in poorish health because it eats too many sweets, a sensitive, cosseted creature and a perfect fool like its mistress. It is of interest that Maggie's dog is a male, and thus very different from that of Minny, who is very much a female—a silly bitch. And lastly there is Bob Jakin's dog, Mumps, a clever common dog who is full of animal sagacity; his master says of him, "Lors, it's a fine thing to hev a dumb brute fond on you; it'll stick to you, and make no jaw." Bob tells Mumps to be a friend to Maggie, and Mumps does his best, but he comes too late.

Dickens was far too astute a melodramatist to neglect the Animal Friend and *Oliver Twist* shows us a splendid example of the kind in Bill Sykes's dog. This was "a white, shaggy dog, with his face scratched and torn in twenty different places," a skulking dog which his master kicks so savagely that it is driven right across the room. What are we to make of this creature? Except for the harlot Nancy, it is the only creature in the world that is attached to Sykes. But Sykes is a character familiar in melodrama, and perhaps some of us have met him in daily life: He is the Damned Man, bent on his own destruction. In the end he murders Nancy in a scene of terrible brutality, and then he is on the run. Because everybody knows that Bill Sykes is always accompanied by a white dog, disguise is impossible, so he determines to kill the dog—determines, so to say, to be rid of the last redeeming bit of good that is in him. The dog won't stay to be killed; it runs away. But it comes back again; it cannot bear to be without Sykes, so it searches all the places in which he might hide until it comes to the foul thieves' hangout on Jacob's Island. When at last Sykes tries to escape by leaping from the roof, and is hanged in his own rope, the dog leaps to join him, and is dashed to death in the stony ditch beneath.

There is melodrama indeed! In all of Dickens the conflict of Good and Evil is presented vividly, and for some readers, too vividly. Their taste is too refined for these naked, hair-raising expositions of Nestorian dualism: or, to put it another way, they lack stomach for the gaudier aspects of the Eternal Struggle. But Bill Sykes is by no means the most shocking depiction of Evil in *Oliver Twist*. That, surely, is Fagin, the receiver of stolen goods and the corrupter of children. Of late it has become a fashion in the criticism of Dickens to seek for evidence of homosexual elements in the relation of Fagin to his crew of pickpockets. Is it important? Only if you think that sexual corruption is the worst sort of corruption. I stick to the opinion that what Fagin manifestly does is the worst that such a creature could do: He makes evil appear to be good, and throws over it such a mantle of humorous charm, and makes himself appear to be such a gentle, unworldly, genial old soul, that Oliver becomes a thief to please this dear old gentleman, rather than through any brutal compulsion. Isn't that how Maggie Tulliver saw the Devil? There is a wonderful portrait of Fagin at the end of the book, when he is in the hands of the police, and clings to them as if they were his friends, because if they once divert their attention from him, the angry crowd will destroy him. If you find Bill Sykes and his dog crude melodramatic workmanship, what do you make of this splendid depiction of the ambiguity of Evil, which we find in Fagin?

How well did Dickens understand Evil? He was fascinated by it all his life and when we read of his visits to wretched slums and thieves' dens, as a guest of the police in the days of his fame, we must also bear

in mind the child who lived alone in London when his parents were imprisoned in the Marshalsea for debt. We must remember the boy in the blacking factory, employed in pasting labels on packets of shoe polish. This time in Dickens's life was so horrible to him that it was many years before he could confide the secret of it even to his closest friends. Some people think this was because of shame that he, the famous, feted author, should once have been so low in the social scale. I think better of Dickens than that. I think it was because what he saw then, with the clear eyes of a child, was so horrible that it burned itself forever into his nature, and he could not be rid of it, except through the art that was his. Human degradation: yes. Ignorance and Want: You recall how the Spirit of Christmas Present shows these to Scrooge, in the guise of two horrible children, in whom the terror of the future is implicit. But also Crime, and Dickens is not one of those who tells us that Crime arises only from Ignorance and Want, though they are its friends; it is an element of humanity with autonomous power of its own. It is Evil, though it is not the Whole of Evil.

Dickens explores Evil in a way that no other literary artist of anything like comparable stature does, because he contrasts constantly with Good. The Evil of Pride we find in the casual seducer Steerforth in *David Copperfield*. And in that same book we find another sort of Pride in the extraordinary character of Mrs. Gummidge, that lone, lorn creetur with whom everything went contrairy; Mrs. Gummidge seeks and embraces quite unnecessary misfortunes in order to throw herself into prominence and exploit the kindness of others. Pride is, among other things, egotism.

All of the Seven Deadly Sins are constantly on parade in Dickens. Pride is extensively dealt with, and to those I have mentioned I should like to add perhaps his masterpiece in this realm—Mr. Dombey. Envy? Lots of it, with Uriah Heep at the head of the list. Wrath? We have talked of Bill Sykes, and we think of Mr. Murdstone, whose cruelty to people for their own good is so impressively described in *David Copperfield*. Lechery? You'll find plenty of it in Uriah Heep and in Mr. Carker, in *Dombey*. (Whether Lechery, which might be defined as sexual desire untouched by affection, is still a sin or not is a matter of dispute; there are those today who prefer to call it an alternative

life-style.) Avarice? Scrooge is the obvious example, but the finest portrait of this quality in Dickens, to my mind, is that of Jonas Chuzzlewit. Sloth? Very subtly handled, in Mrs. Jellyby, whose pity is all for the unfortunate of distant lands, but she is bored by her own wretched children. And what of Harold Skimpole, that superb portrait of a particular sort of artist who thinks the world owes him a living? Gluttony? We think at once of the Fat Boy in *Pickwick*, but he is a pathological case. In what novel of Dickens's do you not find people exulting and gloating over food and drink? Think of the gourmandizing at Dingley Dell, after the Pickwickians went for that twenty-five-mile walk. Think of the pints of sherry, hot and cold, that everybody drinks apparently without feeling in the least tipsy. Think of Old Krook, the marine-stores dealer in *Bleak House*, who drinks for years until at last he bursts into flames and perishes of Spontaneous Combustion, in one of Dickens's most lurid scenes. Oh, yes; plenty of Gluttony.

Apart from these sins, so carefully defined in the Middle Ages, Dickens is superb in his depiction of a sin very prevalent in the Victorian era, and a profuse growth in modern democracies. I mean Hypocrisy. How well and in what a variety of tints he paints it! The full-length portraits, of course, are represented by Seth Pecksniff and Chadband. But how many hypocrites there are who are merely sketched, but sketched with a master hand; like Mr. Spenlow, in *Copperfield*, who was all compliance himself, but dared not take action for fear of his invisible, and perhaps even imaginary, partner, Mr. Jorkins.

All of these sins, of course, are aspects of Evil, and bring about not only obvious and palpable Evil, but also that unbounded, grey unhappiness, that arthritis of the spirit, which we might call everyday or bread-and-butter evil. How did Dickens know so much about it? Well, he was a very keen observer; but that quality alone makes a detective, not a novelist. Not only could he see what was under his nose (which only a limited number of people can do) but he could find a response to it in himself. He was, as only the greatest artists are, continually in communication with what psychiatrists call his Unconscious, and not simply his personal Unconscious, but that vast Collective Unconscious

which glues the race together. Goethe once said that he knew of no crime of which he could not imagine himself capable, and if Dickens had been as cool a customer as Goethe, he could have said the same. But Dickens was not a cool customer. He was, in fact, a ripsnorting, raging, egotistical cad, and if he had not also been a supremely great writer he would have been intolerable. What he was is the price of what he could do. Thackeray, who was also a great writer, couldn't do it because Thackeray, by birth and instinct, was a gentleman, and he always handles Evil with tongs. Dickens didn't: He lived it.

I mean that. He sweated and toiled and wept over his writing, and in his later years he killed himself by giving public readings in which the intensity of his emotion was far too great for a man already ill to sustain. His favourite reading was the Murder of Nancy, from *Oliver Twist*; it was melodramatic acting of the most extraordinary—though not the highest—kind. I say "not the highest" because acting is an art, and the actor works to excite and move his audiences, while remaining in control of himself. Otherwise a week of playing Othello or Lear might kill him. But Dickens lived his readings, and paid the terrible price. This is not imagination; his doctor begged him to drop the Murder from his repertory. But the Murder was not the only killer. Dickens's normal pulse was 72, but when he read the Death of Paul Dombey it was never below 82, and might rise above 100. On Friday, January 21, 1870, when he read the Murder, his pulse was 90 when he began, and rose to 112. On February 15 of the same year, he confided to his manager, "I shall tear myself to pieces," and when he spoke his pulse was already 90, and when he came off the stage it was 124. If this was not self-destruction, what was it? It was, among other things, an acting out of Evil that brought audiences to their feet in applause. It was a fainting era, and lots of people fainted. Dickens's reading of the Murder was a stupendous feat of making external and actual something which had existed as an artistic creation. The story of the Dickens readings—there were, in all, 444 of them—is a fascinating psychological study. But there is one aspect of them that interests me in a ghoulish fashion, and that is that Dickens never read anything from *The Old Curiosity Shop*. He never, in public, brought himself face to face with Daniel Quilp.

There will be those among you who have not read *The Old Curiosity Shop*. Students nowadays are often warned off it; it is not "essential Dickens." I say you can't know Dickens without it; it is the essence of at least a large portion of Dickens. The story is simple in outline. The proprietor of the Old Curiosity Shop is an old man named Trent, who falls a victim to gambling mania; he rationalizes his obsession by pretending that he gambles only to secure a fortune and future safety for his granddaughter, Nell. He is an unlucky gambler, and the dupe of cheats, so he is in continual need of money and borrows it from a moneylender named Quilp, a filthy, cruel, lecherous, and demonic dwarf. When ruin comes the old man and the child flee from London and wander in poverty through England, pursued by the dwarf, and also by Nell's brother, who is convinced that possession of the child will bring him the money he is sure the old man still has. At last the wanderers are taken in by a kind village schoolmaster, but Nell is exhausted by her travels and her anxiety about her grandfather, and she dies. A very good plot, apt for melodrama, which Dickens bountifully supplies.

It is the character of Little Nell that gets under the skin of those who detest the book, and in especial they resent Dickens's description of her death. His contemporaries thought it magnificent. The great actor Macready, when he read it, was too stunned to weep; Carlyle, not a notably easy audience, was overcome by it; Landor, Washington Irving, and many other people of distinguished taste thought it superb. Everybody knows the story of how a crowd assembled on the dock in New York harbour, when the monthly instalment of the story was due aboard ship, shouting across the water to know if Nelly were really dead or not. But our refined age does not like it; our generation is described by George Santayana, a brilliant critic of Dickens, as aesthetically snobbish, and desirous of "a mincing art." And indeed there may be something wrong with us; we hate to have our feelings touched.

Aldous Huxley, a notable novelist in his chosen realm, loathed *The Old Curiosity Shop* and wrote scathingly about it in his interesting but unsound essay *Vulgarity in Literature*. He shows us, in his own novel *Point Counter Point* how he thinks the death of a child may be described without vulgarity. And indeed it is very finely done. But can you recall the name of the child? If you can, did you much like the child when he was alive? He was a nice little boy, but no more. Little Nell was a very different creature, and the inspiration for her came from a very different place. Huxley's mind was broad but his spirit was not deep; he simply could not comprehend what Dickens was doing.

Little Nell was one of Dickens's earliest Good Women. There were to be many of them, and even to an enthusiast like myself they are trying. They are, in the true melodramatic style, embodied goodness. Why are the good people in books so rarely appealing? I shall try to say something about that in a later lecture. We must confine ourselves here to some consideration of Little Nell; the worst I can say of her is that I cannot imagine any man hoping that Little Nell had lived and grown up in order that he might marry her. But somebody did want Nell, not perhaps for marriage, but for sexual enjoyment of most alarmingly sadistic kind. That man was Daniel Quilp, the dwarf usurer.

Quilp had a wife, a very pretty one, who was frightened out of her wits by him. Dickens had to walk carefully in his descriptions of their married life, because the sensibilities of his age were very tender about sexual things. But we get the message, and when we read that Mrs. Quilp had to sit up all night waiting for his return, and then make his breakfast, and watch him as "he ate hard eggs, shell and all, devoured gigantic prawns with their heads and tails on, chewed tobacco and water-cresses at the same time with extraordinary greediness, drank boiling tea without winking, bit his fork and spoon till they bent again, and in short performed so many horrifying and uncommon acts that the women were nearly frightened out of their wits," we can dimly guess at the sort of thing that went on when the curtains of the connubial bed were drawn. Where, and how often, do you suppose pretty Mrs. Quilp was bitten and bruised?

All the great nineteenth-century novelists found their way around the prudery of their time, and they send us signals which we must be alert to receive. When Quilp says: "Be a good girl, Nelly, a very good girl, and see if one of these days you don't come to be Mrs. Quilp of Tower Hill," we know that he could easily get rid of Mrs. Quilp

Number One. The first Mrs. Quilp, the pretty Mrs. Quilp, might just happen to die, you see. It is like Richard III's wooing of Lady Anne beside the coffin of Henry VI. There is a scene of terror in which Quilp has seized the Old Curiosity Shop for debt, and has romped and exulted on Nell's pretty bed; and a later scene, when Nell has to creep into her old bedroom to steal a key, and finds Quilp sleeping in her bed, his head lolling upside down over the edge of the mattress, and his eyes open, but with only the yellow whites showing.

Quilp is a masterly and demonic creation. Where did he come from? Out of the depths of Charles Dickens, where every novelist's characters come from. If the waters in those depths are shallow, or heavily chlorinated, or else simply stagnant, the characters are not particularly arresting. But the imagination of Charles Dickens contained wells of very dark water indeed, and they were of a terrifying depth, lit by strange lights. It is because of them that I have attached Carlyle's phrase "Phantasmagoria and Dream Grotto" to this lecture. But if Quilp came from the depths, where did Nelly come from—"chubby, rosy, cosy little Nell," as Quilp calls her? From the same grottoes, but the light is different. We know something about Charles Dickens that throws quite a lot of light on Nell and most of his other idealized women. When he was young and impressionable, he encountered a charming family—all lucky young men encounter at least one such family—that possessed charming daughters. He married the wrong one. He married Kate. But the one he later wished he had married came to live with him and his wife, and died not long afterward. He wrote her epitaph, and here it is:

Mary Scott Hogarth
died 7th May 1837
young, beautiful and good,
God in his mercy
numbered her with his angels
at the early age of
seventeen

It is the idealized image of Mary we meet again and again in Dickens. He learned much about women, and his earliest love, Maria

Beadnell, is hilariously but rather cruelly caricatured as she appeared in middle age, in the character of Flora Finching in *Little Dorrit*. But the angelic form of Mary Hogarth never deserted him until, perhaps, he found it again in the mistress of his last years, Ellen Ternan. For Dickens a woman of the highest order was always that figure from melodrama Lady Soul.

I have never seen a criticism of *The Old Curiosity Shop* that called attention to the fact that it contains two remarkable death scenes. That of Little Nell is famous; though prolonged, I do not find it overwritten in terms of the book as a whole. It is long, and Death is sometimes long; it is pathetic, and if we do not find the death of a child pathetic, we should ask ourselves why. Oscar Wilde once said that anyone who could read of the death of Little Nell without laughing must have a heart of stone; it is a good-enough wisecrack, but it springs from that limitation of sensibility that was the flaw in Wilde's own art; Dickens gushed, but Wilde trickled, and only the most strenuous pumping could force the trickle to look like a fountain. I am surprised that Wilde did not observe the contrasted death scenes in the book to which I now direct your attention.

Quilp dies, too. He is on the run, and he takes a false step on the rotten wharf where he lives, falls into the filthy river, and is drowned. Read it. The passage is quite a short one, but it is in Dickens's finest Caravaggio style. Artistic control and emotional scope are finely linked here. Next time somebody speaks to you of the death of Little Nell, ask them if they have compared it with the death of Daniel Quilp. For linked they are: Good and Evil quit the scene very near together.

We know who Nell was. Who was Quilp? Dickens loved acting out his characters in private life, and he used to do Quilp to frighten his mother-in-law, who was not a favourite of his. He found Quilp where he found all the rest of his characters, in the strange land where his Conscious and Unconscious met and united, in the land of Phantasmagoria and Dream Grotto.

Our time is at an end. Do not go away supposing that because I have told you that in my opinion Charles Dickens drew upon his own depths of potential but unacted Evil for Quilp and the rest of his villains, I intend to fob you off with the old conclusion that Evil is simply an unredeemed portion of the human spirit or, to be even more theological, simply an absence of good, *a privatio boni*. That is not what I think at all. But to arrive at my conclusion I must next make a dive into an area not often considered by literary critics; next time I shall talk about tales of the uncanny, of ghosts, of what Henry James called Gleams and Glooms.

16

Gleams and Glooms

Some of the oldest stories we have are ghost stories; mankind never seems to tire of them. They have been neglected by critics, because critics, as we all know, are wonderfully wide-awake fellows, alert to the sources, the promptings, the mainsprings of works of literary art; they love to take the clock apart and demonstrate what makes it tick. With a ghost story we know without telling what makes it tick; it is a recognition of the supernatural—what Carlyle called "the Unseen World or the No-World"—and this source of inspiration is not readily accessible to the sort of knowledge critics usually possess. Though they deal with works of art, they approach them as rationalists, and rationalism and the supernatural are cat and dog. If we look for common sense on the matter we cannot do better than to turn to that monument of common sense, Dr. Johnson, and his words are well known. He said "It is wonderful that five thousand years have now elapsed since the creation of the world, and it is still undecided whether or not there has ever been an instance of the spirit of any person appearing after death. All argument is against it, but all belief is for it."

When Johnson discussed the matter with his friends, of course people spoke up who had seen ghosts. Cave, whom the Doctor thought "an honest man and a man of sense," had seen one. Oliver Goldsmith's brother, who was a clergyman, had seen a ghost. And it is much the same today; if the question of ghosts comes up in conversation, it must be a very dull group indeed in which somebody does not come forward with a tale, or a fragment, that seems to support the belief that there are such things as spirits of the dead which do, under appropriate circumstances, show themselves to some people, though not to everybody, and certainly not on demand. The possession of a ghost is thought to confer prestige on the owner of the house to which it belongs. For many years in my youth I lived in an old house in Kingston that had a ghost; it was of an elderly doctor who was reputed to have drowned his troublesome daughter in the bath. Several people had seen it. I confess that I was not of their number, but I knew two ladies of unimpeachable veracity who saw him—one at four o'clock in the afternoon, and because the ghost wore evening dress, she supposed him to be a servant. The other, who did not know the first lady, saw him some years later. I myself saw a ghost in that house, at a subsequent time, no less than twice in the same night, and I sat up the rest of the night because I had a very strong premonition that if I saw it a third time, it would be the worse for me. But it was not the ghost of Dr. Betts, who had such a short way with tedious daughters, and I do not propose to tell you who it was. So you see, in the dispute as to the reality of ghosts, I am not of the skeptical party, though I hope I am not foolishly credulous, either.

Nor was Shakespeare skeptical. He has given us some of the most famous ghosts in literary history. Caesar's ghost appears to Brutus. Hamlet's father appears to his son, with what is undoubtedly the commonest of ghostly messages: Revenge my death. *Macbeth* is a very great play of the supernatural, and although I have seen that play many times I have never seen it really well done, because I have never seen it directed by anyone who truly believed in the supernatural. Theatrical directors, like critics, seem unable to accept the fact that Shakespeare believed in ghosts, but I am strongly of the opinion that he did, and as I admire Shakespeare more than I admire his critics, I think he knew what he was writing about. As did Homer, and Vergil, and some writers whom I propose to discuss very soon, whose insight into life is that of creators, rather than critics. To be a creator is to be in touch, sometimes in uncomfortably close touch, with what psychiatrists call the Unconscious—and not always one's personal Unconscious, but the vast, troubled Unconscious of mankind.

Let us look at a characteristic ghost story. I take my example from the period of literature which concerns us in these lectures, the nineteenth and twentieth centuries, and from a writer who was not an artist in fiction, but a famous writer of guidebooks and biographies. His name was Augustus Hare, and his dates were 1834 to 1903; he was a well-known figure in good English society, for a time tutor to the Crown Prince of Sweden, and author of an autobiography that fills six volumes. There are many people who dislike Hare; they say he was shockingly indiscreet; that is why I like him very much. The indiscretion of yesterday is the rich feeding of today. Hare delighted in tales of ghosts and uncanny happenings, and his autobiography is full of them, and each one is attributed to somebody—usually somebody very well known—who told him the tale. I recommend his life to you as bedside reading and agreeable browsing. Here is a simple, short story from the riches he provides:

Lady Georgiana Grey told me a curious story of some friends of hers: Lady Pennyman and her daughters took a house at Lille. The day after they arrived they went to order some things from a warehouse in the town, and gave their address. "What," said the man, "are you living there, ma'am? Did I not misunderstand you?"—"Yes," said Lady Pennyman, "that is where I live. Is there anything against the place?"

"Oh dear, no, ma'am," said the warehouseman; "only the house has been for a long time without being let, because they say it's haunted." Going home, Lady Pennyman laughed to her daughters, and said, "Well, we shall see if the ghost will frighten *us* away."

But the next morning Lady Pennyman's maid came to her and said, "If you please, ma'am, Mrs. Crowder and me must change our rooms. We can't remain where we are, ma'am; it's quite impossible. The ghost, he makes such a noise over our heads, we can get no sleep at all."—"Well, you can change your rooms," said Lady Pennyman; "but what is there over your room where you sleep? I will go and see," and she found a very long gallery, quite empty except for a huge iron cage, in which it was evident some human being had been confined.

A few days after, a friend, a lady living in Lille, came to dine with them. She was a very strong-minded person, and when she heard of the servants' alarm, she said, "Oh, Lady Pennyman, do let me sleep in that room; I shall not be frightened, and if I sleep there, perhaps the ghost will be laid." So she sent away her carriage and stayed; but the next morning she came down quite pale and haggard, and said certainly she had seen the figure of a young man in a dressing-gown standing opposite her bed, and yet the door was locked, and there could have been no real person there. A few days afterward, toward evening, Lady Pennyman said to her daughter, "Bessie, just go up and fetch the shawl which I left in my room." Bessie went, and came down saying that as she went up she saw the figure of a young man in a dressing-gown standing on the flight of stairs opposite to her.

One more attempt at explanation was made. A sailor son, just come from sea, was put to sleep in the room. When he came down in the morning, he was quite angry, and said, "What did you think I was going to be up to, mother, that you had me watched? Why did you send that fellow in the dressing-gown to look after me?" The next day the Pennymans left the house.

There you have it, a classical ghost story, or a part of one, for nobody troubled to find out what the ghost wanted or why it appeared. But we can make a guess: It was by no means uncommon in the eighteenth and nineteenth centuries to lock up a troublesome relative—a madman, or a monster—in the attics. It is not so uncommon nowadays as it ought to be, as careful reading of the daily papers will assure you. The ghost obviously wanted to be given justice—to be understood. It wanted somebody to know that it had not been mad, or wholly mad, and that it had been cheated out of whatever its proper fortune in life happened to be. That is what ghosts are: They are the dead who cannot rest because their story on this earth has not been told. There is a wrong to be righted, and often what is sought is vengeance. And thus, you see, ghosts are linked with that idea of Poetic Justice which we discussed in connection with nineteenth-century melodrama; they are a manifestation of the deeply rooted notion that somehow and somewhere, every living creature should have his due, and if he cannot get it before death he may return to demand it after death.

How do ghosts fit into our discussion of forms of evil as they make their appearance in literature? Ghosts are generally regarded as evil things, or if not evil, uncanny and apt to bring ill luck to those who see them. There are a few ghost stories which attempt to offer us a benevolent ghost; I remember one in which the ghost was a mother who returned to earth to brood tearfully over the cradle of her little one. As a ghost she was a failure. It is the Senecan ghost, with its terrible cry of "Revenge!", that makes us glance over our shoulders in apprehension. We know that the Lord has claimed vengeance as His own, presumably because mankind is so ready to assume the God-like prerogative, in the name of justice. The ghost is prompting someone to an act which is contrary to religion, an act linked to the age-old yearning for poetic justice. Revengeful ghosts arouse that sneaking belief in the supernatural that lingers among people who have no use for religion. Religion may include the uncanny and the evil, but its emphasis is on the redemptive and doctrinal aspect of belief. The people who have lost religion, or who have simply grown up as religious illiterates—a very common class today—have lost their sense of the beneficent part religion plays in life, but they have not shaken off their primitive fears. They dimly guess at an area of being which is not readily approached, and which is certainly not good; this is the haunt of Evil, the Devil's Kingdom. Christianity has not for many decades paid much attention to this realm or its Dark Master. Hebraism, in its orthodox form, has not been so ready to abandon the Devil or his many agents, and in this respect I think the Jews are wiser than we. How their belief lives, and what extraordinary forms it takes, are readily and enjoyably discovered in the works of one of the greatest writers living today, Isaac Bashevis Singer, most of whose brilliant stories are available in English translations from the Yiddish.

Do I hear you say that orthodox Jews are stuck in the eighteenth century? And that we have advanced beyond their curious compound of peasant credulity and infinitely complex scholarship? If that is your belief, take a look at what the movie houses offer in this city, at any time of the year, and answer honestly what you think *Rosemary's Baby*, and *The Exorcist*, and *The Omen*, and *The Devil Within Her* are all about? They are enormously popular exercises in the age-old cheat of having your cake and eating it too. They give their audiences a faint sense of having encountered something profound, of having peeped into an abyss, of having dallied with evil, without having really been obliged to accept the reality of evil. They are poisoned sweetmeats, these films, but they satisfy a longing in the public heart for some approach to an essential human problem: What is Evil and how does it manifest itself in the world? The evil these trumpery films offer is feeble, because the people who put the films together are not sincere in what they are doing; they are a pack of Dickensian Fat Boys who want to make our flesh creep. But when there is nothing better, the hungry public appeases its appetite with what it can get.

Let us look at the history of the ghost story, and some of its ablest practitioners, during the period with which these lectures are concerned. In doing so I expect I shall mention some names that will be unfamiliar to most of you. They are the names of writers of great quality and high attainment, but not of the greatest quality or the highest attainment, and for this reason they are seldom mentioned in universities. We must not blame the universities, who are expected to teach something that looks like the body of English literature in three or four years to students who often come to the university without any substantial acquaintance with literature on any level. They have to be force-fed, like Strasbourg geese, if they are to put on any intellectual flesh at all; unfortunately, like Strasbourg geese, they often develop pathological symptoms in the process. They must hit the high spots, and gobble the best that has been thought and said as fast as they can; they have no time for lesser figures in literature. But when they have left the university, they surely have time to read for pleasure and for enlargement of the spirit; they have time to read what they like, rather than what they must. It is to be hoped that they will read some authors who are neither among the certifiably great, nor among the certifiably fashionable. Only people with no taste shun reading which is not in the highest taste; the true reader has favourites whose faults and deficiencies are obvious, but whose virtues are highly individual and uncommon.

A writer in our realm for whom the universities have some indulgence is Edgar Allan Poe, and he is often referred to as a master of the uncanny and the horrible. Indeed, he was so, but I do not think that he was as great a master as several others whose names I shall mention shortly. Poe never, so far as I know, wrote a classical ghost story, though he wrote many familiar tales of premature burial, of murder and vengeance, of terror and the macabre. He wrote them in a manner which I myself do not like; it is a style of nervous excitability that is never far from hysteria. Behind all of Poe's writing lurks a sense of grievance, of having had a raw deal, of being a lost child in a hostile world, which is amply justified by the story of his life. But though we may pity him, we do not have to like his work. The admiration that he received in France, which still persists, has done much to sustain his reputation in American literature. But is he really the wonder-worker in his realm that we are told he is? I put the question but I do not offer an answer; I content myself with asking you to compare his work with that of Mervyn Peake, a writer born in 1911 and not long dead, whose trilogy of *Titus Groan*, *Gormenghast*, and *Titus Alone* possesses qualities of sustained macabre fantasy, of poetic expression, and of sheer creative power which I do not think Poe can rival. Peake achieves the real poet's feat of creating a world with its own laws, its own nature, and even its own weather—a World in which the reader lives as he reads, and which he never forgets, and this is achievement indeed.

If you object that it is improper to compare two writers who are separated by more than a century, let me mention a contemporary of Poe's, who seems to me to be, in his best vein, fully Poe's equal. That is the Irish writer of uncanny stories, Joseph Sheridan LeFanu (1814–73). Like Poe, he was an oddity. (Indeed the writers of ghosts stories are often oddities: Poe was a neurotic, Peake a sadly afflicted invalid, and LeFanu a man whose life was darkened by a domestic tragedy of the sort we should now put in the psychoanalytic category, but which was in the nineteenth century thought to be chiefly religious.) LeFanu had flirted with the ideas of Swedenborg, whose *Caelestia Arcana* has crept into a remarkable number of ghost stories. But what concerns us here is that LeFanu was successful in creating an atmosphere of evil in his books and short stories which can only have been possible to a man who believed in evil, not as an intellectual concept, but as a living reality. Many of his admirers recommend *Carmilla*, which is a tale of vampirism complicated by what we should now recognize as Lesbianism, but which the nineteenth century saw as passionate friendship. This story was plundered later in the century by another Irishman, Bram Stoker, who wrote *Dracula*; Stoker was good on creating sensation, but lacked the higher qualities of an author, and we shall not return to him. I am an admirer of LeFanu, and I greatly prefer his novel *Uncle Silas* to his short stories. He was a novelist of fine attainment; his characterization, and the skill with which he moves, slowly and teasingly, to his denouement, are masterly. The threat that hangs over his heroine, Maude Ruthyn, is finely suggested and sustained. Indeed we are astonished that, in the end, Maude pulls through. As we read we recall Poe's dictum that the most poetical topic in the world is the death of a beautiful woman. But Maude does not die, and the clouds of evil that surround her are dispelled.

LeFanu is remarkable among writers of this genre because so many of his stories are about women. Many writers assume that the supernatural, as a serious matter, is necessarily a masculine business. Not LeFanu; he makes us fear for threatened women, and the fear we feel is not a simple worry that some simpleton may lose her virginity, but that a human creature may lose its soul. LeFanu, by the way, suffered all his life from a recurrent nightmare that he was trapped in a falling house, from which he was rescued in the nick of time; when he died, his physician commented, perceptively, that the house had fallen at last. I mention that because I think it gives a hint of the quality of LeFanu's mind.

It seems odd that the greatest of nineteenth-century writers of fiction was not at his best in the ghostly mode. Charles Dickens was a man who, when he was off his guard, had extraordinary intimations of the Unseen World or the No-World, but as a general thing he liked to pose as a hard-headed rationalist. When we read in *The Old Curiosity Shop* that magnificent passage in which the animal showman makes a dog that has disgraced itself grind out the tune of the "Old Hundredth" on the barrel organ, while the showmen talk about what becomes of old giants, we know that we are in the presence of a great and uncanny imagination. But when Dickens faces the Unknown head-on, he becomes jokey and the wine grows thin. In *A Christmas Carol* he leads off with a splendid ghost, that of Jacob

Marley, the tight-fisted man of business, who in his ghostly state is condemned to drag a terrible chain of ledgers and cash boxes; but the story degenerates to a disappointing denouement, where we are told that the spirits that visited Scrooge had their origin in a bottle. I think we may say we know better; they originated in a great imagination which, in this area, mistrusted itself. Dickens might write to a friend about his determination to make the public "writhe and stagger in their shoes" with a horror story, but his vision of Evil is clearest when he explores the depravity of the living.

The desire to joke about ghosts is very common. One of the most popular jokers of this sort was the Reverend Richard Harris Barham, who, under the name of Thomas Ingoldsby, wrote that extraordinary series of ghostly pieces called *The Ingoldsby Legends.* From the early portion of the nineteenth century until about 1914 it seemed that people could not get enough of these tales and they appeared in eighty-eight editions. But now the *Legends* seem to be forgotten, save for "The Jackdaw of Rheims," which is neither the best nor the most characteristic. I suggest that you hunt them up and look at them afresh, because they provide two kinds of pleasure: They are good ghost stories and they are brilliant light verse—for all but a very few of the legends are in verse form, and Barham was a master of the tripping measure and the unexpected rhyme.

Barham died in 1845, and as a clergyman—he was a Canon of St. Paul's—he was in the midst of the religious ferment of his time, much of which was concentrated in what was called the Oxford Movement, a call for a return to pre-Reformation usages in the Church of England, and a revulsion against both the easygoing ways of the Church in the eighteenth century and the increase of liberalism and rationalism in the nineteenth. The Oxford Movement tried to arouse the English people to the emotional power and the aesthetic beauty of religion. Barham was not of the Oxford party, but he seems to have been fascinated by its awakened sense of the splendours of the religious life, and especially the example and influence of the saints.

He wrote many of his legends about saints, and in them he makes fun of saints, and Popes, and Cardinals, and all the apparatus of the pre-Reformation Church, as a conservative Anglican clergyman of his time might see them. His ideas are historically absurd, his approach to any sort of Catholicism is uncharitably ignorant, and his idea of the spiritual life is flawed by a jocose vulgarity. But he has two things on his side: First, he is very funny and not infrequently witty, and second, he has a fine imagination, even if its flights are hampered by a huge Anglican ball-and-chain on his left leg. What is more, he understood terror and evil, and they often assert themselves when he is doing his excellent best to be amusing.

Allow me the indulgence of a personal reminiscence. When I was a small boy my father used to read to me before bedtime on Sunday nights, and one of his star performances was "Nell Cook!! A Legend of the Dark Entry" from the *Legends*. I didn't understand all of it, and when my father thought he was amusing me he was frightening the wits out of me. The tale is of Canterbury Cathedral in its pre-Reformation days; a highly placed cleric of that establishment, who lives in the Dark Entry, has brought a beautiful lady, whom he calls his niece, to live with him and they have a high old time. Now the Canon has a servant, a pretty girl called—well, this is what Barham says:

> Although within the Priory the fare was scant and thin
> The Canon's house it stood without;—he kept good cheer within;
> Unto the best he prest each guest with free and jovial look,
> And Ellen Bean ruled his *cuisine*. He called her "Nelly Cook."
>
> For soups and stews and choice *ragouts*, Nell Cook was famous still;
> She'd make them even of old shoes, she had such wondrous skill;
> Her manchets fine were quite divine, her cakes were nicely brown'd;
> Her boiled and roast, they were the boast of all the Precinct round.
>
> And Nelly was a comely lass, but calm and staid her air,
> And earthward bent her modest look—yet she was passing fair;
> And though her gown was russet brown, their heads grave people
>   shook;
> —They all agreed no Clerk had need of such a pretty Cook.

One night Nelly puts the fire tongs in the gay lady's bed, and there they remain, undisturbed and without any complaint from anyone for some time. So where has the lady been sleeping? The

merriment goes on. A passage which—for no reason I can understand—struck me with dread was that which described the niece's
musical performances:

> And fine upon the Virginals is that gay lady's touch,
> And sweet her voice unto the lute, you'll scarce hear any such;
> But is it "O Sanctissima!" she sings in dulcet tone?
> Or "Angels ever bright and fair"? Ah no,—it's "Bobbing Joan"!

So Nell Cook makes a huge warden pie for the happy couple, in
which she puts poison, and they both die. The Canons of the
Cathedral, faithful to their order, bury Nell alive under the pavement
of the Dark Entry, with nothing but the remains of the pie to comfort
her. And so Nell becomes a ghost.

I did not understand the mainspring of the plot. I did not know
that the niece was not a niece, or that there was anything odd about
the sleeping arrangements, because to me sleep meant sleep, and
nothing else. I believed that Nell was a cook and no more. But I half-
understood her jealousy. The spirit of evil that the tripping verses
conveyed struck upon my childish heart like the blows of a coffin-
maker's hammer, and I think my critical instinct was right, even
though it was immature and ill-informed. And since then I have
become increasingly aware of the splendid mixture of wit and terror
that lurks in the *Legends*.

A few years ago I was shown over Canterbury Cathedral by Dr.
Burgon Bickersteth, whom some of you know. When we came to the
Dark Entry all the dread of childhood arose in me and I understood
as never before what another nineteenth-century versifier meant
when he spoke of the moment when

> ... the pain that is all but a pleasure will change
> For the pleasure that's all but pain.

Dr. Bickersteth was much engaged with the real history of the Dark
Entry, but all my thoughts were for the Canon, and the merry lady,
and for Nell Cook, below the flagstones, with her evil pie.

By that time, you see, I knew a great deal more about the *Legends*
and about their author. Barham is described in the *Life* written by his

son as the good father and family man, the good clergyman who rose to be a Priest of the Household to the Royal Family, and the genial, good fellow who knew all the wits of London, and combined clerical decency with a great deal of roistering conviviality. The reality, which has fairly recently emerged, is decidedly different. Barham was the child, not of his father's wife, but of his father's cook; his childhood was darkened by a powerful sense of not being what he seemed; a coach accident ruined one of his arms; he was early separated from his beloved sister Sarah, another illegitimate child, and his childhood in Canterbury and later life at the family manor of Tappington Everard was lonely; the peasant tales of the Romney Marsh were almost daily fare when he was living there. His married life was by no means an idyll, and he suffered the deaths of six of his children before he died himself, of something that sounds very much like melancholia, called then "a decline."

When we look at the *Legends* again we see that the jolly tales of the saints are not so predominant as a casual glance might suggest; it is the ghost stories of the Romney Marshes that take the foremost place, and the sensibility of a man who was outwardly merry, but whose childhood had been sad, gives the *Legends* their characteristic nervous grotesquerie.

I am not, of course, indulging in the silly game of suggesting that Barham wrote *The Ingoldsby Legends*, or that Poe wrote his tales of terror, because they had wretched experiences in childhood; if an unhappy childhood were all that is needed to make a genius, or a man of talent, the world would be crowded with such people. Between the experience and the creation something intervenes that we cannot explain, and though the experience may do something to shape the creation it does not cause it. However, we may go so far as to say that unhappiness in very early life brings with it a premature recognition of the double-sidedness of human nature and of life in general, and that a large number of our writers of ghost stories, about whose early experiences we have undisputable information, had unenviable childhoods. Even when they seem to have had normally pacific childhoods, these writers of ghost stories are themselves queer fish.

Consider one of the best of the group, the late Montague Rhodes James, born in 1862, who lived until 1932, and was famous both as a Provost of King's College, Cambridge, and as Provost of Eton. He was not just your normal little boy. His first work was *Short Sketches of the Principal Northern Saints, Volume I, Illustrated*, which he wrote—and illustrated—at the age of seven! He grew up to become a great medievalist and antiquary, a great humorist and mimic, and a splendid writer of ghost stories, with which he used to amuse his Eton and Cambridge friends. I commend them to you as among the best of the genre. He is a daring writer, for he makes no concessions to the public, and indeed one of his best stories, *The Treasure of Abbot Thomas* begins with fifteen lines of rather dense Latin, of which no translation is offered. But even more daring is his refusal to offer any explanation of any of his ghosts; they simply exist, and he makes us believe in their existence, giving no quarter to the anti-ghost party. He was, of course, a clergyman, and repeated reading of his work suggests to me that he regarded the dangerous and terrify-ing side of the supernatural as the shadow of its redemptive side. Many writers about ghosts seem to be dualists in their hearts, even when they are orthodox in their professions.

Dualism has rarely had such a thorough and successful presenta-tion as in *The Strange Case of Dr. Jekyll and Mr. Hyde*, written by Robert Louis Stevenson in 1886. Everybody knows the story: The admired philanthropist Dr. Jekyll experiments with what would, in our day, be called "mood-changing drugs" and turns himself into the diabolical Mr. Hyde. If we read with our eyes open, we know that the evil of Hyde is the unlived life of the exemplary Jekyll, released and given its head by the drug. It is a famous thriller. But the same theme, of the Unlived life, the inadmissible portion of a personality, is explored with vastly greater subtlety by Joseph Conrad in two of his most celebrated tales, *The Secret Sharer* and *Heart of Darkness*; Conrad had a penetration not given to Stevenson, and in *The Secret Sharer* we see that the supposedly evil part of a character is not without its attraction and sympathetic spirit; the evil is as much a consequence of suppression, of having been disowned, as it is inher-ently wicked and unacceptable. This is the ambiguity of evil, a subject that few writers have been able to convey; but the ambiguity of evil, when we consider it, gives us a different conception of that much-maligned and grossly caricatured metaphysical power whom we speak of as the Devil.

This same theme is apparent, though it is never quite brought into focus, by a writer who seems now to have been forgotten, though once he had a considerable vogue. He was Arthur Machen, a Welshman, born in 1863, who died in 1947. He wrote magnificently during a period when style was greatly valued for its own sake, and I some-times think that this was his undoing. If someone had said: "Come on, Machen, chuck the crepuscular mists and unspeakable horrors, and give us a sharp, clear horror," he would have left a greater name. The titles of his books, *Far Off Things*, *Things Near and Far*, *The Three Impostors*, *The Great God Pan*, and *The Hill of Dreams*, suggest the kind of writer he was—one capable of what John Masefield called "beautiful and terrible stories" but inclined to a wooziness which was at one time supposed to be Celtic by people who know little about the Celts. Machen is apt to lead us up to a splendid mystery, and then to sheer off, declaring it to be too dreadful for description. This leaves it to our imagination; but of course we don't want our own imagina-tions, with which we are too tediously familiar; we want the imagina-tion of an author with a turn for the horrible.

Of course, some of the best writers of uncanny tales have done precisely this, but they wield a greater magic wand than was given to Arthur Machen. At the very top of the list we must place Henry James, whose tales of horror, and haunting, and the uncanny, seem to me to make him the great genius in this department of literature. He is so important a figure in the world of the novel generally, that his author-ity in the world of terror and evil is sometimes forgotten.

His most famous tale is, of course, *The Turn of the Screw*, and here he does precisely what I have blamed poor Machen for doing: He leaves the final explanation up to us, if there is to be a final explana-tion. Was the governess in that story a little mad? Was she unsettled by a suppressed and dangerous affection for her employer? How did the ghosts of Peter Quint and his female accessory debauch the chil-dren Miles and Flora? There is a strong whiff of sexual corruption

hanging over the story, but do we accept sexual corruption as the ultimate in evil? The story presents us with a net of questions that we are
left to answer from the hints we have been given, and the interpretation we put on what we are plainly told. It is an undoubted masterpiece.

For my taste, however, it is not James's greatest work in this realm.
For me that is *The Beast in the Jungle*. There are people who read it
without any feeling that it belongs among James's ghostly tales,
though this is not the opinion of the great Jamesian Leon Edel, who
included it in his collection that bears that name. Do you recall it? It
is about a man called John Marcher who confides to his friend May
Bartram that he had, from the very earliest time, had a sense of being
kept for something rare and strange, possibly prodigious and terrible,
that was to happen to him. They are friends for a lifetime, and the
great thing never happens, until, when she is dying, she tells him what
it is: It is the recognition of the unlived life; he has had from her all
that a man can have from a woman, except love. Not that she was not
ready to give it, but because his sense of his own isolation and his
egotism prevented him from knowing that, and taking what was there
to be taken. She dies, and it is some time after her death before he
understands the truth of what she has said. He is a man who has
allowed egotism to devour him and isolate him from life, and that is
the strange and terrible thing that he has been waiting for. When he
understood, we are told, the very tears in his eyes seemed to freeze.
Such a précis as this does violence to a great work of art, but as a tale
of the horrible and the uncanny, masked as a sober account of a man's
life, I do not think it has an equal. The ghost that haunts John
Marcher—the ghost of the unlived life, and the love he was too self-
delighted to see—is a dreadful ghost indeed.

Such tales as these are a long way from the simple ghosts we find
recorded in the pages of Augustus Hare's autobiography. Are they to
be taken, therefore, as marks of a greater sophistication in public
taste? I should not say so; they mark a change, rather than an advance-
ment, though I realize that there might well be dispute on that point.
It is of interest in terms of our central theme—the depiction of evil in
literature—that the appetite for tales of the uncanny persisted into

the twentieth century and that literary artists who were both gifted and strongly aware of fashionable trends took pains to satisfy the demand. One of the most successful was Sir James Barrie. His play *Dear Brutus*, which made its appearance in 1917, has a theme that is reminiscent of Henry James, for it is a play about unlived lives. A curious host, named Lob, invites a group of people to visit his house on Midsummer Eve; they enter an enchanted wood where they are given a second chance at life—a chance to avoid the mistakes they made the first time. And do they do so? With one pathetic exception, they do not. It is in Barrie's familiar bittersweet manner; never has there been a dramatist so adept at making audiences swallow the sugar-coated pill. His play *Mary Rose* is another adventure into the uncanny, about a girl who visits a curious island in the Hebrides, and vanishes for several years. Its first audiences thought it very pretty to begin with, then they found it distasteful, for it said clearly that the unseen and the unchancy stands very close to us, and we never know when it may assert itself even in our own well-managed and somewhat commonplace lives. People do not like to be told that the uncanny is as near to you as the coat you wear. To the end of his life Barrie pondered the theme of the unlived life, and in 1931, when he was not far from his death, he wrote one of the masterpieces of the uncanny, his short novel *Farewell, Miss Julie Logan*. It is a brilliant story of a delusion which may, on the other hand, have been a haunting; a young Presbyterian minister, something of a bigot, falls in love with a beautiful girl and rejects her when he discovers that she is a Papist. His difficulty is that nobody else sees the girl. I commend it to you as the work of a master who is at present out of fashion.

Perhaps the concept of the "unlived life" calls for some expansion. It is not suggested that we should all obey every prompting of our desires, though it is healthy for us to give full attention to those desires which we will not fulfill, but which sometimes arise to plague us. We must be aware of the darker side of our natures. We must know what lurks in the shadows. Goethe said that he had never heard of a crime which he could not imagine himself committing, under appropriate circumstances; that is the sort of self-knowledge we should seek. But the "unlived life" is something different: It is very often the life that has been put aside in order to serve the demands of a career, or an idea of one's place in the world, or simply—as in the case of the hero of Henry James's story—to serve one's own comfort and egotism. Very often it is love that is sacrificed in this way, but it may also be adventure, or a concern with the arts, or friendship, or simply a greater freedom of action: These unlived elements revenge themselves and sometimes they do it with compounded interest.

We all know the saying that preachers' children are the worst harum-scarums, but do we ever look to see what ghosts of the parsonage they are laying by their rowdy behaviour? The banker's boy who becomes the school thief is bodying forth a repressed part of his father's concern for money. The young people who make a cult of promiscuous sex may be doing what their elders were afraid to do but longed to do. The druggies and the layabouts are living out the unlived life of too scrupulously moral and work-ridden families.

This does not mean that these disreputable people are in the right, or that their elders are to blame for their bad behaviour. What is demonstrated is simply the principle of *enantiodromia*, which is the tendency of things to run into their opposites if they are exaggerated. Excessive self-love becomes no love at all; extreme prudence ends up by spoiling the ship for a ha'p'orth of tar; a rejection of all that is coarsely vital in life brings a shrivelling of sensibility. As a very eminent psychiatrist once said to me: "We attract what we fear." What we fear is the portion of life that remains unlived. Our task, if we seek spiritual wholeness, is to be sure that what has been rejected is not, therefore, forgotten, and its possibility wiped out.

The more recent years of the twentieth century have not lacked their distinguished practitioners of the ghost story. We have not time to look at them all, but I suppose that many of you are familiar with the stories written by Roald Dahl, which are elegant, frequently funny, and always somewhat cruel in theme. One of the few successful novels in this genre is the work of Sylvia Townsend-Warner, a writer who has never, in my opinion, been sufficiently recognized; it is called *Lolly Willowes*, written in 1925, and it is about a woman who, without wishing to do so, becomes a witch. Miss Townsend-Warner, who is now eighty-three, still occasionally publishes tales of the other world in *The New Yorker,* a magazine not usually associated with this sort of fiction. And of course in our own time the remarkable Alphonsus Joseph-Mary Augustus Montagu Summers has published his highly Catholic ghost stories, as well as his better-known and controversial works of scholarship, many of which relate to ghost literature and the Gothic novel. When I was at Oxford it was common to see Father Summers taking his afternoon walk, dressed in the soutane and shovel hat of a European priest, accompanied either by his secretary (a pale young man dressed entirely in black), or by a large black dog. You never saw him with both secretary *and* dog, and it was rumoured that this was for the best of reasons; Father Summers was said not merely to be a scholar of the supernatural, but an adept in its horrid mysteries.

Nor can I complete even such a hop, skip, and a jump as this through the uncanny literature of our time without mentioning what I consider one of the finest ghost stories of recent years; it is "The Portobello Road" by the very popular novelist Muriel Spark.

Upon the whole, the ghost stories of the twentieth century have taken a psychological turn; the ghost, or the possession, or whatever the uncanny element in the story may be, is represented as having its origin not in Hell, but in the psyche. The difference seems often to be one merely of terminology. The twentieth century has seen the psyche become a scientific reality, and the world has embraced it with a whoop and a holler. What is strange is that so many people—possibly a majority—suppose that the psyche must be a region of terrors and a breeding ground of unhappiness. As the word *psyche* means, after all, Soul, one wonders what has happened; the Soul in the old days had a better reputation. Indeed, for many people, Soul is the most embarrassing of the four-letter words. I want to talk about that, because it is very near the root of our central discussion, and gives some evidence about the nature and origin of evil.

This century has seen one of the great intellectual revolutions of the last two thousand years—a revolution at least as far-reaching in its consequences as the Renaissance. For convenience, let us call it the Freudian Revolution, because the theories and explorations of Sigmund Freud are central to it.

What is perhaps the most revolutionary of Freud's books, *The Interpretation of Dreams*, appeared in 1900; it was not very well-received and sold slowly; it was not translated into English until 1913. Indeed, it was not until the twenties that it was read widely, and of course it, and his two volumes of *Introductory Lectures on Psychoanalysis*, and all his subsequent works were attacked and derided, as much by members of his own profession as by others. But Freud was fond of saying that his desire was to disturb the sleep of the world, and the world found itself unable to resist the force of what he had to say. The import of his teaching is familiar to us all: In brief, it is that the conscious part of the mind is only a part, and not always the dominant part, of the whole mind, and that many of our troubles have their origins in those areas which lie below the surface, and which declare themselves in dreams, or often in undesirable symptoms of one sort and another, or in madness. The supernatural world, to Freud and his followers, was an illusion arising from the Unconscious. More than that: The whole structure of religion, including belief in God, was an illusion, persisting from the early period of man's development, and something that man must set aside if man hoped ever to attain full freedom and self-determination.

The argument, set out in his brilliant essay *The Future of an Illusion*, is that God is an obsessional neurosis of which mankind must be cured. Freud says: "Religion consists of certain dogmas, assertions about facts or conditions of ... reality, which tell one something that one has not oneself discovered, and which claim that one should give them credence." Now one might be prepared to agree with all of that except the important word 'consists'; if religion were nothing more than what Freud says it is, one wonders if it would have lasted so long, and in such a variety of forms. But in that word *consists* we find a basic Freudian attitude; the cast of his mind is strongly reductive, and whatever came under the inspection of that remarkable mind emerged notably smaller and less impressive than what it had been before.

Do not think, I beg you, that I am deriding Freud. I am strongly conscious of what he has done for mankind; he is one of the greatest liberators of the human mind in our history. He roused the world from its sleep, and he swept away a great amount of troublesome and decaying rubbish that had been under our feet. He was a man of probity and a man of genius. But he was still a man, and subject to error, and as with other men whatever he said took its colour and its dimensions from his own extraordinary but nonetheless finite mode of perception. And the prevailing mode of Freud's mind was reductive.

To him, with his nineteenth-century scientific training, that was what science meant. But one wonders sometimes—wonders timidly and tentatively—how well Freud knew himself. How clearly did he understand that he was not only a genius and a scientist, but also a spellbinder, and a controversialist of enviable wit and elegance of style? Like all such people, he can slip things past you that you do not notice; he can persuade you to accept his arguments because they are so well marshalled that you do not see what has been left out—or if you do see it, you are ashamed to mention it, because Freud has made it seem inconsequential. Freud did not believe in God. Very well; perhaps God as the nineteenth century knew Him was an illusion— or nine-tenths an illusion. But Freud did believe, with his whole heart and soul, in Science, and it never seems to have occurred to him to question that structure of causality and proof which is called Science. It is notorious that if you give a theologian an inch, he will have you bound and gagged in fifteen minutes, unable to voice a doubt. But scientists are just such monsters of dialectic; admit a few assertions which you have to accept on faith, and in no time they have put you to silence and shame. What does Freud say in *The Future of an Illusion*: "Science is no illusion. But it would be an illusion to suppose that we could get anywhere else what it cannot give us." There you are; with that sentence, if you accept it, bang go all the insights of art and literature.

Or do they? Do they really go bang? For some people, it seems, they do. But not for me. It was on this point that I finally had to make up my mind about my allegiance to Freud, whose writings I perused with fascination and great benefit to myself for many years in my younger days. But it just wouldn't do. Art and literature were the things that sustained me in this life, and as time went on I became convinced of the existence of another dimension of life without which I could not live as a free and courageous being; if people wanted to call it God, the term had no evil echo for me, and indeed the weight of tradition behind it seemed to me to be an argument in its favour. If foolish people want to define a silly God, and then declare that he does not exist, I am not interested in their game. Defining God has always seemed to me a pompous and self-defeating exercise. I am content that God should encompass me: I do not think it likely that I shall encompass Him. Where God is concerned, I am the object, not the subject.

I am not, I assure you, indulging in this personal confession for its own sake, but because I think my experience of the Freudian Revolution was a powerful one. I took it seriously. But at last the time came when I could accept its reductive, vainglorious, scientific outlook no more, and fortunately I was able to turn my attention to the work of Freud's great pupil C.G. Jung. Jung had broken with Freud, after a period of discipleship, because he could not swallow the dogmatic atheism, the science worship, and the trick of looking at the whole world through the wrong end of the binoculars. The Freudians have suggested that Jung, who was the son of a Lutheran pastor, could not accept atheism because of loyalty to his father—and to Freudians loyalty to a father is pretty dubious conduct. But they were wrong. Jung's father had lost his faith; that was part of his personal tragedy. Jung's insistence on God as, at the least, a psychological fact, and at the best as a transcendent authority manifesting itself in man through the activity of the psyche, was the result of his work with his patients. Jung was an empiricist, and thus far he too was a scientist. For Jung, God was a fact for which evidence existed in the mind of man—which is not to say that God is nothing more than that: For Freud, God was an imposture upon the mind of man. The rights and wrongs of this matter are not for us to pursue here. What concerns us is that Freudian teachings, half-understood and freely adapted, have had immeasurable effect on the popular thinking of our time, and have strongly influenced our ideas about good and evil.

Freud banished for many people the belief that a transcendent authority exists to which mankind is accountable for its actions. We see the consequences all about us. Many dogmatically supported rigidities of thought, and some manifest cruelties, have lost their authority under the Freudian attack. But inevitably the common acceptance of ideas of right and wrong has suffered, as well. Extraordinary horrors and indecencies are now regarded, not as simply evil, but as a consequence of some inequity in society, or in nature, for which we are all, in very vague terms, thought to be responsible, and against which, therefore, we should not seek redress. The supposed death of God has loaded us all with a new kind of guilt. If a policeman is killed in attempting to apprehend a homicidal robber, the emphasis is likely to be on what has made the robber anti-social, rather than on the fact that the policeman, and his immediate family, have suffered an irreparable loss. We are all, somehow, thought to be responsible for the robber. His personal responsibility has almost vanished. Any notion that the homicidal robber may be the instrument of a force of Evil which is rather more than his personal psychological disturbance is rarely discussed, and the anti-God party does not want it to be discussed. The wallow of sentimentalism that attended the recent abandonment of capital punishment in Canada was typical of the kind of thinking that springs from half-baked Freudian morality. Under the Freudian flag, the Devil has gained a good deal of ground, which was not, of course, what Freud intended. But great revolutions are never achieved without some unforeseen losses, and terrible outbursts of sentimentality which is, as I have said elsewhere, the philosophy of boobs.

The Jungian point of view has not gained much ground because it is not so readily susceptible to popular simplification as is its Freudian counterpart. The Jungians assert the existence of God, but they have also sought to re-examine some beliefs which were long ago discarded by Christian orthodoxy. They have some good words for the Gnostics—who are hateful to orthodoxy. They have asserted that the alchemists were not wholly fools—which is detestable to modern science. And they suggest that the Devil is not a joke, and that he may be encompassed in the being of God, which gets up the dander of all those modern clergy who want a God, but can't bear the notion of a Devil. Of course I am putting these things in very simple terms, because I must. These are not our primary concerns here, and we must get back at once to the question of ghost stories and their continued popularity in an age when the benign aspect of the supernatural has been banished from popular thinking.

In brief, I think the explanation is this: The rejection of God as a transcendent authority does not, for most people, settle all the problems that come under the general term of the supernatural. It does not settle the problem of Evil, which most people decline to associate with their concept of God, and which they most decidedly do not reject when they reject the idea of God. The Freudian Revolution has dismissed, for those under its influence, the all-wise, all-loving Father; it has done nothing to rid them of the Devil, or the burden of guilt and fear that might suitably be considered as the Devil's realm. It seems to be characteristic of the human mind to allow itself to be robbed of what is beneficent, but to regard what is maleficent as an inalienable burden.

I have emphasized that many people who reject God have a sneaking acceptance of the supernatural. The Freudian Revolution offers them little comfort. In the matter of ghosts, for instance, of which we have been speaking, it would be acceptable Freudian argument to say that a ghost is a constellation of a fear, or a neurosis, which has its origin in the personal unconscious. But what about the ghosts, of whom there are so many, who appear to more than one person, and who—like the ghost I spoke of in my home in Kingston—appear to people of honest mind, who have no expectation of seeing any such thing, and who have not collaborated on a story to deceive others. On the face of it, it looks as if the supernatural had a genesis other than somebody's disordered psyche. Ghost stories approach, usually by some oblique path, an area of which we have only an oblique perception, but which seems to have some relevance to the world we inhabit.

Ghost stories are also an approach, often tentative and hesitant, to a question which most people put to themselves at some time, and it is: What happens to me when I die?

It is a question that strikes very deep. We all know people who declare with bravado that they expect oblivion in death—that they hope for it and indeed refuse to consider any other possibility. If their attitude were widespread, why would there be the inveterate belief in ghosts, and the ready market for stories about them? I think most people, when they are not putting up a show, have other ideas—and indeed there are few civilizations so crude that they have no notion of a life after death. We all know that we were not nowhere before we were born; scientists will give us, in concrete terms, their notion of where we were—or where a part of us was. Are we to conclude that all that long chain of being ceases when what we call ourselves ceases to be present in the guise we now wear? Such an answer would not, I think, appeal to a scientist—and we know that the concept of what science is and what its limits are has changed radically since the time when Freud made his bold claim that science holds all we may know or expect from life. Ghost stories are very often attempts to answer our question, ranging from the crude concept of the spirit that cannot rest until its wrongs are avenged on earth, to such subtle concepts as that of Henry James—though even that is still rooted in the idea of unfinished business.

The Freudian Revolution stops short of being a really satisfactory explanation of anything except certain sorts of mental illness. Saying that God is dead is like saying that there is no Santa Claus; the jolly old man with the white beard may vanish, but the gifts are under the Christmas tree just the same. All that has happened is that the child who thinks it has discovered a great secret no longer feels that it need be good in order to receive its gifts; Santa has gone, but parental love is just where it always was.

In life, however, the gifts, or the circumstances of life, are not always delightful; there are many surprises of a devastating character in store for us as we unwrap the parcels that contain the things that make up a life. If that is the case in the life we know—and it is—what makes us think that the life we do not know, the life that insists on asserting itself in our persistent belief in ghosts, is a blissful oblivion? Ghost stories, and the universal fondness for them, are indirect evidence of our vastly deeper concern.

Tomorrow we conclude these lectures, and in the last of the series I shall attempt to answer some of the questions that have been raised already, or if I cannot answer them I shall try to suggest lines of speculation that may lead toward answers. But I shall attempt to give some hints about the nature of Evil as it shows itself in the literature of our own day, the literature of the Freudian Age. And because it dwells so much on damnation, without any prospect of blessing, I have called it by T.S. Eliot's phrase, Thunder Without Rain.

17

Thunder Without Rain

In this, the last lecture in this series, I want to talk about the novel in this century, attempting some assessment of its attitude toward Evil, and its ways of depicting Evil. The theme is much too large for the time we have, and therefore I warn you at the beginning that I shall speak only of a few novelists, not always the best-known, as any attempt to include the many famous writers of our era would demand another method of approach, and might result in nothing better than a rich confusion. Even as matters stand I must pick and choose in a manner which is certainly arbitrary, but which I hope will make it possible to touch some of the high spots. The title of the lecture is "Thunder Without Rain"; the phrase is T.S. Eliot's, and signifies threat from the heavens, without any blessing to soften its severity.

Those among you who are accustomed to keeping up with the modern novel are aware of the atmosphere of Existentialist gloom, of malice against mankind, of the concentration on misfortune, and the delight in gallows humour, that characterizes so much of the work of even the most talented of our writers. There are no gods, they seem to say, but there is a Lurking Something that acts against mankind, to render his works futile. The people in these novels rarely love, but if they do their love is complex and productive of pain and disillusionment. They lust a great deal, but without gusto; they copulate compulsively, but without joy and often with pain. They are ill at ease in their world. Only very rarely do they grow old, and age brings no wisdom. If they die, they die without hope or resignation. They are ridden with guilt. They seek what they call Identity, by which they frequently mean some reconciliation with what is least admirable in themselves. Of course my description involves a measure of caricature, but not a great deal of it. The Evil they put forward as a pervasive element in life is that very old sin which used to be called Wanhope, and later Despair. A medieval name for it was Acedia, and it was attributed to monotony of life. This seems to me to be psychologically very perceptive, and I have ventured to wonder whether our modern proneness to this plague is not attributable, at least in part, to the monotony of life that afflicts so many people. Has there ever, I wonder, been a period of history when so many people worked so hard, at such dull tasks, in order to maintain a quality of life which is better than anything the majority of mankind could have enjoyed in the past, but which is bought at the cost of unremitting work, economic complexity, lifelong burdens of debt, and an hysterical craving for more and costlier physical objects of a kind that can never requite the toil and servitude it takes to acquire them. In the midst of our heaped-up abundance of things made of metal and wires and plastic, we starve for the bread of the spirit. As I argued yesterday, the Freudian Revolution has changed our ideas about the spirit, and for many people it has killed the spirit as a source of enrichment, leaving only what breeds guilt and dread. Guilt and dread are what we find in the most up-to-date exercises in the age-old art of storytelling, where they are cloaked as revelations of the inner life of man.

Let me repeat what I said yesterday: We must not blame Sigmund Freud for this. He said he came to rouse the world from its sleep, and to some extent he did so. But most of mankind are slow to wake, and find themselves now not awakened, but roused only to a terrifying, unrefreshed Katzenjammer—a hangover from the indulgences of the past.

As it is mirrored in fiction, this awakening did not come in a hurry. Let us take a few minutes to look at some of the most popular fiction of the first half of this century. This is not, I am convinced, a waste of our time. I have great faith in popular art as a clue to what people desire, and as a picture of the world as they wish it were. We can find this evidence in the class of books called bestsellers.

What is a bestseller? Can we agree that it is a book that has sold over a million copies? They are of all sorts, and we should be foolish to deride a book because it has sold widely and given delight to great numbers of people. When people knock bestsellers I remember that Dickens and Tolstoy were bestsellers in their day, and are bestsellers still; beside their names we could place a score of other names, unquestionably meritorious. But I want to talk now of the bestseller as the lily of a day—the book which captures the enthusiasm of the reading world but which never becomes the theme of academics or sophisticates.

Let us begin with Edgar Rice Burroughs's extraordinary fantasy *Tarzan of the Apes*, which appeared first in 1912. Something in the neighbourhood of fifty million copies of these books—there are several of them—have been sold, in sixty languages. They are fantasy books; their author was a man who was a failure in business, and wrote—in the beginning—to give rein to his stifled imagination. I don't have to tell you what they are about. The powerful ape man, Tarzan, is in reality an English nobleman, Lord Greystoke, lost in the jungle as an infant and nurtured by kindly primates. He possesses simplicity of mind, nobility of spirit, and immense physical power. Let the Freudians explain his habit of swinging rapidly through the trees, howling with high spirits as "levitation-fantasy"; of course it is. But it has been the spiritual nurture of many a poor brute whose family are apes only in a metaphorical sense, and it has released him from the shackles of the modern world in which, as several statesmen have loved to tell us, "we never had it so good."

Is Tarzan too coarse for you? Bestsellers can be very refined, if refinement is what you want. Have you read Florence L. Barclay's enormously popular novel *The Rosary* (1909)? It is about a fat woman who finds love. Of course she is never called fat in the book, but we are told that the Hon. Jane Champion is thirty years old, and "of almost massive proportions." She is so massive that nobody "has ever apprehended her wonder as a woman." Where Tarzan howled, the Hon. Jane sang, and what she sang was Ethelbert Nevin's richly evocative ballad "The Rosary." You remember it—

The hours I spent with thee, dear heart,
Are as a string of pearls to me;
I count them over, every one apart—
   My rosary.

That was what she sang in a voice described as "low and vibrant as the softest note of a 'cello." She never knew she could sing like that until she did so at a charity affair, and from then on her romance blossomed, and a very fine fellow who is of artistic temperament—he wears red socks with evening dress—apprehends her wonder as a woman.

Not all the heroes and heroines of bestsellers were as lucky as Lord Greystoke and the Hon. Jane. In 1921 the world was enchanted with the misfortunes of Mark Sabre, hero of A.S.M. Hutchison's bestseller *If Winter Comes*. Mark is that popular character, known from Bible times, the Suffering Servant. He says himself, in the rueful, slangy style that makes him so likeable, "My sort's out to be kicked, and I wouldn't be any other sort." And kicked he certainly is. His wife snubs him because he is friendly toward the servants, and finally she deserts him; he is cheated by his business partners, because he is so trusting and they, of course, are such crooks; in this sort of book all real businessmen are crooked—success is in itself a kind of dishonesty. He befriends a girl who is going to have an illegitimate child, and of course everybody thinks it must be his; but he stands by the girl, whose name is Effie, and whom he thinks of as "a jolly little sister," and at last he ends up in court, where he is humiliated by a beastly prosecuting lawyer who is not a gentleman and shows it by having a hump-back. Mark is that darling of the literary symbol-seeker, a Christ Figure, which always seems to mean an incompetent no-hoper. It is of interest that the book appeared in the year that Freud's early works first attained some popularity in the English-speaking world. Freudians, I am sure, spotted Mark Sabre at once as a masochist and a grievance seeker, but there is enough of that spirit in all of us to ensure the success of a book. It is of some interest that the late Mackenzie King, not usually known as a literary critic, declared the book to be one of the greatest ever written. Which shows, if it shows anything, that a resolute winner can still be stirred to admiration by the tale of a resolute loser.

The loser as winner—this has always been a popular theme. The year after *If Winter Comes* there appeared another book which delighted the general reading public; it was *Tell England*; its author was Ernest Raymond. It was called by its publishers "A Great Romance of Glorious Youth, in Two Episodes, School and War." It is about a couple of clean-limbed, fine English lads, who discover something of the complexity of life in their schooldays, and then go to War, full of chivalrous determination, and die at Gallipoli. The title comes from a translation one of them did of the epitaph written to commemorate the Spartans who fell at Thermopylae:

> Tell England, ye who pass this monument,
> We died for her, and here we rest content.

I am not the man to jeer at it, because it moved me profoundly when I read it as a schoolboy, and though I think differently now, I know that one derides one's long-lost self at the cost of some self-respect. The book was one of the last flings of the chivalrous spirit that was so completely destroyed by the First World War. Chivalry was not wholly a good thing; in foolish people it had foolish consequences. But the world is the poorer for its passing, and I know I could not read *Tell England* now without mingling mirth with a painful sense of loss.

A book I could read now, and have indeed reread quite recently, is another bestseller that came before the Freudian Revolution had completed its work. It is *Precious Bane*, by Mary Webb (1926), which, after a somewhat slow start, was pushed into prominence by the enthusiasm of the then Prime Minister of England, Stanley Baldwin. Whatever you may think of Baldwin as a statesman, he was not a trivial literary critic, and unquestionably this book is of a special order of excellence. I mention it here to emphasize what I said earlier: a bestseller is not by definition a bad book. I must admit at once to a special interest; *Precious Bane* is a tale of the borderland between Shropshire and Wales, and that is country I know well, because my forebears lived there from the dawn of time. It is a country of extraordinary and subtle beauty, and the book conveys that quality as only a writer who was a poet could do it. It is a tale of the era of the Napoleonic Wars, and it is about love and avarice. Gideon Sarn is a young farmer who sacrifices everything to money; his sister Prue has almost abandoned hope of love because she has a harelip, which is not merely disfiguring but is a mark of a witch. But she finds love all the same, and as she writes in her diary, "I took my crumb, and behold, it was the Lord's Supper." It was this book that was chiefly responsible for Stella Gibbons's brilliant pseudo-Freudian parody of a whole school of books of rural life, *Cold Comfort Farm*, which appeared in 1932. As parodies go, it is in the front rank, but parodies never go very far. A parody is a compliment; nobody troubles to mock what nobody takes seriously.

Precious Bane is a novel of powerful, but artistically controlled, feeling. It came at a time when feeling was being severely frost-nipped by the chill blasts of the Freudian Revolution. A modern poet of high reputation and merit, Stevie Smith, has written, "I suppose it was Aldous Huxley who is the watershed of feelings in novels. Before his time feelings were permissible. But he, not being able to express emotion, made a virtue of necessity and set up the half-man for hero, the little creature who itches and fidgets but cannot feel."

This is somewhat unjust. Huxley's characters do feel; shame, embarrassment, frustration, rejection, ineffectuality—whatever is negative and life diminishing—they feel all of these things, often very amusingly. They do not feel love, except when their love is to be mocked by the author. They are a cruel, heartless lot, but very funny. I speak of course of the early Huxley, of *Crome Yellow*, of *Antic Hay*, and of *Point Counter Point*. In middle age Huxley underwent a change not unfamiliar to psychologists, and became fascinated with those things which he had formerly derided, and wrote at length about religion and social justice and how to embrace the Perennial Philosophy. But as a philosopher and a magus he suffered from his earlier defect— he thought too much and felt too little, and what had made him a splendid comic novelist made him rather a bore as a world saviour.

It would have taken more than Huxley to kill the novel of feeling. It lived on and lives still, for many of the admired novels of our day, with their everlasting whine about the meaninglessness of life, are obviously deeply felt. The bestseller that dealt in coarse, obvious feeling certainly did not die. At the time of Huxley's greatest popularity one of the huge successes in this realm was Vicki Baum's *Grand Hotel*, which has something for everybody. It has not aged well, but we can see what gave it power: First of all, the story of Herr Kringelein, the little clerk who is told that he has cancer of the stomach and cannot live long; he goes to the Grand Hotel to splurge his savings on a last fling, and in no time at all he opens his bedroom door to find a naked girl on the threshold. "She staggered toward him, fell heavily ... and the helpless collapse of the warm golden body filled him with a sweet enchanting terror." One thing leads to another and after a blossoming of love—it blossoms in minutes in such novels as this—"he fell asleep blissfully in a blaze of gold that looked like Flämmchen's breast and was also a hill of broom in flower." From then on he never looks back; he tells off his domineering boss (which is always a sure card) and leaves the hotel with a girl who is determined he shall not die. Against him we must balance his boss, who is rich but never mistakes a girl's breast for a hill of broom, and Baron Gaiger, the aristocratic burglar who is so sensual that he licks the petals of flowers for fun; and Madame Grusinskaya, the great ballerina, who wants to kill herself because she is frigid, until the Baron shows her that she has been under a misapprehension. And for sophistication, we have Dr. Otternschlag, the man with a face ruined by war, who sits in the foyer, and reflects that nothing ever happens, although we know that the Grand Hotel is a hotbed of passion and intrigue.

I have taken some time to speak of these books because they were once influential as well as popular. They were no more naive than many popular books of our day—consider *The Naked and the Dead*, or *Exodus*—but their naïveté was of a different order. The popular books of our time draw upon the resources of the Freudian Revolution; even when they attempt a great sweep of action, their tone is reductive. When I was an undergraduate a popular song began, "Life Is Just a bowl of Cherries"; campus wags altered it to "Life is just a bowl of pits." To the popular modern novelist, life is just a bowl of pits. But it is to writers more enduring and influential than they—the writers whom they imitate, at a distance and with greatly diminished talent—that we must look for the kind of evidence we are seeking about the appearance of Evil in modern fiction.

Where do we begin? The slow publication and slow acceptance of James Joyce's *Ulysses* suggests itself, and its date, 1922, is an attractive one. But it was many years before the full influence of *Ulysses* was felt, although many writers were quick to adopt the stream-of-consciousness technique of narration, and use it with varying degrees of success. But I would rather not talk of it here, first because it is a superbly comic novel and thousands who have acclaimed its novelty have missed its humour, and second because it is by no means a book wanting either in feeling or in a sense of a transcendent reality behind the world of appearances. I would prefer to speak instead of a great writer who has never, it seems to me, been given his due, and that is John Cowper Powys. Powys, who was born in 1812, lived until 1963, and wrote forty or more books of poetry, essays, and fiction. He daunts many readers because his novels are so long. *Owen Glendower* runs to 938 pages; *Wolf Solent* is 966 pages; the book that some critics consider his masterpiece, *A Glastonbury Romance*, numbers 1,174 pages: nor are these pages which flick quickly under the reader's fingers—they demand concentration or something important will be missed. And what is important is not narrative, but feelings, infinitely varied and minutely described feelings.

What kind of feelings? It is here that Powys appears as an innovative and essentially modern novelist. He does not adopt new ways of writing prose, as Joyce does; nothing in the manner of his books will confuse you. But as an explorer of sensibility Powys is very much a novelty for his time, and a writer of such mastery that his work still has surprises for us. Sometimes he is said to be of the school of Thomas Hardy, because he writes about rural or village life in the area of Hardy's Wessex. I have not much patience with the tracing of schools and influences in the work of writers who are plainly able to stand on their own feet. It is true that Hardy is not a novelist of Christian feeling, but what of that? Powys is not a novelist of Christian feeling either, but he is no more like Hardy than he is like Huxley. It is worth noting, I think, that serious or tragic novelists are so often expected to write under the influence of some sort of religion, whereas comic novelists are not thought to have any such requirement. Such an attitude springs from the old, fallacious idea that joy and merriment are not religious feelings, whereas a miserable fate or a tragic life must carry with it some paraphernalia of the displeasure of God, or of the gods.

Powys does not exclude religion from his novels; they are full of parsons and church people, but the parsons have a range of feeling, and an attitude toward nature, that are not, in my observation, the outcome of any seminary training. Even in *A Glastonbury Romance*, where the mainspring of the plot is the presentation of a Passion Play in the old and numinous town of Glastonbury, conventional Christian feeling has little place, but pagan feeling, and the weight of legend and mythic history, are breath of the book's life. How does Powys make these things manifest to his readers? Because he does make them manifest to anyone who reads him sympathetically, and it is this intensity and immediacy of feeling that gives the books their value and importance. He does it through loving and evocative description of states of emotion.

In religion Powys was a skeptic; in psychological type he was a sensualist, and as a sensualist he was very much a sadist. His books contain extraordinary descriptions of pain, either directly felt or observed in others, and this pain is productive of heightened sensibility and of a special kind of joy. Perverse, would you say? Possibly so, but great art, as well.

Let us look at a book by Powys, and I propose to take one that is less popular than *A Glastonbury Romance*. I decide for *Wolf Solent*. The title is the hero's name, because Powys's characters have extraordinary names; the girl he marries is called Gerda Torp. Their love scenes are described at considerable length, and a certain tedium may overcome even the most sympathetic reader as he works his way through them. Love scenes are great tests of a novelist, and many of the greatest have solved the problem by merely hinting at them. After all, in a love scene, it is what is understood that is important; what is said may be jejune or embarrassing. A Shakespeare may write great love scenes, because his lovers have to convey their passion by words;

in the more realistic world of the novel a talkative lover may prove unconvincing. Powys does not agree, and his love scenes range from the transporting to the tedious. Apart from this, his descriptions of scenes and people are vivid. Consider what he says about a country squire: "From one corner of his twitching mouth a trickle of saliva descended, towards which a small fly persistently darted." That fly is almost Powys's signature; thousands of novelists make people drool, but only he makes them attract flies. Who is this unseemly squire? When he is tormenting the Vicar, who is a poor creature, Wolf knows, we are told that Wolf "was tolerant enough of the various forms of normal and abnormal sensuality; but what at that instant he got a glimpse of, beneath this man's gentlemanly mask, was something different from viciousness. It was as if some abysmal ooze from the slime of that which underlies all evil had been projected to the surface."

It is not easy to quote from Powys; the language seems strained and high-coloured. All his talk of perversities and acute states of sensibility is puzzling and almost without meaning when it is removed from context. But in the preface to *Wolf Solent* he makes a plain statement of what he calls "the purpose and essence, the inmost meaning of this book," and it is "the necessity of opposites. Life and Death, Good and Evil, Matter and Spirit, Body and Soul, Reality and Appearance have to be joined together, have to be forced into one another, have to be proved dependent upon each other, while all solid entities have to dissolve.…" The book demonstrates this proposition with remorseless intensity. What he has said is easy enough to accept; we nod as if it were a commonplace when we hear it. But as demonstrated in the novel it is something new in experience; Solent, his remarkable mother, his wife Gerda and her rustic family, his maniacal employer, and all the queer *dramatis personae* of this book attest to what Powys has said in a way that is unexampled even in the work of George Eliot. Without each other, they could not be themselves, and without the Reserved Sacrament in the Church, the evil of Lenty Pond would be as nothing. This novel is at the farthest extreme from *The Old Curiosity Shop* with its all-good Little Nell and its all-bad Mr. Quilp. It is a work of art in which the vice and virtue of the characters is interdependent, and where good and evil, though always in contention, will never fight to a lasting victory for one or the other. Is *Wolf Solent*, then, a greater work of art than the novel by Dickens? I am not here to award marks or establish ranks among novelists. Both are books directed at the ages in which they were written, and each partakes of the character of its age. *Wolf Solent* is a novel of a time when we have seen the need to establish some reconciliation among opposites, not by attempting to alter their nature, but by more clearly understanding their interdependence.

It is this seriousness of vision that divides Powys, as an author, from the vastly more popular Aldous Huxley. Brilliant as Huxley is, he is in the grip of the fashionable Wanhope of his time, and he seems at least in the earlier part of his career to have accepted wholly that immutability of cause and effect which, in these latter days, some of the most eminent scientists have begun to question. His later quest for transcendency, through Eastern mysticism, and Western mysticism, and finally through drugs, never fully convinces, because he seems to be in quest of Absolutes. Powys knew in his bones—which is perhaps the only place to begin with such knowledge—that there are no Absolutes, but rather an infinitely complex mingling of contrarieties—at least insofar as such things can be ascertained by the means we possess.

A strong recognition of the interdependency of human creatures and moral concepts need not always lead to a recognition of the sort of transcendent power in the universe that can be likened to the God of the Old or the New Testament. One of the most extraordinarily gifted novelists in the serious modern vein is Marcel Proust, whose great novel of social life is called *A la recherche du temps perdu* (*Remembrance of Things Past* in the English translation). To trace that novel through its long course is to be rewarded, at last, with an enduring, heightened sense of the interdependence of its characters, down to the least of them; no one could be quite what he or she is without the others, and no single character seems to have the powerful individuality that would raise him to unchallenged supremacy. This is, of course, because they are all in search of the same idea of what is good and enduring in life, and it is simply a rather limited personal satisfaction. Nobody wants to depart very far from the norm established by the society he worships; nobody wants to be a saint, or a devil, except as society understands these terms. Their kingdom is a kingdom of this world; their religion, where it exists, is an aspect of society. In consequence the book offers some careful studies of Acedia, of monotony, of boredom, of Wanhope. Even the Baron de Charlus, who is surely the finest portrait in fiction of a particular sort of sensualist, gets very little fun out of his wickedness; when, at the last, the author gives us a portrait of him, blasted by vice, being wheeled about in an invalid chair, raising his hat in a pathetic parody of his earlier, splendidly aristocratic and demonic style, we wonder for a moment if Proust has not set up in business as a moralist. But we are quickly reassured on that point.

One of the questions this great novel raises in our minds is: What on earth did they all get out of it? What were they struggling for? Of course Madame Verdurin ends her career as the Duchesse de Guermantes, but by that time our concept of that splendour has shrunk to the dimensions of the shrivelled old schemer and society harlot that she is. The supreme social position is no greater than she who has attained it, after Time has worked its reductive magic. Life is just a bowl of pits. But—and this is one of the many points—art is not a bowl of pits, and the art of this book fully justifies its reputation. It is as a work of art that it leaves us enlarged. Nor is it a book in which we cannot see the working of a transcendent power. In Proust the dominating, all-pervasive element is Time: The god here is Time, who devours all his children, and we may decide that he is an evil god.

Proust's method is however wholly his own. His imitators cannot do what he has done. There have been several of them, but the one most in the public eye at present is the English writer Anthony Powell, whose long novel—there are twelve volumes—is called *A Dance to the Music of Time*. It presents us with a prospect of English society, beginning with a group of schoolboys, one of whom is the narrator; the boys do not all last into their sixties, but some of them do, especially the egregious Widmerpool, who is a splendid comic creation. We follow him from his inept schooldays through a career in which he achieves various kinds of power, in business, in the Army, and at last in government. But he seems never fully to hit the mark; there is an essential clownishness about him; even when his career is at its height he is involved in humiliations with which he cannot cope; he becomes a cuckold—and it takes a King Arthur to be a cuckold and maintain a high measure of dignity. Widmerpool is seen at the end as a deluded old ass engaged in that common pursuit of deluded old asses—he is trying to mix on terms of physical equality with his juniors, who despise him. As a picture of Widmerpool the long, long book is a fine creation, but as a portrait of society it lacks the certainty of Proust, and because Proust went before it along this path, we are aware from the beginning what the theme of the book must be: Life is just a bowl of pits.

Superior to Powell in this sort of creation is his friend Evelyn Waugh. Waugh's novels are, for the most part, short works, and they are of a special order of perfection. He is a fine stylist, though his style is unobtrusive. Yet, though they are brief and compressed, his works are not miniatures. Their strength and dimension arises from the coherence of the point of view from which they are written. Waugh was a moralist. His morality was always that of dogmatic Christianity, and early in his career it became the morality of the Church of Rome. It is not a morality that excludes any sort of human experience, or that imposes a sober attitude toward life, but it is a morality that insists that man should live, at all times, in awareness of a transcendent power from whom his life is derived and toward whom his life will return. An awareness of God, in short, which cannot protect a human creature from folly and sin, but which keeps him aware of a scale of things in which follies and sins must assume their proper place.

In Waugh's later work this awareness increases, until *The Loved One*, for instance, assumes almost the dimensions of a tract against superstition and triviality. *Brideshead Revisited*—which startled and disappointed those readers who had stupidly regarded Waugh as no more than a gifted funny man—contains a scene of deathbed penitence and acceptance of faith that aroused strong antagonism among people who insisted that death was no more than a passage to oblivion—a point of view we have already discussed at some length. And his trilogy, *Officers and Gentlemen*, surveys the War of 1939–45 as one man's struggle against a world being enclosed in folly and sin, triviality and spiritual shoddiness, and is, in my opinion, the most complete and poignant work of literary art to be inspired by that conflict.

Waugh does not, as you will observe, partake of the follies of the Freudian Revolution, and he draws his insights from Catholic doctrine, rather than from the Freudian enlightenment. He most decidedly does not believe that life is a bowl of pits, merely because that is what a great many people seek to make it. It is the moral weight of his novels that raises them above the level of those of Powell, of whom we have spoken, and whose subject matter is much the same as his. Waugh's concept of Evil is a powerfully Catholic concept; the great Evil is to forget God, or to turn one's face from Him.

Is it necessary, therefore, to be a Catholic, or an adherent of Christian dogma, in order to depict life seriously—for Waugh is always serious, though he is rarely solemn. No, because one of the great novelists of this century, the late Thomas Mann, achieves the same end, in a very different manner, and with full acceptance of the Freudian Revolution—or perhaps it would be wiser to say the Psychoanalytical Revolution. I make that qualification because on a famous occasion, when he was called upon to pay tribute to Freud at a public dinner, he somewhat astonished the guest of honour by including a very warm encomium upon the work of Freud's rival and apostate pupil, Carl Jung. Mann was prone to such failures of commonplace tact, as anyone who has studied his life is aware. Mann writes in a manner inimitable by anyone else; the density and prolixity of his novels would be intolerable in a writer who did not also possess his extraordinary sweep and complexity of mind. It is unsatisfactory to call this quality Teutonic, for it is not common among Teutons. It is wholly his own. Mann was a philosopher, steeped in the thought of Goethe and of Nietzsche, and yet his conclusions are not those of either of his masters.

Think of *The Magic Mountain*, which I choose because I assume that many of you will have read it. The concept is not altogether unlike that of Vicki Baum's *Grand Hotel*, but the execution is of a very different order: A group of people are assembled in a tuberculosis sanatorium in Switzerland; they represent a wide variety of human attitudes, which they expound in an atmosphere of invalidish reasoning and invalidish living. These sick people present a paradigm of Europe and its civilization. They expound and haggle about life and death until we could bear no more if we were not certain that some conclusion is in prospect, and indeed it comes. The hero, Hans Castorp, who is not himself a gifted disputant, arrives at it in a time of isolation and stress, and here it is, in the words of the English translation: "For the sake of goodness and love, man shall let death have no sovereignty over his thoughts." It is, you see, a rejection of Wanhope, a statement of moral courage, a rejection of the notion that life is just a bowl of pits. Goodness and love are not, of course, put forward as simple-minded, Pollyanna concepts; the whole thrust of the book is to show their profundity and final worth.

Even more clearly, though with an intensification of Mann's accustomed denseness of argument and prolixity of expression, this concept of life as a noble thing is put forth in what is perhaps his most difficult novel, *Dr. Faustus*. I shall not assume that you have read it, for it is a book that has been known to damp the courage of even determined and serious readers. It is easy to see it as a political allegory, expressing in the form of human tragedy the tragedy of the German people, who asserted an arrogance of intellect which drew its inspiration from spiritually archaic and obsolete sources; this, says Mann, is "the Devil's domain" and leads to ruin. But the story of the musician Adrian Leverkühn is decidedly more than that. Leverkühn is shown to us as born in 1885, in what Mann calls "Luther's Germany," and his first love is theology; but he turns to music—a demonic art— and finds that his powerful intellect is a gift he enjoys at the expense of the God-given creative spontaneity of natural genius. He becomes infected with syphilis; indeed, he seeks it; later he makes a bargain with the Devil—and it is interesting that the Devil is drawn to him by his proud intellectual powers, as a correlative of his infected body. He receives, in return for his soul, the assurance of twenty-four years of genius, with only one stipulation; during that time he may not love. He has his gift and the Devil claims his price; Leverkühn goes mad and the last ten years of his life are spent in dotage. Power is bought at the price of complete humanity, and the downfall is of tragic dimension. Yes, it is a political allegory, but it is something more profound than that. Here again we have Evil depicted as the failure of Love, or to use the older word that has no merely romantic overtone, of loving kindness.

In another statement, not in one of his novels, Mann sets forth the doctrine of the union of contraries, which I have spoken of in my remarks on John Cowper Powys. In the essay "What I Believe" he speaks of "the new humanity" in which he sees "the union of darkness and light, feeling and mind, the primitive and the civilized, wisdom and the happy heart." I do not want to oppress you with my own Jungian prejudices, but this sounds uncommonly like that Mystical Marriage of Opposites, resulting in wholeness, which Jung found in his investigation of the discarded writings of the Alchemists, and which he puts forward as the way of life in which the hope of mankind lies.

I warned you at the beginning of these lectures that I am no theologian; I have not even amateur qualification in that complex realm. But from what I have already said, or adduced from the writings of a number of novelists of high repute, it is clear to anyone that this union of opposites is something different from the dualism which Christian theologians have condemned. It may not be any less a heresy, but that is not for me to decide. Dualism is the continual opposition of Good and Evil, the war in heaven between God and the Devil, with the implication that at some time one of the opposed forces will emerge as undoubted victor—but without saying which it may be. The union of opposites of which these writers speak is something else; it is the merging of apparent opposites to produce a new and stronger spirit in man, because it is in the soul, or heart, or mind of man—in all three we may presume—that the struggle is carried on, and the eventual new element appears in the form of a wider sensibility, a greater wisdom, and an enlarged charity. But as you have immediately observed, this is to happen in individual men, and be manifested through them, and that is not what I have been hinting at through these lectures; I have been suggesting the existence of a power of good and a power of evil external to man, and working through him as an agency—a God, in fact, infinitely greater than man can conceive, and a Devil vastly more terrible than even the uttermost terrors of human evil. It is part of mankind's vanity to assume that all of Nature is merely a background against which he works out his destiny—the scenery for his drama. Religion, in some of its aspects, has encouraged this vanity, but I suggest that the idea is open to question.

This vanity on the part of mankind is not unreasonable. We are the only creatures, so far as we know, to achieve the intricate and extensive consciousness of self that makes us in so great a degree the masters of our lives. Unless we are greatly mistaken, there is no other creature on earth that begins to rival us in power of communication, of degree of interrelation and co-operation, and of abstract thought. But whether we are or are not the end toward which all evolution has been striving is open to doubt. Any assertion we may make that the forces we call, for brevity and convenience, God and the Devil are forces contained in ourselves, and without external being, is open to even greater doubt. Visionaries and philosophical thinkers like Powys and Mann appear to have doubts on this point, and writers who are professing Christians have no doubt about it at all.

Indeed, doubt as to whether science can answer all man's questions, and remove his God from him as if God were a tumour, is likely to crop up in unexpected places. Last night I gave you examples of the atheistic dogma of Sigmund Freud. Because I respect him so much, I am happy tonight to give you a sample of a later doubt. He wrote, in a lecture of 1933, "If one regards oneself as a sceptic, it is a good plan to have occasional doubts about one's scepticism too. It may be that I too have a secret inclination toward the miraculous that goes half way to meet the creation of occult facts." Not much of a chink in his armour, you may say. But consider whose armour it was, and how thick it was.

Our time is running short and I cannot detain you with a multitude of further examples. I should like to speak of two, however, both of whom have achieved eminence as writers, mingling critical appreciation with widespread popularity in the way that remarkable writers do.

The first is Graham Greene, who is sometimes called a Catholic novelist, though I think that too narrow a label. He is a Christian novelist, and Christian belief is at the heart of his best work. He has some tiresome characteristics; one of these is a fondness for losers as principal characters; sometimes as I read him I wonder if I have not picked up the wrong book, and have *If Winter Comes* in my hand, with its exaltation of the loser-hero. It is just as romantic, and just as wrong, to exalt trivial failure as it is to exalt trivial success. Greene's whisky priests, struggling against booze and lechery, are interesting to read about, but in a life that has brought me into contact with a great many priests I have never met one who was in the least like them. Success is not always bought at the cost of the soul, and if the winners are always wrong, we must regard evolution as a gigantic swindle, because it is a long chronicle of victory. But when we have disposed of Greene's romanticism, we have still to face his theology, and what is it?

In a recent novel, *The Honorary Consul*—it appeared in 1973—he offers an unusually clear statement, and I shall quote it to you at some length. A priest who has sinned deeply, but has served his people nobly, is talking to a group of Argentine peasants, one of whom is the mother of his child, and a doctor. He says: "I believe in the evil of God, but I believe in his goodness, too.... The God I believe in must be responsible for all the evil as well as for all the saints. He has to be a God made in our image with a night-side as well as a day-side.... I believe the time will come when the night-side will wither away ... and we shall see only the daylight of the good God. You believe in evolution ... and I believe God is suffering the same evolution that we are, but perhaps with more pain." The doctor intervenes; in novels doctors are generally spokesmen for strict rationality, though how they come by this reputation puzzles me when I talk to those I know. The doctor says: "Suppose the night-side of God swallows up the day-side altogether? Suppose it is the good side which withers away. If I believed what you believe, I would sometimes think that had happened already." The priest has an answer: "But I believe in Christ; I believe in the Cross and the Redemption. I believe that the day-side of God, in one moment of happy creation, produces perfect goodness, as a man might paint one perfect picture. God's good intention for once was completely fulfilled so that the night-side can never win more than a little victory here and there. With our help. Because the evolution of God depends on our evolution. Every evil act of ours strengthens his night-side, and every good one helps his day-side: We belong to him and he belongs to us. But now at last we can be sure where evolution will end one day—it will end in a goodness like Christ's. It is a terrible process all the same, and the God I believe in suffers as we suffer while he struggles against himself—against his evil side.... God when he is evil demands evil things; He can create monsters like Hitler; He destroys children and cities. But one day with our help He will be able to tear his evil mask off forever. How often the saints have worn an evil mask for a time, even Paul. God is joined to us in a sort of blood transfusion. His good blood runs in our veins, and our tainted blood runs through his."

To me, at least, this sounds uncommonly like Bernard Shaw's theory of Creative Evolution. The notion that Shaw was an atheist dies hard, especially in people who have not troubled to read the works of his old age. A God who is bound to us, and whose redemption we assist and share in, is a Shavian concept which seems not to be repugnant to the declared Catholic Graham Greene.

The idea of complete perfection, even when it is an attribute of Christ himself, has been known to cause disquiet in some souls, who long for wholeness in the Redeemer of Mankind, and who see wholeness as including human attributes of which the Biblical Christ knows nothing. There has been a great fuss recently in England, because a Scandinavian filmmaker has announced his intention of making a film there about Christ's sex life. The terms in which the film is described are distasteful, and as several people have said, there would be an even greater outcry if such a film were projected about Mahomet, or Abraham. But so far as I have followed the controversy, nobody has yet suggested that this plan may have its root in the human desire for wholeness, and a wish for a Redeemer not so far removed from the common fate of man. Wholeness is not wholly admirable—or at least not in orthodox terms—and to be wholly admirable is, in the eyes of some truly sincere people, to be repellent. Of course, Christ rejected Satan when Satan tempted him. Whether his rejection included so powerful an element of humanity as the sexual urge is a question for better-equipped theologians than I.

The idea of a wholly good God, however, is by no means wanting in modern adherents, and one of them is a writer much admired and discussed in our time, Aleksandr Solzhenitsyn. In the famous broadcast he gave last April, he accused the modern world of a loss of courage and a loss of reason, and this was his comment on that state of affairs: "There is a perfectly simple explanation ... not the superficial one so fashionable in our day, according to which man himself is irreproachable, and everything is blamed on a badly organized society. The explanation I have in mind is a purely human one. Once it was proclaimed and accepted that above man there is no Supreme Being, and that instead man is the crowning glory of the universe and the measure of all things, then man's needs and desires—and indeed his weaknesses—were taken to be the supreme imperatives of the universe." He draws a humiliating conclusion: "In the years which followed the world wide upheaval of 1917 that pragmatic philosophy on which present-day Europe was nourished, with its refusal to take moral decisions, has reached its logical conclusion: since there are no higher spiritual forces above us and since I—Man with a capital M— am the crowning glory of the universe, then should anyone have to perish today let it be someone else, anybody but not I, not my precious self, nor those who are close to me."

These are heroic words, uttered by a man who has heroically earned the right to utter them. They are strong meat for reflection, but we must not forget our theme, which is the appearance of Evil in literature, and a discussion of its manifestations.

Why does evil appear in literature at all? The question seems a foolish one at first utterance, but its answer is not simple. A book about wholly good people would be intolerably dull reading. We demand of literature a reflection of life, and life without some evil, or some falling away from strict morality of conduct, is unthinkable. As Graham Greene points out, even the saints knew evil, and Paul was the greater saint because he had been one of those who took part in the martyrdom of Saint Stephen—and Paul was on the wrong side in that encounter. The Christian urge for nearly two thousand years has been toward a perfection that we profess to admire; but when we are off guard, it is wholeness rather than perfection that we are interested in and the full development of human possibility is what we ask of literature.

That is what we have been talking about during these evenings. And we have met with the paradox that when there is a sharp dichotomy between good and evil in a novel—as, for instance, between Little Nell and Daniel Quilp in *The Old Curiosity Shop*—the evil character seems to enlist the superior creative powers of the writer, and therefore is more attractive than the good. Every writer of melodrama knew that without a good strong villain, his play was lost; the subtler novelists of the nineteenth century offered us villains who are very near to being monsters, in the case of Dickens, but we feel a truth in their enormities; in the ghost stories we talked about there was no doubt that a good ghost was worse than no ghost at all, and a ghost that could inspire terror with its cry of "Revenge," or that could chill us by the nearness of its threat as in the masterpieces of Henry James, was the ghost that won our terrified confidence. So often the good seems contrived, whereas the evil is vital and engrossing.

The solution, I think, lies in the fact that novels taken as complete works of art possess a wholeness that we respond to as a reflection of life. Little Nell is almost too good to be true; I say "almost" advisedly, because good people are not as rare as cynics pretend. Daniel Quilp is almost too bad to be true—though some of us have met a Quilp here and there, and policemen and lawyers and judges can tell some strange tales. But Nell and Quilp together give us a heightened picture of life that produces the satisfaction of a genuine, if high-coloured, work of literary art. The gaudiness is immaterial; it is only people of ultra-refined taste who cannot stand these strong portraits. If, in the world of some literary artists, their good people seem pallid and feebly conceived, whereas their villains have the breath of robust life, it is surely because the creative energy that rises from the unconscious of the writer tends toward what is evil; he is wanting in the wholeness of spirit we have been discussing. He is not a bad man; he is a man who can evoke and transmute into art the evil in himself.

It is by putting Man in the highest position in the universe that we diminish the vigour and tension of literary art. Some works of undoubted artistic interest have certainly been produced under the influence of such a belief, and I mention the novels of Virginia Woolf as examples. But as time wears on, literary fashion changes, and the novels of Mrs. Woolf seem to have lost some of their gloss recently, whereas the novels of Arnold Bennett, whom she derided with the remorseless cruelty of a Bloomsbury wit, have shown themselves to have unexpected powers of endurance. To put it with the uttermost bluntness, the writers who are enclosed in a kingdom of this world do not have the big literary artillery, and when we have wearied of them, we are likely to turn again to the authors who, overtly or by implication, write as if man lived in the presence of a transcendent authority, and of an Adversary who sought to come between him and the light.

The concept of wholeness is so very great, so demanding of our uttermost powers of understanding, that most of us must be content to glimpse it, indirectly, so to speak, through art of some kind; and literary art as often as not. It is a benign concept, though many terrors are in the path of those who seek it. But because we recognize evil, and confront it as wisely as we may, we do not necessarily succumb to it. When we watch two men wrestling, they seem almost to be in a lovers' embrace, but we know that at last one will fall. Our hope is that Evil may fall at last. To conclude I shall quote the final passage from John Cowper Powys's *Autobiography*. In part, it is a reflection on death. "It comes to pass, even while we are still in life, that when our soul loses itself in the long continuity of kindred lives, it does not lose itself in any power less gentle, less magical, less universal than itself, or less the enemy of cruelty; for what it finds is what it brings, and what it sees is what it is; and though the First Cause may be both good and evil, a Power has risen out of it against which all the evil in it and all the unthinkable atrocities it brings to pass are fighting a losing battle."

But literature is the chronicle from the battlefield.

Physicians

18

An Allegory of the Physician

On Friday, November 16, 1984, Robertson and Brenda Davies went to Baltimore so that he could take part in a seminar at Johns Hopkins University, at the invitation of Dr. George Udvarhelyi. He was the first speaker at the event on Sunday, and as the whole thing was titled "An Allegory of the Physician," that was the title he gave his opening words. He also lectured in the evening, and I have included that speech as the next selection, "Can a Doctor Be a Humanist?"

Davies's diary relates the events of the three-day stay over three single-spaced typewritten pages, so I have chosen the entry directly related to this speech.

Friday, November 16: ... *Arrived at eleven, and were met by George Udvarhelyi, a charming Hungarian, a rapid, tireless talker, and a most genial and delightful fellow, to whom we warmed at once. These yearly symposiums are what he now does for Johns Hopkins, to try to bring some measure of general culture to the attention of the medical students and faculty.* ...

Sunday, November 18: ... *The Symposium began at one; a fine auditorium, with lots of light (too much, it became blinding and hot) on the speakers. As usual, a microphone before which one had to crouch, and [John] Houseman [actor and moderator of this event] and I, as the tallest, were in some difficulty. I led off, and managed very well, and made the audience cheerful. Geraldine Fitzgerald [actress] followed,*

324

with a beautifully acted but irrelevant talk about how she had acted Mrs. Tyrone in Long Days's Journey *[into Night by Eugene O'Neill] and by extreme cleverness discovered that O'Neill didn't know as much about morphine addiction as he supposed: something about the pupils of the eyes. Actresses are wonderful creatures; she charmed everybody, but really added nothing to what we were talking about. Then she flew away, charmingly, to appear in New York in the eve. Then [Edwin] Wilson [critic for the* Wall Street Journal*] talked very well; intelligent, learned, a touch on the dull side but solid after the Fitzgerald soufflé. Then we had a break, during which all of us were hounded without mercy by people who wanted to have private talks about a variety of concerns. It was a test of skill to get to the Men's. We re-assemble, and Marsha Norman [playwright, 'Night Mother] talks well about playwrights and their medical concerns and charms everybody, but is much brighter in the head than Miss Fitzgerald. Then Frank Rich, [critic for the* New York Times*] who was extremely nervous, sweated a good deal, but spoke pretty well. What was troublesome was that people were invited to write questions on forms that were supplied and direct them to members of the panel, so that each of us had a group of questions that varied from intelligent to trivial and from the abstractly philosophical to the noisily personal. We did the best we could with these; I refused to answer a question about the Foe child, who has been given a baboon's heart, as I said it was too immediate and painful in implication, and to my surprise this drew applause. But by the time it was five we were all very tired, and the lights were becoming intolerable. Houseman undertook to sum up; he is 82 and had stood during most of the* P.M. *at the lectern; his summing-up was pretty good, but too late, and he reminisced a good deal, so it was six when finally we got free, dying for the w.c. and then a drink.... Both of which were immediately forthcoming, for Johns Hopkins has a great command of hospitality.*

☙

It is my task to speak first in this symposium, and when I was thinking about what I should say to you this afternoon I could not get out of my mind the striking illustration that appears on the public notices of this event, and which I presume you have all seen. At the bottom of the page is a pageant-like depiction of four figures—an Angel, a Man, a God, and a Devil, and it bears the title "An Allegory of the Physician." It is a brilliant choice, and I have made it the foundation of what I am about to say.

I suspect that before the symposium is over the distinguished symposiasts will have presented you to yourselves in all four guises— Angel, Man, God, and Devil—and you will be pleased with the identification. You will not mind being likened to angels or gods, you suppose yourselves to be men of various kinds, but you will be most pleased to be equated with devils. There is something about having devilishness attributed to oneself that is rather jaunty and stylish—a hint of unsuspected depths—and among no classification of mankind is that feeling stronger than it is among doctors. Why is that so? I shall tell you something about that this evening, after dinner, when your nerves have been calmed by food and possibly even by drink. At this moment, however, I am going to face you with what happens when you are considered merely as men.

This symposium is called "Medicine in the Mirror of the Stage." The title is an echo of some words of Shakespeare's. In the tragedy of *Hamlet*, the Prince of Denmark, who is an actor, a critic, a playwright, and a scholar—in fact a whole symposium in a single man—gives some advice to a group of actors, and he tells them what acting and theatrical illusion is. He speaks of "the purpose of playing, whose end, both at the first and now, was and is to hold as 't were, the mirror up to nature: to show virtue her own feature, scorn her own image, and the very age and body of the time his form and pressure." A symposium, as you all know, was originally a drinking party, where the guests delighted themselves with amusing but by no means trivial conversation. If there is no drink here this afternoon, do not blame us; we never said a word against it. But amusing conversation—well, I hope we may provide that. I assure you that we have thought of little else but this occasion for several weeks past.

As you have discerned, I am trying to put you in a good mood, to soften you up, just as a doctor does when he is about to reveal a disagreeable diagnosis. I may as well tell you at once that in my inves-

tigation of the role played by the medical profession on the stage—
that is, as you are reflected in the Mirror of Nature—you have not,
until comparatively recent times, cut much of a figure. Why this
should be so I cannot explain; writers, and playwrights as much as
any, are all hypochondriacs, continually fretting about their health,
rushing to the doctor at the slightest twinge, and consuming pills and
potions in extraordinary quantity. Why, then, have they not been
kinder to you? Why have they not put you in a flattering light at centre
stage? Why, indeed, when you are obviously the character most relevant to the action, have they not called you in? I have raked the great
tragic drama of Greece from end to end, and in all those tragedies I
have not discovered a single doctor. Yet, to choose but one familiar
example, think what a doctor might have done for Oedipus! A few
words from a Priest of Aesculapius, explaining that although incest is
inadvisable it is by no means fatal, and that tragedy might have had
quite a happy conclusion. Of course, about twenty-five hundred years
later, Dr. Sigmund Freud would have had to find some other field of
work. The Greeks, as reflected in their tragedy, were a violent people,
and where violence rages the surgeon thrives. But in the whole range
of classic drama I could find only one doctor and he is in a Roman
comedy by Plautus; he diagnoses a patient as insane, and prescribes
gigantic doses of hellebore. The Romans thought of that sort of thing
as excruciatingly comic because, as I am sure you know, hellebore is a
violent purge, and the notion of some poor creature being purged
almost to extinction was surefire comedy to the toughs who made up
the audience in a Roman theatre.

Things are not much better two thousand years later. Shakespeare
has a few doctors in his plays. There is a purging doctor—you see
how long the joke lasted; in *The Merry Wives of Windsor* one of his
patients says, "He gives me the potions, and the motions." One gets
the impression that in past ages people had bowels of brass or they
could not have withstood the horrors of heroic purging. And
Shakespeare has a doctor in *Macbeth* who is asked to treat the Queen
of Scotland, who walks in her sleep—but he throws up the case:
"More needs she the divine than the physician," he says. Macbeth
himself appeals to him:

Canst thou not minister to a mind diseased,
Pluck from the memory a rooted sorrow,
Raze out the hidden troubles of the brain,
And with some sweet, oblivious antidote
Cleanse the stuffed bosom of that perilous stuff
Which weighs upon the heart?

Obviously *Macbeth* is asking for chemotherapy. But the doctor was a pre-chemotherapy physician, and the best he can say is:

Therein the patient
Must minister to himself

a suggestion so horrendous that the King cries

Throw physic to the dogs, I'll none of it.

Not a happy doctor-patient relationship, I am sure you will agree. But Shakespeare, who was always ahead of his time, does offer us one splendid portrait of a woman doctor in *All's Well That Ends Well.* Her name is Helena, and she is one of the most charming of Shakespeare's heroines. Her specialty is an odd one, for her time and her sex; she is a proctologist. The King of France is gradually succumbing to a stubborn fistula of the anus; Helena has a sovereign ointment, and after a few dabs of this magical substance, the King is up and dancing, and offers Helena any husband she chooses as her reward. I should like to meet Helena. Not that I would have anything to offer her in her professional line, but as a general physician— witty, compassionate, and learned—she meets all my most optimistic medical requirements.

It is not long after the death of Shakespeare that we encounter a very great playwright who positively hated doctors. That was the French genius Molière. Characteristically of his profession, Molière was a hypochondriac, and his neurosis was as great as his genius. Perhaps I am wrong to say he hated doctors; he wanted his daughter to marry one, so that he would have a physician constantly in atten-dance. In several of his best plays doctors appear, usually armed with those huge, ominous brass squirts with which they administered enemas, for medicine was still in the grip of that obsession with enemas which it has not wholly shaken off to this day. The doctors usually converse in the bad Latin which was part of their mystery at that time. Your profession made a grave mistake when it discarded Latin. Did the medical brotherhood like Molière? No, they disliked him only slightly less than the clergy, who loathed him. I might present Molière's death as a warning to all men of genius but faulty discretion. It was on the night of February the 17th, 1673, when he was himself acting the leading role in his most ferociously mocking anti-doctor play, called *Le Malade imaginaire*, that Molière suddenly became ill, and died. Now—was it the malign power of an outraged medical profession that brought about his end? A poisoned enema, perhaps? I think it by no means impossible: You all know how dangerous it is to thwart the medical brotherhood. Certainly the doctors and the priests had the last word, Molière was refused Christian burial and had to be huddled into his grave at night, unhouseled and unaneled, like Hamlet's father.

Now, lest you should become unduly proud of your feat in having killed Molière, I should point out that the greatest theatrical enemy of your profession in recent times, Bernard Shaw, wrote a play called *The Doctor's Dilemma* in 1906, and although some of your professional forebears hated him as fiercely as ever they hated Molière, he lived in robust health for another forty-four years, succumbing at last at the age of ninety-four. Of course I should point out that Shaw was an Irishman, and thus not subject to the common rules that govern mankind. In justice I must say also that a great number of doctors admire Shaw's play without reserve, for they have understood the truth that lies behind the brilliant comedy. And that truth is that medicine, like everything else, is subject to fashion, the form and pressure of the time; the best of doctors are still men, and their medical practice is strongly coloured by what they themselves are.

Perhaps you are becoming a little restless. Were there no doctors, you may ask, who were presented as serious characters in the greatest drama? Oh yes, indeed there were, and if you want to study a splendid example I recommend you to Henrik Ibsen's great drama *A Doll's House*. Most people remember it as a protest against the psychological subjection in which women were held in nineteenth-century society. But in the character of Dr. Rank there is another protest that should not go unnoticed. Dr Rank is that pitiable object, a sick physician, and there is no cure for what ails him. He has inherited syphilis, a disease very common in 1878, when the play was written and not unknown in our own time. Some of you who have a literary cast of mind will recall that this was the disease that brought such tragedy to the life of the Baroness Karen Blixen, who wrote under the name of Isak Dinesen. She did not inherit it; it was a wedding present from her husband, but there is a link between her suffering and that of Dr. Rank. In *A Doll's House* Rank puts a question which may be familiar to some of you from your own clinical experience: Why should I suffer for the pleasures and sins of my parents? Why should I pay another's debt with my life? I offer you Dr. Rank as a splendid, artistically controlled portrait of a physician mercilessly reflected in the Mirror of Nature—the Theatre.

But it is not in Comedy or Tragedy that the doctor appears most frequently or most compellingly, in theatrical art of every kind. But theatrical art has found new forms in our century and the most widespread and most popular are film and television. There, on the large screen and the small one, you may see the doctor presented in the fullest range of character, every day of your life.

In film and television the doctor appears in full Technicolor as the Hero. Of course Ibsen, who saw everything and seems to have known everything, had a Doctor-Hero before anybody else. In *An Enemy of the People* (1882) Dr. Stockmann is engaged in the classic doctor struggle against the stupidity and corruption of society. He discovers that the mineral springs on which the fortunes of his town depend are in fact polluted by the local sewage disposal and he wants everybody to know about it. But he is beaten by the entrenched interests; he is told to keep his mouth shut. He is represented as an enemy of society, and he loses his fight. So Dr. Stockmann, though a Hero, is a loser, and that is not what movie and TV audiences want to see. They want their heroes to be winners, and it is as winners they appear in a hundred popular films—*Arrowsmith*, *The Citadel*, *Magnificent Obsession*, *Men in White*, *Doctor Zhivago*, and in all those films about Louis Pasteur,

Paul Ehrlich, and Albert Schweitzer in which we see Edward G. Robinson or some other powerful actor triumphing, after a heroic battle, over the stupidity of people who have the impertinence to oppose him and his infallible scientific knowledge. Anybody who opposes the great doctor is a villain, and is naturally played by some lesser-paid actor with a nasty face. The lesson of these extremely popular movies is that the doctor is always right.

In television this lesson is greatly simplified, but it is even stronger. Who but a villain would dare to contradict handsome young Dr. Kildare? He is certainly the Angel in the Allegory of the Physician which you have all seen. Who would dare to contradict good old Dr. Gillespie, who is Dr. Kildare's guru, and who is certainly cast in the mould of God, another figure in the Allegory? Of course these characters have their faults; now and then Dr. Kildare is flirting with a pretty nurse when his attention ought to be on some ugly old man, obviously a troublemaker. Now and then Dr. Gillespie loses his glasses, or his temper, but in medical matters he can conquer anything but Death and one is led to think that he regards Death as a fellow doctor, who has a cure for everything. And as well as Dr. Kildare we have Ben Casey, who is such a regular guy, as well up in medicine as he seems to be illiterate in everything else. And we have probably made the acquaintance of that charming group who appear in *The Nurses*, and *The Doctors and the Nurses*. We, the television viewers, understand from these programs how hard you work, what splendid people you are, how little you care for money, and what a lively, eventful life you lead! We envy you, and though we realize that we are unworthy to be doctors, we vow that we shall be humble, unresisting patients. You are our heroes.

That is not the whole story, of course. There are evil doctors, whose character is the complete opposite of dear old Dr. Christian, whom we remember as a saintly man, living only for others. These evil doctors are likely to be great medical discoverers, like the villainous Dr. Mabuse, who will be remembered only by those of you who are well into middle age. But you have probably encountered Dr. Cyclops, whose specialty it is to reduce human beings to midgets, and then to subject them to fearful humiliations. There are lots of evil doctors, and it is psychologically significant they are virtually all foreigners. Now why could that be, do you suppose? You are all profound psychologists, and I leave the problem to you. These doctors, of course, are related to the figure of the Devil in the Allegory of the Physician.

But there is one doctor who is the most popular of all—so popular indeed that no less than sixteen films have been made about him—and he is not a foreigner, unless you regard Englishmen as foreigners. He is Dr. Henry Jekyll, and he first appeared in Robert Louis Stevenson's brilliant short story "The Strange Case of Dr. Jekyll and Mr. Hyde" (1886). It is such a thrilling story that sometimes we miss its psychological comment, and I am afraid most of the sixteen movies have done so. Dr. Jekyll is an admired London physician, famous for his upright character, his kindness of heart, and his charity toward all mankind. But he has one fault; he *will* tinker with his chemicals and he finds a formula which, when he drinks it, changes not only his character but also his physique, and he becomes the repellent, hateful Mr. Hyde, a malign dwarf whose urge is to do whatever is evil. Dr. Jekyll is horrified; can there be such a monster repressed within his own blameless—no, his noble—character? Indeed it is so, and in the end Mr. Hyde triumphs. What the story is telling us, of course, is that to seek to attain perfection is to try to be more than a man; not perfection, but wholeness, should be our aim. Be angel, be God if you will, but never forget that you are a man, or you will have an ugly encounter with your devil. If Dr. Jekyll had taken the trouble to make the acquaintance of the horrible Mr. Hyde without having Hyde forced upon him by scientific accident, he could have made allowance for Hyde, and without yielding to him, he could have recognized him as a dangerous possibility, and made some sort of moral reconciliation with him. The lesson of the story—all Stevenson's stories have lessons, though they are so charmingly disguised—is the old Greek injunction, "Know thyself." I wish every doctor had that mighty counsel written in large letters over his desk. But the striving for perfection is a professional hazard of the medical profession, and one of your hardest tasks is to resist it. Never forget Mr. Hyde.

Even Robert Louis Stevenson was not immune from the popular desire that doctors should be perfect. You notice that his hero is DOCTOR Jekyll, but his villain is plain MISTER Hyde. Or have I forgotten something: In England surgeons are addressed as Mister—perhaps Hyde was a surgeon.

Do you wonder what I am getting at? Perhaps you have forgotten that I promised to talk to you about your profession as it appears in the Mirror of Nature—that is to say, the Theatre in all its forms.

I assure you that I have not forgotten. I said that portraits of doctors are comparatively rare in Tragedy and Comedy, but we cannot forget that other, huge category of dramatic entertainment which must be called Melodrama, for it too is a Mirror of Nature. When doctors appear on the stage, on the large screen or the small one, they are most often bathed in the lurid light of melodrama.

What is Melodrama? The word has bad connotations in common speech. People think it means plays and films in which impossible situations and crude emotions are exploited—shows quite unworthy of the attention of such sophisticated persons as you and me. Not at all. I have spent a great deal of time studying melodrama, and I have come to the conclusion that it is the dramatic depiction of life as most of us wish it to be, and indeed as, in our personal experience, it is.

Few of us live in a dimension of Tragedy, for Tragedy demands a nobility of feeling and a depth of suffering, which is not ours, though we take great delight in it when we see it in the theatre. Few of us live in a dimension of Comedy, for Comedy is only funny when you are an observer; to be involved in a truly comic situation can be as demanding and exhausting as living in a situation of tragedy. What both Comedy and Tragedy share is a strong spirit of Inevitability; the situation is going to work itself out as the gods wish it, not as we ourselves desire it. But in Melodrama our wishes are supreme; the good are rewarded and the wicked punished; the heroes and heroines win their battles and win each other; the villains and villainesses are crushed beneath the weight of their own unworthiness. And the Heroes and Heroines have no faults—or only small, lovable faults.

That is why, in the popular plays and films and TV programs about doctors, you always appear as heroes—a little flawed, but only enough to be cozy. That is what we, the public, the great group whom you refer to as "laymen," want you to be. After all we trust you with what is most precious in ourselves. We have, I think foolishly, banished many of the heroes we used to admire, and we have forced the heroic image on a few professions, and the medical profession is our favourite. So there you are: If your professional image is heroic and if in consequence you are sometimes impatient when you are questioned, or if you immodestly assert your preeminence in society, and if you demand rewards that seem excessive, it is because you are what we have made you.

I have been talking about your profession in terms of the theatre. Let me conclude by giving you some sound theatrical advice: Don't believe your own publicity. Don't succumb to the desire of wretched, suffering mankind to see you as angels or gods or—when you make dreadful mistakes as now and then you do—to see you as devils.

The most important figure in the allegory of medicine is the Man. It is your quality as men that is the real truth about you, and what ought to be reflected in the Mirror of Nature. If, from time to time, the reflection should be unflattering, perhaps we are both at fault.

19

Can a Doctor Be a Humanist?

Robertson Davies's last novel, *The Cunning Man*, published in 1994, is about the life of Jonathan Hullah, a physician. From Hullah's boyhood encounter with Mrs. Smoke, an Ojibwa medicine woman in Northern Ontario, the theme of healing runs through the book, and great respect is shown for unconventional methods. This is not unexpected since Davies himself had benefited so greatly from learning the Alexander Technique to alleviate physical ailments.

His 1984 lecture makes it clear that Davies was devoting much provocative thought to the topic of healing long before the 1994 book. One of the most famous medical schools in North America, Johns Hopkins Medical Institution in Baltimore was a fitting location for the David Coit Gilman Lecture on November 18, 1984, arranged by his friend Dr. George Udvarhelyi. Besides the lecture, there were other enjoyable aspects of his visit to the old Maryland seaport city, as these excerpts from his diary show: *George takes me to the 14 West Hamilton Street Club, described as "an intellectual Men's Club" housed in a charming old early nineteenth-century house and small in membership. Meet John Houseman who is to moderate the Symposium, and he is very much like his film self, a charming, distinguished, beautifully spoken man of wide culture and we get on very well. We both speak briefly at lunch.... After dinner Prof. Richard Macksey takes us to his house for drinks and to see his library which is a wonder; reputedly thirty-six thousand books, everywhere in a splendid old house, but especially in a library he adapted from a garage, two storeys tall, books floor to ceiling, heaped on tables, deep on the floor—quite wonderful. Shows me some of his association books, chiefly Ruskin, but he has much in this line including some Johnson. Asks me to inscribe books for the College which I do with a will.*

☙

I am at a loss as to how I should describe what I am about to say to you. A lecture I fear it is not, for that would suggest that I was about to tell you something new about something I understand better than you do. A lecture should be on a subject that has discernible boundaries, and it should say something that only the boldest dares to contradict. A lecture should be informative and perhaps edifying, and if it should ever be published it ought to be richly bejewelled with footnotes. Above all, a lecture should be solemn. I have given lectures in my time, but I assure you this is not going to be one of them. If I had to describe my remarks this evening frankly—as if I were in police court and on oath, so to speak—I should have to call it a ramble over several subjects, portions of which may seem to you to be impudent, and portions of which will be ignorant, and portions of which may contrive to be both at once.

You see I know nothing about medicine, though I have, in the highest degree, the hypochondriacal curiosity about it that is characteristic of authors. Indeed I know nothing about any science whatever. I presume you asked me to talk to you now because you thought it might be amusing to hear what a literary man thinks about your profession. A literary man is supposed to know about people, and the profession of medicine is still loosely associated with people, though it seems to be moving rapidly toward a condition where it is principally involved with science. That is what I want to talk about: I want to beg you not to break off entirely your association with people, simply as people, because we need you, and you—even if only as raw material—need us.

When I was asked to speak tonight, I assented with glee, because I knew that it was an honour to give the Gilman Lecture, and I have a simple delight in honours which may be unbecoming but is also human. I agreed to do it many months ago, and then, as tonight drew nearer, your coordinator, quite naturally, asked me for a title. Because I was very busy writing a novel, I was flustered and hastily replied with a title—"Can a Doctor Be a Humanist?" It is a bad title because it invites an immediate affirmative response. Of course a doctor ought to be a humanist. What I should really have called my speech is "How Can a Doctor Possibly Be a Humanist in a Society that Increasingly Tempts Him to Be a Scientist"—but as you see that is clumsy and much too long. Nevertheless, that is what I am going to talk about.

When I was a boy, if I went to a doctor he examined me gravely, asked questions that were searching without being positively embarrassing, and when we had both had enough of that he retired to a dirty little kitchen behind his consulting room, where he mixed up a few things he had lying around, and emerged with a bottle from which he instructed me to drink three times a day. It usually contained something that tasted of rusty nails and boiled rhubarb, and I received it reverently, because I regarded the doctor as a magician, and I knew that his nasty mixture had magical properties. But for many years of my adult life my various doctors have given me medicine—it tends to be in pill form nowadays—which plainly comes from a pharmaceutical company, and I leave his office thinking of him as a middleman between me and a large pill works. He has lost his magic. I want to make a few suggestions as to how he might regain at least some of his magic, and my recommendation is that the doctor should be, plainly and unmistakably, a humanist.

Do not suppose that I am hostile toward the modern marvels that come in the form of pills. Certainly not hostile but I have—I promised to be honest with you—a hint of skepticism. Of course I take the pills; I am frightened not to do so. But the reverence has gone.

Over the years, I have seen many medical certainties come, heralded by trumpetings and hosannas, which have in a few years died upon the ear, as the great discoveries faded almost into oblivion. Not all of these panaceas were strictly medical, but medical men seemed to believe in them. The first I recall, when I was a small boy, was Autosuggestion, the discovery of one Emile Coué, and it was delightfully simple. All that was involved was that the sufferer from practically anything should fall asleep every night murmuring to himself a magical formula—what Oriental religion calls a *mantra*—and it was *Every day in every way I am growing better and better*. And people did grow better and better—for a while. Coué himself gained fame, but very little money: He made his discovery available for nothing. His cure—he was not a medical man but a French pharmacist—had its place in the long, foggy history of autosuggestion, but the forces of evil were too much for it, and lots of people went down into their graves gasping out the wonderful *mantra*, and in a few years Monsieur Coué passed into oblivion, joining the advocates of colonic lavage and the people who thought that everything could be cured by eating bran.

His disappearance was not noticed, perhaps because he was not really medical in his advice; he was a primitive psychologist. And as he vanished, another truly medical wonder appeared upon the scene. It was called Focal Infection, and it was thought to be the cause of many of our mortal ills. As I heard about it, Focal Infection came principally from diseased teeth, and in my part of the world we were greatly impressed—indeed we were awed and humbled—by a famous dental surgeon who devoted all of his Sundays—for nothing, just for the sheer philanthropy of the thing—to pulling the teeth of the inmates of our largest mental hospital. Many of them, it was asserted, recovered their wits as a result of his ministrations, and rushed out of the asylum, praising God and His agent upon this earth, the great dentist. But something happened—I don't know what it was—and Focal Infection faded from view.

I shall not bore you with all the changes in medical enthusiasm I have seen. In the city in which I lived, as a young man, a doctor achieved fame that lasted for almost a year, treating cancer—apparently with success—with something or other he wrung out of rabbits. Penicillin came, and great claims were made for it, and indeed it is still extensively prescribed, and it was at one time believed to be a specific for syphilis and tuberculosis. Tuberculosis, a scourge in my own family, was banished, but a medical friend tells me it has not utterly gone, and from time to time one hears dark whisperings of syphilis.

Of course there were cures which have come and have remained, some of them for the most dreaded diseases of childhood, and everybody is immeasurably grateful. But—I do not wish to sound cantankerous, but the truth must out—as one disease goes, another seems to arise to take its place, and many of my contemporaries are struggling with ailments that were unheard of, or simply not identified when we were young. Upon the whole, medicine has not succeeded in its nineteenth- and twentieth-century crusade to make mankind immortal, though life expectancy has been much increased, and some of the worst afflictions have been confined and mitigated. And for this we are deeply grateful to you, and the researchers and pharmaceutical geniuses who stand at your elbow.

It is not to the triumphs of the heroes of medicine that I wish to address myself tonight, but rather to the day-to-day, jogtrot practice not simply of family physicians but diagnosticians, specialists, and surgeons; for I have often heard members of your profession complain of the diurnal routine which, over a long professional life, may become rather a bore. You grow tired of the endless parade of the ailing, all of whom regard themselves as uniquely afflicted, but whom you know to be suffering from one or other of perhaps two dozen common, though not necessarily trivial, ailments. You may grow sick of a very bad disease yourself; that is to say, you may become sick of the human race, and its endless whining and beseeching. Behind your professional half-smile there may lurk an impulse to play some mercurial trick on a patient—in fact, to give him something really serious to complain about. The forbearance you show in the face of this temptation is beyond all praise.

What do you look like to your patients? You hope that you look like a trustworthy professional man, and so you do, in most cases, though not all. But you look like something else, to the wretch who sits in the chair on the other side of your desk. You look like a god. Oh, yes you do. Don't contradict me. Medicine may be your game, but the detection and identification of gods in modern life is mine, and I assure you that you look like a god. Your patient may not think so—not consciously. But about your head shines a divinity, and it is extremely likely that somewhere in your consulting room the identifying symbol of the god appears.

There are doctors who have no modesty about assuming the godlike *persona*. I have made a desultory study of the pictures that doctors hang in their offices, and to the reflective eye, they are revealing. They are usually of a kind that reflects warmly on the medical profession or perhaps on the doctor himself—a few watercolour sketches from his own hand, or that of his talented wife, for instance. The office picture I like least shows an old-time country doctor, driving his buggy and his tired old horse along a country road through the night. He is engaged in a race; in the sky above him flies a stork, and in a sling in its bill it carries a baby. Will the dear old doctor arrive in time? We are supposed to smile, while wiping away a tear. I do not like to speak evil of any man, but I believe this disgusting assault on the senses was the work of Norman Rockwell. Another standard decoration of a doctor's office in my youth was a monochrome reproduction of Sir Luke Fidles's famous picture *The Doctor* in which a doctor, professional and also godlike, sits in an attitude of reflection at the bedside of a sick child whose humble parents hover anxiously in the background, waiting for the great man to utter. But the one I like best had no title and needed none; its message was clear. On a bed lay the form of a beautiful young woman, stark naked and revealing—at least to the layman's eye—no sign of illness. But over the bed hovers the menacing figure of Death, horrible and skeletonic; Death is seeking to deflower the toothsome beauty. Will he? No, most decidedly he will not, for standing at the bedside, defying him with all the power of his fully clothed youthful manhood, is the doctor, who is going to save the girl. I imagine that picture sustained the doctor, who was a surgeon, through many a weary month of tonsillectomies and removals of glued-up gallbladders He was wondering when he would be summoned to that passion-fraught bedside.

But it is not of these boastful, obvious valentines addressed to himself that the doctor hangs on the wall of his waiting room that I speak when I talk of the symbol of the god. I mean the caduceus, which has for centuries—indeed for at least five thousand years—been the special mark of your profession and the symbol of the power you have inherited from the past, and from the world of myth which is still a potent, if rarely recognized, force in our daily lives. Let us examine this symbol and see what it has to say to us. You know it well, have seen it countless times, but what have you thought about it, as having a bearing on your everyday life?

Of course it is the staff of Mercury. It is frequently described in literature. What does Spenser say?

> He took *Caduceus* his snakie wand
> With which the damned ghosts he governeth ...

But who was Mercury? And what were the damned ghosts? In Greece he was called Hermes, but he did not have his origin in Greece. Hermes was a Greek adaptation of the Egyptian god Thoth, and when we speak of Thoth we are already five thousand years in the past. You have seen images of Thoth in museums; he is the god with a man's body, and the head of a bird, an ibis. He was worshipped as the inventor of the arts and the sciences, of music, of astronomy, of speech and of the written word. Thoth was translated by the Greeks as Logos, the Word. The god, in fact, of the intellect in its farthest reaches.

So the staff, representing the power of the god, has an ancient ancestry, but as Thoth bore it, it had no twining snakes. Those were Greek additions, and the legend is that one day the god Hermes—the Greek Thoth—came upon two warring serpents, who writhed and fought upon the ground at his feet. To restore peace the god thrust his staff between them, and they curled around it, forever in contention, but held in a mutuality of power by the reconciling staff. And there they are still, held in check by the power of Hermes from achieving a final victory in their struggle for supremacy.

What are the serpents? Are they damned ghosts? No: They are vividly alive and relevant. They are Knowledge and Wisdom, and in your profession the caduceus is a perpetual reminder that the god Hermes—who is Hermes Trismégistus, Hermes the Thrice Great—requires you to hold them in balance and to keep one from devouring the other.

But, you may say, are Knowledge and Wisdom opponents? Not necessarily, but they may easily become so, for they are opposites and unless they are reconciled and each made a supporter of the other, they can make the staff of Hermes lopsided, and wanting in its true power. To lapse for a moment into the language of Analytical Psychology, Knowledge is an extroverted element in the doctor's psyche; it comes from without; it is what he acquires during his long and demanding education in order that he may direct it outward upon his patients. Its what you bring to bear upon the disease that confronts you in your patients. But Wisdom is an introverted element in the doctor's psyche; it has its origin within, and it is what makes him look not at the disease, but at the bearer of the disease. It is what creates the link that unites the healer with his patient, and the exercise of which makes him a true physician, a true healer, a true child of Hermes. It is Wisdom that tells the physician how to make the patient a partner in his own cure.

Instead of calling them Knowledge and Wisdom, let us call them Science and Humanism.

When the Greeks were ill, they often went to the temple of Hermes to pray, and their first prayer was "To which god must I sacrifice in order to be healed?" There were many gods then, and there are many gods now, though we usually pretend that there is only one, or else none at all. But the prayer is still one of great power, and I suggest that it is now the prayer of the physician: "To which god must I sacrifice in order to heal?" To which of the warring serpents should I turn with the problem that now faces me?

It is easy, and tempting, to choose the god of Science. Now I would not for a moment have you suppose that I am one of those idiots who scorns Science, merely because it is always twisting and turning, and sometimes shedding its skin, like the serpent that is its symbol. It is a powerful god indeed, but it is what the students of ancient gods called a shape-shifter, and sometimes a trickster. Science, during the past 150 years, has gained formidable new authority, and it is to Science that we owe the increased longevity of the race, and the control of many of the terrible ills that afflict mankind. Science may cure disease, but can it confer health? Like all powerful gods, Science seeks to be the One True God, and as it writhes about the staff of Hermes it seeks to diminish and perhaps drive out the other god, the god of Humanism.

I am telling you nothing you do not know already. I remember with pleasure a conversation I had a while ago with a young man who was studying medicine, who told me that one of the finest of his teachers said to his class: "When you find yourself at the bedside, don't immediately *do* something: Just *stand* there!" In other words, hold Science in check, and wait to see what Wisdom does.

I am reminded of what I have been told about one of the most astonishing diagnosticians of this century, the late Dr. Georg Groddeck. When a difficult case was brought to him—which was often when other doctors had had a crack at the case and given up— he put the patient in bed in his clinic and for two or three days did not see him; the patient was calmed by warm baths, cleaned out by gentle but searching enemas, fed small quantities of bland foods. Then, at last, Dr. Groddeck appeared, sat by the bedside, and told the nurse to strip the covers from the patient. Then he placed his ear on the patient's abdomen, and there he listened for sometimes three hours, without speaking a word. He listened to joints. He sniffed the patient's breath and sometimes, dismayingly to the sensitive, he sniffed their private parts. Groddeck, as many of you know, was not a pretty man, and it must have been rather like a nosy inspection by a hedgehog, or perhaps one of those gnomes one meets in fairy tales. But at last, when all the sniffing and listening and prodding with the fingers and thumbs was over, he began to talk to the patient and to ask questions that had been suggested by all the animal-like prelimi- naries. After a while, the great doctor began to make suggestions. He had found a diagnosis, frequently an unexpected and astonishing one. I hope I do not provoke nausea in any of my hearers by using the word *psychosomatic* but sometimes—certainly not always—his diagnosis was on psychosomatic lines. Like all really great doctors, he acquired a reputation as a magician, but he laughed heartily when that was said to him. He might well have said, as the great Ambroise Paré said three centuries before him, "I dressed his wounds, and God healed him."

You see, of course, what Groddeck was doing. He was allowing the patient to speak, in bodily sounds and smells, before the patient was invited to open his mouth. And what had happened was that what was deepest in the patient—not merely his disease—had been invited to speak to what was deepest in the doctor.

Do you say, We cannot be expected to train yearly graduating classes of Groddecks? Of course not. So many of your students come to you, already such convinced worshippers of the Science snake, that they do not want to hear about anything else. You have to be minded of what we might call the Doctor Psychology, the cast of mind that impels young men and women to want to join your profession. As an outsider, I am sometimes impressed by the similarity of mental qualities that make doctors so very much like farmers. I am sure you all know a few farmers, and many of them are admirable people, but surely you have observed how fiercely impatient they are to questioning or restraint. They are loners. When they are standing in their fields they will not allow anyone to offer an opinion on their work. They are deeply suspicious of co-operative efforts and they are sometimes convinced that the whole of mankind is in league against them. Is that cast of psychology familiar to you, in any degree? It may be admired as a manifestation of the Hero Psychology, the determination to conquer, to rule, and to brook no interference. It is heroic, certainty, but it is also pigheaded. Farmers of genius, like doctors of genius, are uncommon. When we meet a great farmer we find that he possesses no command of nature; he lets nature speak to him. It is so with doctors.

You see where I am tending: I now want to talk about the other snake, the Humanist snake, the snake which symbolizes not the knowledge of Science, but Wisdom, that breadth of the spirit which makes the difference between the first-rate healer and the capable technician.

Those of you who are of a strongly scientific cast of mind are doubtless already impatient with me, because the personal slant that I am giving to my remarks is so painfully unscientific. It is a widely held belief among scientists that whatever derives from a single, personal experience is of slight value compared with what may be deduced from a statistical analysis of a large number of cases. Well, it is your own fault; you must not ask novelists to talk to you if you want statistical analyses, for their personal response to life is the strongest element in their character, and some of them display that ability to see through a brick wall that is so disturbing to the scientific mind. Again to employ the terminology of Analytical Psychology, the scientist is a man in whom thought and sensation predominate, whereas an author is usually a man of feeling and intuition. So you will not be surprised if I continue with a personal anecdote—a single experience—on the basis of which I mean to generalize.

When I was a young man, a student at Oxford, I became ill in a way characteristic of me and my family; I developed a ferocious cold and cough. Ordinary treatments achieved nothing, and I was sent by my tutor to his own doctor. "You'll find him first-rate," he said, "a very wise fellow." And so he was. His name was Dr. Raymond Greene, and with my Canadian experience of doctors he was not at all what I expected. He saw me in what must have been his consulting room, but it looked much more like a library, for it was lined with books and because I can read the title of a book at forty yards, I knew at once that they were not books about medicine. He had some excellent pictures, not of the Norman Rockwell or Luke Fildes variety. And his manner was most agreeable, but in terms of my experience utterly unprofessional.

He heard my complaint, and took a quick look at me and said in an offhand manner: "Oh yes, I'll give you an inhalant and something to control the cough. Your family tends toward respiratory illnesses, I suppose?" I said that was so. Then he said, "Now why do you suppose you are unwell?"

I launched into the usual North American students' rigmarole about the chill of the Oxford winter, the coldness of Oxford rooms, the prevalence of drafts—all of that. "But why are you ill?" he persisted. "Germs, I suppose." I had never been asked before to diagnose my own case. "Certainly germs," said Dr. Greene, "but you know perfectly well there are germs everywhere. Why have they been able to get their hooks into you? Why are you ill in the way you tell me all your family become ill, when they have need of an illness? That is to say when they need to look seriously at their life and where they are. Is it a girl? What about your work?"

It was my work, which—for reasons that need not detain us—was in a dreadful mess, for reasons that were not all my fault. We talked about that, and out of our conversation emerged some plans which, in quite a short time, put my work back on the rails. But then he said:

"You know, you shouldn't put so much emphasis on your work. Only second-rate people do that. And then, of course, their work eats them up. Whereas they, of course, ought to eat up their work. My work would eat me up, but I keep it in its place by climbing mountains. And, do you know, climbing mountains makes me a better doctor."

I found out a few things about Dr. Greene, later on, all of which I read again in his obituary in the London *Times*, which appeared in December 1982. He was indeed a very distinguished mountain climber, a greatly admired physician, and—this is not perhaps as irrelevant as it may seem—the brother of the novelist Graham Greene. And the *Times* made it clear, to me at least, that he was a first-rate doctor because he never allowed doctoring to eat him up. He was a humanist first, and a physician second.

I recovered from my symptoms—the cold and the cough—and ever since I have been trying to follow the doctor's more enduring prescription, which was that I should not allow my work to eat me up. It has sometimes been a struggle, but my wife, who like all really good wives is an admirable physician, constantly reminds me of the danger. And I have often thought with gratitude of Dr. Raymond Greene, and blessed the day when I set foot in his consulting room. Since then I have fallen into the hands of many doctors—few of whom have been humanists though some of them were remorseless scientists—and I have felt the full fury of the Snake of Knowledge, the Scientific Snake, when it rages and coils unchecked by the Snake of Humanism.

Dr. Greene, of course, was in a great tradition—a tradition I recommend you to explore if you have not already done so. It would be long and tedious to discuss even a handful of the great humanist physicians, but I should like to speak briefly of three, the first of whom was the man with perhaps the most resounding name in all the annals of medicine—Philippus Aureolus Theophrastus Bombast von Hohenheim, commonly called Paracelsus, who lived from 1493 to 1541, and was thus, as you see, at his great revolutionary work just as knowledge of the New World became general. In his day he was a great revolutionary against authority, and his revolt was on behalf of science: Were he living today I have no doubt that he would be lecturing, with all his terrible eloquence and daring, against the tyranny of unchecked science in an age when another new world, that of space, is in process of exploration.

He was essentially a humanist, you see. That does not mean that he was an atheist. Mankind as God's noblest creation, and inseparable from his Creator, was the theme of all his teaching. He said: "There is no field on earth in which heavenly medicine grows or lies hidden, other than the resurrected flesh or 'new body' of man; only in the 'new body' have all its words force and efficacy here on earth. This heavenly medicine works according to the will of the man of the 'new birth'; in him lie all the active virtues. For it does not operate in the mortal body, but only in the eternal body." This was not a priest speaking, or a man bound by the old medicine of Avicenna and Galen, but a man who was a pioneer in the dissection of the body. His life was a constant, turbulent search for wisdom—the wisdom of the Humanist Serpent—and it was he who said "The striving for wisdom is the second paradise of the world." I dare not recommend that you read all of his work, for it is extensive, but I urge you to take a look at some of it—there is an excellent anthology published in volume 28 of the Bollingen Series—because though at first it may seem puzzling, it is full of the sweet milk of humanist wisdom.

My next great humanist physician, who was almost an exact contemporary of Paracelsus, is François Rabelais, whose great novel about Gargantua and Pantagruel is probably familiar to you. Although he was a priest, and for a time a monk, he was primarily a doctor and another mighty rebel against the domination of the accepted wisdom of his time—which was university scholasticism. If he were living now, I am certain that he would be lambasting the self-delighted scientists with all the vigour of his wit and the irrepressible hilarity and irreverence that kept him perpetually in trouble. The commonplace opinion about Rabelais in our time is that he wrote a dirty book. Of course it is dirty: A true humanist is always mindful of the inescapable ties that hold mankind close to the grossest facts of life; his feet are in the dunghill, but his eyes are fixed upon the heavens. This is what makes the life of man absurd, and I am surprised that the modern Absurdists have never claimed Rabelais as the greatest of their ancestors. But absurdity was not all Rabelais saw in Life—and in that he differs from the modern Absurdists; he saw life as glorious, and hilarious. It may be said of him as it has been of a later humorist, "His foe was folly, and his weapon, wit."

He must have been a wonderful creature. Sometimes I think that if I were lying on my deathbed, and opened my eyes to see Dr. Rabelais standing beside me, I should either leap to my feet, or perhaps expire laughing with delight at the splendour of the world, and the folly of mankind. As I am sure you know, Rabelais himself is said to have died murmuring, "I go in search of the Great Perhaps." That is certainly splendid, but there is another tradition which I hold in equal esteem, which is that as Rabelais lay dying, the last rites of his Church were being administered to him, and the moment had come when the priest anointed his feet with the holy oil. It is said that then he was heard to murmur, "I must be going on a long journey; they are greasing my boots."

My third and last of these great humanist physicians from the past is one whose name is, I am sure, held in honour at Johns Hopkins. That is Sir Thomas Browne, the great physician of Norwich, who lived from 1605 until 1682, and whose first book, *Religio Medici*, is one of the treasures of English literature. The temptation of all who talk of Browne is to quote from him, and I must be strong with myself. Nevertheless, some quotation cannot be avoided. It was Browne who made that great humanist statement: "We carry within us the wonders we seek without us: There is all Africa and her prodigies in us." And some of his words might be taken as warnings against the stern certainties of Science, as when he says: "To believe only possibilities, is not faith, but mere Philosophy." May we not think he is protesting against that mighty force in the medical science of our day, the passion for the new, the latest, when he says: "If there be any among those common objects of hatred I do condemn and laugh at, it is that great enemy of reason, virtue and religion, the multitude: that monstrous piece of monstrosity which, taken asunder, seem men, and the reasonable creatures of God, but, confused together, make but one great beast, and a monstrosity more prodigious than Hydra." Whenever I read that, I remember the mighty clamour about Focal Infection, of which I spoke earlier. Paracelsus, Rabelais, and Browne were all men deeply committed to religion, but in each of them was a wise skepticism, which kept them from fanatical enthusiasms. Christian theology is not much in vogue nowadays, but I think we would be wise to recall that two of the Virtues Christianity adopted from the Greeks and the Jews were Temperance and Prudence. In other words, do not let anything, even your work, eat you up and silence your common sense.

To talk of Sir Thomas Browne at Johns Hopkins is of course to recall a name held in high honour here, that of Sir William Osler. It is a source of pride to me that he was a Canadian, who received his earliest medical education at the Universities of Toronto, and McGill in Montreal. It has been said that his work here almost a century ago revolutionized medical education in Johns Hopkins, and indeed on the North American continent. He was truly a great physician, and he was also a splendid Humanist, and Browne's *Religio Medici* was a fixed star in a literary taste—a book collector's taste—that included much that was finest in the literatures of several languages. He constantly adjured medical students to read *Religio Medici*. I wonder how many did so? But even if only a few did so a blow had been struck for the humanism that lay at the root of Osler's art as a physician.

I have told you that the great god of medicine was Thoth, and that in time he was transformed by the Greeks into the Thrice-Mighty Hermes. But he underwent a further transformation, and a psychologically very interesting one, because among the Romans he was called Mercurius, and in the course of that change he took on new attributes. He kept all his splendour as the god of intellect, but the psychological expansion and perception of the Romans saw in him also the shadow side of intellect, which is sometimes trickery and charlatanism, and always of wit, of ambiguity, and of the merriment which accompanies quickness of wit. When you are working under the influence of Mercurius you cannot always subdue the element of fantasy, of duality of meaning, that accompanies genuine, deeply felt knowledge, and without which that deeply felt knowledge cannot be transformed into wisdom. Mercurius was the god of the alchemists, whose supposed desire was to change base metals into precious metals. But we know now that the best of the alchemists were at work

349

to change many things that were in themselves inert and dull into the splendour of wisdom. Knowledge may enable you to memorize the whole of Gray's *Anatomy* or Osler's *Principles and Practice of Medicine* but only wisdom can teach you what to do with what you have learned.

Osler, great man that he was, could not escape the mischievous aspects of Mercurius, and in your library here you preserve a full record of the medical opinions of Osler's Mercurial self, whom he called Dr. Egerton Yorrick Davis, many of which were published as papers in the most respectable and learned medical journals. I am sure some of these are well known to you. For instance, his hair-raising and hilarious account of the childbirth customs and sexual shenanigans of the Caughnawaga Indians, which he managed to impose on some of his colleagues who were children of Hermes, but had not yet graduated to be children of Mercurius. I am sure you all know his writings on that distressing inconvenient ailment, strabismus of the penis. These were signed by Dr. Egerton Yorrick Davis, but the hand was the hand of William Osler. He simply could not be solemn, twenty-four hours a day, year in and year out, about medical science. The writings were in the true spirit of Rabelais, and distressing though they may be to the wholly solemn members of his profession, they convince many of us that Sir William would have been the ideal doctor for us, because he took neither himself nor his vast knowledge with total, unremitting solemnity. And that, ladies and gentlemen, is one of the marks of the true humanist, who pays appropriate heed to the left-hand snake that coils about the staff of the caduceus. To confuse mere solemnity with real seriousness is to forget that the trickster god lies always in wait to pull the rug from under your feet.

That word *caduceus*, by the way, means also the staff of the herald, and it is the privilege, and also the duty of the true physician to be the herald who brings great news, transporting enlightenment, to his patients. Does he not also bring news of Death? Why do you think that news may not be, to the philosophic mind, transporting and enlightening? Grave news but is it always bad news?

Will you allow me, before I finish, to surrender myself to the influence of Mercurius—who is also the god of writers, as I am sure you know—and suggest to you a truly Mercurial, humanistic approach to your work as physicians. It is an approach which might, given a chance, revolutionize medical practice. Even if it did not do that it would give you a great deal of not wholly innocent fun.

What is the great evil, the pervasive malaise, that overshadows the whole of mankind at present and is frighteningly on the increase, everywhere and among all kinds and conditions of men and women? Is it cancer? No, it is not. Is it the ravages wrought in society by smoking tobacco, which is now under such discussion and attack by the most zealous of your kind—the group which, so many years ago, leapt on the bandwagon of Focal Infection? It some-times seems to me, as I look back over my life, that smoking has achieved the status of the Ultimate Curse which was, in my boyhood, conferred upon masturbation. That indulgence, the youth of all civilized countries were assured, would sap the intellect, bring about rot of the spine and loss of the reason, and within measurable time destroy the vigour of the race. Perhaps it did so, for I see the evidence everywhere about me. But to my astonishment I find that masturba-tion is no longer reprehended, but tolerated, and even advocated by some of the most advanced medical and psychological minds. Novels have been written about it, and grave matrons speak of it without a blush. But now tobacco has usurped its place and yet I say to you that tobacco, dangerous addiction though it be, is not the worst affliction of our age.

What is it, then? I shall tell you. It is, quite simply, *stupidity,* which seeps like a corrosive poison through every level of society, and lays its blighting hand on every aspect of social, professional, political, and cultural life. To whom may we confide the task of attacking this pervasive blight better than upon yourselves, to whom we look for so much that is concerned in the betterment of mankind?

It is not always easy to diagnose. The simplest form of stupidity—the mumbling, nose-picking, stolid incomprehension—can be detected by anyone. But the stupidity which disguises itself as thought, and which talks so glibly and eloquently, indeed never stops talking, in every walk of life is not so easy to identify, because it marches under a formidable name, which few dare attack. It is called

Popular Opinion, and sometimes the Received Wisdom of the Race. It looks as though it came from some form of mental activity or spiritual grace, but it does not, and its true name is Intellectual Stasis.

Unquestionably you have observed this dread evil among your patients. But have you ever mentioned it? Have you ever prescribed for it? In the nineteenth century it was not easy for a physician to tell his patient that he had syphilis; social delicacy inhibited him. So it is today with the even more dreadful social disease of stupidity. Something must be done, and yours is the profession that has the authority to do it.

You cannot expect governments to do anything about it. After all, their dependence on stupidity is notorious. Stupidity is the great vested interest, with holdings everywhere, and the full support of the media. And so it will be a long time before popular television programs are prefaced by a flash which says, "The Surgeon General warns that viewing what follows is injurious to your mental health." No, a wiser, more responsible agency than government must do what needs to be done, and that agency is the medical profession.

What can you—what, as humanist physicians, must you do—to fight stupidity? First, you must assure your own complete inoculation against this plague by massive daily applications of art, music, and literature. Then you must do the most difficult thing of all: You must be wholly honest with your patients.

"Madam," you will say to the woman who sits in your patient's chair, "We have dealt, on the whole successfully, with your allergies, yet you tell me that you still feel dull, logy, unable to eat more than three large meals a day and drink more than three Martinis at a time. I am not in the least surprised. Your intellect, which is no worse than the average despite lifelong abuse, is under a cloud. Read Rabelais, and if that proves too strenuous, read the works of Mark Twain. For a weekend health workout, go to a festival of Marx Brothers films. Learn to laugh, especially at yourself."

That is not too hard. But what about the elderly man who complains to you that although he is in his mid-seventies his sex life is still volcanic in its vigour, and he has just divorced his wife to give his full attention to a charming little creature of seventeen.

Nevertheless, the fear of Death is upon him, even as he frolics in the harlot's embrace. He wakes up in the night sweating, with a chill about his heart. Now, here is a case that demands graver measures than that of the lady who merely feels that her life is dull.

"Sir," you will say: "You have been taken in by the popular magazines that assure you that sex in old age will bring you happiness, and perhaps immortality. Now, I am going to give you this card, which you must carry about with you, and read at least three times a day. Listen—

"'I could be content that we might procreate like trees, without conjunction, or that there were any way to perpetuate the World without this trivial and vulgar way of coition: it is the foolishest act a wise man commits in all his life; nor is there anything that will more deject his cool'd imagination, when he shall consider what an odd and unworthy piece of folly he hath committed.'

That is by a very great physician, Sir Thomas Browne of Norwich. My prescription is that you should be content to leave to youth those delights that belong to youth. As for the Spectre of Death, when it frightens you, read this other card:

"'DEATH, be not proud, though some have callèd thee
Mighty and dreadful, for thou art not so:
For those whom thou think'st thou dost overthrow
Die not, poor Death; nor yet canst thou kill me.
From Rest and Sleep, which but thy pictures be,
Much pleasure, then from thee much more must flow;
And soonest our best men with thee do go—
Rest of their bones, and soul's delivery!
Thou'rt slave to fate, chance, kings and desperate men,
And dost with poison, war and sickness dwell;
And poppy or charms can make us sleep as well
And better than thy stroke. Why swell'st thou then?
One short sleep past, we wake eternally,
And Death shall be no more:
    Death, thou shalt die.'"

If he obstinately continues to tremble, tell him that the man who wrote that died of typhoid fever, an illness that your profession has tendered almost unknown.

But what about the lady who presents herself to you complaining that although she jogs six miles every day, and has reduced her fat by forty pounds or so, she still *feels* fat, and her friends do not seem to notice any change in her appearance? "Madam," you must say, "It is true that you jog in the flesh, but are you jogging in the spirit? Your adiposity is metaphysical. You no longer are fat in the body, but you are still fatheaded. I recommend some strenuous mental jogging; I advise you to read a chapter daily of Gibbon's *Decline and Fall of the Roman Empire*, and then read it again, and continue until your friends tell you that you look lithe and sinewy, that a new light shines from your eyes, and that your conversation and your comprehension of political and social life has improved immeasurably. Go at once, and busy yourself with your cure."

There you are, ladies and gentlemen, I have told you what to do: Now go and do it, and bring about the great Humanist revolution in the practice of medicine. In your diagnoses, give full attention to the Left-Hand Snake.

I make no charge for this invaluable advice. I am myself above taking fees, because I am a Humanist, but I know that you must live, and when you have brought about enough Humanist cures not you, but your grateful patients, will insist that your fees be doubled. So— onward on behalf of the Left-Hand Snake. Forward, Children of Mercury, in the great assault upon stupidity.

With this stern injunction I bid you adieu.

Unusual Treatments

20

Prologue to the Good Natur'd Man

Robertson Davies was always accomplished in the art of parody. This entry shows one of his most successful imitations of another writer's style, on this occasion put to good, and undetected, use.

The following note was attached to the original copy of the prologue in Robertson Davies's handwriting: *Written for the Old Vic production in the Autumn of 1939 and spoken by Miss Marie Ney in the character of Mrs. Groaker. Dr. Johnson's prologue was thought too gloomy—this one seemed to create a proper mood for the comedy.* No one ever realized it was not part of the original play written by Oliver Goldsmith and presented at Covent Garden in 1767.

♪♪

Since first Man was, the Drama's task has been
Aptly to mirror Life's fantastic scene;
In dances wild and crude, disgusting mime
The savage shewed the spirit of his time;
With strutting stilt and hollow, echoing mask
The Greeks gave grandeur to the actor's task,
While a lewd drama found a lewder home
In the round O's of great, but wicked, Rome,
'Til chiding priests crushed those libidinous stages
(For which their reign is known as the Dark Ages).
Then Thalia nodded by her dying fire
'Til roused to dance by daedal Shakespeare's lyre;

Strode by the Commonwealth, harsh and full of rage,
Great Charles returned, and cheered the fainting Stage
Playwrights appear'd, a wild, ungovern'd genus,
Who made a molehill of the Mount of Venus.

    Our modern writers, too, reflect a time
Chaotic, rude, unfit to live in rhyme,
Or ev'n blank verse (some slight excuse for those
Who wrap their thought in even blanker prose)
Pale and confused they flutter round Life's flame
Coining their fears, and shivering for fame;
By comic chance each wildly scribbling creature
Mistakes his limits for the bounds of Nature,
But yet exploits his complexes so ill
That things complex become more complex still.
Thus Drama, as successive curtains roll
Reflects the changing fashions of the Soul.

    Our play, though moderns find its theme amiss,
Reflects an age perhaps more kind than this,
When Wrong was merely Right that needed mending,
Love's path, though tortuous, sure a happy ending,
And justice, though inclined to some contortion,
At last was meted out in due proportion;
Abrupt Peripety cut the Gordian knot
And solved the jigsaw puzzle of the plot.

    Our fate lies in your *hands*, to you we pray
For an indulgent hearing of our play;
Laugh if you can, or failing that, give vent
In hissing fury to your discontent;
Applause we crave, from scorn we take defence
But have no armour 'gainst indifference.

21

Animal U.

This was written as a story for children, but several people assured me that children would find it difficult. I have a better opinion of children than that. They are, after all, adults in the making, and those who will have a sense of humour when they grow up have it when they are small. I wrote the story because when my wife and I and our daughters moved into Massey College in 1963, the building was full of animals that had lived on the land where the building now stood, and they were very hard to dismiss. It seemed almost as if they were determined to join the College community, and if they had done so, the consequence might well have been like this.

ↄ৮

Once upon a time in a great university, a new college was built. It was a beautiful building, with lots of studies and bedrooms, a library and a dining hall, and a large garden.

The builders worked as hard as they could to finish it. "The students will fill it as soon as autumn comes," they said.

The builders did not know that it was full already. The college was built on a vacant lot, and as the walls went up and the rooms were finished, animals came down from the trees, and out of the sky, and up out of the earth, and took possession of the building. There were tribes of squirrels and chipmunks, mice, a skunk, two families of moles, a whole nation of rabbits, a fox, and a raccoon, not to speak of birds.

"How kind of these men to build us a college," they said. "It is really very unlike humans to understand our place in the university so well."

"But the college is *not* for us," said a large Hare. "You have all made a terrible mistake. The college is for humans. I have been listening to the builders, and I know."

All the other animals laughed cruelly. "You think you know all about humans," said they. "We shall have to call you Human Hare." And they laughed and rolled on the grass and sharpened their fingers at the Hare, who felt very badly, but did not change his mind.

"Waste no time on him," said Richard Raccoon, who had taken charge of the big meeting of the animals in the College Library. "This is a great moment in animal history. For the first time we have a university of our own. We must find a great name for it."

"That's easy," said a young Rabbit who was particularly clever because he ate the crocuses at the Law School every spring. "Let's call it Animal University; it shortens down nicely to Animal U."

He spoke so impressively that all the animals cheered without being sure why.

"Excellent!" said Richard Raccoon. "And now we must choose our university staff. I do not think we could do better than to appoint Mr. Reynard Fox to the important position of President. Three cheers for President Fox!"

All the small animals began to cheer, because they were getting the habit. But the Hare interrupted.

"I am just an old grey Hare," said he, "but I am not a fool, and I warn you that this college is not for us."

"Boo!" shouted all the small animals. "Shut up, Human Hare! Hurrah for President Fox."

"Thank you, thank you, my dear friends," said Reynard Fox, waving his paw with easy grace. "You may rely upon me to serve the interests of animal education with all my well-known artfulness. But I always say that a university president is no better than his teaching staff. Therefore it gives me the greatest pleasure to appoint all crows to the position of Full Professor. And as for my dear old friend Socrates Owl, I beg him to accept the position of Dean."

Socrates Owl opened his beak, then closed it, as though his feelings were too much for him. He said nothing because he could think of nothing to say.

Poor Human Hare groaned, but nobody heeded him, because they were cheering.

"Let us not dilly-daily," barked President Fox. "Let us begin our university work at once."

"One moment," said Dean Owl, who had understood the expression on the face of his friend Richard Raccoon. "We have forgotten the most important thing of all. Who is to be our Chancellor?"

"What's a Chancellor?" asked a little Fieldmouse, who did not mind appearing ignorant.

"A Chancellor is the highest official in any university," said Dean Owl. "The wisest, the best-loved, the most dignified, and—he rolled a big eye at the Raccoon—the biggest."

"Richard Raccoon for Chancellor," shouted President Fox, and seized the Raccoon by the paw. "Our Chancellor!" he cried, waving encouragingly at the other animals who cheered wildly, because they were anxious to do the right thing.

"You make me feel very humble," said Chancellor Raccoon. "This is certainly the greatest day in animal history. My students—rabbits, skunks, moles, mice, all birds who are not black—let us hurry off at once and improve our minds!"

They did. The mice rushed to the kitchen and began research into all kinds of food, to see what tasted best. The rabbits set to work on a fine set of tunnels in the garden, to study earth science. The moles studied the college wiring, and sometimes got electricity in their teeth, and had to lie down for a while, till it went away. The squirrels and chipmunks rode up and down in the elevator that took things to the kitchen, studying engineering. The skunk spent hours every day studying garbage disposal. The rats worked very hard in the library, devouring books and sometimes spreading paste on the leaves with their tails, if the books seemed very dry.

The Professor Crows had a fine time, arguing all day, and laughing at jokes the student animals did not understand. President Fox sat in his office, worrying about money and eating chicken sandwiches.

Dean Owl found a room with no light in it at all, and sat in it all day, sometimes sending for a fat mouse whose work was unsatisfactory. Such mice must have been expelled, because whenever anybody disappeared forever, the little animals whispered: "He's been to the Dean!"

Happiest of all was Chancellor Raccoon. When the smaller animals had learned as much as they could hold, he held grand ceremonies in which he touched these animals on the shoulder saying, "Hokus, pokus, skilamarokus" (which is animal Latin), "Arise, B.A." (which meant Better Animal). Then the small animals went away to learn some more, and were very grateful to Animal U.

All this time poor Human Hare hung around the university, looking gloomy. Most of the animals sneered at him, but some of the nicer ones said, "Cheer up! we forgive you for being wrong."

Then one autumn day a lot of young people came into the College and moved books and suitcases and guitars into the lovely rooms. After them came some old men with even more books, and a lot of middle-aged men with brooms and lawn mowers, who were very unkind to the students and professors of Animal U.

"It's an outrage," shouted the animals, at a great meeting they held in the garden. "It can't be ALLOWED!"

This was President Fox's greatest moment. "It's no good saying something can't be ALLOWED when we have no way of stopping it," said he. "These young people have honoured us by coming to Animal U; it shows they know that animals are wiser than they are; they want to learn from us."

"But what are we to do?" said Chancellor Raccoon.

"We do what any good university does," said President Fox. "We get advice from our greatest expert on Human Behaviour. Professor Human Hare, will you have the goodness to address the meeting?"

Human Hare, who had been standing nervously at the back of the crowd, was astonished at becoming a Professor so suddenly. But he drew himself to his full height, and spoke:

"It is simple," said he. "The Humans like to work by day; it is just as easy for us to work at night, and as a courtesy to them, that is what we shall do. Also, when human universities want to be specially nice to somebody they give him something called an LLD. As all you intelligent animals can see, those letters are simply a short form allowed, and they mean the person is aLLoweD to come to the university as much as ever he likes. We must give each of these humans an LLD. from Animal U."

So that very night, when all the young people were asleep, a splendid procession tiptoed through the College, led by Chancellor Raccoon in his black and silver gown, and President Fox in his red gown, and that very distinguished scholar in Human Behaviour, Professor Human Hare. Into each room they went, and after Professor Human Hare had assured Chancellor Raccoon that each sleeping young creature was really human (which he did by peeping under the blankets), the Chancellor touched him on the brow, saying, "By my power as Chancellor I create you an LLD. of Animal U. Hokus, pokus, skilamarokus! You are aLLoweD to stay here."

When it was all over, the student animals danced around Human Hare in the moonlight; singing:

> For he's a jolly good animal!
> For he's a jolly good animal!
> For he's a jolly good animal!
> Which nobody can deny!

And Human Hare smiled gently, thinking how like human beings they were, to forgive him at last for being right.

22

The Fourth Wiseman 1974

Davies wrote this very short story in his diary, describing it as a dream or a vision. From his study of Carl Jung, he was most interested in his dreams and recorded many of them, but no other was such a complete story. Some years before he described seeing the young woman with the manticore while thinking about his novel *The Manticore* as a vision. I leave it to the reader to make up his own mind, both about the meaning and where it came from. I have left the diary structure to give a sense of Davies's thoughts and reading at this time. He had just attended Bill Broughall's funeral; a lawyer with National Trust and the Massey Foundation and close friend.

⤜⤛

Wednesday, July 24: Slept very badly; woke about two and did not really sleep again. Thoughts of Broughall. Tried to divert myself by telling myself a story about the Fourth Wise Man, an aesthete who spent 33 years looking for the perfect gift for the infant Christ, and arrived at Calvary too late, but in time to be advised by the Good Thief to look for the acceptable gift within himself. Might even write this, but I know there is a story about the Fourth Wise Man which used to be very popular, and which was *Reader's Digest* in tone.

Friday, July 26: Eve continue my reading of *Ego and Archetype* by Edward F. Edinger, an admirable book which is driving me mad. Did ever puritan divine counsel one to such strict courses of life as these

Jungians? To become integrated, as described by EFE, is too damned much like being dead. What shakes me is that there is no room whatever for a sense of humour, no place for the upsurge of the irrationally ludicrous; yet I know the Unconscious is full of such matter for I have been on the receiving end of the wire ever since I was a child, and it has been one of the glories and refuges of my life. Of course old CGJ was not like that; his *Letters* brims with humorous insight and he is not above referring to a colleague whom he disagrees with as "an old shitbag." That's the man for me, not these clergy from the First Gnostic Church of Boston. They are drearier than Christian Scientists.

Saturday, July 27: I cannot get on with the play [Question Time]; something stands in my way & I cannot write, though usually I get out of such binds by simply putting myself to the task.... The Gordons come to lunch, & I query Walter about the process of Question Time in the House of Commons and what he tells me is what I already knew from the Encyclopedia. Eve finish Edinger, a notable book, but what he labours to say Esther Harding and Elinor Bertine say much more simply.... It has struck in upon me that the story of the Wise Man I told myself Wednesday night partook much more of the nature of a vision, for it came full-grown to me, and I did not so much make it up as hear myself telling it. As I have been thinking so much about individuation, and my desire to attain some measure of it, I would be stupid to neglect this upsurge, which comes in the vein which is especially mine—the literary vein. So here it is.

IT IS WELL KNOWN, that when Jesus was born in Bethlehem Wise Men sought him out, and presented the infant King with gifts of gold, frankincense and myrrh. Scores of splendid pictures show us the scene, and we are moved by the beauty of the homage paid by the kings—one usually old and wise and wizard-like in appearance, one youthful, perhaps a Frank, nobly strong and proud, and one very often a black man of dark mystery—to the Holy Mother and her Son. But what is not so well known is that there should have been four Wise Men, and that one of them was late in coming. He was the youngest, no more than a youth, and his father thought it would be good experience for him to go on an unimportant embassy to learn his trade of kingship. He was wise, too, for he had early shown great taste in things of beauty, and everything had been done to enlarge and support his connoisseurship. Therefore he was determined that his gift to the newborn king should be exquisite and suitable—something truly worthy, and obviously worthy. So he set off on his pilgrimage, and though he saw the Star he had to take time to make his choice of a gift, and in time he lost it. But this did not worry him, as he knew how to navigate by the stars, and the gift was of first importance. He looked everywhere, and examined everything, and rejected every- thing, and as the years passed he won the reputation of being a Great Expert, and he was covertly laughed at in many lands and many places where objects of art were sold because nothing ever quite came up to his exacting standards. But he stuck to his task in a way that commanded respect. Once, when he was in Jerusalem, some friends urged him to come with them to the Jewish Temple where there was, they said, an extraordinary boy who was preaching with such power and lucidity that he confounded all the learned doctors. But our friend said: "Spare me your infant prodigies; I have seen many of them and their talent is usually a flash in the pan; show me this boy in another twenty years and if he is still a great teacher I will listen to him then." And away he went, to see some of the fine things of which he had heard; but of course they were disappointments.... The search went on and on, and although he felt some urgency about his embassy, he was stubborn in his insistence that nothing but the very finest would do, and he would not fail in his mission. He travelled widely, and knew everyone, and stayed in the best houses, and many people would have said that his life was an enviable one, but as time passed he became dejected, and wondered if he would ever find what he so sorely needed.... It was more than three decades after he had set out on his journey that he found himself in Jerusalem, and as always he was staying in the house of the governor. Pontius Pilate was pleas- ant company, for though he was primarily an administrator and his taste was not fine he lived in good style, and his wife would have been even more agreeable than he if she had not had a foolish leaning toward occultism. Our friend was so unlucky as to arrive in Jerusalem at the time of the Passover, and had been quite discommoded early in the week at becoming involved in what seemed to be a procession of unruly people howling and shouting around a figure riding on an ass, who seemed to be a prophet or a political insurrectionist of some sort. But if there was one thing our friend hated, it was uproars and revolutionary movements, and he got away from that scene as fast as he could. Pilate told him the city was uneasy, and that his own concerns as Governor made it necessary to neglect his guest more than he would have wished. So our friend kept at home for the greater part of the week, and amused himself in his host's very respectable little library of fine things…. Nevertheless, he was restless at this constraint, and on the Friday, when the city seemed quiet, he went for a walk. The weather was overcast, as if a storm were coming, and he did not mean to walk far, but as he walked he became so depressed, and overcome by a sense of failure that he walked farther than he meant, and found himself outside the city in a region that he did not like at all. It was ugly—not a garden to be seen, or a decent house— and the ground was littered as if the Passover crowds had thrown down all the bits of food and trash they did not want, so that the sense of the crowd was very real. But there was no crowd to be seen; only a few people walking back to the city…. There was a hill in sight, and as our friend walked up it the sense of his failure and unworthiness became so oppressive that he felt positively unwell. So much of his life gone, and his first mission still unachieved; so much connoisseurship, and not one thing of satisfactory quality discovered; so much money spent, so much talk, so much reputation gained without anything coming of it. He was a king's son, and a wise man, and yet he was miserable…. There were three crosses on the hill, and he thought idly that his friend Pilate and his Romans had been about their strict justice. There was no malefactor on the middle cross, and he could see, some distance away, a group of people, some of them women, carrying away an object which he supposed must be the body of their dead friend. But there were two men on the crosses that remained. One of them was cursing, but in a low and incomprehensible voice because he was stupid with the drug he had been given. But the other was looking down at our friend, and if a dying man can wear an ironical expression, that was what could be seen in the dimness. But our friend was not looking upward but downward, and he was muttering "Too late; too late." "Not so late as I," said the man on the cross, "but it wasn't too late for me." Our friend looked up. "But it is too late," he said, and was amazed to find himself talking to a ruffian whom his friend had sent to death; "my life is almost gone, and where is the treasure I was to have given to the young King?" "Fool," said the thief; "you've had it all the time."

So there: that's it, and now I must find out what to make of it.

23

Look at the Clock!

(A Suggestion for a Film Scenario)

When Brian Mcging, a Classics Professor at Trinity College in the University of Dublin, and a former Junior Fellow of Massey College, became the editor of *Hermathena*, he turned to the Founding Master of his old College for a contribution. Robertson Davies never had difficulty with such a request as he had many ideas he wished to express, and when he had a chance to have some fun with an idea, he did not hesitate.

On December 7, 1991, Davies wrote: *Complete revision of* Look at the Clock! *for* Hermathena; *an odd piece but I like it and have always wanted to have some sport with the overblown Oedipus business.*

※

The room is empty when first we see it, but we need a moment to take it in. At first glance it looks like any room reserved for the private use of some great person in any one of a hundred European palaces; the carpet is richly coloured, the furniture in French eighteenth-century style, of gilt wood and silk upholstery; a handsome bookcase has not been able to contain all the books the owner of the room needs, and some large folios are heaped on the floor; an imposing clock stands near the door. But as we look more closely, we see that this furnishing is in a room with old stone walls, not fully concealed by tapestries; the ceiling is supported on heavy old beams. An archaic room, in fact, immeasurably old, that has been brought to modernity as royalty encounters modernity. Through the window we see a landscape, harsh but beautiful, that tells us that this must be Greece. It is morning.

The door bursts open and a woman dashes into the room in high agitation; she is splendidly but simply dressed; her clothing is less significant than her beauty and palpable vitality. She unwinds the heavy sash that is her girdle, throws it over a hook which is fastened in a central roof beam, and rapidly and expertly makes a noose. She draws up a chair, climbs on it, puts the noose around her neck, then pauses for a moment, seems to reflect, takes her neck out of the noose, steps from the chair, seats herself at ease on a sofa, takes a cigarette from a box on the table, and lights it, drawing in the smoke with obvious satisfaction. She is smiling, now.

Cries are heard outside, and they come nearer until the door bursts open and a magnificent young man dashes into the room, his sword drawn. He has the air of a king and wears a uniform which might be that of a field marshal. But it is not in the best of military taste; there is a flashiness about it, and a multiplicity of Orders and Medals that suggests vanity rather than glory in the field. He is shouting.

THE KING: A sword, a sword, and show me here
      That wife, no wife, that field of bloodstained earth
      Were husband, father, sin on sin, had birth,
      Polluted generations!
THE QUEEN: Ah, we're having Gilbert Murray today, are we?
THE KING: We are having The Great Myth, and we are having it in English. You know I prefer Murray to any of the others.
THE QUEEN: Certainly he offers great opportunities to a man of your rhetorical gifts. Sophocles in English. Personally I prefer Seneca's version of our little trouble—
THE KING: Seneca gives you a suicide scene all to yourself. Obviously you like it. But Sophocles was immeasurably the superior playwright.
THE QUEEN: I don't grudge you your Sophocles. I don't even grudge you Gilbert Murray. But now and again I wish I didn't have to play such a docile second fiddle to you, my dear boy.

THE KING: Don't call me your dear boy!

THE QUEEN: I've called you that for years. It's a simple endearment.

THE KING: In the light of what we know—what we discover every time we play out my personal tragedy, such a term is indecent in the highest extreme.

THE QUEEN: And we play out your personal tragedy, as you insist it is (though I carry a lot of the weight of it), on the last day of every lunar month, and have done for the last twenty-eight hundred years, give or take a little. "When 'Omer smote 'is bloomin' lyre," as a contemporary of Gilbert Murray wrote. Don't you ever tire of it?

THE KING: It is not for me to tire of it. I have my place in the great world of myth, and it is my duty to body it forth for the enlargement and guidance of mankind. Tire of it! You are frivolous.

THE QUEEN: O, my dear—you can't imagine how I long for a little frivolity.

THE KING: Well, you can't have it now. Don't you hear the Citizens of Thebes crying for me?

(The Screen shows us the Citizens of Thebes, and they are indeed crying for this unhappy King. Anyone who has had experience with films knows how hard it is to assemble a good Mob, and this one is composed of theatrical extras of all sorts and degrees of education. The English ones cry Eedipus, the Americans cry EDDYpus, and those who have been to Drama School and are waiting for their big chance OIDYPOOS. Now we cut back to the Queen's Chamber.)

THE QUEEN: Well, go to them and say that there has been a change in the script.

THE KING: After—after—A change in the script? You are out of your mind! After—(He is trying to do a sum in his head.)

THE QUEEN: You needn't cudgel your brains. You were never any good at reckoning—

THE KING: It is an unkingly accomplishment.

THE QUEEN: Very well. But you have only to look at the clock over there to see that it comes to about twenty-eight hundred years or—or quite a few thousand lunar months. Are we never to have anything new? I am bored to death with this old script and my part in it.

THE KING: How often must I explain that we have the ineffable honour to be creatures of myth, fixed forever in the deepest consciousness of mankind, eternal and unchangeable. You are talking like a woman—

THE QUEEN: Indeed I am. And please don't shout at me. Not for nothing have you been called Oedipus Tyrannus.

THE KING: I glory in the title. I rule single-solus. I brook no contradiction or opposition. What else should I be called?

THE QUEEN: Well, I know you don't like hearing about him, but my first husband was called Laius Basileus. He wasn't a tyrant; he was a king, and wasn't afraid to take advice.

THE KING: Oh, that old ass—

THE QUEEN: Please! He was your father, and my first husband. Not so old and not in the least an ass. A very capable ruler, until you murdered him— and with your usual unfailing tact, managed to do it before the altar of two major gods. Your way of meeting a difficulty is to kill somebody. I have been killed thirty-six thousand, four hundred times, if you want accuracy, and I'm fed up with it!

THE KING: I see. One of your tantrums. I'll get Creon to talk to you.

THE QUEEN: You mean you'll get Creon to advise you. You—a tyrant! My lad, without Creon you'd have been assassinated years ago!

THE KING: We are wasting time. *(He rings a bell and The Messenger, who has been listening at the door, almost falls into the room.)* Ask the Lord Creon to join us.

THE MESSENGER: O King—

THE QUEEN: And ask the Prophet Teiresias to join us also.

THE MESSENGER: But what shall I say to the people?

THE KING: The people must wait. Go at once.

(The Messenger goes.)

THE KING: Why do you want that old fool?

THE QUEEN: I don't know, but I hope to find out.

THE KING: Ye gods! *(And he must be careful to say it as an invocation, like a Greek, and not 'Yee gahds" like an exasperated American schoolgirl.)* The vagarious irrationality of women!—Listen to that Crowd.

(The Camera cuts again to the Mob, whose outcry is increasing. The drama students, remembering that "The city breathes/Heavy with incense, heavy with dim prayer/And shrieks to affright the Slayer" are breathing with difficulty, and a few of the more creative souls utter the most frightening shrieks they can manage. Then we see the Lord Creon, a thoroughly capable bureaucrat, making his masterful way up the palace steps. Not far after him is the aged Teiresias, who is supposed to be blind, but manages astonishingly well with the aid of a staff. Creon wears Court dress, with plenty of gold braid. The Prophet looks as if he had just come from a university lecture room, wears odd socks and a rusty, somewhat tattered academic gown. We now see them enter the Queen's room. Creon gives Oedipus the most perfunctory of bows, and kisses his sister. Teiresias whacks about him with his stick until he finds a chair, and sits immediately.)

THE KING: *(Ironically)* Be seated gentlemen.

TEIRESIAS: Oh, dreadfully sorry. Quite forgot.

(He bobs up and sits again at once. Creon sits in the middle of the stage, like a man accustomed to chairing meetings.)

CREON: I needn't tell you that the people of Thebes are waiting for the reappearance of their King. What has caused this delay?

THE KING: She won't go ahead with it.

CREON: Won't hang yourself? Why, may I ask.

THE QUEEN: Look at the clock, brother. Look at the clock! We are very near the end of the Eon of Pisces. Are we to go into Aquarius acting out this same rowdy puppet show of cruelty, and vengeance, and incest and remorse? Is there never to be any change?

CREON: Let me see, isn't this the day you do the Gilbert Murray version? In Gilbert Murray's day they believed in the Myth of Progress. Don't tell me you've fallen for that, sister?

THE QUEEN: I have not "fallen for" anything. I have been thinking, which is quite another matter.

THE KING: And usually the beginning of trouble.

CREON: What have you been thinking about, sister?

THE QUEEN: Time.

THE KING: *(amazed)*
CREON: *(inquiring)* } Time!
TEIRESIAS: *(delighted)*

THE QUEEN: Yes, time. It is rather the fashion these days to be derisive about it. People scold about Time as if it were a prison. Yet without it, how should we see men and things in more than one light? Without Time, life would stand still.

THE KING: But you surely understand that with people like ourselves, life does stand still. We are myth. We are Eternal.

THE QUEEN: I have been eternal for quite long enough. Without Time, mind stands still. And don't sneer at the notion of Progress, Creon. If you think of it as a sort of plant food to secure quick, lavish growth, of course, it's silly. But things do change, you know. Slowly, slowly, very, very slowly. But surely, all the same.

CREON: Do I understand that you are proposing that we should change our great Myth?

THE QUEEN: We could talk about it.

THE KING: Blasphemy!

THE QUEEN: Blasphemy against what?

THE KING: Can you ask? Against one of the supreme myths of mankind. Against one of the forces that has shaped man's mind and man's destiny. Against one of the most profoundly rooted of the archetypes that govern the life of man, the highest achievement of Creation.

THE QUEEN: Oh balls!

THE KING: What did you say?

THE QUEEN: You heard me. This great myth of yours was just another old story—a very fine story I freely admit—until that cigar-smoking wizard at Berggasse 19, Vienna District IX, blew it up into something which he insisted was universal—meaning that every man was supposed to share it. Women didn't matter.

THE KING: Madam, you are belittling my Complex. The Oedipus Complex, the discovery of which revolutionized the world's attitude toward— toward—toward a great many very significant things. And don't say women didn't matter. They mattered as fiercely desired mothers.

TEIRESIAS: Yes, and without a mother, where's your Complex? She's the bone father and son are fighting over. Thus far, she's central. Passive, but central. She's the prize that goes to the stronger. Daddy hangs on to Mummy, and Baby sulks for life. Baby wrests Mummy from Daddy, and Daddy shrivels up and blows away. But Mummy is always pig in the middle, as in the children's game.

THE KING: You are quite wrong. I detest your reductive names for the characters in the struggle, but if that's the way you understand it, you must know that Baby kills Daddy and has Mummy all to himself.

THE QUEEN: Always killing somebody!

THE KING: Well, what about it?

TEIRESIAS: I'll tell you what about it—

THE KING: Have you entirely forgotten your palace manners? Don't speak to royal persons until you're spoken to.

TEIRESIAS: But then I should never get a chance. I like to talk, but we prophets are never asked to talk unless everybody else is utterly exhausted. I want to talk about fathers. This father business is greatly misunderstood.

THE KING: Not at all. The man who does not kill his father and thus deliver himself from servitude must be content to live as his father's shadow. Simple.

TEIRESIAS: Not simple at all, O King. The Queen is right; things do change, but not quickly. I grant you that every man must kill his father, not in the flesh but in the spirit, if he is to be his own man. And as things are now—you see, O Queen, that I share your respect for Time—every man has many fathers—one of the flesh but more than one of the spirit. The teacher, the benefactor, the father in craft or art—every one a father and the free man must, as humanely as he can, kill them all. That is to say, he must take what they have to give and make it his own, and then be quit of them. And the wise father—teacher, benefactor, craftsman, or artist—will take the blow as handsomely as he can, for it is his last blessing on his son.

THE KING: I detest these amplifications and explanations. I am for the simplicity and splendour of life, and the nobility of tragedy. Man is never so truly man as when he is implicated in a tragic situation. You people have no understanding of that. None whatever. Look at you. All sitting down. In tragedy one never sits. Sit down and you immediately reduce a situation to comedy.

THE QUEEN: Always the actor.

THE KING: The principal actor in the greatest tragedy the world has known. I am proud of my role.

TEIRESIAS: You are young, O King, and the young are great ones for standing. And for tragedy. They love a great uproar and tempest of feeling. The old know tragedy too well to enjoy it.

THE KING: Spare us the tedious wisdom of age, prophet.

TEIRESIAS: Willingly. I know better than anyone how unavailing it is. Have I not, in my long life, been both a man and a woman? Yes, many long years I spent in a woman's body, and it was because I had loved women's bodies too much. Athena caught me spying on her beauty while she bathed, and turned me into a woman so that I should learn what a woman's body really was. I was soon sick of it, I can tell you.

(The Camera shows us a dark alley in Athens. TEIRESIAS, now a woman, stands at a corner and as a soldier passes, she beckons to him. After a brief colloquy, he possesses her fiercely against the wall, and when she puts out her hand for her fee he strikes her brutally across the face, and walks away, laughing.)

TEIRESIAS: I was glad when Zeus mercifully turned me back into a man, and I was able to get on with my real vocation, which is prophecy. Female prophets are too easily discredited.

CREON: But when you were a woman you were able to answer the great question: Which enjoys sexual congress the more—the man, or the woman?

TEIRESIAS: Yes, I was able to settle that. The women are the fortunate ones. They get nine times more pleasure from that exercise than do men.

THE QUEEN: Yes, and they pay for it with nine months' tedious work. Whatever way you look at it, it's a swindle.

CREON: May I remind you that the people of Thebes are waiting for the resolution—the ancient, time-honoured resolution—of this situation. If we begin talking about sex we shall go on quarrelling and boasting for hours. What are we to tell the people? The Messenger is hanging about outside waiting for his summons. Surely I do not have to remind you drama-conscious people that nothing destroys a tragedy so much as superfluous talk. What's it to be? Make haste!

THE KING: It's as plain as day. I burst into the room, crying for the blood of the woman who has betrayed me into incest and thus brought a horrible plague upon Thebes. I find her hanging from the roof, her own girdle tight about her neck. She has discharged her role, and her duty—But there she sits, smoking and laughing at me.

CREON: Well—order her to discharge her role, and her duty.

THE KING: I don't know that I altogether want to do that. Of course I'm furious with her, but I am fond of her. It goes against the grain. I'd rather she did it out of a sense of—well, a sense of fitness.

CREON: And you call yourself a tyrant!

THE KING: You tell her to hang herself. You're her brother.

CREON: When a brother tells his sister to hang herself; it is mere family pleasantry. You're the offended party. You do it.

THE KING: I am a doer, not a talker. When I came into this room, I was whirled in a tempest of tragic fury. At that moment, I could have chopped her into messes. But I was taken off guard. What I was prepared to do, by tragic necessity and long custom, was to seize the gold pin from her breast and blind myself with it. I was not prepared to meet an arguing, laughing, obstinate woman.

CREON: That is an explanation, but not a proposal. I repeat—what are we to tell the people?

THE QUEEN: Why not tell them the truth?

THE KING: ⎫
CREON: ⎭ The truth?

THE QUEEN: Yes. Tell them that the plague in Thebes is not because of the incest of their King, but is the predictable consequence of their own stupidity. If they persist in dumping their household refuse and their close stools in the streets, and throwing dead donkeys and corpses into the waterways, they must expect plague, and dirt is far more dangerous than a trivial sexual transgression.

THE KING: Trivial? You call our tragic mating trivial?

THE QUEEN: The fuss about incest is absurd. If it doesn't hurt anybody, or debauch anybody, what's so bad about it?

THE KING: It's all these damned books you read! I knew you were perverse, but not depraved!

TEIRESIAS: Incest is not really likely to catch on in a big way, even if you decide to recognize it, as people now recognize homosexuality. Kindly Nature has so ordained things that most siblings are deeply repugnant to one another. O Queen, would you consent to wed your brother Creon?

THE QUEEN: What a perfectly revolting idea!

CREON: Thank you. And I return the compliment.

TEIRESIAS: You see? Even though King Creon and Queen Jocasta would make an infinitely better royal couple than the present arrangement.

CREON: The Messenger is waiting. We have no time to spare for these compliments. What are we to tell the people? You hear them.

(The Camera once again shows us the Mob, which has increased its clamour, but at considerable personal discomfort. Vendors of throat lozenges, who pass among them, are doing a brisk trade.)

TEIRESIAS: The Queen has suggested the truth.

CREON: When has any Mob ever been ready for the truth?

THE QUEEN: You are right, brother. And we must have some regard for the King. He demands tragedy. It is his milieu. If we tell the people that their agony is caused by a dirty water supply, we reduce this tragedy to a drama of social betterment, like something by Henrik Ibsen.

CREON: And what do you suggest?

THE QUEEN: Couldn't the King and I go out, hand in hand, and explain to the people that the whole thing was an unfortunate mistake, and neither of us knew what we were doing then, but we know now, and intend to go right on doing it?

THE KING: I should look like a fool. Marrying a woman old enough to be my mother!

THE QUEEN: I wasn't so old. And I am your mother.

TEIRESIAS: When Helen ran off with Paris, and brought about the Trojan War, she was only twelve—though a well-developed twelve. We folk of the mythic world are allowed quite a bit of latitude with Time. If you were to ask me, I should say, give it a try.

THE KING: We haven't asked you—Very well, if that is how it is to be, I shall speak to the people—but alone.

CREON: No, brother-in-law, you'll make a mess of it: I shall speak to the people.

THE QUEEN: And what exactly are you going to say?

CREON: I shall want a few minutes to collect my thoughts.

THE QUEEN: The Messenger is waiting. You'd better listen to me. Tell them that the World Clock is moving toward the new Eon. The Eon of Pisces is nearly done, and extraordinary new things are to be expected. The Eon of Aquarius is very near, and we must prepare for the new beliefs, attitudes, feelings, and all that it brings. Tell them that the King and I will appear, more deeply united than before, but that our example must be followed, if at all, with the uttermost circumspection.

CREON: No, no: very crude. I shall find my own way.

THE QUEEN: Spoken like a ruler. Now—think up your speech.

THE KING: This leaves me in a pretty predicament, I must say.

TEIRESIAS: Not so bad, really; if the old drama had been played out, and you were now blinded, you would have to retire to Colonus, and become a sage. You would have time for reflection. But now, of course, you must continue your reign, and your much-admired association with the Queen. Wouldn't you rather be a King than a sage?

THE KING: I shall miss the long nights of reflection at Colonus.

THE QUEEN: What did you reflect about?

THE KING: Ah—I've never told anybody. But when the Sphinx asked me her famous riddle, and I gave the right answer and she destroyed herself, she actually asked me two riddles. The first, of course, was—

TEIRESIAS: What walks on four legs at dawn, on two legs at noonday, and on three legs at sundown?

THE QUEEN: It seems easy now, when everybody knows the answer. But I don't suppose it was easy when the Sphinx asked you.

THE KING: No indeed. I think I acquitted myself not badly that time, stupid though Creon supposes me to be. But that isn't the whole story. The Sphinx was furious. She raged, because she knew she had to destroy herself. But she shrieked, before she leapt into the chasm, "O clever one, answer this: 'What shall be yours that no one else would have? What shall be yours that King Creon will pay for? What shall be yours that you cannot see?'"

TEIRESIAS: And you have never guessed it?

THE KING: Never. Though I have puzzled for countless hours.

TEIRESIAS: Shall I tell you?

THE QUEEN: No. The Sphinx will be answered in plenty of time.

TEIRESIAS: It will be something for you to work on at Colonus.

THE KING: If we are changing the script I don't think I shall go to Colonus.

CREON: I am ready now.

THE QUEEN: You have it?

CREON: Oh yes. I shall tell the people that the gods have spoken. They have forgiven the King and Queen their transgression, and what has been regarded as their sin is a sin no longer, but a royal prerogative. For which reason, if it is uncovered among lesser folk, it will be subject to an extremely heavy fine.

THE KING: But the Complex? My Complex—the Oedipus Complex: What is to become of that?

CREON: Well, I don't want to be immodest but I think this rather a fine stroke. Homosexuality was botched. An opportunity for a tax thrown away. But henceforth anyone who lays claim to, or is discovered to possess, an Oedipus Complex must pay a substantial yearly tax so long as it persists. A tax on neurosis!

TEIRESIAS: What a mind! What an introduction to a new age!

CREON: Not bad, if I may say so. Of course the Complex will continue to be popular among the neurotic well-to-do, so the tax should bring in a substantial yearly sum.

(Creon claps his hands and The Messenger dashes through the Doorway.)

CREON: Tell the people that I shall address them immediately. Tell them that I bring great news from the gods. And you, sister and brother-in-law, you lurk inside the doorway, until I give you your cue, then come forward hand in hand, and be gracious. Assume a noble port—

THE QUEEN: A what?

CREON: Look your best. Don't snigger. No—wait. You, O King, come first, and when the shouts are over their peak make a splendid gesture, and you, sister, come forward in your role as mother, consort, and goddess. Better put on your Moon tiara.

TEIRESIAS: *(to The Messenger)* Is there a side door? I don't want to miss any of this.

(The Messenger beckons, and Teiresias goes.)

CREON: Come, O King. Think of this as a new role.

THE KING: You know, I feel I may be glad of a change.

(The King and Creon go, and as we hear a great roar of acclaim from the Mob—some cry, "Hail O King" and others whisper, "Look, he hasn't blinded himself"—we see the front of the Palace, with Oedipus more kindly than ever before in his career, at the top of the steps. Then we cut back to the Queen's chamber. She goes to a large cupboard which, when opened, reveals a store of treasure and jewels of every kind. She selects with great care a silver tiara on the top of which, cut from a single moonstone, is a crescent. As she is adjusting it to her liking before a mirror, there is a tap on the door, and when she cries, "Come," a very old man—a cobwebby old man who might almost have been carved out of the root of a yew tree—enters softly. He bows.)

OLD MAN: If you please, O Queen—

THE QUEEN: Yes, what is it?

OLD MAN: The clock. It's time for me to wind the clock.

THE QUEEN: Very well—I don't think I have ever known that clock to be wound before.

OLD MAN: Well, you see—I only wind it once in two thousand years. Every Eon, that's to say. And when I wind it, there are quite a few changes. Because the gods change their minds, every Eon. Not much, you know, but it's surprising what that little brings about.

THE QUEEN: And a new Eon is coming.

OLD MAN: O yes, my lady. Indeed, it's a little bit on its way already. But when I wind up the clock, the big changes will begin. The gods must change their minds from time to time. They'd shrivel away with boredom else.

THE QUEEN: You don't sound like a servant. Certainly not a slave.

OLD MAN: Oh no indeed, my lady. I've had my day, and I'm not really finished yet.

THE QUEEN: I wish I had more time to talk, but I have a most important appearance to make.

OLD MAN: Yes. One of the big changes. Or perhaps not such a big one. I don't know. I just wind the clock.

THE QUEEN: We must talk again, clock winder.—What is your name?

OLD MAN: Cronus, my lady. Or Saturn, if you prefer.

(But the Queen has gone before she hears his name. The Old Man opens the great clock, takes a key from his pouch, and sets to work to wind it. Superimposed on the image of the Old Man at his work we see that of Oedipus and Queen Jocasta acknowledging the welcome of the Mob, as they set out on their new myth. But the noise of winding the Clock grows louder and louder until it drowns out the Mob, and the trumpets, as the film ends.)